ECONOMIC BACKWARDNESS
IN
HISTORICAL PERSPECTIVE

ECONOMIC BACKWARDNESS
IN
HISTORICAL PERSPECTIVE

A Book of Essays

ALEXANDER GERSCHENKRON

THE BELKNAP PRESS
OF HARVARD UNIVERSITY PRESS

Cambridge, Massachusetts, and London, England

Library of Congress Catalog Card Number: 62–17217
ISBN 0–674–22600–3

FOR GONGELINE

Acknowledgments

I am indebted to the following for the kind permission to reprint my essays in this volume:

1. University of Chicago Press for "Economic Backwardness in Historical Perspective," *The Progress of Underdeveloped Countries*, B. Hoselitz, ed., 1952.

2. *L'industria*, Milan, for "Reflections on the Concept of 'Prerequisites' of Modern Industrialization," no. 2, 1957.

3. The International Economic Association for "Social Attitudes, Entrepreneurship, and Economic Development," *Economic Progress*, Leon H. Dupriez, ed., Louvain, 1955.

4. *Journal of Economic History* for "Notes on the Rate of Industrial Growth in Italy, 1881–1913," December 1955.

5. *Rivista Storica Italiana* for "Rosario Romeo and the Original Accumulation of Capital," LXXII, no. 1, 1960.

6. Harvard University Press for "Problems and Patterns of Russian Economic Development," *The Transformation of Russian Society*, C. Black, ed., 1960.

7. Harvard University Press for "The Problem of Economic Development in Russian Intellectual History of the Nineteenth Century," *Continuity and Change in Russian and Soviet Thought*, E. Simmons, ed., 1955.

8. *Review of Economics and Statistics* for "Soviet Heavy Industry: A Dollar Index of Output, 1927/28 to 1937," May 1955.

9. *L'Economie Appliquée* for "Notes on the Rate of Soviet Industrial Growth" ("Notes sur le taux de croissance actuel de l'industrie soviétique"), October-December 1953.

10. Harvard University Press for "Industrial Enterprise in Russia," *The Corporation in Modern Society*, E. S. Mason, ed., 1960.

11. *American Slavic and East European Review* for "A Neglected Source of Economic Information on Soviet Russia," February 1950.

12. *World Politics* for "Reflections on Soviet Novels," January 1960.

13. University of Chicago Press for "Notes on *Doctor Zhivago*," which appeared in *Modern Philology*, February 1961.

14. The International Economic Association for passages in the Postscript to this volume from "The Early Phases of Industrialization in Russia."

15. *Journal of the American Statistical Association* for "Problems of Measuring Long-Term Growth in Income and Wealth," December 1957.

Contents

Introduction

THE essays in this volume were written and published in various journals and symposia between 1951 and 1961. Revision of the original texts has been held down to a minimum. The piece on the speed of Soviet industrialization (Chapter 10) is the only one that has been largely rewritten. The other essays remain unchanged, save for some added or deleted footnotes, numerous but small editorial changes, and in one case (Chapter 6) the elimination of two final sections, the subject matter of which has been shifted to another chapter.[1]

A volume of this sort is exposed to two dangers threatening from opposite directions: lack of inner cohesion and repetitiousness. Neither has been fully avoided, and some brief discussion of the ways in which the individual pieces are interrelated may be in order. The first eight essays deal with problems of European industrial development in the nineteenth century. The writer's general ideas on the subject were laid down as early as 1951 in a paper which appears now as Chapter 1 of this collection. The reader will find the same ideas restated in several of the subsequent chapters, where they serve as springboards either for further elaboration of the general theme (as, for instance, in Chapter 2) or for treatment of case studies of industrialization in individual countries (Italy, Russia, and Bulgaria). These essays are dominated by the general hypothesis that very significant interspatial variations in the process of industrialization are functionally related to the degree of economic backwardness that prevailed in the countries concerned on the eve of their "great spurts" of industrial growth. In this fashion, the industrial history of Europe is conceived as a unified and yet graduated pattern.

[1] The two pieces "Rosario Romeo and the Original Accumulation of Capital" and "Some Aspects of Industrialization in Bulgaria" (Chapters 5 and 8) appeared in Italian only. The essay "Notes on the Rate of Industrial Growth in Soviet Russia" (Chapter 10) appeared in French only.

I

A general approach of this kind inevitably imparts a measure of inner cohesion. Still, a group of essays is not a monograph. It represents a series of successive explorations. Accordingly, it depicts the processes of research more clearly than its results. The latter are likely to change — sometimes imperceptibly — from essay to essay. Perhaps the Postscript at the end of this volume will serve to point out some of those changes and to discuss both the limits of the approach and the possible paths of future research.

The last six essays deal with the problems of economic and social change in Soviet Russia. As is intimated in Chapter 1, Soviet evolution may be considered a special case within the general pattern of European economic development. But the differences are formidable and the hiatus between the two groups of essays is undeniable. For in Russia the individual elements in the pattern have been both magnified and distorted beyond all recognition. The reasons for the deviations are not necessarily "ideological," in the customary sense of the term. It can be argued (as in Chapter 11) that viewing the Soviet economy as "socialist" does little to advance our understanding of that economy. Nor is the very high rate of growth in itself its characteristic feature. Rather, it is the fact that the policy of rapid industrialization has been inaugurated and maintained by a totalitarian dictatorship and that the mechanics of dictatorial power have come to dominate the economic processess; this has created curious incongruities and actually prevented, or at least delayed, the mental adjustment of the population to the normalcy of a fully industrialized society.

This is the main point made in the "Reflections on Soviet Novels" (Chapter 13) which, therefore, should not be approached as an effort in literary criticism. The latter description might apply with more justice to the last essay in the collection. The reader may, however, consider "Notes on *Doctor Zhivago*" in conjunction with the preceding essay: precisely because of the specific deficiencies of the Soviet value system, Pasternak in his bold protest against dictatorial oppression rejects "material" progress and shows nothing but disdain for the fruits thereof.

Although much in Soviet economic development is thus *sui generis,* there are aspects of Soviet economic research which relate it rather closely to studies of European industrializations. It is the quantitative measures of growth which provide a common bond for the two groups of essays. This requires brief explanation.

Because of the inadequacies of official Soviet indices of output and income, Western scholars have tried to develop some more satisfactory gauges. Among these attempts belongs this writer's construction of a dollar index of output of heavy industries in Soviet Russia during the 1930s. The respective studies are summarized here in Chapter 9. Whatever the light they may have cast on processes of Soviet industrialization, they rather dramatically revealed the quantitative significance of the index-number problem over long periods, and particularly in times of rapid growth. Since the general approach to European industrial history as presented in this volume deals with processes of long-term change, and also focuses on periods when the rate of growth was relatively high, the greater awareness of the effects of changes in the weighting system has been useful far beyond the area of Soviet statistics.

It may be added that an economic historian, once the importance of the index-number problem has been called to his attention, does not necessarily view it — as does the statistician — simply as a regrettable failure of our tools. He will realize that the long-run changes in weights of output indices are themselves an integral part of economic history and as such a very worthwhile object of historical study. The reader will see, therefore, that Chapter 9, in addition to summarizing this writer's five statistical studies of Soviet output, also attempts to place the index-number problem within the framework of historical processes of industrialization.

It is, furthermore, fair to say that preoccupation with the inadequacies of Soviet statistics has sharpened our eye not only for the index-number problem but also for a number of relatively simple but important general requirements of satisfactory index making. In particular, the present state of the procedures used in otherwise very respectable studies for deflating long-term national-income data at current prices in a number of continental countries appears woefully inadequate. This point is made more specifically in a short review which is attached to this volume as Appendix III. Data on industrial output are more reliable than those on national income, but they, too, are capable of considerable improvement. The first remedy would seem to lie in ruthless publicity. Those who present statistical series on long-term economic change must offer the reader an unobstructed look into the statistician's laboratory. Accordingly, this writer's indices of Italian and Bulgarian output (Chapters 4 and 8) are supported by rather complete statements on sources, nature of the raw data, and methods of computation, which the reader will find in Appendices I and II.[2]

The general importance of these statistical problems must not be underrated. But in the present context they also serve to emphasize the fact that such unity as this volume possesses lies not only in the affinity of the themes treated but also, even though less conspicuously, in the methods of research that have been applied.

[2] So far these appendices have been available only in mimeographed form.

I

Economic Backwardness in Historical Perspective

~~~~~~~~

A HISTORICAL approach to current problems calls perhaps for a word of explanation. Unlike so many of their predecessors, modern historians no longer announce to the world what inevitably will, or at least what ideally should, happen. We have grown modest. The prophetic fervor was bound to vanish together with the childlike faith in a perfectly comprehensible past whose flow was determined by some exceedingly simple and general historical law. Between Seneca's assertion of the absolute certainty of our knowledge of the past and Goethe's description of history as a book eternally kept under seven seals, between the *omnia certa sunt* of the one and the *ignorabimus* of the other, modern historical relativism moves gingerly. Modern historians realize full well that comprehension of the past — and that perforce means the past itself — changes perpetually with the historian's emphasis, interest, and point of view. The search is no longer for a determination of the course of human events as ubiquitous and invariant as that of the course of the planets. The iron necessity of historical processes has been discarded. But along with what John Stuart Mill once called "the slavery of antecedent circumstances" have been demolished the great bridges between the past and the future upon which the nineteenth-century mind used to travel so safely and so confidently.

Does this mean that history cannot contribute anything to the understanding of current problems? Historical research consists es-

sentially in application to empirical material of various sets of empir-
ically derived hypothetical generalizations and in testing the closeness
of the resulting fit, in the hope that in this way certain uniformities,
certain typical situations, and certain typical relationships among individual factors in these situations can be ascertained. None of these
lends itself to easy extrapolations. All that can be achieved is an
extraction from the vast storehouse of the past of sets of intelligent
questions that may be addressed to current materials. The importance
of this contribution should not be exaggerated. But it should not be
underrated either. For the quality of our understanding of current
problems depends largely on the broadness of our frame of reference.
Insularity is a limitation on comprehension. But insularity in thinking
is not peculiar to any special geographic area. Furthermore, it is not
only a spatial but also a temporal problem. All decisions in the field
of economic policies are essentially decisions with regard to combinations of a number of relevant factors. And the historian's contribution consists in pointing at *potentially* relevant factors and at
potentially significant combinations among them which could not be
easily perceived within a more limited sphere of experience. These
are the questions. The answers themselves, however, are a different
matter. No past experience, however rich, and no historical research,
however thorough, can save the living generation the creative task
of finding their own answers and shaping their own future. The following remarks, therefore, purport to do no more than to point at
some relationships which existed in the past and the consideration
of which in current discussions might prove useful.

THE ELEMENTS OF BACKWARDNESS

A good deal of our thinking about industrialization of backward
countries is dominated — consciously or unconsciously — by the grand
Marxian generalization according to which it is the history of advanced or established industrial countries which traces out the road
of development for the more backward countries. "The industrially
more developed country presents to the less developed country a
picture of the latter's future." [1] There is little doubt that in some

[1] Karl Marx, *Das Kapital* (1st ed.), preface.

broad sense this generalization has validity. It is meaningful to say that Germany, between the middle and the end of the last century, followed the road which England began to tread at an earlier time. But one should beware of accepting such a generalization too whole-heartedly. For the half-truth that it contains is likely to conceal the existence of the other half — that is to say, in several very important respects the development of a backward country may, by the very virtue of its backwardness, tend to differ fundamentally from that of an advanced country.

It is the main proposition of this essay that in a number of important historical instances industrialization processes, when launched at length in a backward country, showed considerable differences, as compared with more advanced countries, not only with regard to the speed of the development (the rate of industrial growth) but also with regard to the productive and organizational structures of industry which emerged from those processes. Furthermore, these differences in the speed and character of industrial development were to a considerable extent the result of application of institutional instruments for which there was little or no counterpart in an established industrial country. In addition, the intellectual climate within which industrialization proceeded, its "spirit" or "ideology," differed considerably among advanced and backward countries. Finally, the extent to which these attributes of backwardness occurred in individual instances appears to have varied directly with the degree of backwardness and the natural industrial potentialities of the countries concerned.

Let us first describe in general terms a few basic elements in the industrialization processes of backward countries as synthesized from the available historical information on economic development of European countries [2] in the nineteenth century and up until the beginning of the First World War. Thereupon, on the basis of concrete examples, more will be said on the effects of what may be called

[2] It would have been extremely desirable to transcend the European experience at least by including some references to the industrialization of Japan. Unfortunately, the writer's ignorance of Japanese economic history has effectively barred him from thus broadening the scope of his observations. The reader must be referred, however, to the excellent study by Henry Rosovsky, *Capital Formation in Japan, 1868–1940* (Glencoe, 1961), in which the validity of this writer's approach for Japanese industrial history is explicitly discussed.

7

"relative backwardness" upon the course of industrial development in individual countries.

The typical situation in a backward country prior to the initiation of considerable industrialization processes may be described as characterized by the tension between the actual state of economic activities in the country and the existing obstacles to industrial development, on the one hand, and the great promise inherent in such a development, on the other. The extent of opportunities that industrialization presents varied, of course, with the individual country's endowment of natural resources. Furthermore, no industrialization seemed possible, and hence no "tension" existed, as long as certain formidable institutional obstacles (such as the serfdom of the peasantry or the far-reaching absence of political unification) remained. Assuming an adequate endowment of usable resources, and assuming that the great blocks to industrialization had been removed, the opportunities inherent in industrialization may be said to vary directly with the backwardness of the country. Industrialization always seemed the more promising the greater the backlog of technological innovations which the backward country could take over from the more advanced country. Borrowed technology, so much and so rightly stressed by Veblen, was one of the primary factors assuring a high speed of development in a backward country entering the stage of industrialization. There always has been the inevitable tendency to deride the backward country because of its lack of originality. German mining engineers of the sixteenth century accused the English of being but slavish imitators of German methods, and the English fully reciprocated these charges in the fifties and sixties of the past century. In our own day, Soviet Russia has been said to have been altogether imitative in its industrial development, and the Russians have retorted by making extraordinary and extravagant claims. But all these superficialities tend to blur the basic fact that the contingency of large imports of foreign machinery and of foreign know-how, and the concomitant opportunities for rapid industrialization with the passage of time, increasingly widened the gulf between economic potentialities and economic actualities in backward countries.

The industrialization prospects of an underdeveloped country are frequently judged, and judged adversely, in terms of cheapness

8

of labor as against capital goods and of the resulting difficulty in substituting scarce capital for abundant labor. Sometimes, on the contrary, the cheapness of labor in a backward country is said to aid greatly in the processes of industrialization. The actual situation, however, is more complex than would appear on the basis of simple models. In reality, conditions will vary from industry to industry and from country to country. But the overriding fact to consider is that industrial labor, in the sense of a stable, reliable, and disciplined group that has cut the umbilical cord connecting it with the land and has become suitable for utilization in factories, is not abundant but extremely scarce in a backward country. Creation of an industrial labor force that really deserves its name is a most difficult and protracted process. The history of Russian industry provides some striking illustrations in this respect. Many a German industrial laborer of the nineteenth century had been raised in the strict discipline of a Junker estate which presumably made him more amenable to accept the rigors of factory rules. And yet the difficulties were great, and one may recall the admiring and envious glances which, toward the very end of the century, German writers like Schulze-Gaevernitz kept casting across the Channel at the English industrial worker, "the man of the future . . . born and educated for the machine . . . [who] does not find his equal in the past." In our time, reports from industries in India repeat in a still more exaggerated form the past predicaments of European industrializations in the field of labor supply.

Under these conditions the statement may be hazarded that, to the extent that industrialization took place, it was largely by application of the most modern and efficient techniques that backward countries could hope to achieve success, particularly if their industrialization proceeded in the face of competition from the advanced country. The advantages inherent in the use of technologically superior equipment were not counteracted but reinforced by its labor-saving effect. This seems to explain the tendency on the part of backward countries to concentrate at a relatively early point of their industrialization on promotion of those branches of industrial activities in which recent technological progress had been particularly rapid; while the more advanced countries, either from inertia or from unwillingness to require or impose sacrifices implicit in a large investment program, were

9

more hesitant to carry out continual modernizations of their plant. Clearly, there are limits to such a policy, one of them being the inability of a backward country to extend it to lines of output where very special technological skills are required. Backward countries (although not the United States) were slow to assimilate production of modern machine tools. But a branch like iron and steel production does provide a good example of the tendency to introduce most modern innovations, and it is instructive to see, for example, how German blast furnaces so very soon become superior to the English ones, while in the early years of this century blast furnaces in still more backward southern Russia were in the process of outstripping in equipment their German counterparts. Conversely, in the nineteenth century, England's superiority in cotton textile output was challenged neither by Germany nor by any other country.

To a considerable extent (as in the case of blast furnaces just cited), utilization of modern techniques required, in nineteenth-century conditions, increases in the average size of plant. Stress on bigness in this sense can be found in the history of most countries on the European continent. But industrialization of backward countries in Europe reveals a tendency toward bigness in another sense. The use of the term "industrial revolution" has been exposed to a good many justifiable strictures. But, if industrial revolution is conceived as denoting no more than cases of sudden considerable increases in the rate of industrial growth, there is little doubt that in several important instances industrial development began in such a sudden, eruptive, that is, "revolutionary," way.

The discontinuity was not accidental. As likely as not the period of stagnation (in the "physiocratic" sense of a period of low rate of growth) can be terminated and industrialization processes begun only if the industrialization movement can proceed, as it were, along a broad front, starting simultaneously along many lines of economic activities. This is partly the result of the existence of complementarity and indivisibilities in economic processes. Railroads cannot be built unless coal mines are opened up at the same time; building half a railroad will not do if an inland center is to be connected with a port city. Fruits of industrial progress in certain lines are received as external economies by other branches of industry whose progress in turn accords benefits to the former. In viewing the economic history of Europe in the nineteenth century, the impression is very strong that only when industrial development could commence on a large scale did the tension between the preindustrialization conditions and the benefits expected from industrialization become sufficiently strong to overcome the existing obstacles and to liberate the forces that made for industrial progress.

This aspect of the development may be conceived in terms of Toynbee's relation between challenge and response. His general observation that very frequently small challenges do not produce any responses and that the volume of response begins to grow very rapidly (at least up to a point) as the volume of the challenge increases seems to be quite applicable here. The challenge, that is to say, the "tension," must be considerable before a response in terms of industrial development will materialize.

The foregoing sketch purported to list a number of basic factors which historically were peculiar to economic situations in backward countries and made for higher speed of growth and different productive structure of industries. The effect of these basic factors was, however, greatly reinforced by the use in backward countries of certain institutional instruments and the acceptance of specific industrialization ideologies. Some of these specific factors and their mode of operation on various levels of backwardness are discussed in the following sections.

THE BANKS

The history of the Second Empire in France provides rather striking illustrations of these processes. The advent of Napoleon III terminated a long period of relative economic stagnation which had begun with the restoration of the Bourbons and which in some sense and to some extent was the result of the industrial policies pursued by Napoleon I. Through a policy of reduction of tariff duties and elimination of import prohibitions, culminating in the Cobden-Chevalier treaty of 1860, the French government destroyed the hothouse in which French industry had been kept for decades and exposed it to the stimulating atmosphere of international competition. By abolishing monopoly profits in the stagnating coal and iron production, French industry at length received profitable access to basic industrial raw materials.

To a not inconsiderable extent, the industrial development of France under Napoleon III must be attributed to that determined effort to untie the strait jacket in which weak governments and strong vested interests had inclosed the French economy. But along with these essentially, though not exclusively, negative policies of the government, French industry received a powerful positive impetus from a different quarter. The reference is to the development of industrial banking under Napoleon III.

The importance of that development has seldom been fully appreciated. Nor has it been properly understood as emanating from the specific conditions of a relatively backward economy. In particular, the story of the Crédit Mobilier of the brothers Pereire is often regarded as a dramatic but, on the whole, rather insignificant episode. All too often, as, for instance, in the powerful novels of Émile Zola, the actual significance of the developments is almost completely submerged in the description of speculative fever, corruption, and immorality which accompanied them. It seems to be much better in accord with the facts to speak of a truly momentous role of investment banking of the period for the economic history of France and of large portions of the Continent.

In saying that, one has in mind, of course, the immediate effects of creating financial organizations designed to build thousands of miles of railroads, drill mines, erect factories, pierce canals, construct ports, and modernize cities. The ventures of the Pereires and of a few others did all that in France and beyond the boundaries of France over vast areas stretching from Spain to Russia. This tremendous change in economic scenery took place only a few years after a great statesman and a great historian of the July monarchy assured the country that there was no need to reduce the duties on iron because the sheltered French iron production was quite able to cope with the iron needs of the railroads on the basis of his estimate of a prospective annual increase in construction by some fifteen to twenty miles.

But no less important than the actual economic accomplishments of a few men of great entrepreneurial vigor was their effect on their environment. The Crédit Mobilier was from the beginning engaged in a most violent conflict with the representatives of "old wealth" in French banking, most notably with the Rothschilds. It was this conflict that had sapped the force of the institution and was primarily responsible for its eventual collapse in 1867. But what is so seldom realized is that in the course of this conflict the "new wealth" succeeded in forcing the old wealth to adopt the policies of its opponents. The limitation of old wealth in banking policies to flotations of government loans and foreign-exchange transactions could not be maintained in the face of the new competition. When the Rothschilds prevented the Pereires from establishing the Austrian Credit-Anstalt, they succeeded only because they became willing to establish the bank themselves and to conduct it not as an old-fashioned banking enterprise but as a crédit mobilier, that is, as a bank devoted to railroadization and industrialization of the country.

This conversion of the old wealth to the creed of the new wealth points out the direction of the most far-reaching effects of the Crédit Mobilier. Occasional ventures of that sort had been in existence in Belgium, Germany, and France herself. But it was the great eruptive effect of the Pereires that profoundly influenced the history of Continental banking in Europe from the second half of the past century onward. The number of banks in various countries shaped upon the image of the Pereire bank was considerable. But more important than their slavish imitations was the creative adaptation of the basic idea of the Pereires and its incorporation in the new type of bank, the universal bank, which in Germany, along with most other countries on the Continent, became the dominant form of banking. The difference between banks of the crédit-mobilier type and commercial banks in the advanced industrial country of the time (England) was absolute. Between the English bank essentially designed to serve as a source of short-term capital and a bank designed to finance the long-run investment needs of the economy there was a complete gulf. The German banks, which may be taken as a paragon of the type of the universal bank, successfully combined the basic idea of the crédit mobilier with the short-term activities of commercial banks.

They were as a result infinitely sounder financial institutions than the Crédit Mobilier, with its enormously swollen industrial portfolio, which greatly exceeded its capital, and its dependence on favorable developments on the stock exchange for continuation of its activities. But the German banks, and with them the Austrian and Italian banks, established the closest possible relations with industrial enterprises. A German bank, as the saying went, accompanied an industrial enterprise from the cradle to the grave, from establishment to liquidation throughout all the vicissitudes of its existence. Through the device of formally short-term but in reality long-term current account credits and through development of the institution of the supervisory boards to the position of most powerful organs within corporate organizations, the banks acquired a formidable degree of ascendancy over industrial enterprises, which extended far beyond the sphere of financial control into that of entrepreneurial and managerial decisions.

It cannot be the purpose of this presentation to go into the details of this development. All that is necessary is to relate its origins and effects to the subject under discussion. The industrialization of England had proceeded without any substantial utilization of banking for long-term investment purposes. The more gradual character of the industrialization process and the more considerable accumulation of capital, first from earnings in trade and modernized agriculture and later from industry itself, obviated the pressure for developing any special institutional devices for provision of long-term capital to industry. By contrast, in a relatively backward country capital is scarce and diffused, the distrust of industrial activities is considerable, and, finally, there is greater pressure for bigness because of the scope of the industrialization movement, the larger average size of plant, and the concentration of industrialization processes on branches of relatively high ratios of capital to output. To these should be added the scarcity of entrepreneurial talent in the backward country.

It is the pressure of these circumstances which essentially gave rise to the divergent development in banking over large portions of the Continent as against England. The continental practices in the field of industrial investment banking must be conceived as specific instruments of industrialization in a backward country. It is here essentially that lies the historical and geographic locus of theories of economic development that assign a central role to processes of forced saving by the money-creating activities of banks. As will be shown presently, however, use of such instruments must be regarded as specific, not to backward countries in general, but rather to countries whose backwardness does not exceed certain limits. And even within the latter for a rather long time it was mere collection and distribution of available funds in which the banks were primarily engaged. This circumstance, of course, did not detract from the paramount importance of such activities on the part of the banks during the earlier industrialization periods with their desperate shortages of capital for industrial ventures.

The effects of these policies were far-reaching. All the basic tendencies inherent in industrial development in backward countries were greatly emphasized and magnified by deliberate attitudes on the part of the banks. From the outset of this evolution the banks were primarily attracted to certain lines of production to the neglect, if not virtual exclusion, of others. To consider Germany until the outbreak of World War I, it was essentially coal mining, iron- and steelmaking, electrical and general engineering, and heavy chemical output which became the primary sphere of activities of German banks. The textile industry, the leather industry, and the foodstuff-producing industries remained on the fringes of the banks' interest. To use modern terminology, it was heavy rather than light industry to which the attention was devoted.

Furthermore, the effects were not confined to the productive structure of industry. They extended to its organizational structure. The last three decades of the nineteenth century were marked by a rapid concentration movement in banking. This process indeed went on in very much the same way on the other side of the English Channel. But in Britain, because of the different nature of relations between banks and industry, the process was not paralleled by a similar development in industry.

It was different in Germany. The momentum shown by the cartelization movement of German industry cannot be fully explained, except as the natural result of the amalgamation of German banks. It was the mergers in the field of banking that kept placing banks in the positions of controlling competing enterprises. The banks refused to tolerate fratricidal struggles among their children. From the vantage point of centralized control, they were at all times quick to perceive profitable opportunities of cartelization and amalgamation of industrial enterprises. In the process, the average size of plant kept growing, and at the same time the interests of the banks and their assistance were even more than before devoted to those branches of industry where cartelization opportunities were rife.

Germany thus had derived full advantages from being a relatively late arrival in the field of industrial development, that is to say, from having been preceded by England. But, as a result, German industrial economy, because of specific methods used in the catching-up process, developed along lines not insignificantly different from those in England.

THE STATE

The German experience can be generalized. Similar developments took place in Austria, or rather in the western sections of the Austrian-Hungarian Empire, in Italy, in Switzerland, in France, in Belgium, and in other countries, even though there were differences among the individual countries. But it certainly cannot be generalized for the European continent as a whole, and this for two reasons: (1) because of the existence of certain backward countries where no comparable features of industrial development can be discovered and (2) because of the existence of countries where the basic elements of backwardness appear in such an accentuated form as to lead to the use of essentially different institutional instruments of industrialization.

Little need be said with reference to the first type of country. The industrial development of Denmark may serve as an appropriate illustration. Surely, that country was still very backward as the nineteenth century entered upon its second half. Yet no comparable sudden spurts of industrialization and no peculiar emphasis on heavy industries could be observed. The reasons must be sought, on the one hand, in the paucity of the country's natural resources and, on the other hand, in the great opportunities for agricultural improvement that were inherent in the proximity of the English market. The peculiar response did not materialize because of the absence of the challenge.

Russia may be considered as the clearest instance of the second type of country. The characteristic feature of economic conditions in Russia was not only that the great spurt of modern industrialization came in the middle of the 1880s, that is to say, more than three decades after the beginning of rapid industrialization in Germany; even more important was the fact that at the starting point the level of economic development in Russia had been incomparably lower than that of countries such as Germany and Austria.

The main reason for the abysmal economic backwardness of Russia was the preservation of serfdom until the emancipation of 1861. In a certain sense, this very fact may be attributed to the play of a curious mechanism of economic backwardness, and a few words of explanation may be in order. In the course of its process of territorial expansion, which over a few centuries transferred the small duchy of Moscow into the huge land mass of modern Russia, the country became increasingly involved in military conflicts with the West. This involvement revealed a curious internal conflict between the tasks of the Russian government that were "modern" in the contemporaneous sense of the word and the hopelessly backward economy of the country on which the military policies had to be based. As a result, the economic development in Russia at several important junctures assumed the form of a peculiar series of sequences: (1) Basic was the fact that the state, moved by its military interest, assumed the role of the primary agent propelling the economic progress in the country. (2) The fact that economic development thus became a function of military exigencies imparted a peculiarly jerky character to the course of that development; it proceeded fast whenever military necessities were pressing and subsided as the military pressures relaxed. (3) This mode of economic progress by fits and starts implied that, whenever a considerable upsurge of economic activities was required, a very formidable burden was placed on the shoulders of the generations whose lifespan happened to coincide with the period of intensified development. (4) In order to exact effectively the great sacrifices it required, the government had to subject the reluctant population to a number of severe measures of oppression lest the burdens imposed be evaded by escape to the frontier regions in the southeast and east. (5) Precisely because of the magnitude of the governmental exactions, a period of rapid development was very likely to give way to prolonged stagnation, because the great effort had been pushed beyond the limits of physical endurance of the population and long periods of economic stagnation were the inevitable consequences.

The sequences just mentioned present in a schematic way a pattern of Russian economic development in past centuries which fits best the period of the reforms under Peter the Great, but its applicability is by no means confined to that period.

What must strike the observer of this development is its curiously paradoxical course. While trying, as Russia did under Peter the Great, to adopt Western techniques, to raise output and the skills of the population to levels more closely approaching those of the West, Russia by virtue of this very effort was in some other respects thrown further away from the West. Broadly speaking, placing the trammels of serfdom upon the Russian peasantry must be understood as the obverse side of the processes of Westernization. Peter the Great did not institute serfdom in Russia, but perhaps more than anyone else he did succeed in making it effective. When in subsequent periods, partly because of point 2 and partly because of point 5 above, the state withdrew from active promotion of economic development and the nobility emancipated itself from its service obligations to the government, peasant serfdom was divested of its connection with economic development. What once was an indirect obligation to the state became a pure obligation toward the nobility and as such became by far the most important retarding factor in Russia's economic development.

Readers of Toynbee's may wish to regard this process, ending as it did with the emancipation of the peasantry, as an expression of the "withdrawal and return" sequence. Alternatively they may justifiably prefer to place it under the heading of "arrested civilizations." At any rate, the challenge-response mechanism is certainly useful in thinking about sequences of that nature. It should be noted, however, that the problem is not simply one of quantitative relationship between the volume of the challenge and that of the response. The crucial point is that the magnitude of the challenge changes the *quality* of the response and, by so doing, not only injects powerful retarding factors into the economic process but also more likely leads to a number of undesirable noneconomic consequences. To this aspect, which is most relevant to the current problem of industrialization of backward countries, we shall advert again in the concluding remarks of this essay.

To return to Russian industrialization in the eighties and the nineties of the past century, it may be said that in one sense it can be viewed as a recurrence of a previous pattern of economic development in the country. The role of the state distinguishes rather clearly the type of Russian industrialization from its German or Austrian counterpart.

Emancipation of the peasants, despite its manifold deficiencies, was an absolute prerequisite for industrialization. As such it was a negative action of the state designed to remove obstacles that had been earlier created by the state itself and in this sense was fully comparable to acts such as the agrarian reforms in Germany or the policies of Napoleon III which have been mentioned earlier. Similarly, the great judicial and administrative reforms of the sixties were in the nature of creating a suitable framework for industrial development rather than promoting it directly.

The main point of interest here is that, unlike the case of Western Europe, actions of this sort did not per se lead to an upsurge of individual activities in the country; and for almost a quarter of a century after the emancipation the rate of industrial growth remained relatively low. The great industrial upswing came when, from the middle of the eighties on, the railroad building of the state assumed unprecedented proportions and became the main lever of a rapid industrialization policy. Through multifarious devices such as preferential orders to domestic producers of railroad materials, high prices, subsidies, credits, and profit guaranties to new industrial enterprises, the government succeeded in maintaining a high and, in fact, increasing rate of growth until the end of the century. Concomitantly, the Russian taxation system was reorganized, and the financing of industrialization policies was thus provided for, while the stabilization of the ruble and the introduction of the gold standard assured foreign participation in the development of Russian industry.

The basic elements of a backward economy were, on the whole, the same in Russia of the nineties and in Germany of the fifties. But quantitatively the differences were formidable. The scarcity of capital in Russia was such that no banking system could conceivably succeed in attracting sufficient funds to finance a large-scale industrialization; the standards of honesty in business were so disastrously low, the general distrust of the public so great, that no bank could have hoped to attract even such small capital funds as were available, and no bank could have successfully engaged in long-term credit policies in an economy where fraudulent bankruptcy had been almost elevated to the rank of a general business practice. Supply of capital for the needs of industrialization required the compulsory machinery of the government, which, through its taxation policies, succeeded in directing incomes from consumption to investment. There is no doubt that the government as an *agens movens* of industrialization discharged its role in a far less than perfectly efficient manner. Incompetence and corruption of bureaucracy were great. The amount of waste that accompanied the process was formidable. But, when all is said and done, the great success of the policies pursued under Vyshnegradski and Witte is undeniable. Not only in their origins but also in their effects, the policies pursued by the Russian government in the nineties resembled closely those of the banks in Central Europe. The Russian state did not evince any interest in "light industry." Its whole attention was centered on output of basic industrial materials and on machinery production; like the banks in Germany, the Russian bureaucracy was primarily interested in large-scale enterprises and in amalgamations and coordinated policies among the industrial enterprises which it favored or had helped to create. Clearly, a good deal of the government's interest in industrialization was predicated upon its military policies. But these policies only reinforced and accentuated the basic tendencies of industrialization in conditions of economic backwardness.

Perhaps nothing serves to emphasize more these basic uniformities in the situation and the dependence of actual institutional instruments used on the degree of backwardness of the country than a comparison of policies pursued within the two halves of the Austrian-Hungarian monarchy, that is to say, within one and the same political body. The Austrian part of the monarchy was backward in relation to, say, Germany, but it was at all times much more advanced than its Hungarian counterpart. Accordingly, in Austria proper the banks could successfully devote themselves to the promotion of industrial activities. But across the Leitha Mountains, in Hungary, the activities of the banks proved altogether inadequate, and around the turn of the century the Hungarian government embarked upon vigorous policies of industrialization. Originally, the government showed a considerable interest in developing the textile industry of the region. And it is instructive to watch how, under the pressure of what the French like to call the "logic of things," the basic uniformities asserted themselves and how the generous government subsidies were more and more deflected from textile industries to promotion of heavy industries.

THE GRADATIONS OF BACKWARDNESS

To return to the basic German-Russian paradigm: what has been said in the foregoing does not exhaust the pattern of parallels. The question remains as to the effects of successful industrializations, that is to say, of the gradual diminution of backwardness.

At the turn of the century, if not somewhat earlier, changes became apparent in the relationship between German banks and German industry. As the former industrial infants had grown to strong manhood, the original undisputed ascendancy of the banks over industrial enterprises could no longer be maintained. This process of liberation of industry from the decades of tutelage expressed itself in a variety of ways. Increasingly, industrial enterprises transformed connection with a single bank into cooperation with several banks. As the former industrial protectorates became economically sovereign, they embarked upon the policy of changing alliances with regard to the banks. Many an industrial giant, such as the electrical engineering industry, which could not have developed without the aid and entrepreneurial daring of the banks, began to establish its own banks. The conditions of capital scarcity to which the German banks owed their historical position were no longer present. Germany had become a developed industrial country. But the specific features engendered by a process of industrialization in conditions of backwardness were to remain, and so was the close relation between banks and industry, even though the master-servant relation gave way to cooperation among equals and sometimes was even reversed.

In Russia the magnificent period of industrial development of the nineties was cut short by the 1900 depression and the following years of war and civil strife. But, when Russia emerged from the revolutionary years 1905–1906 and again achieved a high rate of industrial growth in the years 1907–1914, the character of the industrialization processes had changed greatly. Railroad construction by the government continued but on a much smaller scale both absolutely and even more so relatively to the increased industrial output. Certain increases in military expenditures that took place could not begin to compensate for the reduced significance of railroad-building. The conclusion is inescapable that, in that last period of industrialization under a prerevolutionary government, the significance of the state was very greatly reduced.

At the same time, the traditional pattern of Russian economic development happily failed to work itself out. The retrenchment of government activities led not to stagnation but to a continuation of industrial growth. Russian industry had reached a stage where it could throw away the crutches of government support and begin to walk independently — and, yet, very much less independently than industry in contemporaneous Germany, for at least to some extent the role of the retreating government was taken over by the banks.

A great transformation had taken place with regard to the banks during the fifty years that had elapsed since the emancipation. Commercial banks had been founded. Since it was the government that had fulfilled the function of industrial banks, the Russian banks, precisely because of the backwardness of the country, were organized as "deposit banks," thus resembling very much the type of banking in England. But, as industrial development proceeded apace and as capital accumulation increased, the standards of business behavior were growingly Westernized. The paralyzing atmosphere of distrust began to vanish, and the foundation was laid for the emergence of a different type of bank. Gradually, the Moscow deposit banks were overshadowed by the development of the St. Petersburg banks that were conducted upon principles that were characteristic not of English but of German banking. In short, after the economic backwardness of Russia had been reduced by state-sponsored industrialization processes, use of a different instrument of industrialization, suitable to the new "stage of backwardness," became applicable.

IDEOLOGIES OF DELAYED INDUSTRIALIZATIONS

Before drawing some general conclusions, a last differential aspect of industrialization in circumstances of economic backwardness should be mentioned. So far, important differences with regard to the character of industrial developments and its institutional vehicles were related to conditions and degrees of backwardness. A few words remain to be said on the ideological climate within which such industrialization proceeded.

Again we may revert to the instructive story of French industrialization under Napoleon III. A large proportion of the men who reached positions of economic and financial influence upon Napoleon's advent to power were not isolated individuals. They belonged to a rather well-defined group. They were not Bonapartists but Saint-Simonian socialists. The fact that a man like Isaac Pereire, who contributed so much, perhaps more than any other single person, to the spread of the modern capitalist system in France should have been — and should have remained to the end of his days — an ardent admirer of Saint-Simonian doctrines is on the face of it surprising. It becomes much less so if a few pertinent relationships are considered.

It could be argued that Saint-Simon was in reality far removed from being a socialist; that in his vision of an industrial society he hardly distinguished between laborers and employers; and that he considered the appropriate political form for his society of the future some kind of corporate state in which the "leaders of industry" would exercise major political functions. Yet arguments of that sort would hardly explain much. Saint-Simon had a profound interest in what he used to call the "most numerous and most suffering classes"; more importantly, Saint-Simonian doctrines, as expanded and redefined by the followers of the master (particularly by Bazard), incorporated into the system a good many socialist ideas, including abolition of inheritance and establishment of a system of planned economy designed to direct and to develop the economy of the country. And it was this interpretation of the doctrines which the Pereires accepted.

It is more relevant to point to the stress laid by Saint-Simon and his followers upon industrialization and the great task they had assigned to banks as an instrument of organization and development of the economy. This, no doubt, greatly appealed to the creators of the Crédit Mobilier, who liked to think of their institution as of a "bank to a higher power" and of themselves as "missionaries" rather than bankers. That Saint-Simon's stress upon the role to be played by the banks in economic development revealed a truly amazing — and altogether "unutopian" — insight into the problems of that development is as true as the fact that Saint-Simonian ideas most decisively influenced the course of economic events inside and outside France. But the question remains: why was the socialist garment draped around an essentially capitalist idea? And why was it the socialist form that was so readily accepted by the greatest capitalist entrepreneurs France ever possessed?

It would seem that the answer must again be given in terms of basic conditions of backwardness. Saint-Simon, the friend of J. B. Say, was never averse to ideas of laissez-faire policies. Chevalier, the co-author of the Franco-English treaty of commerce of 1860 that ushered in the great period of European free trade, had been an ardent Saint-Simonian. And yet under French conditions a laissez-faire ideology was altogether inadequate as a spiritual vehicle of an industrialization program.

To break through the barriers of stagnation in a backward country, to ignite the imaginations of men, and to place their energies in the service of economic development, a stronger medicine is needed than the promise of better allocation of resources or even of the lower price of bread. Under such conditions even the businessman, even the classical daring and innovating entrepreneur, needs a more powerful stimulus than the prospect of high profits. What is needed to remove the mountains of routine and prejudice is faith — faith, in the words of Saint-Simon, that the golden age lies not behind but ahead of mankind. It was not for nothing that Saint-Simon devoted his last years to the formulation of a new creed, the New Christianity, and suffered Auguste Comte to break with him over this "betrayal of true science." What sufficed in England did not suffice in France.

Shortly before his death, Saint-Simon urged Rouget de Lisle, the aged author of the "Marseillaise," to compose a new anthem, an "Industrial Marseillaise." Rouget de Lisle complied. In the new hymn the man who once had called upon "enfants de la patrie" to wage ruthless war upon the tyrants and their mercenary cohorts addresses himself to "enfants de l'industrie" — the "true nobles" — who would assure the "happiness of all" by spreading industrial arts and by submitting the world to the peaceful "laws of industry."

Ricardo is not known to have inspired anyone to change "God

Save the King" into "God Save Industry." No one would want to detract from the force of John Bright's passionate eloquence, but in an advanced country rational arguments in favor of industrialization policies need not be supplemented by a quasi-religious fervor. Buckle was not far wrong when in a famous passage of his *History* he presented the conversion of public opinion in England to free trade as achieved by the force of incontrovertible logic. In a backward country the great and sudden industrialization effort calls for a New Deal in emotions. Those carrying out the great transformation as well as those on whom it imposes burdens must feel, in the words of Matthew Arnold, that

> . . . Clearing a stage
> Scattering the past about
> Comes the new age.

Capitalist industrialization under the auspices of socialist ideologies may be, after all, less surprising a phenomenon than would appear at first sight.

Similarly, Friedrich List's industrialization theories may be largely conceived as an attempt, by a man whose personal ties to Saint-Simonians had been very strong, to translate the inspirational message of Saint-Simonism into a language that would be accepted in the German environment, where the lack of both a preceding political revolution and an early national unification rendered nationalist sentiment a much more suitable ideology of industrialization.

After what has been just said it will perhaps not seem astonishing that, in the Russian industrialization of the 1890s, orthodox Marxism can be said to have performed a very similar function. Nothing reconciled the Russian intelligentsia more to the advent of capitalism in the country and to the destruction of its old faith in the mir and the artel than a system of ideas which presented the capitalist industrialization of the country as the result of an iron law of historical development. It is this connection which largely explains the power wielded by Marxist thought in Russia when it extended to men like Struve and in some sense even Milyukov, whose Weltanschauung was altogether alien to the ideas of Marxian socialism. In conditions of Russian "absolute" backwardness, again, a much more powerful

ideology was required to grease the intellectual and emotional wheels of industrialization than either in France or in Germany. The institutional gradations of backwardness seem to find their counterpart in men's thinking about backwardness and the way in which it can be abolished.

CONCLUSIONS

The story of European industrialization in the nineteenth century would seem to yield a few points of view which may be helpful for appreciation of present-day problems.

1. If the spurtlike character of the past century's industrialization on the European continent is conceived of as the result of the specific preindustrial situations in backward countries and if it is understood that pressures for high-speed industrializations are inherent in those situations, it should become easier to appreciate the oft-expressed desires in this direction by the governments of those countries. Slogans like "Factories quick!" which played such a large part in the discussions of the pertinent portions of the International Trade Organization charter, may then appear less unreasonable.

2. Similarly, the tendencies in backward countries to concentrate much of their efforts on introduction of the most modern and expensive technology, their stress on large-scale plant, and their interest in developing investment-goods industries need not necessarily be regarded as flowing mainly from a quest for prestige and from economic megalomania.

3. What makes it so difficult for an advanced country to appraise properly the industrialization policies of its less fortunate brethren is the fact that, in every instance of industrialization, imitation of the evolution in advanced countries appears in combination with different, indigenously determined elements. If it is not always easy for advanced countries to accept the former, it is even more difficult for them to acquiesce in the latter. This is particularly true of the institutional instruments used in carrying out industrial developments and even more so of ideologies which accompany it. What can be derived from a historical review is a strong sense for the significance of the native elements in the industrialization of backward countries.

A journey through the last century may, by destroying what

Bertrand Russell once called the "dogmatism of the untravelled," help in formulating a broader and more enlightened view of the pertinent problems and in replacing the absolute notions of what is "right" and what is "wrong" by a more flexible and relativistic approach.

It is, of course, not suggested here that current policies vis-à-vis backward areas should be formulated on the basis of the general experience of the past century without taking into account, in each individual instance, the degree of endowment with natural resources, the climatic disabilities, the strength of institutional obstacles to industrialization, the pattern of foreign trade, and other pertinent factors. But what is even more important is the fact that, useful as the "lessons" of the nineteenth century may be, they cannot properly be applied without understanding the climate of the present century, which in so many ways has added new and momentous aspects to the problems concerned.

Since the present problem of industrialization of backward areas largely concerns non-European countries, there is the question of the effects of their specific preindustrial cultural development upon their industrialization potentialities. Anthropological research of such cultural patterns has tended to come to rather pessimistic conclusions in this respect. But perhaps such conclusions are unduly lacking in dynamic perspective. At any rate, they do not deal with the individual factors involved in terms of their specific changeabilities. At the same time, past Russian experience does show how quickly in the last decades of the past century a pattern of life that had been so strongly opposed to industrial values, that tended to consider any nonagricultural economic activity as unnatural and sinful, began to give way to very different attitudes. In particular, the rapid emergence of native entrepreneurs with peasant-serf backgrounds should give pause to those who stress so greatly the disabling lack of entrepreneurial qualities in backward civilizations. Yet there are other problems.

In certain extensive backward areas the very fact that industrial development has been so long delayed has created, along with unprecedented opportunities for technological progress, great obstacles to industrialization. Industrial progress is arduous and expensive; medical progress is cheaper and easier of accomplishment. To the ex-

27

tent that the latter has preceded the former by a considerable span of time and has resulted in formidable overpopulation, industrial revolutions may be defeated by Malthusian counterrevolutions.

Closely related to the preceding but enormously more momentous in its effects is the fact that great delays in industrialization tend to allow time for social tensions to develop and to assume sinister proportions. As a mild example, the case of Mexico may be cited, where the established banks have been reluctant to cooperate in industrialization activities that are sponsored by a government whose radical hue they distrust. But the real case in point overshadowing everything else in scope and importance is, of course, that of Soviet Russia.

If what has been said in the preceding pages has validity, Soviet industrialization undoubtedly contains all the basic elements that were common to the industrializations of backward countries in the nineteenth century. The stress on heavy industry and oversized plant is, as such, by no means peculiar to Soviet Russia. But what is true is that in Soviet Russia those common features of industrialization processes have been magnified and distorted out of all proportion.

The problem is as much a political as it is an economic one. The Soviet government can be properly described as a product of the country's economic backwardness. Had serfdom been abolished by Catherine the Great or at the time of the Decembrist uprising in 1825, the peasant discontent, the driving force and the earnest of success of the Russian Revolution, would never have assumed disastrous proportions, while the economic development of the country would have proceeded in a much more gradual fashion. If anything is a "grounded historical assumption," this would seem to be one: the delayed industrial revolution was responsible for a political revolution in the course of which the power fell into the hands of a dictatorial government to which in the long run the vast majority of the population was opposed. It is one thing for such a government to gain power in a moment of great crisis; it is another to maintain this power for a long period. Whatever the strength of the army and the ubiquitousness of the secret police which such a government may have at its disposal, it would be naive to believe that those instruments of physical oppression can suffice. Such a government can maintain itself in power only if it succeeds in making people believe that it performs an important social function which could not be discharged in its absence.

Industrialization provided such a function for the Soviet government. All the basic factors in the situation of the country pressed in that direction. By reverting to a pattern of economic development that should have remained confined to a long-bygone age, by substituting collectivization for serfdom, and by pushing up the rate of investment to the maximum point within the limits of endurance of the population, the Soviet government did what no government relying on the consent of the governed could have done. That these policies, after having led through a period of violent struggles, have resulted in permanent day-to-day friction between the government and the population is undeniable. But, paradoxical as it may sound, these policies at the same time have secured some broad acquiescence on the part of the people. If all the forces of the population can be kept engaged in the processes of industrialization and if this industrialization can be justified by the promise of happiness and abundance for future generations and — much more importantly — by the menace of military aggression from beyond the borders, the dictatorial government will find its power broadly unchallenged. And the vindication of a threatening war is easily produced, as is shown by the history of the cold-war years. Economic backwardness, rapid industrialization, ruthless exercise of dictatorial power, and the danger of war have become inextricably intertwined in Soviet Russia.

This is not the place to elaborate this point further with regard to Soviet Russia. The problem at hand is not Soviet Russia but the problem of attitudes toward industrialization of backward countries. If the Soviet experience teaches anything, it is that it demonstrates *ad oculos* the formidable dangers inherent in our time in the existence of economic backwardness. There are no four-lane highways through the parks of industrial progress. The road may lead from backwardness to dictatorship and from dictatorship to war. In conditions of a "bipolar world" this sinister sequence is modified and aggrandized by deliberate imitation of Soviet policies by other backward countries and by their voluntary or involuntary incorporation in the Soviet orbit.

Thus, conclusions can be drawn from the historical experience of both centuries. The paramount lesson of the twentieth century is that the problems of backward nations are not exclusively their own. They are just as much problems of the advanced countries. It is not only Russia but the whole world that pays the price for the failure to emancipate the Russian peasants and to embark upon industrialization policies at an early time. Advanced countries cannot afford to ignore economic backwardness. But the lesson of the nineteenth century is that the policies toward the backward countries are unlikely to be successful if they ignore the basic peculiarities of economic backwardness. Only by frankly recognizing their existence and strength, and by attempting to develop fully rather than to stifle what Keynes once called the "possibilities of things," can the experience of the nineteenth century be used to avert the threat presented by its successor.

2

Reflections on the Concept of "Prerequisites"
of Modern Industrialization

THE concept of historical prerequisites of modern industrialization is a rather curious one. Certain major obstacles to industrialization *must* be removed and certain things propitious to it *must* be created before industrialization can begin. Both in its negative and its positive aspects, the concept seems to imply, if not the historical inevitability of industrialization, at least the notion that it must proceed in a certain manner; that is to say, through certain more or less discrete stages. Along with it goes the idea of the uniformity of industrial development in the sense that every industrialization necessarily must be based on the same set of preconditions. What is meant, of course, is not the common-sense notion that in order to start an industrial plant certain very concrete things are needed. The concept refers to long-run historical changes.

It would be easy to reject the concept out of hand as a classic example of historical determinism and to leave it at that. This, however, might be regrettable. To be sure, determinism, historical or other, is beyond the boundary line that circumscribes scientific endeavors. It is quite possible that complete knowledge of the world would reveal to us that every event has been inevitably preordained. It may not reveal that at all. How can we know what we would know if we knew? At the same time, however, we cannot approach historical reality except through a search of regularities and deviations from regularities, by conceiving events and sequences of events in terms of

3 1

constructs of our mind, of patterns, of models. There is an infinite variety of possible models, each one of them subject to change and rejection. And yet, as long as we think in terms of a given model, we are all determinists in the sense that we pose a certain interrelation, or sequence, of events and phenomena which is "inevitable." Within this "denaturalized" meaning all scholarly work is deterministic, except that we remain determinists subject to notice, as it were, in the never-ending process of constructing models and discarding them.

Therefore, it may be quite worthwhile to look more closely into the question of prerequisites of industrial development, however rigid the concept may appear on the face of it. It is precisely the purpose of the following pages to discuss the connotations of the concept and to see whether or not it can be divested of its dogmatic character and perhaps be placed within some broader and less stringent explanatory patterns.

I

Although the concept of prerequisites seems to have rather firm connotations, the individual factors that have been considered prerequisites have been rather loosely defined. Very frequently, a rather curious procedure has been followed. One first takes a look at something like an "ideal type" of preindustrial economy, say, the medieval economy in Western Europe of the fourteenth century, and emphasizes a social framework within which the opportunities for growth were rather restricted. Thereupon, in a cinematographic shift, attention is moved to a modern industrial economy. The change in landscape naturally is striking. The inventory of economic progress is enormous: a large politically and economically unified territory; a legal system assuring the rights of the individual and satisfactory protection for property; a store of technological lore; increase in productivity in agriculture rendered possible by the elimination of the open-field system and distribution of common pastures; availability of labor supply of various skills; an entrepreneurial group willing and able to calculate and to innovate; availability of capital for long-term investment; nonexistence of guild restrictions; wide and absorptive markets; and so forth and so on.

Then, with a slight twist of the pen, all those basic traits of a modern economy are declared to be "prerequisites" of industrial development. This, no doubt, has rather discouraging implications as far as development of backward countries is concerned. Have they really to create all those conditions *before* they can embark upon the process of industrialization? Obviously, some of the factors listed are not prerequisites at all, but rather something that developed in the course of industrial development. Moreover, what can be reasonably regarded as a prerequisite in some historical cases can be much more naturally seen as a product of industrialization in others. The line between what is a precondition of, and what is a response to industrial development seems to be a rather flexible one. It might be possible to indicate some regularities according to which the relevant phenomena might be found on the one or the other side of that line.

As was said before, the idea that there are some fundamental prerequisites of industrial development implies a view of that development characterized both by a high degree of generality and by specific discontinuities. Let us select from the rather hybrid listing of various prerequisites the one of "capital availability" and try, with the help of this example, to discuss at some length the nature, the validity, and the usefulness of the concept.

When availability of capital is turned into a prerequisite it assumes the form of "original accumulation of capital," a concept given currency in Marx's famous Chapter 24 in Volume One of *Das Kapital*. There, Adam Smith's concept of previous accumulation hitched to the period of production of the firm, so matter-of-fact and so short-run, was turned into a magnificent historical generalization. It referred to an accumulation of capital continuing over long historical periods — perhaps over several centuries — until one day the tocsin of the industrial revolution was to summon it to the battlefields of factory construction.

The concept found a considerable resonance in terms of a large body of literature. Perhaps its last faint echo, mainly designed "to amuse the curious," was Keynes's reference to Drake's booty as the fount and origin of England's foreign investment.[1] We are concerned here neither with the specific treatment of the problem by Marx nor with the further discussions and controversies in which Sombart's

[1] John M. Keynes, *A Treatise on Money* (London, 1930), II, 156–157.

somewhat grandiloquent and, alas, so thoroughly unsuccessful attempt to "solve the riddle of bourgeois wealth" [2] played such a large part. It matters little that Marx chose to connect his concept so intimately with the early land-enclosing movements in England, to place so much emphasis upon the redistribution of *existing* wealth, and to allow himself to be deflected into the question of preindustrial accumulation of labor. Modern research has cast a good deal of doubt on some of Marx's empirical findings, particularly on his evaluation of the English enclosures in the sixteenth century. The relative significance of the alleged sources of original accumulation — piracy and wars, exploitation of colonies, trade, enclosures, urban rents, influx of precious metals — is rather immaterial for our purpose, except of course for one basic fact: industrial profits could *not* be regarded as a source of original accumulation without negating the very nature of the concept. And this is indeed the problem.

If for the moment we consider original accumulation analytically rather than historically, and try to perceive the pattern of industrial development of which the concept is an integral part, the pertinent question is: why should development proceed in this fashion at all? Why should a long period of capital accumulation *precede* the period of rapid industrialization? Why is not the capital as it is being accumulated also invested in industrial ventures, so that industry grows *pari passu* with the accumulation of capital? To the extent that this happened, Marxian "originality" of accumulation would be reduced to the modest size of Smithian "previousness." In other words, nothing would remain of the specifically Marxian concept. Therefore, if one wishes to defend it one must exclude the contingency of a gradual industrialization and assume that, for one reason or another, industrialization either comes as a big spurt or does not come at all. There must be a certain specific discontinuity about the development which makes it possible to discern with reasonable clarity the beginning of the process.

In the light of the discussions in recent years, it is not difficult to think of conditions which would make for a "rapid spurt or nothing" situation. One can either argue technologically, as it were,

[2] Werner Sombart, *Der moderne Kapitalismus: Die vorkapitalische Wirtschaft* (Munich-Leipzig, 1928), I:2, 581f.

from the point of view of the minimum capital needs of an industrializing economy, having in mind the technologically required minimum size of the individual industrial firm and the availability of technologically required inputs which represent outputs of other firms. These considerations of indivisibility *cum* complementarity appear on the supply side and were presented with particular clarity and ingenuity in Dahmén's concept of development blocks.[3] Alternatively, or conjointly, one can argue from the demand side, postulating an industrial development along a broad front as the necessary condition of successful industrialization; the new enterprises created in the process in different branches of the industrial economy sustain their growth by the mutual demand for each other's products. If industrialization comes as a spurt, it must demand considerable capital and is therefore predicated upon the existence of sizable "preindustrial" accumulations of capital. In the spurt these accumulations appear essentially as claims on current output and render possible a deflection of resources from consumption to investment which is sufficiently large to sustain the high rate of industrial growth. This is a rather self-contained view in which the prerequisite and the resulting industrialization are indeed logically connected.

On the other hand, the idea that a conjunction of many different factors is necessary for successful industrialization lies on a somewhat different, though obviously related, plane. It may make sense to say that industrialization cannot begin as long as, say, most of the population is held away from industrial employment by a rigid system of serfdom. The sudden abolition of the institution may indeed adumbrate the beginning of industrial development. Such a beginning may be marked clearly enough. But one could not on the basis of such a reasoning *alone* argue that the capital requirements of such an industrial development will be particularly high. One would have to introduce some additional considerations in order to make this plausible. The abolition of serfdom may have released some latent entrepreneurial talent, some pent-up demand, and the like. But discontinuities of this sort do not stem from the nature of the process of industrialization.

[3] Erik Dahmén, *Svensk industriell företagarverksamhet* (Stockholm, 1950), I, 70.

One would look in vain in Marx's discussion for any explicit mention of the fundamental connection between preindustrial accumulation of capital and the subsequent industrialization. Curiously enough, the only explanation provided refers to the abolition of feudal restrictions, that is to say, to a rather incidental circumstance (incidental from the point of view of the concept). But this is of little interest. It cannot be gainsaid that the concept of original accumulation, if properly restated, has a rather modern touch. It testifies to the brilliance of Marx's intuition.

Moreover, the intuition is not just analytical. It is also historical. The more we learn about the nature of the industrialization process in a number of now advanced countries, the greater becomes the assurance with which we can assert that in very many cases the industrial development, after a certain period of preparation, assumed the form of a big spurt, during which for a fairly considerable length of time the development proceeded at an unusually rapid pace. Whether we look at the history of modern industrialism in England, France, Germany, Russia, or Italy, we can discern such upsurges in the growth of industrial output. Actual historical cases cannot, of course, conform with precision to the postulates of an analytical pattern. It is only with a grain of salt that those spurts of industrialization can be regarded as truly "initial." And still, bearing the necessary qualification in mind, it does make sense to say that most of the important industrializations in Europe started in the form of more or less violent industrial revolutions.

Perhaps a few words on that controversial term may be in order. The concept of the Industrial Revolution in England has been frequently criticized. What happened was very much in the nature of what Huizinga once called "inflation of historial concepts." Just as the concept of the Renaissance, originally securely anchored in the sixteenth century, was torn away from its moorings and allowed to drift backward into the preceding centuries, so also the start of the Industrial Revolution began to be shifted from the eighteenth to the seventeenth century, and further on into still earlier periods, the original meaning melting away in the process. All this was done in veneration of historical continuity which was, and perhaps still is, a fashionable concept with some writers. Now, historical continuity is used rather confusedly in at least three different senses. Continuity may mean that the historical roots of a given phenomenon reach very far back into the past. That, of course, is indubitably true as a general proposition and is, in fact, the basic justification of all historical work. Yet it says little about the actual course of historical processes, in particular whether such a course is revolutionary or evolutionary. To give an example from political history: Peter Struve, the great Russian economic historian, once remarked that the Russian political revolutions of this century occurred *because* Empress Anne, in 1730, had torn to shreds the draft of a constitution presented to her for signature by members of the high aristocracy.[4] This view may or may not be valid, but, assuming for a moment that it is, the fact that the roots of an event must be sought in a remote past does not necessarily make it evolutionary. As revolutions go, the Russian revolutions of 1905 and 1917 were revolutionary indeed. At the same time, continuity is used to indicate periodic recurrence of events on a broad historical scale. It is in this sense that one — again rightly or wrongly — operates with concepts like neomercantilism, particularly when, as in the case of Lipson,[5] it connotes the return to the "normalcy of planning," a fulfillment of a natural pattern in the course of which the wind returneth according to its circuits. Finally, continuity is also made to imply a very gradual change, the degree of which is hardly perceptible, in the sense of the motto, *natura non facit saltus*, Alfred Marshall chose for his *Principles*. Now, one may abhor revolutions and any rapid change; alternatively, one may find history without revolutions insufferably dull. The problem, however, is not one of personal likes and dislikes. Nor is it simply one of ascertaining the correct facts. In a sense, speed and changes in speed are arbitrary concepts. To the extent that we deal with measurable phenomena, they depend on the specific averaging techniques used in determining the rate of speed and acceleration. They depend on the length of the period chosen. These choices in turn must depend on the requirements of the problems under study. What is a revolution for one purpose may be seen as a very gradual change in another. A concept is as good as what can be

---

[4] *Sotsial'naya i ekonomicheskaya istoriya Rossii* (Social and Economic History of Russia) (Paris, 1952), p. 314.

[5] E. Lipson, *A Planned Economy or Free Enterprise* (London, 1946).

discovered with its help. If by "revolution" we understand in the first instance nothing more than a sudden upward change in the rate of growth of industrial output and if, in addition, such accelerations in speed as we do ascertain can be regarded as an independent factor in the process of growth because important characteristics in the process of industrialization tend to vary significantly with changes in speed, then economic historians can ill afford to ignore the existence of industrial revolutions. And indeed the revolutions which stare out at the historian from many of the long-term indices of industrial output in Western Europe cannot be ignored precisely because so many important factors of industrial development are so peculiarly correlated with those big spurts of early industrialization.

So far so good. But perhaps not good enough as far as the concept of original accumulation is concerned. True, the existence of initial periods of rapid growth *prima facie* speaks in favor of the concept. If no such periods were ascertainable, the concept could have been dismissed out of hand. As it is, further discussion is in order. There is still the question of whether in actual fact original accumulation can be considered as having materially aided the countries concerned during the period of their rapid industrial growth.

II

Before we touch on this crucial aspect of the problem, a few specific difficulties with the concept of original accumulation might be briefly mentioned. Also, this concept has been subject to "inflation," the beginnings of the process being shifted farther and farther back to the very start of the modern era and, with some writers, even farther back to the high noon of the Middle Ages.

A good deal of historical material assembled in support of the concept actually purports to show that in some earlier historical periods some people managed to become quite wealthy. But over long historical periods wealth is not only created but also destroyed. The Fuggers had acquired an amount of wealth that was unprecedented in the history of Europe. That wealth was largely acquired through connections with political powers but it was also destroyed by these connections. The South German wealth accumulated at the turn of the fifteenth and sixteenth centuries had written an important page in the story of European economic development. Export of technology and of modes of business organization from South Germany fertilized far-away areas. Those activities broke the period of deflationary pressures that had greatly contributed to the economic stagnation of Europe in the preceding period. But all this hardly fits any reasonably understood concept of original accumulation. The wealth of the Fuggers, dissipated in power politics and war finance, went up in the smoke of innumerable battlefields and was given the *coup de grâce* in the Spanish bankruptcies.

If we could assume for a rash moment that Sombart was right in his theory of urban rents as a source of medieval wealth, one still would have to ask: "What of it?" There would be still an obligation to follow through the history of that wealth up till the time of the great upsurge of German industrialization in the second half of the nineteenth century. Naturally, no one has attempted to do that, and one may be right in supposing that we know what the answer would be without too much investigating. In other words, the concept of original accumulation is not just a magnificent generalization; it is *too* magnificent a generalization, in the sense that in order to accept it one has to make abstraction from equally magnificent details, such as the economic impact of the Thirty Years' War upon Germany.

It is extremely doubtful, therefore, whether thinking in terms of very long historical periods of preparation for the industrial spurt makes good historical sense. On the other hand, when the period of original accumulation is foreshortened and reduced to a less extravagant length, other difficulties remain. It is easy to say that a wealthy country will find it easier to launch the period of rapid industrialization. As an abstract statement such a proposition is unexceptionable. In historical reality, however, simple availability of wealth will be helpful for industrialization only if it is assembled in the hands of the people who either will be willing to invest it in industrial ventures themselves or, alternatively, are willing and able to pass it on in one form or another to those who are immediately engaged in industrialization. In any case, it must be wealth in a form which either directly or through some financial transformation is capable of being so passed on. One can think of many historical cases where wealth, even though

39

potentially available and available in an appropriate form, will not in fact reach the industrial entrepreneurs. An inveterate tradition of hoarding may constitute an effective barrier. Apprehensions on the part of the landowning classes lest industrial development deprive them of their position of pre-eminence within the community may have similar effects. Merchants who have a good deal of liquid capital at their disposal may be quite unwilling to make their capital available for industrial ventures because such ventures would disrupt the putting-out system in which they may have direct and important interests. In short, there is no assurance at all that previously accumulated wealth will in fact be made available for industrial investment finance.

The problem, however, is not so much that "original accumulation" must be further qualified before it can serve as a historical prerequisite of modern industrialization. It is rather to find out under what special conditions the concept, even when duly qualified and deprived of its original magnificence, can be regarded as a true prerequisite of industrial development, and under what conditions it may be difficult, impossible, or unnecessary to attribute a great deal of significance to it. With this question we approach the second previously mentioned implication in the concept of prerequisites of industrial development: namely, the assumption of a uniform process of industrialization evolving in such a way that the industrialization, when it occurs anywhere on the globe, repeats in all essential characteristics a process of industrialization that had taken place previously in some other country or region. It would seem that such an assumption leads to a much too simplified view of industrial processes in general, and particularly in their initial phases.

This, of course, is not to raise once more the specter of the "unique and individual" in history. Enough has been said before to suggest that the point is not to reject broad patterns as such, but to select patterns appropriate to the problem. Moreover, up to a point, a uniform pattern of industrial development is quite reasonable. Industrialization everywhere means increase in the volume of fixed capital; it means changes in technology, economies of scale, transformation of agricultural laborers and small artisans into factory workers; it means appearance of men, willing and able to exercise the entrepreneurial function.

Time and again the industrial development of Europe has been described in terms of a general pattern constructed upon the empirical material gleaned from English economic history. Such an approach is not without merit. Precisely because there are common features in all industrializations, it possessed and still possesses some explanatory and even predictive value. To concentrate upon these general aspects of industrialization may be quite useful for some purposes. But it is equally true, as always when the level of generality is pitched very high, that as one moves deeper and deeper into the subject one is bound to come across things in one area or another that do not fit the general model. When that happens, the historian, after he has refused to ignore the uncomfortable irregularities, is faced with two alternatives. He may regard those things as exceptions and treat them as such. Or else he can attempt to systematize the deviations from the original pattern by bringing them into a new, although necessarily more complicated, pattern. This is not something peculiar to economic history; rather, it is the path along which all scientific progress must move. Perhaps the historian who deals with broad and important phenomena has reason to be particularly aware of the problem and to remember that in principle every historical event that takes place changes the course of all subsequent events. The Industrial Revolution in England, and for that matter in other countries, affected the course of all subsequent industrializations.

This writer has felt for some time that some additional insights and a more profound understanding of the processes of European industrializations can be obtained if, instead of working with an undifferentiated uniform pattern of industrialization, one would consider the processes of industrial development in relation to the degree of backwardness of the areas concerned on the eve of their great spurts of industrialization. Such a view has distinct advantages inasmuch as it makes it possible to regard crucial features in the industrial evolution of the individual areas not as specific peculiarities, idiosyncrasies, or exceptions to the norm, but as part and parcel of a system of gradations of backwardness. Such a view has a direct bearing on the question of preindustrial accumulation and the problem of prerequisites of industrial development in general.

It is not necessary to present here more than the briefest possible outline of this general conception, and the reader may find a fuller treatment elsewhere.[6] But two relevant points may precede such a summary. The question as to what is "an intelligible area of study" is faced in any attempt at interpretive history. Intelligibility, of course, must be defined in terms of the problem at hand. Simon Kuznets once detailed the reasons for which a country, taken as a political unit, should be regarded as a basic area of observation in studies of economic development. He referred to the fact that neither the subdivisions within the country nor blocs of several countries constituted more significant units; he mentioned that data are usually available in terms of "states," and he clinched his argument by saying that a country presented a compact "bundle of historical experience." All this is indubitably correct.

Yet it is equally true that one cannot understand the industrial development of any country, as long as it be considered in isolation. Backwardness, of course, is a relative term. It presupposes the existence of more advanced countries. Moreover, it is only by comparing industrialization processes in several countries at various levels of backwardness that one can hope to separate what is accidental in a given industrial evolution from what can be reasonably attributed to the historical lags in a country's development. And, finally, it is only because a backward country is part of a larger area which comprises more advanced countries that the historical lags are likely to be overcome in a specifically intelligible fashion.

The other point refers to the measurability of backwardness. Is it an operational term? If the levels of output or income per capita of the population could be regarded as a satisfactory measure of backwardness, one would not be too far away from a satisfactory solution. In fact, one would be just as far away as the availability and quality of the data *and* the index-number problem would allow. Even so, serious problems of measurement must be encountered. Projecting outputs of different countries against the screen of the price system of one given country may lead to a widely different ranking of countries as compared with the ranking that would result from the use of the price system of another country. In practice, only the price system of the most advanced country in the group could be chosen because of

[6] See Chapters 1, 4, 7, and 8 of this volume.

the more limited range of output and accordingly of available price data in a more backward country.

But can a definition in terms of per-capita output suffice? Obviously, the level of per-capita output may be the result of unfavorable climatic conditions or of poor endowment with natural resources. While not impossible, it would be hazardous indeed to weigh the output data by the reciprocals of resource endowment and climatic propitiousness. Moreover, such conditions which make for high or low output in a preindustrial branch of the economy may, within limits, become more or less relevant after the big structural change has been ushered in and the industrialization launched.

Finally, it is not clear that output, however measured, is a fully satisfactory gauge of the degree of backwardness. One might want to define the degree of backwardness in more dynamic terms. And that would involve asking to what degree a country at a certain moment had developed the preconditions for subsequent economic development. Assume a country A where, say, per-capita output and resource endowment are equal to those of country B, but in the latter country a much larger percentage of the active population is illiterate, thus creating an obstacle to a rapid acquisition of industrial skills; or assume that in country B, for religious reasons, the people consider urban ways of life displeasing to the Lord and are deeply rooted in the soil, while such sentiments are quite alien to the inhabitants of country A, where there is a great and widespread willingness to respond to the call of pecuniary incentives. Would it not make good sense to include such factors, and many others of similar importance and bearing, in the concept of degree of backwardness? Obviously, this would be a hopeless enterprise. There is no precise system of weights by virtue of which disparate factors could be brought together over a common denominator; nor could we possibly determine the precise quantities of the pertinent factors to which those weights could be applied. One has to conclude, however reluctantly, that "degree of backwardness" defies exact measurement. But just how discouraging is a conclusion of this nature? It is important to have drawn it to prevent misleading notions and false hopes. On the other hand, it is far from clear that a high degree of precision is required for the purposes of historical analysis.

43

The purpose of such analysis is to associate certain differences in the historical process with the absence or presence of certain features in the economies concerned. If the cases with which we have to deal are sufficiently discrete and if, in addition, the individual factors on the whole tend to point in the same direction, then we may hope, without aspiring to any exact measurement, to be able to wield our material in such a fashion as to glean from it some meaningful and not altogether unimportant answers. And, indeed, as we look upon the economic scenery of nineteenth-century Europe, riveting our attention, say, to the midpoint of that century, few would disagree that Germany was more backward economically than France; that Austria was more backward than Germany; that Italy was more backward than Austria; and that Russia was more backward than any of the countries just mentioned. Similarly, few would deny England the position of the most advanced country of the time. Whether we think of levels of output, the degree of technological progress achieved, the skill of the population, the degree of its literacy, the standards of honesty and the time horizon of the entrepreneurs, or a number of other similar factors, we get roughly identical answers. In practice, we *can* rank the countries according to their backwardness and even discern groups of similar degree of backwardness.

The main proposition we can then make with regard to countries so ranked is that, the more delayed the industrial development of a country, the more explosive was the great spurt of its industrialization, if and when it came. Moreover, the higher degree of backwardness was associated with a stronger tendency toward larger scale of plant and enterprise and greater readiness to enter into monopolistic compacts of various degrees of intensity. Finally, the more backward a country, the more likely its industrialization was to proceed under some organized direction; depending on the degree of backwardness, the seat of such direction could be found in investment banks, in investment banks acting under the aegis of the state, or in bureaucratic controls. So viewed, the industrial history of Europe appears not as a series of mere repetitions of the "first" industrialization but as an orderly system of graduated deviations from that industrialization.

III

To return at length to the main problem of this essay, we may ask what happens to the concept of uniform prerequisites of industrial development in a world that is far from being uniform. In particular, what happens to the concept of preindustrial accumulation of capital? We have seen that what makes preindustrial accumulation of capital potentially meaningful is the discontinuity of industrial development. We have suggested that, the higher the degree of backwardness, the more discontinuous the development is likely to be. Does this mean that, the more backward a country, the more important was the previously accumulated wealth? Could this conclusion be further strengthened if one considers that in nineteenth-century Europe the capital-output ratios tended upward and, accordingly, the later a country industrialized, the higher was the rate of growth during its big upsurge of industrialization and the greater were its capital requirements per one percent of increase in output?

There is little doubt that in reality the opposite seems to have taken place. The building of factories in England no doubt benefited considerably from the existence of manifold sources of private wealth. One of the characteristics of the English development was that, in conditions of considerable antecedent progress, there was much willingness on the part of individuals to invest in industrial pursuits. But, in the more backward countries on the European continent, neither the size of previous accumulations nor the sympathy with industrial development was consonant with the much greater capital requirements of a delayed industrialization. The focal role in capital provision in a country like Germany must be assigned not to any original capital accumulation but to the role of credit-creation policies on the part of the banking system. It is true that the banks also collected and passed on to entrepreneurs both current savings and some previously created assets that could be converted into claims on current output, but this is much less significant.

When one moves on to even more backward areas where the spurts of industrialization were even more delayed and even more violent, such as Russia in the last decade of the century, one again would find it difficult to attribute a crucial role to any preindustrial

45

accumulations of capital. There it was the budgetary policies of the state that must be considered as the strategic factor in capital supply. This is not to say that this was the only available source. Capital imports were considerable. Preindustrial wealth played some part. Plowed-back profits could not be denied all importance even in the early stages of the process. Much remains to be done in the study of capital formation in Russia in the nineteenth century. But this much seems clear: all the other sources do tend to pale into insignificance compared with the role of budgetary finance of the new and growing industrial enterprises. If a somewhat sweeping expression is permissible, one might say that original accumulation of capital was not a prerequisite of industrial development in major countries on the European continent.

It would appear, therefore, that not very much has remained of the concept of original accumulation of capital. First, it had to be reduced temporally by limiting the length of the periods to which it could be reasonably applied. Then, it had to be further reduced, this time spatially. One might want to conclude that there is no general set of prerequisites valid for all times and climes and that each case must be studied independently. Yet it would be unfortunate if this negative conclusion were taken as a renunciation of a comparative approach to the problem. The framework which has been sketched out in the preceding paragraphs would seem to open up different possibilities. As has been intimated before, one way of defining the degree of backwardness is precisely in terms of absence, in a more backward country, of factors which in a more advanced country served as prerequisites of industrial development. Accordingly, one of the ways of approaching the problem is by asking what substitutions and what patterns of substitutions for the lacking factors occurred in the process of industrialization in conditions of backwardness.

One thing is obvious. Illiteracy and low standards of education, and the resulting difficulty in training skilled labor and efficient engineers, can be overcome to some extent by immigration from more advanced countries and to some extent by using the training facilities of those countries. The same is true, even more importantly, of the lack of a store of technical knowledge. It can be imported from abroad. In this sense, however, one can say that in a backward country there exists a "prerequisite" to industrial development which "the" advanced country did not have at its disposal, that is, the existence of the more advanced countries as sources of technical assistance, skilled labor, and capital goods. In addition, the existence of capital-abundant areas abroad has a bearing on the problem of original accumulation. To the extent that capital can be imported from abroad, the importance of previously created domestic wealth is *pro tanto* reduced. It is true, however, that the *tantum* never was excessively large. Even in Russia of the 1890s, according to this writer's computations, capital imports constituted but a relatively small portion of total capital made available for the purposes of industrialization; this is true even if very low capital-output ratios are assumed for calculating total capital formation during the period. On the other hand, capital import, unlike transformation of previously created wealth into titles on current output, implies the possibility to invest without lowering the rate of current consumption; similarly, the opportunities for imports of capital goods from abroad, if they are financed by such previous accumulations of bullion and plate as may exist in the backward country, also avoid reduction in levels of consumption. That is something which neither the credit-creating policies of banks nor the government policies of tax-financed expenditures can achieve. It is another question that a government engaged in the policy of vigorous industrialization, as was the Russian government in the 1890s, was in a position to tap otherwise inaccessible founts of credit.

Considerations of this sort, however, do not begin to exhaust the range of possible substitution patterns. The question as to why industrialization occurred under the aegis of the banks in the moderately backward areas in Central Europe and under that of the state in the more backward areas farther east can at least partly be answered in terms of absence or presence of certain prerequisites. What effectively prevented banks from engaging in industrial investment in Russia of the nineteenth century was *inter alia* the impossibility of building up an effective system of long-term bank credit in a country where the standards of commercial honesty had been so low and where economic, and particularly mercantile, activities and deceit were regarded as inseparably connected. "He who does not cheat does not sell," taught the economic wisdom of the folklore. Well-staged and repeated

47

bankruptcies were regarded as almost normal steps on the road to wealth. In these circumstances, the government even felt impelled to issue specific injunctions against involvement of banks in long-term credit operations.

In a sense, in Russia the activities of the government effectively substituted for the lacking prerequisite of minimum acceptable standards of commercial honesty. The existence of the prerequisite in Central Europe made possible a different, much more decentralized type of industrialization finance. But one could go further and inquire into the reasons of the differences in standards of commercial honesty in, say, Germany and Russia. To be sure, many an answer to such a question could be found. For instance, the badly delayed emancipation of the Russian peasantry must have had a good deal to do with it. The institution of labor services bred mendacity and deception. The serf-entrepreneurs had many excellent reasons to deceive their owners. The legal uncertainty with regard to peasants' property rights was hardly designed to educate the mass of the population in the spirit of respect for contractual obligations. Yet probably no less important was the absence in Russia of a tradition of urban independence. A sociology of economic honesty still remains to be written, but there is little doubt that over large areas of Europe the historical experience of the craft guilds, with their attempts to increase and to maintain standards of quality and reliability, was of considerable importance in forming the business ethics of the community. One could argue, therefore, that in a country like Germany it was the historical training school of the craft guilds that served as a prerequisite to industrial development by making it possible to substitute the prerequisite of original accumulation by the more efficient banking policies rather than by the less efficient and more costly bureaucratic controls. When in the seventeenth century a keen foreign observer, Yuri Krizhanich, cogitated on the ways and means to reform the sloth and dishonesty of the Russian artisans and traders, the introduction of craft guilds suggested itself to his mind as the most natural remedy.[7] An attempt to create the guilds by government fiat, as was later tried by Peter the Great, could not yield the same positive results as did their

[7] *Russkoye gosudarstvo v polovine XVII veka* (The Russian State in the Middle of the Seventeenth Century) (Moscow, 1859), pp. 28f.

spontaneous evolution in Western Europe. One might say, then, that in Russia the government's policies of industrialization also had to function as a substitute for the missing prerequisite of craft-guild experience.

To give another example: cause and effect are usually intermingled in the discussion of the relationship between the enclosure movement and the industrial progress in England. But it is clear that the latter was materially aided by the growth of productivity in English agriculture that took place during the eighteenth century. But here again government action may be regarded as a substitute, however unpleasant, for the prerequisite of increases in food supplies. To be sure, the transformation of virgin steppes in the south of Russia into arable widened the food basis somewhat. Still, the period of the rapid industrial spurt in Russia in the last decade of the century occurred in conditions of a grave crisis in agriculture. To some extent, the crisis was caused by the fact that industrialization was financed, and, among other things, food supplies to the cities and for export were made available, through confiscation of peasant income and to some extent even through capital depletion. It is true, of course, that all such processes were later dwarfed by the agrarian policies of the Soviet government and its incomparably more ruthless exploitation of the Russian peasantry. Yet the Soviet case is a very peculiar one, and for many reasons prerevolutionary Russia seems to provide a much more "normal" case for a discussion of specific patterns of substitution in the process of industrialization.

Along with increases in food supplies, the increase in supply of labor for the needs of the nascent industries is usually mentioned as the factor which imparts to agrarian reforms the character of a prerequisite. The deliberate preservation and even strengthening of the Russian village commune through the emancipation procedure of the 1860s and several subsequent measures certainly tended to inhibit the formation of an industrial labor force in Russia. Permanent renunciation of the right to land allotment involved considerable financial losses; a member of the village commune working in cities was subject to recall to the village; for decades, departures for work in towns required permissive action on the part of village authorities and family heads. All these were serious impediments to a movement which in any circumstances had to overcome a good deal of ingrained reluctance and inertia.

The finality which attended the move of a landless laborer from the East Elbian estates to the Ruhr Valley was more seldom reproduced in Russia. As a result, a labor force permanently committed to the factory increased much more slowly than might have been the case otherwise. But, to some extent, this deficiency was substituted for by specific entrepreneurial decisions with regard to the volume and character of capital investment in Russian factories. The difficulties in creating a reliable and steady labor force were at least partly compensated for by a choice of more labor-saving equipment in a number of industrial branches. At the same time, in other branches of industry the large labor-force turnover was met by the introduction of more modern machinery, simpler in operation, for which the necessary learning time was shorter and therefore more reasonably related to the prospective duration of employment. In this way, what might be called the basic propensity of a backward country to concentrate on the areas of most recent technological progress, and thus to utilize a specific advantage of backwardness, was further intensified.

IV

It has not been the purpose of the foregoing pages to present more than a few examples; nor has it been intended to qualify and elaborate the relationships touched upon. The purpose rather has been to point out the great elasticity and variability in the industrialization processes that are known from historical experience. It would seem that the lack of something that might be regarded as a *general* set of prerequisites of industrial development does not necessarily diminish the heuristic value of the concept of prerequisites. It is precisely by starting from that concept and by trying to understand how a given country managed to start its process of industrialization despite the lack of certain prerequisites that one can arrive at some differentiated and still coordinated view of industrialization in conditions of graduated backwardness. As we look at the later stages of the process, we find that what may have functioned as a prerequisite and, in a sense, as a "cause" of industrialization in one country appears as an effect of industrialization in another. This serves to reinforce and to complete the present approach to industrial development. This process of a belated "normalization" of the development is also likely to be understood more clearly if it is related to the degree of backwardness of the areas concerned.

On the other hand, there is, of course, no intention to infer that absence of certain "prerequisites" should be regarded in any way as "advantages of backwardness." It is largely the existence of such advantages that makes it possible to overcome the lack of preconditions for economic progress. But the process as a rule was a costly one. It would be a fruitful undertaking in research to explore and perhaps to measure and compare the difficulties, the strains, and the cost which were involved in the various processes of substitution which have been discussed in the preceding pages. The sovereign disregard for the human cost of such substitutions has been perhaps the most characteristic feature of Soviet industrialization over some three decades.

At the same time, however, it may be in order to suggest that past historical experience may justify a measure of optimism with regard to the general prospects of industrialization of backward countries. What is meant is not simply that past industrializations occurred in the face of considerable obstacles and deficiencies. In viewing the historical record one cannot fail to be impressed with the ingenuity, originality, and flexibility with which backward countries tried to solve the specific problems of their industrial development. There is no *a priori* reason to suppose that the underdeveloped countries which today stand on the threshold of their industrial revolutions will show less creative adaptation in compensating for the absence of factors which in more fortunate countries may be said to have "preconditioned" the initial spurts of rapid industrial growth. One can only hope that in drafting the maps of their own industrial progress they will be eager to select those paths along which they will be able to keep down the cost and to increase the yield in terms of human welfare and human happiness.

3

Social Attitudes, Entrepreneurship, and Economic Development

"Social attitudes" is not a very precise term. It must be treated with restraint. Otherwise it will quickly expand to embrace the whole ambit of governmental economic policies — a topic very properly assigned to a special session of this conference.[1] We shall deal here essentially with the significance for a country's economic development of popular evaluations of entrepreneurs and entrepreneurial activities; that is to say, of the general climate of opinion within which entrepreneurial action takes place. Even when so restricted, the problem remains vast, and a great deal of patient monographic research is necessary before any firm conclusions can be reached. The following impressionistic remarks, therefore, purport to do no more than to present briefly some general lines of thought that have been pursued so far, to issue some warnings against too ready an acceptance of certain abstract models, and to illustrate these warnings by reference to some segments of European economic history of the nineteenth century. With regard to the latter, the emphasis is on earlier stages of industrialization rather than on conditions in mature economies. Except for a brief allusion, the question as to what extent European historical experience can be used for elucidating the current problems of underdeveloped countries must likewise remain outside the scope of this paper.

Research on the problem under discussion is still in its infancy.

[1] The reference is to the "Round Table" of the International Economic Association on Economic Progress, 1953.

However, the Harvard Research Center in Entrepreneurial History under the able leadership of Arthur Cole has devoted, over several years, much time and thought to an "entrepreneurial approach to economic history," and it has paid a good deal of attention to the question of social attitudes toward entrepreneurship. Entrepreneurial research in the United States has received its intellectual stimulus primarily from two sources. It has been, of course, greatly influenced by Schumpeter's theory of economic development, which assigns to the innovating entrepreneur a focal role in the process of economic change. In fact, Professor Schumpeter remained in intimate association with the Research Center at Harvard until his death in 1950, and the wealth of Schumpeterian hypotheses — and intuitions — quite naturally predetermined many of the paths of research to be followed. At a very early stage, however, as the problem of the entrepreneurial position within the community impressed itself upon those working in the field, the need was felt for a more rigorous and comprehensive sociological framework. Such a framework has been developed over a wide range of recent writings in the field of social psychology, anthropology, and sociology and has found perhaps its most powerful systematic expression in the theoretical structure which over the past two decades has been erected by Talcott Parsons and the scholars assembled around him.

Even if the writer felt qualified to do so, there still would be neither need nor possibility to enter within the scope of these pages into a discussion of the Parsonian system. But a few words on some specific concepts to the extent that they have affected entrepreneurial research — and only to that extent — may be in order.[2] The interest in this respect centers upon the so-called theory of roles. The individual members of the community are seen as performing specific social roles, and it is the role which "for most purposes [is] the conceptual unit of the social system."[3] "The primary ingredient of the role is

[2] The following references (unless otherwise stated) are taken from the symposium, *Toward a General Theory of Action*, edited by Talcott Parsons and Edward A. Shils (Cambridge, Mass., 1951), particularly from the fundamental Part 2, "Values, Motives, and Systems of Action," which comes from the pens of the two editors. The volume, it may be added, provides a most convenient point of entry for an economist who wishes to trespass upon the domain of modern sociology.

[3] *Toward a General Theory*, p. 190.

the role-expectation," [4] which denotes what role individuals expect each other to perform. Compliance with role-expectation is enforced through positive and negative sanctions (rewards and retributions). The role expectancies and sanction patterns are institutionalized into generalized value systems of the community. In a well-integrated society these values are "internalized in personality systems," that is, they are accepted and adopted by the individuals. As a result, the value system becomes the crucial determinant of action.[5]

One cannot suppress some wonderment as to why these particular concepts should have proven attractive to those interested in explaining the process of economic *change*. It does seem that these concepts essentially pertain to a static system. Of course, the system is still in evolution. Parsons' writings and those of his collaborators are shot through with multifarious warnings. In *Toward a General Theory of Action*, it is said explicitly that the work has not proceeded far beyond the "categorical" stage on the road to the formulation of the general "laws" of the system (pp. 50–51). One is warned that the "empirical significance of selective or value standards as determinants of concrete action may be considered problematical and should not be prejudged" (p. 63), that there are dangers in imputing "too much rigidity to behavior" and in overestimating its "uniformity within a given society" (p. 225). Most importantly, it is emphasized that very often "many of the most important seeds of social change" (p. 179) lie in the failure to maintain social integration at the achieved level. The impression is that the static character of the system is well recognized. Still it is claimed that, "in principle, propositions about the factors making for maintenance of the system are at the same time propo-

---

[4] *Ibid.*

[5] Parsons may be quite unwilling to accept the last sentence of this paragraph as a correct reproduction of his views. Elsewhere (*The Social System*, 1951), he explicitly rejects the "dominant factor theeories which were so popular a generation ago" (p. 493). Yet, time and again, it is said that "value orientations" are used as "major point of reference" (p. 484); that "the primary emphasis of this volume has been on the integration of social systems at the level of patterns of value orientations as institutionalized in role expectations" (p. 350); and so forth. It would seem that from a methodological point of view the substantive outcome is the same, and value orientations when so used do in fact assume the role of the "dominant factor." The difference may lie in the greater awareness of the limitations of the approach, but its locus then is without rather than within the system.

sitions about those making for change" (p. 231). Thus social dynamics is said to be included within the framework; and it is essentially in the conflicts between value systems — in an analysis of what Florence Kluckhohn called dominant, variant, and deviant (that is, prescribed, permissive, and proscribed) values (p. 415) — that the processes of change will be sought. This, however, is still a promise. For the time being it seems fair to say that it is the social state rather than social change to which main attention is addressed.[6]

Nevertheless, it is both the static and the nascent dynamic elements in the system that have excited the interest of entrepreneurial research. This is clearly in evidence in the pioneering symposium volume *Change and the Entrepreneur* which was prepared by the Entrepreneurial Research Center.[7] Thus in this volume Arthur Cole attaches explicit significance to the degree of social approval which the entrepreneur's striving for economic gain will receive in a given economic milieu, and he refers to various social systems from India to France where entrepreneurial activities labor under various degrees of disapproval (pp. 87–88). In his stimulating contribution, Leland H. Jenks[8] concerns himself in more detail with role factors, that is, with prescriptions concerning appropriate behavior of individuals who occupy a set of special positions. And, in dealing with the specific behavior of men like the elder Morgan or Cyrus McCormick, he stresses that whatever the importance of accidental factors in the make-up of

[6] Perhaps a word on the system as a whole may go unsuppressed. The system is presented as a social-equilibrium system, thus evoking comparisons with the general-equilibrium concept in economics. But time and again it appears that the concept of equilibrium is extended so far as to become coterminous with that of organized society; what, then, is actually discussed is not so much a set of equilibrium conditions as a set of minimum conditions of social existence, which would mean that most important and most variegated social processes might take place without any change in the basic variables that enter into the system.

[7] Harvard University Press (Cambridge, Mass., 1949). A good deal of water has gone down the Charles River since the publication of this volume. In quoting the views expressed by the contributors there is, of course, no intention to suggest that those views are necessarily still held in exactly the same form by the writers concerned. In fact, this would be most unlikely in a new and vigorously expanding field. But the volume in question remains the only reasonably full statement of problems in entrepreneurial research that is available, and it is used here for this reason. A new venture of the same kind incorporating the thought and the research experience of the intervening years would seem extremely desirable.

[8] "The Role Structure of Entrepreneurial Personality."

individuals their actions cannot be adequately understood unless they are placed within the context of the cultural patterns of their society (pp. 131–132). But Jenks moves a step beyond and places particular stress on the dichotomy of personal and social roles and the possibility of discrepancy between them. It is the existence of such discrepancies, he says, that is indicative of the fact that significant social change is in the making (p. 138). One would expect, therefore, the concept of entrepreneurial deviance to emerge as the primary device for understanding entrepreneurial behavior and the entrepreneur's role as an innovator. But we are quickly led back to the fold. It is again the "social roles" and the sanctioning acts by which the expected behavior is enforced that assume a central position in the explanatory mechanism. And all we are left with is the fact that in the case of entrepreneurs social roles are peculiarly "indistinct" and "flexible" which, we are told, is in turn the result, among other things, of the fact that the entrepreneurial position "entails the function and opportunity for introducing novelty into the economic structure" (p. 147).

Finally, mention must be made of the essay by Thomas C. Cochran in the same volume.[9] Cochran's essay, which is enclosed within the same conceptual framework, is of particular interest from our point of view because of his specific redefinition of deviant behavior. He speaks of sanctions designed to "encourage deviant behavior" (p. 160). Thus, the concept of deviance is divorced from the discrepancy between social and personal roles, and deviant behavior becomes fully consonant with social role-expectations. Obviously, deviance means something else to Cochran than it does to, say, Florence Kluckhohn, who identifies it with socially proscribed behavior.[10] In Cochran's mind deviance is simply associated with innovation and is seen as an integral part of the dominant value system.

Where does all this lead? Are we witnessing here a new theory of social change *in statu nascendi*? How can an economic historian use the analytical tools, with which he is being so generously supplied, in his attempts to elucidate empirical processes of economic change and, in particular, to understand entrepreneurial behavior? Surely, only very tentative answers can be given to these questions.

[9] "Role and Sanction in American Entrepreneurial History."
[10] *Toward a General Theory*, p. 415.

A dynamic theory? It seems that it allows of economic change in a twofold fashion. On the one hand, a well-integrated society in which economic innovating has become a generally accepted mode of behavior fits the system to a nicety. Since the process of innovation gives rise to what Schumpeter called "creative destruction," [11] the process of change, one may suspect, will still involve dissident personal values of the victims of economic change, but these may be either neglected or else the community assumed to be integrated to a point where even the loser in the process has so thoroughly "internalized" the social standard of value that

> Mit dem Geschick in hoher Einigkeit,
> Gelassen hingestuetzt auf Grazien und Musen,
> Empfaengt er das Geschoss, das ihn bedraeut,
> Mit freundlich dargebotnem Busen
> Vom sanften Bogen der Notwendigkeit.

Be that as it may, it is this type of "built-in" dynamism that apparently was in Cochran's mind. On the other hand, there is the original, nondenaturalized concept of deviant behavior on the part of the entrepreneur. This concept is intimated, but all too soon abandoned, by Jenks in his discussion of discrepancies between personal and social roles.[12]

Both concepts are, of course, meaningful per se. But it may be noted in passing that in Cochran's society the Schumpeterian concept of innovation loses a good deal of its interest. Innovation is regarded by Schumpeter as a "distinct economic function," *inter alia,* because of the environment's resistance to innovators and innovating processes.[13] Once the resistance of the environment is lowered, "personality and will power must count for less." [14] In other words, specific

[11] See in this connection the interesting treatment by Redlich of what he calls the "daimonic" entrepreneur: Fritz Redlich, *History of American Business Leaders* (Ann Arbor, 1940), I, 2–6, and "The Business Leader as a Daimonic Figure," *American Journal of Economics and Sociology,* January-April 1953.

[12] It may be mentioned that Parsons is well aware of the two types of processes of change. He speaks of "processes within the system" and "processes of change of the system" and objects to a confusion of the two in the common term "dynamics" (*The Social System,* p. 481).

[13] J. A. Schumpeter, *Capitalism, Socialism, and Democracy* (New York, 1942), p. 132. See also, *Business Cycles* (New York and London, 1939), I, 100.

[14] *Capitalism, loc. cit.*

entrepreneurial research offers less opportunity for understanding the processes of social change in such a society. At any rate, Cochran's society has little resemblance to economies which stand at the threshold of industrialization and are heavily burdened with traditional resistances to economic development.

In a sense, deviance which spurns the established value patterns may indeed be regarded as a dynamic force making for economic change. But it is at this point that our theories, both general and entrepreneurial, leave us in the lurch. For, though it may make sense in certain historical situations to take a dominant system of social values for granted, it is much less satisfactory to accept the deviant behavior as given. If we deal with an agricultural community based on century-long traditions, we may be willing to accept those traditions as given without caring much about the whys and the wherefores. But if suddenly deviant values make their entry upon the economic scene, the urge for further explanation is irresistible. We cannot help asking whence the change in value orientations: what has caused the sudden outburst? There is nothing within the theoretical framework that provides the elements of such an explanation beyond, perhaps, some implicit and inchoate ideas about the tolerable degree of tension between deviant and generally accepted behavior. In general, the concept of deviance is taken up gingerly and dropped abruptly, and the accent shifts back to the dominant value system as the determinant of action and to the social sanctioning of entrepreneurial behavior. Thus, the questions with which we are left focus on the problem of social approval.

How important is social approval for the emergence of entrepreneurial activities? In particular, what is its importance at the crucial stages of economic development when a country's economy becomes engaged in a sudden spurt of economic development? Should lack of social approval be regarded as a serious retarding factor? Does it affect in a significant manner the contents of entrepreneurial activities and make for adaptations in entrepreneurial attitudes which can be said to influence speed and character of a country's economic development? These questions cannot be answered, of course, except on the basis of extensive empirical research. In default of such research, the following remarks must be taken as highly tentative impressions from scattered, but perhaps relevant, historical material.

The theoretical formula is persuasively simple: social approval of entrepreneurial activity significantly affects its volume and quality. At times, it even appears as though social approval were regarded as a prerequisite for successful entrepreneurship. But doubts are bound to arise the moment historical material is approached. One might recall the dramatic pages in Augustin Thierry's *Tiers État* which deal with the *fermiers généraux.* Hated and despised, their very existence a slap in the face of all the prevailing standards of goodness and decency, perpetually accused and at times subject to monstrous persecutions, they nevertheless progressed and prospered economically and socially, their entrepreneurial vigor remaining unshaken.[15] *Toujours maudits et toujours nécessaires,* cursed and indispensable, they continued their activity, indulging their greed and maturing their frauds. Why did not social disapproval erase the shame of that office from the face of France? Perhaps because a system of social sanctions is often too weak unless reinforced by the sanctions of the state, and the latter may or may not reflect the dominant value system. Or, perhaps, because the system of social values was not to be taken too seriously; perhaps because behind the articulately expressed but ineffectual value system lay another, an actually operational, system. Possibly so, but we must take care. We have set out to examine the determinants of social action. If we begin to deduce social values from the presence of certain actions, we have closed a vicious circle and at the same time have foreclosed the road to a reasoned explanation.

Let us take a brief glance at Russian conditions in the second half of the nineteenth century. After the emancipation of serfs in the early sixties of that century, former serfs and sons of former serfs are known to have engaged on an unprecedented scale in various entrepreneurial activities, including, it might be added, the magnificent venture of constructing and operating the merchant fleet on the Volga River. Again, there is little doubt that their activities were at variance with the dominant system of values, which remained de-

[15] *Essai sur l'histoire de la formation et de progrès du tiers état* (Paris, 1856), I, 108–110.

termined by the traditional agrarian pattern. The Good Life which God intended for man to lead implied tilling the land, which belonged to God, and receiving the divine blessing of its fruit. The Good Life certainly did not mean craving for riches, did not mean laying up treasures on earth where moth or rust doth corrupt. In innumerable adages, fairy tales, and songs, the wisdom of the folklore insisted upon the unrighteous origin of wealth. And still the activities went on unchecked, great fortunes were amassed, and great entrepreneurial innovations were successfully launched.

There is no doubt that throughout most of the nineteenth century a grave opprobrium attached to entrepreneurial activities in Russia. The nobility and the gentry (*dvoryanstvo*) had nothing but contempt for any entrepreneurial activity except its own. And despite some notable exceptions, it failed to make a significant contribution to modern industrial development. Divorced from the peasantry, the entrepreneurs remained despised by the intelligentsia. The latter's aversion to mercantile pursuits was, if anything, even stronger than that of the peasantry, even though the roots of that aversion doubtless lay in the value system of the peasantry. In a sense, the populism of the intelligentsia was a conscious attempt to espouse the standards of values of the "people." Hence came the intelligentsia's aversion to the bourgeoisie, the acquisitive class. Throughout long decades of the nineteenth century, there was only one among the great figures in Russian intellectual life who did not quite share this negative attitude — Belinski, who, at least at one point, refused to believe that a country that had no bourgeoisie could conceivably prosper. And still it was Belinski who at the very same time used his most fiery vocabulary to decry the merchant, the "base, despicable, vulgar creature who serves Plutus and Plutus alone." [16]

But what of the value system of the entrepreneurs themselves? Were they deviants? They certainly were, as far as their behavior was concerned. But since we are precluded from inferring values from action, we must still ask whether or not they were deviants in the sense that their own standard of values was different from the dominant one. And this appears highly dubious. It took a long time before something like an independent standard of values of the

[16] V. G. Belinski, *Pis'ma* (Letters) (St. Petersburg, 1914), III, 329.

Russian businessman developed. They knew full well that by accepted standards their life was a sinful one, and they tried seriously to make amends by donations to the church — "the graft payments to God," as those donations were cynically and probably unjustly called by Vladimir Solovev. It is much more sensible and in accordance with such evidence as we have from letters and memoirs to speak of a profound malaise resulting from the discrepancy not between two value systems but between the dominant value system and a social action that was at variance with it. It is out of this conflict that emerged the figure of the "repentant merchant" (which followed that of the "repentant nobleman" of the pre-Emancipation times), a figure so impressively depicted in Chekhov's *Cherry Orchard*. And the fictitious figure of Lopakhin appears multiplied in the reality of the early twentieth century in the shape of merchants and industrialists who supplied generous funds to revolutionary organizations, including the Bolshevik Party, of whom Savva Morosov, the leading textile industrialist, was an outstanding but far from solitary example.

No one can deny that some changes in this situation took place in the last decades of the nineteenth century. An independent value system of the entrepreneurial group indeed began to evolve. One need only compare the uneasy despotism of the merchant types in Ostrovski's plays with the much more civilized and self-reliant figures of Gorki's *Foma Gordeyev*. And a somewhat parallel change is clearly in evidence in the attitudes of the intelligentsia, as it broke away from the traditional populism and turned with the same radical fervor to the tenets of Marxism. Paradoxical as it is, it was Marxism in Russia which for large strata of intelligentsia, of which revolutionary groups of course constituted but a small minority, brought about at the turn of the century some reconciliation with the bourgeoisie and replaced in their minds the picture of a despicable mercenary by that of a builder and innovator. But one cannot fail to be impressed by the lateness and incompleteness of this development.

What shall one conclude from all that? That social attitudes toward entrepreneurs, that value systems whether dominant or deviant, are unimportant, that they do not influence the development at all? This almost surely would be a wrong inference. First of all, it could be argued that the existence of widespread social attitudes in

Russia which were so patently unfavorable to entrepreneurship greatly reduced the number of potential entrepreneurs and thereby reduced the rate of economic development in the country.[17] There is little doubt that there is some plausibility to such an argument. Even in the twentieth century, Russian university students showed a good deal of contempt for work associated with practical pursuits and particularly with business activity. When they went to Western universities, they quickly developed scorn for their student colleagues whose attitudes they regarded as glaringly materialistic. "Career" remained a shameful word in the vocabulary of a Russian student. This attitude presumably retarded in some measure the industrialization of the country. Yet it did not prevent the brilliant period of rapid industrialization in the 1890s, when the annual rate of industrial growth was in the vicinity of 9 percent.

It seems more reasonable to suggest that the effect upon economic development of the lingering preindustrial value systems, of aversion to entrepreneurs and to new forms of economic activity in general, was somewhat different. It is likely in some measure to have contributed in Russia — and elsewhere in the history of European industrializations — to the specific compression of industrialization processes into periods of rapid growth. Precisely because some value systems do not change readily, because economic development must break through the barriers of routine, prejudice, and stagnation, among which adverse attitudes toward entrepreneurship are but one important element, industrialization does not take place until the gains which industrialization promises have become, with the passage of time, overwhelmingly large, and the prerequisites are created for a typical upsurge.[18] An adverse social attitude toward entrepreneurs may thus indeed delay the beginning of rapid industrialization. But, viewed over a somewhat longer period, more important than the mere fact of delay is the fact that the character of the industrialization process is affected by those attitudes. At the same time, it would be clearly untenable to try to explain these

[17] This point was frequently and effectively made by Hugh Aitken in the writer's seminar.

[18] If I were writing this today I should not have spoken of "prerequisites" as much as of "patterns of substitution" for the missing prerequisites. See Chapter 2 of this volume. [A. G., 1962]

spurts of rapid industrialization in backward countries simply in terms of a lag in social attitudes. Technological progress, growing advantages of what Nurkse has called "balanced growth," and sudden institutional changes — all these combine to achieve the effect.

Before some general conclusions are drawn, let us shift the scene and follow for a few moments some other empirical work which has been influenced by the general theoretical structure discussed in the preceding pages. The reference is to France and to attempts to explain the problem of the relatively low rate of economic development in that country. It is essentially the work of David S. Landes and John E. Sawyer that is of interest here.[19]

The thesis is simple: the character of entrepreneurial behavior in France has been a very important, perhaps the main, retarding factor in France's economic development and that behavior has been largely shaped by the prevailing value system in the country. It is in these terms that must be seen and explained the French entrepreneur's alleged aversion to risk and credit engagements, his conservative spirit, his dislike of sharp competitive practices, his interest in high profits rather than in large sales, the family character of the French enterprises and their small-scale size, to name only the few important points. In addition, the social status of the businessman is said to be low and hence comes the desire of the best talent in France to turn to the "traditional honorific careers." [20] It is essentially the stress on the strength of the *ancien régime* survivals in the cultural pattern of modern France which Sawyer has added to the picture.

It is perhaps somewhat unfair to seek the source of these views exclusively in general theoretical concepts. In part it is the *tertium comparationis* chosen by the two authors that appears to have influenced their thinking. Throughout, the comparison is with the United States. Obviously such a comparison is quite adequate if all that the

[19] See Landes, "French Entrepreneurship and Industrial Growth in the Nineteenth Century," *The Journal of Economic History*, May 1949, pp. 45–61; and "French Business and the Businessmen in Social and Cultural Analysis," in *Modern France*, Edward Mead Earle, ed. (Princeton, 1951), pp. 334–353. Sawyer, "Strains in the Social Structure of Modern France," in *Modern France*, pp. 293–312; and "The Entrepreneur and the Social Order, France and the United States," in *Men in Business*, William Miller, ed. (Cambridge, Mass., 1952).

[20] Landes, "French Entrepreneurship," p. 56.

writers wished to convey was the indubitable differences that exist between the American and the French economies. But if what they were after was an explanation of the peculiar "weakness of French industry and commerce," the comparison with the United States is hardly a very helpful one, and the proper comparison ought to have been with countries of similar geographic size, position, and historical background, which nevertheless showed a higher rate of economic growth. Germany was the natural choice, and at least an explanation for shunning the obvious ought to have been provided.

Once the comparison is made with Germany, most of the factors mentioned by Landes find their counterpart in the German economy. The strength of preindustrial social values was, if anything, greater in Germany than in France. The family firm remained strong, and the lower entrepreneurial echelons, whose numbers bulked large, behaved in a way which was hardly different from that in France. The pronouncement made at the turn of the century, that modern economic development had transformed the top structure of the German economy while everything beneath it still remained medieval, was, of course, a deliberate exaggeration. But there was some meaning in that exaggeration. Such as it was, it applied to France as much as to Germany.[21]

[21] In the original edition of this paper I presented some figures to show that in Germany as in France the small shop was overwhelmingly predominant as far as the number of industrial enterprises was concerned. David Landes rightly criticized a specific deficiency of my data without being able, however, to controvert the point I was trying to make. For, in the end, I believe, we both agreed that in Germany and France before the First World War 94.59 and 97.98 percent, respectively, of all enterprises in industry and mining occupied no more than 10 persons. It is, furthermore, of interest that the "small establishments" in this category were truly small, the average number of those employed per such establishment having been 1.6 in France and 2.0 in Germany (the French figures refer to 1906 and the German figures to 1907). It is another matter that in that period the modern large-scale industry in Germany consisted of larger plants than was the case in France. But this has nothing to do with the untenable view that the small *boutique* was in any significant way more peculiar to France than to Germany. See Alexander Gerschenkron, "Some Further Notes on 'Social Attitudes, Entrepreneurship, and Economic Development,'" *Explorations in Entrepreneurial History*, December 1954. The reader must be referred to two interesting critical comments that have been directed against the present essay: Thomas C. Cochran, "Social Attitudes, Entrepreneurship, and Economic Development: Some Comments," *Explorations in Entrepreneurial History*, February 1954; and David S. Landes, "Social Attitudes, Entrepreneurship, and Economic Development: A Comment," *Explorations in Entrepreneurial History*, May 1954. [A. G., 1962]

Of course, the picture presented is onesided in any case. In order to maintain his thesis, Landes has to relegate vast and most significant fields of French entrepreneurial endeavor, such as railroads, mines, the iron and steel industry, automobile production, banks and department stores, to qualifying footnotes and dependent clauses. On the other hand, a comparison with Germany would have brought out that in the nineteenth century French entrepreneurial vigor in some fields was doubtless in excess of that in Germany. The question of exact priority for the introduction of department stores is perhaps still a matter of a rather useless dispute,[22] but that the French supplied a whole series of momentous entrepreneurial innovations to the field is beyond doubt; so is the fact that at least until the end of the century Germany still lagged in this respect behind her neighbor to the west. It was a great French entrepreneur, Felix Potin, whom the alleged French value standards did not prevent from coining the famous altogether "American" phrase, "Des affaires avant tout, le bénéfice viendra ensuite," and who successfully carried through his great innovations in retailing long before such ideas began to take hold in Germany.[23] At any rate, when Landes is struck by the far-reaching degree of specialization in French food retailing, which rightly seems so un-American to him, he should also have expressed his astonishment about the presence of the same phenomenon in Germany. Somerset Maugham justly claimed that, to know one foreign country, one must also know at least one other foreign country and added that "Arnold Bennett has never ceased to believe in a peculiar distinction of the French to breakfast off coffee and rolls."[24] This seems very sound advice for the field of comparative economic history.

It is true, of course, that the German rate of industrial growth in the second half of the nineteenth century exceeded that of France. Some of the factors which must in large measure have accounted for the difference in the speed of growth are obvious. One is surely the lack of a coal basin comparable to the Ruhr at a time when coal exercised all or nearly all of the locational pull in iron and steel making.

[22] See Ralph M. Hower, *History of Macy's of New York, 1858–1919* (Cambridge, Mass., 1943), pp. 411f.

[23] G. d'Avenel, *Le méchanisme de la vie moderne* (Paris, 1902), pp. 174f.

[24] *A Writer's Notebook* (New York, 1949), p. 153.

The prevalence of the family farm with its unfavorable effects upon the flow of labor to industry is another. It may or may not be true that, when everything is said and done and a distribution of emphasis among the individual factors concerned is attempted, some differences in entrepreneurial behavior between France and Germany may be found very much worthy of mention. But to assume that such differences, if any, need necessarily be explained in terms of roles, role-expectations, and value orientations is surely unwarranted. Clearly, variations in entrepreneurial behavior may have nothing to do with the dominant value system and the degree of social approval. They can be, and no doubt are, the result of varying income levels, living conditions, degree of endowment with natural resources, and so on.

And, in a sense, the same applies even to comparisons with the United States. There can be no doubt that differences in "dominant value systems" can be easily discerned between France and the country whose economy has remained largely, though by no means completely, free from the influences of precapitalist traditions. Ernest Renan once adverted to those differences in forceful sentences:

> Nous sommes une race des gentilshommes; notre idéal a été créé par des gentilshommes, non comme celui de l'Amérique, par d'honnêtes bourgeois, de sérieux hommes d'affaires. Les personnes qui poursuivent si avidement l'idéal américain oublient que cette race n'a pas notre passé brillant, qu'elle n'a pas fait une découverte de science pure, ni créé un chef-d'oeuvre, qu'elle n'a jamais eu de noblesse, que le négoce et la fortune l'occupent tout entière.
>
> Les meilleurs choses (par exemple, les fonctions du prêtre, du magistrat, du savant, de l'artiste et de l'homme de lettres sérieux) sont l'inverse de l'esprit industriel et commercial, le premier devoir de ceux qui s'y adonnent étant de ne pas chercher à s'enrichir, et de ne jamais considérer la valeur vénale de ce qu'ils font.[25]

These sweeping statements cannot lay claim to absolute accuracy and one should beware easy generalizations.[26] But this is not the

[25] "Philosophie de l'histoire contemporaine: La monarchie constitutionelle en France," *Revue des Deux Mondes*, November 1, 1869, p. 93.

[26] Modern research, for instance, has assembled considerable evidence to show that even the American merchants in mid-nineteenth-century frontier regions held merchandizing in low esteem and tried to escape from it as soon as possible into more honorific careers. See, for instance, Lewis E. Atherton, *The Pioneer Merchant in Mid-America*, University of Missouri Studies, April 1, 1939, pp. 30–31.

point. What is important to note here is that, even in this classical case of differences in "value systems" between the United States and France, there is an obvious need for a good deal of careful and undogmatic research before one can begin to form some idea as to just how much significance can be reasonably imputed to those differences as against the host of other incomparabilities between the two countries.

Perhaps some conclusion can be drawn from the foregoing discussion. A rigid conceptual framework is no doubt useful in formulating questions, but at all times it evokes the peril that those questions will be mistaken for answers. There is a deep-seated yearning in the social sciences for the discovery of one general approach, one general law valid for all times and all climes. But these attitudes must be outgrown. They overestimate both the degree of simplicity of economic reality and the quality of scientific tools. As the economic historian organizes and interprets his material, all he can hope for is the discovery of limited patterns of uniformity which may possess explanatory value for some places and periods but may be utterly inapplicable to others. And this is fully true of the sets of concepts which have been discussed above. It seems reasonably clear that the chances for their usefulness are greatest when applied either to stagnant primitive communities in which no development takes place at all or to well-integrated advanced societies with well built-in dynamic elements. Paradoxical as it may sound, the analysis hitched to a general standard of values is best adapted to, say, the Navaho Indians on the one hand and to the present American society on the other. This perhaps explains the strong affiliation that exists between anthropology and modern sociology; and perhaps also the strong though illusory feeling, so frequently expressed, that *plus ça change, plus c'est la même chose* [27] — illusory because it overlooks the fact that the conceptual schemata may have held much less well for the intervening stages of the development. At any rate, serious doubts are permissible about whether the theory of roles in its present form and everything that it implies can be of much use for understanding processes in the economies within which a rapid change *in economic*

[27] For example, Cochran, in "Role and Sanction in American Entrepreneurial History," p. 174.

systems is in the making; more concretely, within the economies which experience a specific initial upsurge in the rate of growth of industrial output.

But the reservations must go farther. The preceding discussion may have seemed at times to have skirted perilously the old question of precedence: does capitalism "create" the capitalist spirit or does the capitalist spirit "create" capitalism? Nothing could be more unfortunate than for work in economic history once more to be dragged down into the depth of metaphysical or at least hopelessly abstract arguments. The question cannot be: are social values important or unimportant? It must read first of all: what is the degree of persistence in value systems, what is their propensity to change in response to what factors? In dealing with periods of economic transformation which in themselves imply a considerable degree of diversity in values within a given community, one should least of all try to evoke the impression of a unified and general normative system. If something like "coefficients of changeability" — however crude such a measure must be — is attached to various value systems, one cannot fail to discover that the range of such coefficients must be wide indeed. Some values do not seem to change at all over long periods of time. The attitude of peasants who cling to the land even under unfavorable economic circumstances and, even when at length forced into urban occupations, still keep looking back over their shoulders, ready to return to the land at the earliest possible chance, are surely determined by values whose change is exceedingly slow. It is perfectly reasonable to attribute to the existence of such values the well-known difficulties experienced by young industrial countries in building up a reliable permanent labor force in industry. On the other hand, the same hardly could be said of entrepreneurial values. The volatile group of entrepreneurs — composed of men who by definition are "ganz besonders traditions- und beziehungslos . . . und dem System der überindividuellen Werte . . . ganz besonders fremd" [28] — may not be oriented in their actions by any discernible set of values. There may be, as was pointed out above, a far-reaching divorce between their actions and the general value system to which they may still adhere.

[28] J. A. Schumpeter, *Theorie der wirtschaftlichen Entwicklung* (Munich-Leipzig, 1926), p. 134.

And, finally, even if a discernible set of special values can be attributed to the entrepreneur, these values are likely to be so recent in origin, so liable to further change, that it would seem highly unsatisfactory to take these values as a basis for interpreting economic action and economic change.

Precisely because in historical reality we are confronted with important cases where entrepreneurs did not appear as disciplined actors performing their preassigned roles in well-structured sociological plays, but entered the historical stage in response to the challenge of great changes in the economic and social environment, it becomes imperative in dealing with the problem of entrepreneurial values to examine their relationship to the environment in the broadest sense of the term. The Russian entrepreneurs of the 1860s and the subsequent decades and the French entrepreneurs of the 1850s have no doubt wrought great economic changes, but it is the emancipation of the peasantry, in the one case, and the establishment of the Second Empire with its liberalizing policies, in the other, that would seem to explain those changes much more readily and simply than would any reference to value systems.

But to say all those things does not imply at all that the conceptual framework used should be banned altogether from the area of entrepreneurial research. Economic historians must at all times try to combine the use of analytical tools provided by economic theory with those supplied by the other social sciences. Eli Heckscher once even defined economic history as characterized by an interest "in the interplay of economic and other influences on the actual course of events." [29] But too enthusiastic an acceptance of abstract sociological models may tend to discredit the value of interdisciplinary approaches to economic history, and the "theory of roles" may be a case in point. What is suggested here, therefore, is that a serious effort should be made to try to establish through empirical research the spatial and temporal limitations within which the use of such an approach is reasonable and defensible. The discovery of these limits

[29] Eli F. Heckscher, "David Davidson," *International Economic Papers*, no. 2 (London-New York, 1952), p. 126. See also, Heckscher's *Historieuppfattning, materialistic och annan* (Stockholm, 1944), pp. 30–31; and W. K. Hancock's emphasis on the basic "impurity" of economic history, *Economic History at Oxford* (Oxford, 1946), p. 5.

will in itself push the research work into discovery of other sets of propositions and hypotheses, which may be more promising in treating situations, and historical sequences which differ widely from those for which the conceptual framework originally was designed. And it is then that one may begin to hope for a synthesis, that is, for a plausible distribution of emphasis among a variety of factors yielded from pursuit of a variety of approaches.

The crying need for further research should effectively excuse the lack of any substantive conclusions to this essay. But perhaps one or two general impressions may be in order. It would seem that adverse social attitudes toward entrepreneurs and entrepreneurships do not emerge as a major retarding force upon the economic development of European countries in the nineteenth century. This seems also true of Russian industrialization prior to World War I, although in that country one might have expected hostility to entrepreneurs to be of more consequence than in the more advanced countries. In general, one cannot help being impressed by the rapidity with which the numbers of native entrepreneurs multiplied in nineteenth-century Russia and also by the speed with which their behavior became more and more consonant with Western practices.

The temptation is great, of course, to argue from the Russian experience to the present conditions in underdeveloped countries and to arrive at somewhat more optimistic prognostications than those currently in use. But it may be hazardous to succumb to such a temptation. Russia until the First World War had benefited greatly from the presence of foreign entrepreneurs. It is true that some degree of animosity against foreign entrepreneurs and technicians was in clear evidence. But such animosity remained within moderate limits and, if anything, served as a stimulus to native entrepreneurial talent. It may well be that conditions in some of the underdeveloped countries are less favorable in this respect.

Moreover, adverse social attitudes to entrepreneurship in Russia stemmed largely from "preindustrial" value orientations, and those anticapitalist attitudes which usually arise with the spread of the industrial economy did not seem to affect entrepreneurial activities in any marked degree. Quite to the contrary, as mentioned before, the effects of prerevolutionary Marxism on attitudes toward entrepreneurs was presumably positive. It is quite possible that in under-developed countries today the strength of preindustrial values and the resulting lack of sympathy with entrepreneurs is greater than it was in Imperial Russia. And, on the other hand, it is perhaps more likely that those values will more readily coalesce with modern anti-capitalist sentiments and persuasions and that, unlike Russia before 1914, such a combination may find effective expression in acts and policies of the governments concerned. Count Witte's state of the 1890s stood aloof from popular attitudes. But this is much less likely to be true of backward countries in the second half of the twentieth century. Perhaps the generalization may be ventured that adverse social attitudes toward entrepreneurs do not significantly affect the processes of industrialization unless they are allowed to become crystallized in governmental action.

4

Notes on the Rate of Industrial Growth in Italy, 1881–1913

~~~~~~~~~~~~~~~~

I T is obvious that in the decades following its political unification Italy's economy remained very backward in relation not only to that of England, but also to the economies of industrially advancing countries on the continent of Europe. The same conclusion will result, whatever gauge one may choose for the purposes of comparison, be it qualitative descriptions of technological equipment, organizational efficiency, and labor skills in individual enterprises; or scattered quantitative data on relative productivity in certain branches of industry; or the numbers of persons employed in industry; or the density of the country's railroad network; or the standards of literacy of its population. It is true that there were very large differences in this respect among the individual regions of the Peninsula; but according to Pantaleoni's computations, which — subject to a considerable margin of error as they are — probably give a correct idea of the order of magnitudes involved, the private per-capita wealth of the richest and most advanced areas in northern Italy in the second half of the eighties was still very much below one half of the contemporaneous figure for France as a whole.[1]

At the same time, it is equally undeniable that by 1914 a great industrial transformation had taken place in Italy. Under these

[1] Maffeo Pantaleoni, "Delle regioni d'Italia in ordine alla loro ricchezza ed al loro carico tributario," *Scritti varii di economia*, 3rd ser. (Rome, 1910), pp. 242, 252.

circumstances, it seemed legitimate to inquire whether and to what extent the processes of industrialization, when at length launched in the country, betrayed the same characteristic features as those displayed by other relatively backward European countries of the nineteenth century. In other words, the present writer approached the Italian material with a series of historical questions or expectations in mind, some of which may be summarized as follows:

1. The process of modern industrialization in conditions of considerable economic backwardness was likely to assume at a fairly early stage the form of a big initial push, showing a relatively high rate of industrial growth. The beginning of such a period may have been aided by coinciding with the turning point at the bottom of an international cycle, but the push was specifically "long-term" in its nature and therefore not coterminous with short-run fluctuations: once begun, it was likely to make the country fairly immune to the next cyclical recession.

2. In the course of such an initial industrial upsurge, a backward country typically tended to favor output of producers' goods as against that of consumers' goods because in conditions of the period it happened to be in the field of the former that recent technological process had been most rapid. Heavy industries, therefore, offered far-reaching opportunities for utilizing as far as possible the advantages inherent in a late arrival upon the industrial stage.

3. Along with the productive structure of industry, its organizational structure was also likely to be affected in the direction of a considerable stress on concentration in various forms.

4. These basic features of delayed industrializations were likely to be reinforced by the use of specific institutional instruments, such as the investment policies of banks and various policies of the state. In cases of very great backwardness the role of the government was more prominent and the banks did not participate in the process until a certain degree of industrial progress had been achieved.

The following pages, then, purport to discuss the process of Italian industrialization before 1914 in terms of its conformity with, or deviation from, the pattern just described. Admittedly, this is a rather narrow approach and, in addition, only a few of the pertinent aspects of the problem can be touched upon here.

73

I

The approach as sketched in the preceding section called first of all for some measurement of the rate of growth of Italian industry during the period under review. It necessitated, therefore, the construction of an index of Italian industrial output for the years 1881–1913, the choice of the initial year being essentially determined by statistical availability.

A detailed description of the index has been included in this volume (see Appendix I). The reader will find there, along with a complete statement on source materials and methods of computation (some of which unfortunately had to be rather involved), some critical evaluation of the deficiencies of that index as well as a comparison with some previous attempts in the same direction by French and Italian scholars. Let it therefore be mentioned briefly that the index comprises six main series which have been combined by using as weights the writer's estimates of value added pertaining to the years 1902–1903.[2]

There is no question that the paucity of the underlying data and the manifold uncertainties of the weighing process detract seriously from the value of the computations. Nevertheless, it seems that the index serves sufficiently the present purpose, which is to obtain a general view of the speed of the Italian industrialization in various periods and subperiods before 1914.

Table 1 shows the aggregate index for the whole period. The development of the six index industries over the period is presented in Table 2.

[2] The six series are:
(1) mining,
(2) metalmaking,
(3) engineering,
(4) textiles,
(5) chemicals,
(6) foodstuffs.
Also two alternative computations based on weights derived from data on employment and horsepower, respectively, have been prepared. The results as presented in the following are all in terms of an index based on value-added weights.

Table 1. Index of Italian industrial output, 1881–1913

1881	54	1891	67	1901	104	1911	174
1882	57	1892	64	1902	109	1912	182
1883	64	1893	70	1903	114	1913	184
1884	63	1894	72	1904	117		
1885	65	1895	73	1905	126		
1886	67	1896	75	1906	139		
1887	73	1897	78	1907	152		
1888	74	1898	86	1908	163		
1889	72	1899	92	1909	168		
1890	72	1900	100	1910	169		

Table 2. Index of output of six industries, 1881–1913
(1900 = 100)

Year	Mining	Metalmaking	Textiles	Engineering	Chemicals	Foodstuffs
1881	71	22	54	62	9	63
1882	79	18	53	76	11	65
1883	80	27	62	92	13	68
1884	77	25	58	90	15	70
1885	77	40	61	94	17	69
1886	72	55	65	98	20	68
1887	68	66	73	118	22	67
1888	70	91	73	115	24	67
1889	71	119	71	96	26	69
1890	72	91	80	79	28	71
1891	76	72	73	62	28	70
1892	82	56	72	53	27	68
1893	80	67	85	58	26	69
1894	79	65	93	59	31	65
1895	72	68	93	62	42	66
1896	79	70	94	62	49	67
1897	90	77	93	65	56	69
1898	92	95	101	72	61	80
1899	88	101	104	89	72	86
1900	100	100	100	100	100	100
1901	103	103	105	100	102	106
1902	100	99	114	98	110	111
1903	107	120	111	108	115	120
1904	106	127	119	121	121	112
1905	108	170	124	144	132	115
1906	103	212	136	171	159	119
1907	99	218	153	196	185	122
1908	98	283	142	247	228	127
1909	93	346	136	261	257	128
1910	95	374	122	276	281	130
1911	89	377	128	287	260	141
1912	96	392	142	280	276	146
1913	98	381	134	272	281	166

The choice of subperiods into which a fairly long stretch of growth should be divided is necessarily arbitrary. For the purposes of a presentation that aims at isolating the big upsurge, an inspection of the data seems to yield the following division:

1881–1888 Moderate growth
1888–1896 Stagnation
1896–1908 Very rapid growth
1908–1913 Reduced rate of growth

The rates of growth implied in the index for these subperiods are given in Table 3.

Table 3. Annual average rates of growth of Italian industrial output
for 1881–1913 and subperiods

Period	Percentage change
1881–1888	4.6
1888–1896	.3
1896–1908	6.7
1908–1913	2.4
1881–1913	3.8

Note: computed on the assumption of a geometric rate of growth between the first and the last years of the specified periods.

Table 4 presents, for the same periods, the rates of growth implied in the indices of output of the six industrial groups.

Table 4. Annual average rates of growth of the six index industries
for 1881–1913 and subperiods
(percentage change)

Industry	1881–1888	1888–1896	1896–1908	1908–1913	1881–1913
Mining	0.0	1.3	1.8	0.0	1.0
Metalmaking	22.0	−3.2	12.4	6.1	9.3
Textiles	4.4	3.2	3.5	−1.2	2.5
Engineering	9.2	−7.4	12.2	2.0	4.7
Chemicals	15.1	9.4	13.7	1.8	11.3
Foodstuffs	.9	0.0	5.5	5.5	3.1

Note: see Table 3, note.

II

One point seems to emerge with sufficient clarity from the data contained in the preceding tabulations: Italy did have its period of a big industrial push. While there may be some questions concerning the exact choice of the initial and terminal years for the individual subperiods, it seems appropriate to locate the period of the great push between the years 1896 and 1908. Before 1896 lay the years of a laborious return from the low of 1892 to the level of 1888. After 1908, the rates of growth of all the index industries but one were greatly reduced.

Rather characteristic for such a period of "long-term" growth is the ease with which it rode horse and foot across the intervening depression of 1900. It may be instructive in this connection to take a glance at Wesley Mitchell's diagrammatic "Conspectus of Business Cycles in Various Countries" for the period concerned.[3] The United States and Canada remained untouched by the depression of 1900, but elsewhere its effects were grave, particularly on the continent of Europe. It broke the back of the long industrial push in Russia and it affected severely the countries in Central Europe which, as a result of the long tariff war with France, had become Italy's principal trading partners. There is little doubt that the capacity of these countries to absorb Italian exports was considerably diminished; at the same time, the competition of their industrial products with domestic goods in Italian markets was intensified. And yet the effect on Italian industrial development, although discernible, seemed almost negligible. Very similarly, a few years earlier Russia, then in the midst of her great industrial upsurge, felt no more than a light ripple of the wave of the severe international depression of the early nineties; her rate of industrial growth remained unaffected on the whole.[4]

At the same time, the period was characterized by a rapid increase in the share of producers' goods in total output, even though to some extent the change must reflect the workings of the accelerator. This is shown clearly in Tables 2 and 4. For the six index industries,

[3] Wesley Mitchell, *Business Cycles: The Problem and its Setting* (New York, 1927), p. 445.

[4] Alexander Gerschenkron, "The Rate of Industrial Growth in Russia since 1885," *The Tasks of Economic History*, Supplement VII (1947), 151.

that share was 28 percent of the index total (using value-added weights) in 1896. It had been at the same level in 1881, although 1888 showed a higher percentage. But by 1908 the share of producer goods, so computed, had jumped to 43 percent and was to reach 47 percent in 1913.

All this is quite in accordance with the expectations set forth in section one of this essay. This, no doubt, is comforting. But the disappointments are just around the corner.

It is implied in what has been said earlier that the rate of growth in a backward country during the early periods of its industrialization may be assumed to vary directly with the degree of the country's industrial backwardness. The more belated the big industrial upswing, the stronger it is likely to be when it comes. It seems that, considering the great delays in Italian industrialization on the one hand and similar periods in other countries on the other, the rate of industrial growth in Italy during 1896 and 1908 was lower than what might have been expected. It may be noted that Germany of the nineties was far beyond its period of initial growth and still its annual average rate of industrial growth for the years 1888–1896 amounted to almost 5.5 percent, which was indeed lower than the Italian rate in 1896–1908 but not very significantly so. When it comes to countries like Sweden, Russia, or Japan, the pertinent rates are a good deal higher than the Italian rate. Swedish industry grew at a pace of almost 12 percent a year between 1888 and 1896; Japan, between 1907 and 1913, showed an annual rate of growth of 8.5 percent; Russia of the nineties increased its industrial output at the rate of more than 8 percent a year.[5]

True, comparisons of this sort are precarious and too great a reliance on them is hardly warranted. But this is not the whole story. The method of computing rates of growth as used in the foregoing fastens attention on the initial and terminal years of each period and does not take into account the history of the intervening years. An inspection of the behavior of the index in the course of the period 1896–1908 suggests some differences as compared with cases of the

[5] The German and Swedish rates have been computed from data given in *Industrialization and Foreign Trade* (League of Nations, 1945). For the Russian and Japanese rates, see Gerschenkron, p. 156.

great spurt in other European countries: the industrial growth in Italy, while free from any severe setbacks, seems to have proceeded in a less uniform and more jerky fashion, denoting perhaps a more delicate state of public confidence and greater entrepreneurial uncertainties and hesitations. It may be useful to ponder a little some of the reasons that may have prevented Italy's big industrial push from displaying its full potential force.

III

It is not intended, of course, to supply here a comprehensive list of all the retarding forces that may have influenced the industrial development of Italy around the turn of the century. Anything beginning with the poor endowment of natural resources and ending with the mysteries of national or regional character might legitimately go on such a list. Such a broad discussion would overstep the limits set to this paper and probably not shed much additional light on its specific subject. The purpose of this section is rather to concentrate upon those factors that may be of some significance from the point of view of the general pattern of development as described earlier.

As mentioned before, the historical experience of European countries seems to warrant the generalization that in cases of very considerable backwardness the policies of the state tended to play a very important positive role during the years of the big upsurge of industrial development. In the classical case of Count Witte's Russia of the nineties, it would seem altogether meaningful to regard the policies of the government as the strategic factor, primarily responsible for the great spurt in industrialization of the period. Nothing comparable seems to have taken place in Italy. Not that the successive Italian governments showed no interest in the industrial future of the country. At one time or another, the government helped to launch some important industrial enterprises, the huge steelworks at Terni (1884) being perhaps the outstanding example. Government orders did play some role in the development of Italian industry. There was the policy of subsidies to shipbuilding and navigation which was initiated in 1885 [6] and extended in a somewhat revised

---

[6] See "Legge concernante la marina mercantile," *Raccolta ufficiale delle leggi e dei decreti del Regno d'Italia*, LXXIX, no. 3547 (December 6, 1885).

form in 1896; there was the partial waiving of governmental royalties flowing from the iron-ore mines on Elba. State aid of this nature there certainly was; yet what strikes the observer of these policies is not only their desultory character, not only the fact that they were rather less than more in appearance during the period of the great push of 1896–1908, but primarily the onesided nature of the government's interest in industrial development — that is to say, its concentration on the least deserving branches of industrial activity.

The ineptness of governmental industrialization policies becomes quite obvious as one moves from the measures just mentioned to a consideration of the Italian tariff, which must be viewed as the real *pièce de résistance* of those policies. One might rightly wonder how much importance one should in general ascribe to tariff policies in the history of European industrializations. In some cases it was not the tariff, but its abandonment, or at least reduction, that opened the road to industrialization. In other cases, the tariff seemed subordinate to the great variety of more direct and more vigorous measures that were taken by the government. At any rate, it would seem difficult to attribute much positive influence to the tariff structure that existed in Italy during her big industrial upswing. In fact, it is more reasonable to regard that tariff as one of the obstacles in the road of the Italian industrialization.

The pillars of Italian protectionism were three: grain, cotton textiles, and iron and steel. In the case of grain the march of protection began in 1887 when the tariff on wheat was raised from a nominal level to 3 lire per quintal. The first step was taken gingerly. Uncandidly, the purpose of the increase was said to be a purely fiscal one.[7] The lawmakers' consciences were far from easy. The measure was unpopular and had to be adopted against the recommendations of the detailed report prepared by the special parliamentary committee on Agrarian Inquiry.[8] But thereby the dam was broken.

[7] See the speech by Minister of Finance Magliani, July 5, 1887, *Camera dei Senatori, Discussioni*, Sessione 1886–87 (Rome, 1887), p. 1461.

[8] "Atti della Giunta per la inchiesta agraria e sulle condizioni della classe agricola," *Relazione finale sui resultati dell'inchiesta redatta per incarico della Giunta dal Presidente, Conte Stefano Jacini* (Rome, 1884), XV, Fascicolo I; also, "Atti della Commissione d'Inchiesta per la revisione della tariffa doganale," *Relazione del Senatore Lampertico* (Rome, 1885), I. *Parte Agraria*, Fascicolo I, p. 184.

Further increases followed, and by 1895, with a duty of 7.50 lire per quintal, Italy's wheat production had become the most heavily protected among the major countries of the continent.[9] True, this policy was part and parcel of a widespread European response to changed conditions of wheat supply in the world markets. But two things must be remembered. On the one hand, Italy's agriculture had at its disposal methods of adjustment that were not available to an equal degree north of the Alpine wall; on the other hand, if Germany with its rapidly developing industry could afford (economically, not politically) the luxury of agrarian protectionism, Italy with its much less favorable conditions never should have dared subject the tender plant of its industrial growth to the rigors of a protectionist climate in agriculture.

But what about the industrial side of the tariff? It need not be gainsaid that, at least in principle, Italy's industrialization could have been aided by a rationally conceived and executed tariff. Such policies would have had to start from the basic fact that in a historical period in which coal exercised the main locational pull, a country deprived of the mineral, forced to obtain it (on an average) at a price twice as high as that in the coalmining countries, and thus laboring under the disadvantage of high cost in industry and transportation, should have concentrated on those branches of industrial endeavor in which the expenditure for coal was small in relation to other cost items. Furthermore, a backward country, so disabled, should have felt particularly keenly the need to promote output of new products and new industries. The vast and variegated area of engineering offered the greatest promise in this respect.

What happened in fact was the adoption in 1878 of a tariff chiefly devoted to the protection of cotton textiles and ferrous metalmaking. The former was an old industry with a moderate rate of modern technological progress and accordingly relatively limited possibilities in a backward country on the European continent; the

[9] Ghino Valenti, *Granaglie, produzione, commercio, regime doganale*, Comitato nazionale per le tariffe doganale e per i trattati di commercio (Rome, 1920), p. 97; and H. Liepmann, *Tariff Levels and the Economic Unity of Europe* (London, 1938), pp. 64, 68, 72, 81, 87. In 1913, the Italian wheat duty amounted to 41.5 percent ad valorem. The corresponding figures for France, Germany, and Austria were 34.5, 38, and 36 percent, respectively.

latter was a coal-consuming industry par excellence. While a variety of engineering products was included in the tariff, the rates imposed on those products as a rule were such as to provide the machinery industry at best with a partial compensation for the duties accorded to iron and steel.[10]

It is true that the rates on machinery were generally increased in 1887. The cases of protectionism in reverse were eliminated and a margin of genuine protection created. But that margin, if computed ad valorem, was almost negligible. Moreover, it should be noted that the important branches of textile and agricultural machinery came to be protected by duties hardly in excess of those on steel; that the rates on machine parts were very low, thus encouraging assembling of machines rather than their production within the country; that, finally, the rate on "nonspecified" machinery — the very area of innovations — was particularly low. None of this should cause surprise, since tariff makers everywhere as a rule protected the existing and vocal interests, while the promise of future innovations tended to lie beyond their range of vision.[11] As one follows the parliamentary debates on the tariff of 1887, one is struck by the fact that it was with respect to engineering alone that the speakers found it advisable to pay their respects to the liberal tradition inherited from Cavour. That tradition was quickly forgotten as soon as they turned to cotton textiles and iron and steel.[12] But this is not the end of the story. During the debates, Minister Magliani promised that the excesses of the Tariff Act would be mitigated in the course of the subsequent negotiations on commercial treaties.[13] Yet, if a generaliza-

[10] Thus, for example, the rate on steel was 10 lire per quintal while that on locomotives was 10, that on railroad freight cars 9, and on steam engines 8 lire per quintal. "Legge che approva la tariffa doganale d'importazione e d'esportazione," *Raccolta ufficiale delle leggi e dei decreti del Regno d'Italia*, LIII, no. 439 (May 30, 1878).

[11] "Legge che riforma la tariffa doganale," *Raccolta ufficiale delle leggi e dei decreti del Regno d'Italia*, Parte Principale, Series 3a, LXXXV, no. 4703 (July 14, 1887).

[12] A good example among many is the Report of the Committee on Tariff Inquiry, the industrial part of which was written by V. Ellena: "Atti della Commissione d'Inchiesta per la revisione della tariffa doganale," II. Parte Industriale, *Relazione del Deputato V. Ellena* (Rome, 1886), 242, 361, 420.

[13] Atti parlamentari, Camera dei Senatori, Sessione 1886–87, July 9, 1887 (Rome, 1887), p. 1621. Incidentally, a few weeks earlier, in order to allay the un-

tion is possible with regard to those treaties, it is this: the duties on cotton textiles and ferrous metals remained substantially unchanged or at best were slightly changed. The great field of tariff concessions was supplied precisely by the duties on machinery where the slim margins established in 1887 were reduced and sometimes eliminated.[14] The Italian machinery industry was largely left to its own devices.

When in addition it is noted that the equally promising field of the chemical industry, pregnant with many innovational possibilities and well suited to the conditions of the country, was quite ignored by the tariff makers of 1887, the conclusion seems justified that the main action of government policies in the field of Italian industrialization was likely to retard rather than promote its development. The Italian government's participation in, and contribution to, the big industrial push in the country certainly fell far short of what one might have expected on the basis of the industrial history of other backward countries such as Russia or Hungary.[15]

---

easiness of the Lower Chamber with regard to the lopsidedness of the tariff, it was promised that an opportunity for revising the rates on machinery would be provided when the House reconvened after the summer vacation. Such a revision never was undertaken. See Atti del Parlamento Italiano, Camera dei Deputati, Sessione 1886–87, June 23, 1887 (Rome, 1887), p. 3967.

[14] See, for example, in *Trattati e convenzioni fra il Regno d'Italia e gli altri stati*: treaty with Austria-Hungary, December 6, 1891, XII (Rome, 1892); treaty with Switzerland, April 19, 1892, XIV (Rome, 1895), and July 7, 1904, XVII (Rome, 1907); treaty with Germany, December 3, 1904, XVII (Rome, 1907); treaty with Austria-Hungary, February 11, 1906, XVIII (Rome, 1930).

[15] In his interesting article ("The North-South Differential in Italian Economic Development," *Journal of Economic History*, XXI, no. 3, 314), Richard Eckaus is reluctant to accept this negative appraisal of the Italian tariff because the rates of growth of output in cotton textiles and iron and steel were higher than the average rate of growth for the index-number industries as a whole. But obviously what is called for is a historical judgment rather than a mechanically arithmetical one. The trouble lay precisely in the fact that unsuitable industries were allowed to grow fast at the expense of others. A historian has to take into account not only the impasse in which the unduly swollen cotton industry found itself by the end of the index period, but also the fact that flooding the country with expensive domestic steel necessarily retarded the growth of those branches of industry whose potentialities were great indeed. Considering the magnitudes involved, it is very reasonable to assume that, given lower prices of raw materials and shifts in capital allocations in the proper direction, the rate of growth of the young industrial branches, particularly in engineering, would have been a multiple of the one actually achieved. [A. G., 1962]

83

Another weakness of the Italian industrialization of 1896–1908 may have derived from the fact that by that time the great period of Italian railroad building was largely a thing of the past. During the years of the great Russian industrialization, 1886–1900, the railroad network increased by more than 70 percent. There is little doubt that during that period the railroads were the fulcrum around which the industrial level of the country was being rapidly lifted. By contrast, the accretion to the Italian railroads during the years 1896–1908 amounted to less than 10 percent. Special circumstances in Italy tended to accentuate the difference. The law of 1885 by which the operation of state-owned railroads was entrusted to three private companies for a period of sixty years foreshadowed a possible discontinuation of the arrangement after only twenty years. The uncertainties created by this provision greately influenced the investment policies of the companies in the last eight or ten years before 1905, the year in which the agreements could, and in fact did, expire. Partly for this reason, the flow of capital into the special investment funds established under the Act of 1885 was hesitant and insufficient.[16] True, after 1905, when the operation of the railroad system had reverted to the state, ambitious plans were launched to modernize and to expand tracks and rolling stock. These plans, however, matured in the last years of the period 1896–1908 and came too late to change its general character.

One is free to argue that the early completion of the bulk of railroad building was likely to benefit the country's industrialization in subsequent years by releasing to industry capital that otherwise may have been attracted to railroads. But the argument does not carry much force. For the implicit assumption of a unified capital market in Italy seems to do violence to the actually existing conditions. Many a large-scale investor who stood ready to purchase railroad bonds issued or guaranteed by the government was most reluctant to engage his funds in industrial ventures. At the turn of the century, Giulio Einaudi found strong words to castigate this attitude

[16] As a result, a special provision of that act under the terms of which the railroads were compelled to afford an additional preference of five percent to domestic suppliers remained rather ineffective. "Legge per l'esercizio delle reti mediterranea, adriatica e sicula, e per la costruzione delle strade ferrate complementari," *Raccolta ufficiale*, Art. 21, LXXV, no. 3048 (April 27, 1885).

of "veneration of 4 percent." [17] The small saver who took his money to the branches of the Postal Savings System or to cooperative banks was even more security-minded; accordingly, his funds went into short-term commercial loans or into financing of public works by municipalities and provinces. It is significant in this connection that the period 1896–1908 was characterized by massive repatriation of Italian securities held abroad. The compartmentalization of the Italian capital market was great, and herein lay one of the specific functions of the big investment banks, whose role is touched upon in the concluding paragraphs of this essay.[18] Thus, absence of large railroad investments did not necessarily mean increased capital availbilities to industry, and the failure of the industrial "push" to coincide with a period of "railroad fever" with its specific stimulations to industrial activities may well have kept the rate of industrial growth below what it would have been, had the Russian situation reproduced itself in Italy.

Another factor, which tends to point in the same direction, deserves mention here. The political situation in Italy at the beginning of the period 1896–1908 was not propitious to quiet economic growth. The disastrous harvest of 1897, coupled with the government's prolonged hesitations to suspend or to reduce the wheat duties, led in the course of the *anno terribile* — 1898 — to unrest and disorders in several regions. These disturbances culminated in the Milan insurrection in May of that year and were followed by two years of repressive policies under the Pelloux governments. Then came the electoral shift of 1900 and the regicide of the same year. A new page in Italy's political history was opened. It was to be overshadowed by the genius of Giovanni Giolitti's conciliatory statesmanship. An integral part of his policy of pacification was the government's adherence to the principle of strict neutrality in wage conflicts. Consequently, the strike waves rose to quite unprecedented heights. Between 1901 and 1913 there was only one year when the number

---

[17] *Un principe mercante, Studio nell' espansione coloniale Italiana* (Turin, 1900), p. 160. A translation into English of this fascinating essay in entrepreneurial economic history by the former President of the Italian Republic would seem very desirable.

[18] See also, Epicarmo Corbino, *Annali dell'economia italiana*, V, 1901–1914 (Citta di Castello, 1938), 423f.

of days lost by strikes remained below the million mark; in some years of the period it exceeded three and was under four million.[19]

Few would begrudge the poverty-ridden Italian laborer the resulting very modest improvements in his economic position. But the difference in historical situations must be pointed out. While in other countries a period of very rapid industrial growth tended to be *followed by* a period of upward adjustments in the standard of living, in Italy the two processes tended to coincide. Had the industrial upsurge in Italy taken place one or two decades earlier, in all likelihood it would have been much less disturbed by industrial strife. Great delays in industrialization do tend to be compensated for by the rapidity of the ensuing development. Yet the two factors just discussed seem to suggest that the validity of this generalization does not transcend certain limits. Along with the advantages of being late, there are also many definite disadvantages to being very late — a point that may deserve special attention with regard to the underdeveloped countries of our time.

In speaking of the possible sources of the relative weakness of the Italian industrialization of 1896–1908, one final remark may be in order. In studying the periods of rapid initial industrialization of the major countries in Europe, one does not find it too difficult to discern some specific industrialization ideologies under the auspices of which the development proceeded: economic liberalism in England, Saint-Simonism in France, nationalism in Germany, Marxism in Russia of the nineties, all seem to have performed a function in the process and to have performed it well. What strikes the observer of the comparable Italian development is the absence of any strong ideological stimulus to industrialization. Cavour's *liberismo* belonged to an era that was gone. Italian protectionism was an instrument of vested interests and failed to develop into a strong intellectual movement. The nineties in Italy were indeed a period in which Marxism seemed to have captivated the imagination of large strata of the Italian intelligentsia.[20] Some aspects of this sudden ideological swing do

---

[19] See *Annuario Statistico*, 1905–1907, p. 840; 1911, pp. 234–36; and 1915, pp. 313–14.

[20] Benedetto Croce, *Storia d'Italia dal 1871 al 1915* (Bari, 1953), p. 157. Croce himself was, of course, a case in point.

evoke comparisons with contemporaneous events in Russia. But, unlike the Russians, the Italian Marxists showed, if at all, a very restrained interest in the problems of industrial evolution of the country, although, misguidedly and somewhat ashamedly, the leaders of the Italian labor movement did lend their support to the existing industrial-tariff structure. It is not at all clear that they, or the Italian public in general, had any desire to speed up the change that was afoot in the land.

The aggregate effect of these disabilities does not seem to be negligible. In particular, as one considers the ineptitudes of the Italian tariff structure, one cannot but marvel at what was actually achieved during those years within the engineering and chemical industries. The Italian entrepreneurs in those branches deserve praise indeed. But if one were to look for a single important factor that succeeded in offsetting at least some of the great obstacles to the country's industrialization, one could not fail to point to the role performed by the big Italian banks after 1895.

These banks were formed or reorganized after the disastrous banking crashes of the early nineties. The most important of them, the Banca Commerciale Italiana, was established in 1894 under German leadership and with German capital, including some Austrian and Swiss participation.[21]

In a sense, the moment was favorable. There were many industrial enterprises that the preceding storm had left stranded or drifting helplessly. They were content to accept the tutelage of the newcomers. Still the task of the latter was not light. The terrifying *vestigia* of the Credito Mobiliare and the Banca Generale — the two giant victims of the great catastrophe — remained unobliterated for a long time afterward. Burdened with these remembrances; surrounded by a distrustful public and an unfriendly scholarly opinion whose somewhat monotonous insistence on the need for prudence at times seemed to verge on folly; denounced as an instrument of foreign economic penetration; faced by the effects of tariff and subsidy policies which they could not ignore, the Italian banks enjoyed a much more limited

---

[21] These participations were part of an agreement among the founders designed to preclude institutions like the Austrian Credit-Anstalt from competing with the Banca Commerciale in the field of Italian investment.

freedom of action than their counterparts in Germany or Austria. To some extent their interest in cotton textiles and iron and steel was predetermined by governmental decisions, and it was these two industries that found themselves in difficulties after 1908. In the case of cotton it also may have been the German influence that, for some years at least, had guided the Italian banks into a line of activities in which the German banks at home traditionally showed much less interest. It is also true that the Italian banks may have shown more interest than they did in certain innovations such as automobiles. By and large, however, what took place in Italy was a deliberate application of techniques of investment banking as evolved in Germany in the course of attempts to overcome its own economic backwardness.

The Italian investment banks of the previous period, oriented as they were upon French patterns, had never been able to advance fully to the stage of "universal banks" and to become real "department stores" in the field of banking. This was rather dramatically shown by the futility of the attempt to transform the Credito Mobiliare into a commercial bank at a time when its operations were already fully obscured by the shadows of the approaching storm.[22] It is possible to surmise that the upsurge of 1896–1908 was largely made possible by the importation of the great economic innovation of German banking in its most developed and mature form. As in Germany, not only capital but a good deal of entrepreneurial guidance was channeled to the nascent and expanding industrial enterprises. As in Germany, the policy was to maintain an intimate connection with an industrial enterprise and to nurse it for a long time before introducing it to the capital market, which as often as not meant placing its stock among the banks' own clients.[23] As in Germany, the banks tried to influence and modernize the methods of interenterprise credit relations. As in Germany, they were ever eager to "discipline production" of industrial branches, which bland phrase meant reduction or abandonment of competition in favor of various monopolistic compacts.[24] On the

[22] Maffeo Pantaleoni, "La caduta del Credito Mobiliare Italiano," *Studi storici di economia* (Bologna, 1936), pp. 261ff.

[23] See, for example, Banca Commerciale Italiana, *Relazione del Consiglio d'Amministrazione* (Milan, 1905), p. 11.

[24] The literature on the activities of the Italian banks during the period under review is very scant. There is nothing even remotely comparable to Pantaleoni's great

other hand, it would be difficult to discover in Italy *serious* signs of a growing independence from the banks on the part of the industrial enterprises. Such tendencies became very strong in Germany after 1900. Their absence in pre-1914 Italy is not surprising and must be taken to reflect the belatedness of the country's industrialization effort. In these respects at least, the Italian case fits well into the general pattern of European industrialization in varying conditions of economic backwardness.

---

study of the Credito Mobiliare. The writer, however, had the privilege of access to at least a part of the archives of the Banca Commerciale.

5

Rosario Romeo and the Original Accumulation of Capital

⊰⊱

A few years ago, a young Italian historian, Rosario Romeo, was asked to prepare an evaluative survey of the contribution made by Marxian historians in Italy since the end of the last war. The resulting essay, which was published in *Nord e Sud* in 1956, turned out to focus on Antonio Gramsci's widely accepted views — the so-called Gramsci thesis — of the historical inadequacies of the Risorgimento. Romeo already had referred to the thesis in the concluding chapter of his excellent book on the Risorgimento in Sicily,[1] where in a somewhat vague and hesitating manner he refused to identify himself with Gramsci's position. In the 1956 essay, Romeo's dissent became firm and comprehensive. His critique attracted much attention and received, in its turn, a good deal of criticism. Thereupon, in a second article (published in 1958 in the same journal), Romeo tried to expand and deepen his argument by taking a much closer look at certain pertinent aspects of Italian economic development. The two essays have been made conveniently available in the form of a book on the Risorgimento and capitalism.[2]

In this history lie both the book's weakness and its charm. Obviously this is not a piece made *aus einem Guss*. Some of the historians whom Romeo treats in his survey dealt with areas or periods other than Italy or the Risorgimento and its aftermath. Certain parts

[1] *Il Risorgimento in Sicilia* (Bari, 1950), pp. 347f.
[2] *Risorgimento e capitalismo* (Bari, 1959); henceforth abbreviated *ReC*.

of the first essay, therefore, are rather tenuously connected with the main theme of the book: the relation between the economic development in Italy during the twenty-odd years following the unification and the social and political complexion of the liberation movement that preceded it. In addition, the views expressed in the two essays are not always strictly consistent. It might have been more prudent if the author had excised the irrelevancies and smoothed out the inconsistencies before republication. This would have involved a good deal of rewriting, and the reader would have received a more coherent product. Yet obliterating in this fashion the traces of the book's earlier incarnations would have also concealed something else from the reader: the struggle of an independent mind engaged in posing a significant historical problem and in creating an appropriate framework for its discussion. The present form of the book is far from perfect, but it fully reveals the groping freshness of the author's thought which is the most attractive feature of the study.

I

The essence of the Gramsci thesis consists in pointing out the differences between the Risorgimento and the French Revolution. The latter created the bourgeois state, gave it a permanent foundation, and created the modern French nation as a compact entity.[3] The Jacobins by pursuing a policy of faits accomplis pushed an unwilling bourgeoisie into the position of leadership over all the forces of the nation. Revolutionary Paris would have been swept away by peasant rebellions, but the agrarian policy of the Jacobins made rural France accept the leadership of Paris. It saved the revolution and perpetuated its effects.[4] But in Italy the Partito d'Azione failed to follow the Jacobin example. Hence the victory of the Risorgimento: the *andata al potere* was consummated without a previous, or at least concomitant, *andata al popolo* which, according to Gramsci, would have meant "ideologically a democratic program" and "economically an agrarian reform."[5] The lack of vigor of the Italian bourgeoisie in conjunction with the general complexion of post-1815 Europe is said to have been

[3] Antonio Gramsci, *Il Risorgimento* (Einaudi, 1949), p. 86.
[4] *Ibid.*, pp. 73, 84–85.
[5] *Ibid.*, pp. 65, 70.

responsible for the failure to convert the Risorgimento into a real revolution. It remained a "passive revolution," perpetuating the constitutional weakness of the Italian bourgeoisie and creating a country whose national strength remained sapped by "municipal particularism and catholic cosmopolitism." [6]

This is Gramsci's thesis. As Romeo has shown in his first essay, its influence upon Marxian historians has been great. With one or two exceptions, they went on to deplore the downright un-French character of modern Italian history and have been particularly eager to emphasize and to elaborate the view of the Risorgimento as a frustrated agrarian revolution.

Romeo had sat down to write a chapter in intellectual history, but before long he found himself concerned with Italian economic history. Since this writer is interested in the former only to the extent that it may illuminate the latter, there is no need to consider to what extent, if any, writers other than Gramsci may have coproprietory rights in his thesis. Nor is the problem of Gramsci's motivations or the influences that acted upon him of much interest here. It may be, as Romeo suggests (following Venturi), that Gramsci had been impressed by the conceptual connection of *people* (the peasantry) and *nation* in Russian populism of the nineteenth century.[7] More important, perhaps, is the fact that the Russian experience clearly demonstrated the revolutionary potentialities that can result from failures to carry out far-reaching and unambiguous agrarian reforms — be it in one direction or the other. It is therefore quite natural for those who have a professional interest in revolutions to stress the factor of agrarian discontent and to hope that in Italy it would also bring about profound revolutionary cataclysms. On the other hand, there is little reason to be surprised at the naive confidence in historical measurements derived from the use of the French yardstick. The belief that France has established the "normal" or "classic" pattern for modern political development has been as endemic in Marxian literature as the corresponding idea that England has established the normal or classic pattern for modern economic development. Each of these propositions, of course, is a half-truth, and, unfortunately, in historical

[6] *Ibid.*, pp. 87, 106, 136, 167.
[7] See *ReC*, p. 25.

arithmetic two half-truths do not make a full one. In this particular case, moreover, the half-truths are at variance with one another.

It is a frequent occurrence in social sciences that concepts are formed in the nature of similes, by more or less remote analogies, and that afterwards inferences are drawn from the verbal identities which go much farther than was intended or suggested by the original comparison. The name "industrial revolution" was first coined by French writers in the spirit of an obvious metaphoric rapprochement between the political cataclysms of the French Revolution and the period of rapid economic change in England.[8] Although the term was extra-Marxian and even pre-Marxian in origin, it fitted well into a political movement which considered itself revolutionary and into a system of economic thought which showed so much interest in the discontinuities of historical processes. In fact, the fit was so neat and tight that today the concept of industrial revolution is frequently regarded as specifically Marxian; a good deal of fairly inane opposition to the concept and of rather meaningless controversy about it seems to have originated in that belief.

The power of words being what it is, it should not be surprising that Marxians by intellectual predisposition were inclined to regard the Industrial Revolution — the breakthrough of modern industrial capitalism in England — and the political revolution in France as phenomena of the same order. In addition, the connection was further cemented by the general tenets of the materialistic conception of history with its stress on the economic bases of bourgeois revolutions, even though it was awkward from the theory's point of view that the two revolutions remained separated from each other by the English Channel. Still, in a vague and inchoate way, the positive character of the connection was never doubted. Economic transformation laid the basis for the revolutionary adjustment in superstructure which in turn opened the road to further economic progress. Essentially, the logical operation involved consisted in manipulating two oversized concepts: feudalism and capitalism. Capitalist development presupposed — an alternative and preferred way was to say that it *required* — destruction of feudalism. To do this was precisely the function of bourgeois

[8] A. Bezanson, "The Early Use of the Term 'Industrial Revolution,'" *Quarterly Journal of Economics*, 1921–22, pp. 343–349.

revolutions. Leaving aside the economic causes of bourgeois revolutions, the conclusion that they effectively promoted — nay, were necessary for — capitalist development followed cogently from the premises.

There is little doubt that there is some very general level of inquiry at which such a framework can be usefully employed initially. But it is just as undeniable that dogmatic acceptance of those premises must soon lead into a cul-de-sac of meaningless assertions. The bland intimation that both feudalism and capitalism are operational concepts involves assumptions that are hard to accept. At the very least either concept must be absolutely homogeneous in the sense that all its component elements are, as it were, isodromic — pointing, that is, in the same historical direction. *Everything* in feudalism must be opposed to capitalist development and *everything* in capitalism must be premised upon elimination of all that is feudal. This does not make very good sense, and few historians would be willing to accept such a proposition. But once we grant that feudalism can act more or less restrictively upon capitalist development, the concepts that have seemed so compact are decomposed into many not necessarily consistent elements: some of the elements in feudalism may be neutral as far as capitalism is concerned; others may be outright favorable to it. In all such questions, the problem of comparisons, of common denominators, of appropriate yardsticks, measuring cups, and scales, is inevitably raised, and any meaningful discussion of such historical processes presupposes — and in fact consists of — the development of measurable, that is to say, essentially comparable concepts.

In addition, it requires a good deal of simple faith or intellectual recklessness to assume that the situations referred to under the names of "feudalism" and "capitalism" in different areas are sufficiently similar in all the relevant aspects; nor is it less adventurous to believe that passage of time can make no significant change in the relationships concerned. Finally, one must wonder whether "bourgeois revolutions" do really resemble each other so much and whether something that in reality is a complex aggregation of events and of varying sequences of events in very different situations and periods can be usefully subsumed under a single concept. Thus, the concepts that glide with perfect smoothness from a writer's pen — feudalism, capitalism, revolution, bourgeois or otherwise — are highly deceptive. They are neither readily comprehensible nor clearly operational. The suggestion that those who use them and those to whom they are addressed know *senz' altro* what is meant by them is surely unwarranted. And just as the basic concepts are uncertain in content and meaning, no relationship connecting them can be safely considered of operational significance for predicting the future or explaining the past.

The foregoing discussion may seem to have moved too far away from both Gramsci's thesis and Romeo's discussion of it. This, however, is not so. In enlarging upon the conceptual problem, this writer has only attempted to make explicit what he considers the point of departure in Romeo's criticism. It is another matter that Romeo himself has not completely liberated himself from the use of dubious concepts. It is certainly surprising to see him waxing indignant at Aldo Romano's thesis that the Sicilian economy during the Risorgimento was not prevailingly feudal but only "semifeudal." [9] His dissatisfaction is not caused by the attempt to couch highly impressionistic judgments in the guise of seemingly precise propositions. Romano, he says, has failed to grasp that feudalism is perfectly compatible with progress in the "sphere of production." This is not easy to accept or even to follow.[10] There is every reason to welcome Romeo's interest in the development of output, but within the broad rules of etymology and morphology we all are masters over the words we use, and Romeo's insistence on the *correct* rather than the *appropriate* concept is disturbing. All this is a good illustration of the arbitrary rigidity and the semantic fetishism which spread irresistibly whenever concepts are used which are too big for a man to handle. It is curious indeed that Romeo should be seduced into this dogmatic lapse in a study which appears to constitute an attempt to escape from the conceptual three-tree forest in which so many have managed to get lost, very much like those legendary founders of a city in Russia who had contrived to lose their way among three fir trees, according to the tale told by Shchedrin, the celebrated Russian satirist.

[9] *ReC*, p. 66.

[10] All the more so since Romeo himself used the term "semifeudalism" in a different sense to characterize Sicilian conditions. See *Il Risorgimento in Sicilia*, p. 251. Romeo frankly refers to this circumstance in *ReC*, p. 70.

Romeo's thesis is quickly stated: the bewailed fact that the Italian Risorgimento did not involve, or did not lead to, an agrarian revolution with a concomitant expropriation of large landholders in favor of the peasantry must be considered fortunate from the point of view of the development of Italian capitalism. Since Romeo is quite willing to conceive of capitalism primarily in terms of industrial output, he operates in terms of at least potentially measurable magnitudes. The thesis, then, is that the agrarian structure of unified Italy tended to accelerate rather than retard industrial development. More precisely, it was the failure to carry out the agrarian revolution that made it possible to use agriculture as a source for the *original accumulation of capital.*

Before we consider the nature of the concept and the use Romeo has made of it, and before we appraise the degree of plausibility which our author has succeeded in establishing for his proposition, one more preliminary remark may be in order. Romeo's thesis presents itself as a refutation of Gramsci's, and there is a certain irony in using a specifically Marxian tool for the task. Nevertheless, it is probably more correct to suggest that Romeo cannot controvert Gramsci because he is interested in a different set of problems. Eli Heckscher once remarked that the Marxians' contribution to *economic* history turned out to be so meager because as a rule they preferred to study the influence of the "infrastructure" upon the "superstructure" and were really more interested in the latter.[11] There are notable exceptions to the rule, but Gramsci's thoughts on the Risorgimento are not among them. His interests are predominantly political and his few passing references to economic policies are quite unexciting. By contrast, Romeo's primary concern is the development of the Italian economy, and his study deserves to be viewed and judged as a contribution to a highly significant chapter in the economic history of Italy in the second half of the last century.

The present writer recently had an opportunity to express his own views on the concept of original accumulation of capital [see Chapter 2 of this volume], and Romeo has referred to them in his second essay. There is little that can or should be added here, except

[11] "Quantitative Measurement in Economic History," *Quarterly Journal of Economics,* LIII (1939), 169.

that some references to recent discussions of the subject in Soviet Russia may be included for the additional light they cast on the difficulties that seem to be partly inherent in the concept and partly in the dogmatic interpretations thereof. In addition, the deficiencies of the Soviet treatment of the problem should serve to place Romeo's contribution in proper perspective.

II

Few would disagree that Chapter 24 in Volume One of *Das Kapital* constitutes one of the most imaginative contributions to the history and the theory of economic development. But it is one thing to admire Marx's intuitions and to benefit from their highly suggestive brilliance, and it is another to use them as symbols in a ritualistic ceremony rather than as tools in an independent analysis.

Within the last few years, Soviet economists and historians have shown increased interest in the concept of original accumulation of capital. In May 1955, the Institute of History of the Soviet Academy of Sciences convened a special meeting which was somewhat pleonastically described as a "scientific-theoretical conference" for the discussion of "original accumulation of capital in Russia." Thereafter, several studies of various length appeared, some of which contained some interesting material. Nevertheless, it seems fair to say that the excessive intellectual timorousness of Soviet scholars has so far prevented them from a careful delimitation of the problems involved. Generally it is by attempting to refute a concept that one can hope to derive benefit from it. Marxian concepts are no exception to the rule.

Marx, writing as he did *ex abundantia ingenii* and surveying a virtually unexplored landscape, was satisfied to point to a problem and to present, in the light of some empirical material, a few hypotheses about the main elements involved and their possible interconnection. As was his wont, he presented those hypotheses in the guise of categorical assertions. In addition, he was eager to cast further aspersion on the capitalist system, knowing full well how easily origin and essence of phenomena are confounded in the human mind.

Marx assumed that the capitalist system cannot "begin" to function unless preceded by an accumulation of wealth and the emergence of a group of people who are willing — because deprived of other alternatives — to become hired laborers in capitalist enterprises. Wealth obviously could be, and in historical fact was, formed from a great variety of sources. It was, however, both intellectually and politically tempting to Marx to concentrate especially on one of the possible sources of wealth formation: the dispossession of small peasants. There was a certain beauty in solving two distinct problems *uno actu,* and there was a certain extrascientific satisfaction in being able to say that "the so-called original accumulation is nothing but the historical process of separation of producers from the means of production." [12] The point here is not that Marx greatly exaggerated the importance of the English enclosures in the sixteenth century. What matters is that his statement is really at variance both with the definition of the problem by Marx himself and with the historical material he had assembled. Marx presented a long list of other sources of original accumulation, a good many of which, while containing a strong element of violence, did not necessarily involve any "expropriation" of the small in favor of the great. The interest Marx showed in these "other" sources of original capital accumulation demonstrates clearly that he regarded the "precapitalist" accumulation of capital as a prerequisite of capitalist development, quite independently of the formation of a working class.

For the rest, almost everything was left open. Marx did not go into much detail in explaining just how accumulated wealth became "capital" outside agriculture. He was not interested in differentiating the needs for such original capital according to differences in historical situation; to do this would have quantified the character of original accumulation as a necessary precondition, and it went against the spirit and the custom of his thought to admit that patterns of historical events may be more or less "necessary." Nor did Marx, properly speaking, make it in any way explicit why an original accumulation was necessary at all; nor did he explain how operational meaning could be breathed into the twin concepts of "originality" of accumulation and "beginning" of a system. There is more than a fleeting suggestion that, carried away by his quick brush, Marx added many a stroke to his canvas that tended to blur the contours and distort the

[12] *Das Kapital* (Volksausgabe, Moscow, 1932), 753.

perspective of the picture. Was it, for instance, really useful to regard the most variegated activities of the state, from payment of interest on the national debt to protection of domestic industries, as part and parcel of the process of *original* accumulation? Was there not, on the contrary, some insight to be gained in regarding at least some state activities as alternatives to, rather than as an integral part of, *original* accumulation? And, finally, if there was a problem in defining the "beginning" of capitalism, was there not another one in defining the beginning of the original accumulation of capital? These are only some of the questions left unanswered in the Marxian sketch, and no one seriously preoccupied with the concept of original accumulation could possibly avoid probing into them. It is indeed astonishing to see how Soviet scholars, bound by the letter rather than the word, have succeeded in placing a sanctified Marx as an obstruction between his own concepts and their historical research.

The great value of the Marxian concept lies in the fact that it presupposes a type of economic development which encompasses a big spurt of industrialization. It is this assumption which makes the concept of the "beginning" a meaningful one, and it is the large amounts of capital needed to launch and to sustain such a spurt that alone justify the concept of original, that is, prespurt, accumulation. Without the industrial spurt the concept is destitute of meaning. For the simple question as to where the "first capital" came from (before the capital stock started growing from plowed-back "capitalist" profits) is hardly much more sensible or interesting than the question asked in a famous Russian comedy of the eighteenth century: from whom did the "first tailor" learn his trade? [13] But to relate original accumulation to the big spurt does several things. First, it makes the Marxian model a very realistic one, since the industrial history of a number of major countries does in fact register the occurrence of such spurts. Second, it divests the concept of original accumulation of any inherent necessities, iron or otherwise, because in those cases in which big spurts did not occur — and economic history provides us with them, too — capitalist development could very well "begin" without

[13] Curiously enough, Marx did not ignore the problem of the "first tailor" either. With reference to the origin of professions he says: "People had tailored for thousands of years before a man became a tailor" (*Kapital*, p. 47).

any specific previous accumulation. Third, it quantifies the concept, since more or less "original" capital accumulation will be needed depending on just how big the big spurt is and also depending on its precise character, that is to say, on the capital-output ratios which in turn depend on a variety of factors involving technology, the structure of demand, the composition of the nascent industry, and others. In addition, there is the problem of those sources of capital finance which are *not* "capitalist" profits and yet can usefully be separated from original accumulation and, indeed, should be treated as alternatives to it.

One would look in vain in Soviet literature for an attempt to establish a model of economic development and then to determine what place, if any, the concept of original accumulation would have within such a model. At the threshold of the recent discussion of the subject in Soviet Russia stands an article by Pankratova, in which she does say that accumulation of merchant capital is the historical prerequisite for the capitalist method of production because the latter needs previous concentrations of monetary wealth and also presupposes production for trade.[14] But while thus recognizing, though without analyzing, the independent significance of capital accumulation, she proceeds to abuse, as "revisionists," "apologists," and even "traitors of the working class," all those who do not conjoin the problem of wealth formation with that of expropriation of the small producers. The author, in her methodological innocence, does not even bother to explain why the two problems must not be separated. Is it because Marx said so; or is it because this makes good sense within some model that the author unfortunately does not describe; or is it because the connection has been well established by empirical research, so that the presence of the one factor has never been discovered without the other; or is it simply because stressing the connection is prescribed by the code of good — and safe — manners in Soviet Russia? Whatever the answer, Pankratova's style and tone do not make for an atmosphere in which fruitful theoretical discussion is possible.

It is not surprising, therefore, that the previously mentioned

[14] A. M. Pankratova, "O roli tovarnogo proizvodstva pri perekhode ot feodalizma k kapitalizmu" (On the Role of Commodity Production during the Transition from Feudalism to Capitalism), *Voprosy istorii*, IX (1953), 62–63.

conference showed more confusion than clarity. One of the main speakers, Pavlenko, tamely repeated the Marxian proposition of monetary accumulation and creation of "free" proletarians as the two sides of the same phenomenon and was only disturbed by the fact that coincidence of these two factors did not in historical reality always result in the creation of a capitalist system; accordingly, he insisted that for monetary accumulation and expropriation to be a truly "original" capital accumulation, a number of other factors had to be present.[15] This is true, but trite. What it really means is that to transform original accumulation into an operationally useful statement, one should have gone into the problem of transformation of wealth into capital which again, at the very least, would have required a discussion in terms of creation of claims upon current income and in terms of changing rates of investment and changing rates of growth of output. At the same time, the other main speaker, Kafengauz, apparently wished, on the one hand, to stress the element of violence in the process and, on the other, to have the original accumulation of capital understood in terms of creation of large-scale enterprises.[16] It is not at all impossible that an interesting set of problems for research would result from an attempt to operate with the concept of original accumulation in real terms rather than in monetary terms. But to do so would require construction of a model in which a proper distinction would have to be made between "original" and "subsequent" real capital; the connection between the two would have to be elucidated, and the sense would have to be explained in which *original* accumulation could be regarded as such, not simply as a banal "coming early in the game." There seems to be no sign of such at attempt in Kafengauz' paper.[17]

Since neither speaker provided any framework, the discussion seems to have moved back and forth without guide or beacon. Several

[15] N. I. Pavlenko, "O nekotorykh storonakh pervonachal'nogo nakopleniya v Rossii" (On Some Aspects of Original Accumulation in Russia), *Istoricheskiye Zapiski*, LIV (Moscow, 1955), 382–383.

[16] "Nauchno-teoreticheskaya conferentsiya o pervonachal'nom nakoplenii v Rossii" (The Scientific-Theoretical Conference on Original Accumulation in Russia; hereafter abbreviated *Conference*), *Istoricheskiye Zapiski*, LIV, 240.

[17] It should be noted, however, that this writer has not seen Kafengauz' full statement and is relying on a summary report.

participants tried to lay the evil spirits that no doubt were watching them by making the magic sign and accusing the main speakers and other participants in the debate of not paying enough attention to the "expropriation" aspect of the problem.[18] Since the discussion was without methodological orientation, the concept of original accumulation of capital was at the mercy of any fleeting fancy. One participant suggested that the right of the Russian estate owner to require labor services or quitrents from the peasants was a form of original accumulation of capital.[19] Also, the historical limits of the period of original accumulation were subject to much debate. Two women speakers disagreed as to whether the period of original accumulation preceded or followed the period of "manufactories" (large-scale shops as yet unequipped with machinery).[20] Again, the problem presumably was one of conversion of wealth into capital, but it was not described as such and hardly could have been meaningfully posed without a firm conceptual basis. Similarly, the "end" of the period of original accumulation remained quite vague. This was well illustrated by the suggestion of one of the speakers that Stolypin's reforms (1906–1910) also constituted original capital accumulation.[21] That such a suggestion could be made, and that an economic policy which followed rather than preceded the great spurt of Russian industrialization could still be regarded as being in some sense "original," is the final evidence for the prevailing state of confusion.

Nevertheless, this *Hexenkuechen* reversal of "late" and "soon," preposterous as it may seem, is not without some good sense. And, indeed, a redeeming feature of the discussion was the willingness of several participants to speak of a "Russian variant" of the process of original accumulation.[22] This no doubt is an innovation. Not that the differences in English and Russian economic history with respect to original accumulation (however defined) were not obvious. Lyash-

[18] *Conference*, p. 422 (Preobrazhenski); pp. 423–424 (Skazkin); p. 425 (Dubrovski). See also, M. D. Kurmacheva, "Obsuzhdeniye voprosa o pervonachal'-nom nakoplenii v Rossii" (Discussion of the Question of Original Accumulation in Russia) *Voprosy istorii*, XI (1955), 163 (Vilenskaya).

[19] *Conference*, p. 424.

[20] *Conference*, p. 424 (Zaozerskaya) and p. 426 (Vilenskaya).

[21] Kurmacheva, p. 165.

[22] *Conference*, p. 423 (Yakotsevski); p. 425 (Dubrovski); p. 426 (Vilenskaya).

chenko, a distinguished economic historian who had managed to show some independence of mind even during the very trying periods of recent Soviet history, did not hesitate to say that the process of original accumulation in Russia differed from the "classical form" which Marx said it had taken in England.[23] But, in general, the tendency to insist on ubiquitous Marxian "laws of development" had been strong and deep-rooted in Soviet writings. The attitude, no doubt, was established in the remote days when young Russian Marxists opposed the populists, when everything seemed to depend on showing that there was no special Russian way of economic development and that Russia was bound to repeat the experience of the West. It is significant, therefore, that in our time even a hyperorthodox writer such as Pankratova joined in the chorus of references to the "Russian variant." [24] It may well be that an increased sense of national self-importance helped to spread the view that Russian economic history, too, might present a classical case in its own right. Whatever the reason, the change in attitude is tangibly perceptible. Probably its most significant emanation to date is the recent book by Polyanski on the original accumulation of capital.[25]

In the light of the views which had prevailed in Soviet literature for such a long time, it makes odd reading when Polyanski writes: "Bourgeois economists still confine their research to the sphere of the 'western world' which they regard as the epicenter of the globe terrestrial. But this point of view has become antiquated a long time ago. In reality, Western Europe supplied only *one* variant of the genesis of capitalism. Russia, however, provided another variant for the development and stabilization of capitalism." [26] Leaving aside the somewhat naive assertion of Russian parity with the West and the not much shrewder strategy of defending or disguising a departure

---

[23] P. I. Lyashchenko, *Istoriya narodnogo khozyaystva SSSR* (Economic History of the USSR), II (Moscow, 1948), 6.

[24] A. M. Pankratova, "Proletarizatsiya krest'yanstva i yeye rol' v formirovanii promyshlennogo proletariata Rossii" (Proletarianization of the Peasantry and Its Role in the Formation of Russia's Industrial Proletariat), *Istoricheskiye Zapiski*, LIV, (Moscow, 1955), 199.

[25] F. Ya. Polyanskii, *Pervonachal'noye nakopleniye kapitala v Rossii* (The Original Accumulation of Capital in Russia) (Moscow, 1958).

[26] *Ibid.*, p. 4.

from traditionally held doctrines by rechristening them "bourgeois," the stress on the Russian variant has the tendency to liberate the study of Russian economic history from preconceived ideas.[27] Indeed, Polyanski feels much freer than did his predecessors to study the complexities of the relations between the system of serfdom and the industrialization of the country. He is also less inhibited in dealing with the phenomenon of serf-entrepreneurs and can stress the differences in the position of the so-called state peasants with regard to their geographic and social mobility as compared with the privately owned serfs. He can entertain the possibility that pressure for high quitrents on the part of the serf owners may have contributed to the labor supply for industrial enterprises in Russia, thus revealing a "positive" feature of Russian feudalism in its relation to capitalism. For the rest, however, Polyanski's study is nothing more than an intelligent and industrious account in two separate parts of the formation of wealth and of the formation of the labor force in Russia. The account is still vitiated by the traditional unwillingness of Soviet writers to appreciate fully the role of the state in the process of Russian economic development. At one point, with a simplicity that is nothing if not disarming, the author warns against "illicit exaggeration" of state policies under Peter the Great. The danger that must be avoided is "a concession to an idealistic interpretation of the genesis of feudalism in Russia." [28] Thereby, of course, narrow limits are set to the author's emancipation from the doctrine of global uniformity. For to a very large extent, it is precisely the special role of the state that constitutes the essence of the Russian variant of economic development.[29]

[27] This stress on the peculiarities of Russian economic development does not prevent the author from making his obeisance to the traditional view: "Basically the laws governing the sequence of socioeconomic formations are the same in all countries, and this proposition is correct also for the transition from feudalism to capitalism. In all countries, capitalism emerged as a result of the original accumulation of capital. But if the result of the process turned out to be the same, it is obvious that also the essence of the process itself must have been identical" (p. 4). The rites and customs of Soviet scholarship do constitute a rich field for anthropological research.

[28] P. 178.

[29] Similarly, Soviet writers cannot bring themselves to assign proper importance to the preservation of the Russian field commune (*obshchina*) beyond the emancipation of the Russian peasantry. Again, Russian Marxists of the last century were so

The main point remains the one previously made. In the absence of a proper analytical framework, Polyanski, too, is unable to study the problems of the "original accumulation of capital," properly speaking. What he does present is a good deal of empirical materials on the early history of the creation of fortunes and on the industrial labor force. In addition, he offers more information than is usually supplied in Russian sources on the emergence of entrepreneurial groups. All this is useful, though the discussion is incomplete in many respects.[30] Even the very inchoate attempt made in the concluding section to compare the Russian development not only with that of England but also with that of several other West European countries, pointing up similarities and differences, is not entirely devoid of interest. But, by and large, Polyanski's study deserves the same criticism as was leveled at the aforementioned conference against the papers of Pavlenko and Kafengauz.[31] It is essentially a narrative dealing chiefly with the early beginnings of Russian industrial development. As such there is actually very little difference between a book by Polyanski which is said to be devoted to the problem of original accumulation and a general survey of the "feudal economy" in Russia by a writer like Khromov.[32] Since Polyanski never raises the question of the usefulness of the concept, he is at a loss for a criterion for the termination of his period of original accumulation. It is almost at random that he fixes upon the year 1873, the year of "an industrial crisis which showed that Russia had become a capitalistic country." [33] "Naturally," he adds, "also after 1873 various phenomena of original accumulation of capital accompanied the development of capitalism

---

eager to confound the populists by showing that the obshchina already had disintegrated that even now it still seems improper in Soviet historiography to impute any serious retarding effect to it.

[30] See, for instance, the much more imaginative discussion of the wealth creating function of national debt in a recent essay by S. Borovoy, "Rostovshchichestvo, kazennyye ssudy i gosudarstvenny dolg" (Usury, Government Credit, and the National Debt) in L. G. Beskrovny, E. I. Zaozerskaya, A. A. Preobrazhenski, eds., *K voprosu o pervonachal'nom nakoplenii v Rossii* (On the Question of the Original Accumulation in Russia) (Moscow, 1958), pp. 497–537.

[31] *Conference*, p. 421 (Ustyugov); p. 425 (Dubrovski).

[32] P. A. Khromov, *Ocherki ekonomiki feodalizma v Rossii* (Essays on the Feudal Economy in Russia) (Moscow, 1957).

[33] P. 21.

105

in Russia. But such phenomena [then] had no more than an auxiliary character in the development of Russian capitalism." [34] This highly superficial treatment supplies perhaps the strongest evidence for the inability of Soviet writers to do justice to Marx's concept. True to Mephisto's precepts, they have managed "den Geist heraus zu treiben," to exorcise the spirit out of the concept. The result has been accurately predicted:

> Dann hat er die Teile in seiner Hand,
> Fehlt leider! nur das geistige Band.

All the comparisons between the importance of piracy in one case and of national debt in another as sources of fortune making cannot compensate for the lack of a theoretical approach to the problem of economic development. Without such an approach, the concept will not yield any really new insights, however much one may talk about the Russian variant. But to develop such a concept requires courage. The ways of analysis are dangerous. Paradoxically enough, to extract the maximum possible insight value from a concept, one must be prepared to abandon it at a certain point. Despite all the "thaw," the mercury in the intellectual thermometers in Russia is still far below the degree of independence that is requisite for the job.

III

The preceding sketch of the recent vicissitudes of original accumulation in Russia provides a useful background for the discussion of the use Rosario Romeo has chosen to make of the concept. The difference between an apprenticelike mimicry and a mature and creative formulation of the problem is quite striking.

While the Soviet writers never stop to wonder what original accumulation of capital really is all about, Romeo clearly visualizes it as a problem in aggregate economics and proceeds to define its component parts in measurable terms and to determine the interconnections among them. It is then in terms of the resulting pattern that Romeo attempts to view the economic history of the twenty-five years which followed the unification of Italy. The main elements in the pattern stand out distinctly.

[34] P. 157.

At the basis of the pattern is the growth in agricultural output which went apace through most of the period from 1861 to 1880. The next step refers to the utilization of this increase in output. Only a portion of it was used to satisfy the needs of the increase in population which took place during that period. The per-capita real incomes of the rural population either remained constant or actually declined. The difference between the higher per-capita output and the lagging per-capita consumption in agriculture went into increase of land rents.

Precisely because Romeo tries to arrive at a comprehensive view of the problem, he is not satisfied with the mere fact that some high incomes in agriculture rose still higher. Whether he can regard those additionally accrued incomes as actual sources of the original accumulation of capital must depend on the utilization to which those funds were put.

Romeo's second point, therefore, is this: the decades of the sixties and seventies of the last century were the years of preparation for the coming industrialization. It is during those years that the preliminary conditions for industrial development were created. According to Romeo, those preliminary conditions essentially refer to what in modern economic jargon has come to be called "economic infrastructure," an unbeautiful but widely accepted term. The idea is that it is only upon this infrastructure of railroads, roads, canals, and similar creations that the industrial superstructure can be erected. For Italy of the period, the problem largely was reduced to the supply of capital for railroad construction. Romeo admits that much of the capital for the purpose came from foreign sources, but a sizable part, he argues, was obtained from agriculture, both in the form of voluntary savings and through taxes whose burden lay heavily on agricultural incomes.

The accumulation of capital which underlay this investment was thus "original" or "previous" in a twofold sense. First because it preceded and prepared the coming industrial upswing; but second, and in a more specific and more unusual sense, because the funds were not used directly to finance industrial investment but, rather, the creation of services which would facilitate subsequent industrial investment and growth of industrial output. (Later on, something more will have to be said about this view of original accumulation.)

This process is said to have come to an end roughly with the termination of the second postunification decade. The industrial upswing between 1880 and 1887 proceeded in the atmosphere of an agrarian depression. The expansion of agricultural output had stopped, and the government was forced to relax taxes on agriculture and to shift some of the burden to the nonagricultural sectors of the economy.

This is Romeo's scheme. As a refutation of the Gramsci thesis its inferential sequence is clear. Had an agrarian revolution taken place, output in agriculture may not have risen to the same extent or not at all; and, at any rate, the peasants emerging victorious from a revolution would not have brooked the government's encroachments upon their incomes. As a result, the formation of the infrastructure would have been delayed and the industrial upswing of the 1880s would have been weakened or might not have materialized at all.

This reasoning is not implausible, but it refers to something that is a side issue. The real interest of Romeo's presentation lies neither in showing what might have been nor in his ability to score a debating point against dogmatic inflexibility. Romeo's book deserves to be appraised primarily as a study of Italian industrial development. Such an appraisal involves both discussion of the evidence offered by the author and a general evaluation of the plausibility and usefulness of his approach, including his concept of original accumulation.

As said before, what Romeo has presented is a model of Italian industrial development in the nineteenth century which, at least in principle, involves measurable magnitudes. To have thought in those terms no doubt marks considerable progress in the economic historiography of Italy. But Romeo has done more: he has made a serious effort to fill in the numerical data required by his model, thus moving the treatment of the problem to a less abstract level. It was of course a happy accident that, shortly after the publication of Romeo's first essay, the Istituto Centrale di Statistica issued its significant study on the long-term growth of Italian national income.[35] While this study is not the only source upon which Romeo has drawn for his statistical information, there is no question that the wealth of material it contains has been of crucial significance. It seems clear that the validity

[35] *Indagine statistica sullo sviluppo del reddito nazionale dell' Italia dal 1861 al 1956, Annali di Statistica,* IX (Rome, 1957); hereafter abbreviated *SRNI.*

of Romeo's conclusion to a considerable extent depends on the validity of the statistics offered in the institute's study.

The present writer has seen no serious critical analysis of that study. It is true, however, that at least in one or two cases the data contained in the study appear somewhat bewildering.[36] And it is also true that, from Romeo's point of view especially, the astonishingly low rate of growth which the institute's data yield for the 1880s creates a real difficulty. After having used the institute's data throughout, he must suddenly refuse to accept them for 1880–1887, lest he lose his historical verification for the denouement as envisaged by his model. If there was no industrial upswing in the 1880s, it is hard to see in what sense the two preceding decades can be conceived of as representing original accumulation of capital and preliminary investment.

All this is not said in order to cast aspersion on the institute's study. There is no question that, thanks to its pioneering effort, all students of Italian economic development find themselves deeply in the institute's debt. It is true that for the time being it may be the better part of prudence to keep in mind the uncertainty that naturally

[36] For example, one is baffled by the very irregular pattern shown by the relation between investment and growth of national income between 1860 and 1910. It would seem that, however much one might vary the assumptions concerning the lags involved, no plausible hypothesis would result to explain the changing pattern of capital-output ratios implied in the institute data (the pertinent capital-output ratios have been computed from *SRNI*, pp. 251, 266, 270).

More important is the case of data on industrial output in the 1880s to which Romeo refers in his book. Like him and others, the present writer was surprised to find very considerable discrepancies in the rate of growth for that period between the institute study and his own attempt at computing such a rate (see *SRNI*, p. 218, and Chapter 4 of this volume). The rates implied in the institute study are uniformly lower for all the comparable subperiods of the period 1881–1914, but for 1881–1888 my own study shows an average annual rate of growth of 4.6 percent, while the institute's rate is below 1 percent. It is true that the choice of the terminal year changes the picture somewhat: the institute's rate for 1881–1887 (rather than 1881–1888) rises to 1.77 percent. But the discrepancy still remains considerable. The differences in the other subperiods may be quite naturally explicable by the difference between the 1938 weights used in the institute study and the turn-of-the-century weights in my computations. That the institute's rates of growth are *lower* throughout would lend further credibility to such an interpretation. But the discrepancy in the 1880s is much too large to be explained in these terms, and the institute data certainly are at variance with our general information on the period. Still, pending further study, one must reserve judgment.

attaches to first steps in such a vast and difficult field. It is further-more true that future revisions may affect many magnitudes and alter the weights we may be willing to impute to them in our own analyses. For the purposes of this discussion, the present writer is quite willing to follow Romeo in accepting the bulk of the institute's data. To do so, however, does not necessarily mean accepting Romeo's evaluation of those data. It would seem that he has tended to magnify unduly some fairly modest developments as pictured by the statistics.

Romeo, no doubt, is quite correct in stressing the fact of an increase in agricultural output between 1861 and 1880. But its extent is open to question. With regard to output data in physical terms, it is disconcerting to see the staggering discrepancies that exist between two sources which Romeo cites and which contain data on changes in output of a number of agricultural commodities.[37] It is such data that no doubt underlie the value estimates of agricultural output presented in the institute study, and the discrepancies in the basic data certainly detract from the reliability of the value figure. If, however, following the previous decision, we decide to accept the latter as reasonably correct, two conclusions emerge irresistibly. First, the rise in output over the period is indisputable; this is clearly shown by the data on value of marketable gross output of agriculture, at least for the first fifteen years after the unification. Second, the rate of increase was far from overwhelming, amounting as it did to 2.7 percent a year for the first decade and to only 2 percent a year between 1861–65 and 1876–80.[38]

As mentioned before, Romeo places some emphasis upon the accrual of voluntary savings and their role in financing the "prelim-inary" investment. It is perfectly true that, according to the institute study, the rate of saving was negligible in the first quinquennium after the unification and then rose to an average of about 4 percent in the three following quinquennia.[39] In the light of what we know about such rates in other countries in periods of industrialization and in periods preceding industrialization, it is difficult to consider a rate of 4 percent a very high one. Nor was it a high one in comparison to

[37] *ReC*, pp. 118–119.
[38] Computed from *SRNI*, p. 204.
[39] Computed from *SRNI*, p. 264.

rates of saving achieved in other periods of economic development in history. It is interesting that the rate of saving reached its first peak in the first half of the eighties, at a time when the agricultural depression had reduced both incomes and savings. On the other hand, the fact that the peak in the rate was reached during an industrial upswing points more toward "simultaneity" than toward "previousness" in accumulation. The peak level (6 percent), incidentally, was not reached again until the last quinquennium of the century, when the big spurt of Italian industrialization was launched. The saving rate then nearly doubled in the following decade, which means that when Italian industrialization was going full speed the saving rate was about *three times* as high as it had been in the period of Romeo's original accumulation.

At the same time, it is difficult to suppress some uneasiness at the rate of investment that materialized during the first two decades after the unification. The rate of *gross* investment (at current prices) seems to have fluctuated between 7.9 and 9.8 percent.[40] This is hardly impressive. It must also be noted that during the same period public works constituted a portion of gross national product which was very small to start with and which went on declining from quinquennium to quinquennium. It was only in the first half of the 1880s that the share of public works in GNP returned to the (still quite low) level of the early 1860s.[41] Nor, finally, is it easy to accept Romeo's picture of the two decades as a period of busy activity, as an "infrastructure" boom, in the light of the data given in the institute study on the rate of growth of per-capita national income (at 1938 prices): the first decade after unification showed an annual rise of .3 percent (three tenths of 1 percent); the second decade showed a *decline* of .23 percent (minus twenty-three hundredths of 1 percent) per year.[42] The general impression from consulting those five sets of figures or

[40] Computed from *SRNI*, pp. 249, 264.

[41] Computed from *SRNI*, pp. 249, 264. The percentage ratio of public works to GNP was as follows:

1861–65	2.8
1866–70	2.1
1871–75	1.9
1875–80	1.6
1881–85	2.8

[42] Computed from *SRNI*, p. 251.

ratios is that whatever economic transformation was afoot during those "preparatory" decades was not large enough to affect the aggregate magnitudes in any really significant fashion.

To some extent, the difficulty is aggravated by Romeo's special concept of original accumulation. Had he operated with a narrower concept, he would have assumed some sort of hiatus between the formation of wealth and its subsequent conversion into investment funds. Then no one would expect data on national income to show much change during the "accumulation period" as distinguished from the "productive investment period." But, from mere creation of claims upon future national product, the concept in Romeo's hands has evolved into creation of titles to current income, the *originally* accumulated funds being *currently* deflected into investments designed to finance the infrastructure of the economy. Under these conditions one would expect to see high capital-output ratios (fitting the conditions of railroad construction); and even though the railroads were slow in showing profits, their construction and operation was bound to increase the total value added within the economy. The statistics, however, disappoint both expectations. If we abide by the previous decision and abstain from questioning the data, the conclusion suggests itself that the process of what Romeo calls original accumulation may have been in reality less important quantitatively than he believes it to be.

Having said this much, one must say more. The model proposed by Romeo has the advantage of being extremely well ordered. "First things must come first" seems to be writ large over the model: there is a period of preparation, during which the prerequisites for the subsequent growth are created, and then the growth itself takes place. In this view economic development appears as a very logically and methodically arranged sequence of phenomena. Perhaps it was with his own model in mind that Romeo quoted approvingly Sapori's remark that "logic and history in the last analysis are one and the same thing." [43] But Clio is not a tidy housewife. Though it is useful

---

[43] *ReC*, p. 112. For the rest, Sapori's saying is mystifying, to say the least. Does it simply mean that it is through a set of hypotheses that the historian must approach his material and that the hypotheses must be formally, though not substantively, consistent? This, of course, would be quite acceptable. But Sapori appar-

in the first approximation to separate preparation of growth from the "real thing," and though it is also true that some of the empirical material from the European economic development in the nineteenth century can be profitably organized in this way, it is equally true that, in the industrial history of those European countries whose degree of backwardness was considerable, preparation for industrialization and industrialization itself tended to be much more closely interwoven. This is intimately connected with a general observation: the greater a country's degree of backwardness on the eve of its big spurt of industrialization, the more likely it is for factors which may have appeared as prerequisites of industrial development in less backward countries to be either absent or to play a subordinate role. The probability is that in such countries the lacking "prerequisites" were substituted for by other factors and that many a factor which in a more advanced country could be meaningfully regarded as a prerequisite came into being in the more backward country as a *result* of the industrialization. Thus one can suggest that in the more backward countries much of the "preparation" tended to coincide with the industrial upsurge. One is indeed tempted to say that it was precisely this merging of periods that was the actual precondition for the rapid industrialization. In other words, it is altogether possible to believe that in a backward country a period of preparation that is consummated before the industrial upsurge takes place makes it *impossible* for the latter to materialize. This appears paradoxical only if one refuses to recognize the complexities of the specific "logic" of economic backwardness. Italy's industrialization provides perhaps the best possible illustration of these relations. It seems a well-grounded historical assumption to say that one of the factors that kept down the rate of industrial growth in Italy during the big spurt of 1896–1908 was precisely the fact that the construction of the railroad system had been essentially completed before the beginning of the period. If the demand that is associated with railroad construction

---

ently was willing to say much more and to suggest that, whenever statistical material is at variance with the hypothesis and threatens to falsify it, the logic of history must prevail. There is magic and — who knows? — perhaps even some sense in words like *Gestalt*, except that it is difficult to see how Romeo, who has been so patient and persistent about collecting material in support of his model, can possibly share Sapori's view. And how can Sapori himself?

had been maintained, the period 1896–1908 might well have showed a still higher rate of industrial growth, one that would have been more consonant with the degree of relative backwardness of the Italian economy at the time.[44]

What follows from the preceding remarks? The purpose was not to take exception to Romeo's general appraisal of Italian economic development. When he emphasizes the splendidly successful effort of transforming Italy into a modern industrial country — the only one on the shores of the Mediterranean Sea — in the face of truly formidable obstacles, Romeo stands on very firm ground. His case in this respect is so strong that even his citing in support of it the very adventurous figures of Colin Clark cannot weaken it much.[45] But this is not the point. In the end, everything tends to come out in the historical wash, and looking at the result of a process is unlikely to offer much enlightenment on its early stages. And it is the latter that are at issue here.

[44] The present writer cannot help feeling that Romeo treats the problem of demand and the role of the market in the process of industrialization somewhat too lightly. On the one hand, it need not be correct to say that the large imports of industrial consumers' goods from France and England demonstrated the existence of a large internal market (*ReC*, p. 108). The demand for foreign products frequently cannot be transformed into a demand for domestic wares without a previous shift in purchasing power from receivers of relatively high to those of relatively low incomes. On the other hand, Nurkse's statement, which Romeo quotes, that in the last analysis the market can be enlarged only by production, surely cannot be taken to mean that production will find its market under all circumstances (*ReC*, pp. 105–106). The internal market as represented by the peasantry can become unimportant for industrialization — and in fact a retarding force — if someone else, say the state, is willing and able to engender industrial production and at the same time to constitute the market for the goods produced. This is one of the substitution patterns that occur in the industrialization of backward countries. Besides, the demand of the state is not the only possible substitution of this kind. Entrepreneurs acting in accordance with stable optimistic expectations and maintaining for a long time the demand for each other's investment goods can be just as effective a substitute for the demand of the peasantry. Such substitutions often are very likely to take place, but there is no assurance that they actually will. If they do not, the rate of industrial growth is likely to suffer, but the rate that is maintained will surely depend on the existence of the demand emanating from the internal market. The case against the potential importance of the internal market in Italy should, therefore, be argued not in terms of a general proposition, but rather in terms of the probability that preferable, because more effective, substitutes for the internal market would be, or actually were, available.

[45] *ReC*, pp. 197–199.

Romeo's way of viewing the economic development of Italy during the first quarter of the century after unification may be useful in pointing up what was accomplished during that period. But it is at least equally useful to remain aware of the inadequacies and short-comings of that evolution. This is not just to cast a slur on policies — although policies must be criticized — but because, otherwise, very legitimate questions regarding the slowness and belatedness of Italian industrialization would remain unanswered. The crux of the problem, the focus upon which everything converges, is the evaluation of the industrial upswing of the 1880s. That period Romeo himself charac-terizes rather "discreetly" as a time of a "discreetly rapid develop-ment." [46] But he proceeds to describe it in rather exuberant language and does not hesitate to entitle his chapter on the period "The Birth of Large-Scale Industry."

We know that the 1880s did not bring with them the big spurt of Italy's industrial development. For that the country had to wait another fifteen years, and the view seems defensible that the "big spurt" was not as big as it might have been, precisely because it had been delayed. Why, then, did the upswing of the 1880s fail to grow into the characteristic initial upsurge of industrialization? There are many possible answers, and agricultural distress may be one of them. But Romeo himself suggests that "the function of the crisis was to accelerate capital investment in industry." [47] We have seen elsewhere most impressive industrial spurts in very backward agricultural coun-tries in conditions of agricultural depression, and Russia of the late 1880s and early 1890s provides the clearest case in point. The problem, as always, is one of compensations and substitutions. It would seem, therefore, that one of the possible solutions must be sought in the very material utilized by Romeo.

Romeo, of course, is at liberty to call "original accumulation" the process of extracting through taxes portions of the landowners' *current* income and investing them *currently* in infrastructures. But his doing so should not make us forget the other, and perhaps more basic, concept of original accumulation that can be distilled out of Marx's intuitions. That concept, although quite operational in principle, is

[46] *ReC*, p. 188.
[47] *ReC*, p. 175.

more difficult to follow through statistically, as are all processes involving forced savings. But it would seem that at least an important presumption has been well established which must not be obscured by any conceptual redefinitions. The presumption that in Italy there was no sufficient previous long-term accumulation of wealth in *appropriate* hands which at a propitious moment — that is, discontinuously — could be made available to industrial entrepreneurs is fundamental to the understanding of Italy's economic situation at the time. This is not an Italian peculiarity; the situation resembled that in other countries which also were slow to begin their industrialization. But what it means is that the great cognitive value of the basic concept of original accumulation very often is negative. In this case it lies in ascertaining that it was not applicable to Italian conditions. Accordingly, Italian industrial development, if it was to take place at all, was bound to utilize some substitutes for original accumulation —to find some other ways of deflecting sufficiently large segments of national income into investment. By preserving the name of original accumulation for the process he describes, Romeo tends to blur the fact that it is precisely a *substitute* for the original accumulation of capital. As shown before, what emerges clearly from the data is the quantitative weakness of the substitute that was used. A big spurt requires a big effort: either the state or some financial institutions or both must be willing to make it.

It is the feeling of the present writer that Romeo on the whole fails to appreciate how woefully inadequate or misdirected was the policy of the Italian government and that of the pertinent banks before the nineties. In particular, it is difficult to accept his approval of the government's policy with regard to steel. His view that the Italian engineering industry could not have developed without domestic steel production is a most questionable assertion. Facts and reason both point in the opposite direction. The creation of the expensive and inefficient steel industry retarded the rise of the Italian machinery industry, and the argument that the latter could be left with inadequate tariff protection because machinery industry was better suited to Italian conditions seems to misread the purpose and the meaning of a rational policy.[48] Unfortunately, Romeo is

[48] *ReC*, pp. 194–195.

only too right when he refers to the influence exercised by the powerful state-nursed steel industry on Italian tariff policy.[49] Nor is Romeo convincing in his attempts to justify the promotion of the cotton industry and even the protection of grains. One can believe that in Italian conditions a great deal of state intervention would have been in order, and in fact most desirable, and still feel that perfect inactivity of the government in economic affairs might have been more beneficial than what actually took place. It does seem that Romeo has allowed himself to be unduly propelled by the mechanics, or rather the ethics, of his own model. It will not do to regard anything and everything that was done at the time as a blessing for Italian industry; or to be carried away to the point of equally praising as a spur to industrial development both the maintenance of the *corso forzoso* (exchange control) and its abolition.[50] Nor is it helpful to extend complacency to a point where the predominance of small enterprises in the Italian industry is explained and justified by the process of formation of the labor force and the training of skilled labor.[51] If the industrial history of the nineteenth century teaches us anything at all, it is the crucial importance of bigness of enterprise and plant in the big industrial spurt of a backward country. It is precisely within large plants that it has proved possible to economize and to use most efficiently the available skills by substituting both machinery and organizational innovations for qualified labor. It is the large plants and enterprises that can compensate the backward country for its manifold disabilities and obstacles to economic development. But to launch and maintain such enterprises would have required a supply of capital on a scale which neither the Italian government nor the Italian banks of the time would provide. It is hard to see how Romeo can refer to the 1880s as a period of inflationary pressures and considerable forced savings,[52] if one considers that during those years prices were either stable or falling.[53] It is perfectly true, as Romeo says, that the banks were not yet adjusted

[49] *ReC*, p. 184.
[50] *ReC*, p. 191.
[51] *ReC*, p. 191.
[52] *ReC*, p. 178.
[53] *SNRI*, p. 251.

to the support of rapid industrial development.[54] It follows that to have a big spurt of industrialization the state would have had to substitute for the appropriate banking facilities and do so on the requisite scale. This, however, did not happen. As a result, an important historical opportunity was missed, and an industrial upswing that would have been propelled and sustained by the still-continuing needs to create the infrastructure did not materialize.

To a large extent, then, what separates the present writer from Romeo's position is a problem of interpretation of the results yielded by his model. But nothing that has been said in the preceding pages can possibly detract from the cognitive value of the model itself. It represents an original and imaginative attempt to organize in operational terms and to see in its organic interrelation a significant stretch of Italian economic development. Surely this is the way to approach modern economic history, and one can only hope that Romeo will continue his explorations along the path upon which he has entered so auspiciously.

[54] *ReC*, p. 161.

6

Russia: Patterns and Problems of
Economic Development, 1861–1958

THE emancipation of the peasantry stands at the threshold of the period under review. The question of whether, on the eve of the reform, the system of serfdom was disintegrating for economic reasons or whether its vitality and viability were still essentially unimpaired has been the subject of much controversy. But even those who, like the present writer, tend toward the latter view must admit that the development of the nonagrarian sectors of the economy was virtually premised upon the abolition of serfdom.

To say this, however, does not at all imply that promotion of economic development was a paramount objective of the emancipation. As was true of most of the agrarian reforms in nineteenth-century Europe, the authors of the Russian reform either considered industrialization undesirable or, at best, were indifferent to it. The actual procedures chosen reflected these attitudes. In many ways they were bound to hamper rather than facilitate economic growth. The emancipation involved, first of all, a determination of the land area to be given over by the landowner to the peasants for permanent use. There is no question that over wide parts of the country (and particularly in the black-earth belt) the peasants received a good deal less land than had been customarily assigned to them before the reform. Second, there was the question of the magnitude of the quitrents (obrok) to be paid by the peasants as compensation for land allotments. It is true that, once those rents were set, subsequent acquisition of land by the peasants (the so-called redemption proce-dure, by which the right of use was changed to the right of ownership) was rendered very easy and as often as not did not entail any addi-tional burdens upon the peasantry. But the original rents were set far above the contemporaneous market prices of the land. The example of the immediately preceding agrarian reform in Europe — that of Austria in 1848 — where peasants' obligations were mostly determined on the basis of "equity," or cadastral values (much *below* their market prices), was not followed in Russia.

It might be argued that the two features of the Russian reform just mentioned should have provided a favorable climate for subse-quent industrialization; the inadequacy of the peasants' landholdings in conjunction with the considerable financial obligations imposed upon their households could have been expected to favor the flight from the countryside and thus to provide a large reservoir of labor supply to the nascent industry. Such might have been the conse-quences indeed, if the reform and the later legislative measures had not erected considerable barriers to land flight by strengthening the *obshchina*, the village commune, wherever it existed.

An English yeoman who found the cost of enclosing the land excessive could sell his farm and use the funds so obtained for business ventures outside agriculture or, at worst, for covering his transfer cost. A Russian peasant who wished to leave the village commune not only had to relinquish his rights in the land, but in addition had to pay, under the terms of the redemption procedures, what often were very sizable sums before he could receive his release. A member of the household wishing to leave the village perma-nently also had to secure the consent of the head of the household. Where the periodic repartitions of land by the village commune were conducted on the basis of manpower at the disposal of the house-hold, permanent departure of a family member was bound to reduce the extent of land to be made available to the household at the next repartition. In conditions of relative scarcity of land, the willing-ness of the head of the household to permit such departures could not be, and in general never was, very great. Nothing was more revealing of the irrational way in which the village commune functioned than the fact that the individual household had to retain the abundant factor (labor) as a precondition for obtaining the scarce factor (land). On the other hand, the readiness of the member of the household to sever for good his connection with the land and become firmly committed to nonagricultural pursuits naturally was adversely affected by these arrangements.

It is often claimed that the Russian emancipation procedure followed the "Prussian model." It seems that Lenin was the first to give currency to the thought. The analogy is hardly felicitous. The outstanding feature of the Russian reform was that, instead of a class of landless laborers, it had firmly established the landowning peasantry and had taken special precautions to keep the peasants attached to their land. To be sure, this was done *inter alia* in order to satisfy the gentry's need for cheap labor. But here again the similarity with the Prussian reform is rather superficial and deceptive. Unlike the Prussian Junkers, the Russian gentry seldom showed much interest in technological innovations on their estates. The traditions of serfdom may partly account for that. Under these circumstances, the cheap labor assured the estates by the Reform Act may have been a very undesirable gift, inasmuch as it discouraged them from introducing those improvements in the mode of cultivation which tended to have labor-saving effects and to increase the capital intensity of agricultural output.

While permanent migration to the city was made difficult, temporary moves on the part of the members of peasant households were much less so. Yet even in such cases the permissive rights vested in the heads of the village administration and the heads of the household created various opportunities for impounding some portion of the earnings made in the city. The right to demand and enforce the return to the village of the departed member certainly left much room for pressures and extortions of all kinds. If it is considered that age-long tradition and inveterate inertia would have hindered migration to industry in any circumstances, the Russian government by assigning to the obshchina and the mir such a strong role in the emancipation procedure and in the life of the post-emancipation village had created a considerable obstacle to the formation of a permanent industrial labor force in Russia.

If the double pressure to which the peasant economy was

exposed — the inadequacy of land and the magnitude of the financial burdens — was prevented from causing a steady and considerable migration from the land, then that pressure itself was bound to assume the role of a retarding factor in the economic evolution of the country. The peasant economy was unable to increase its productivity because its income after taxation and redemption payments did not permit sufficient investment; at times the low level of income even led to capital depletion. In addition, the prospect of repartitions militated against land improvements, even if and where they were financially possible; and the egalitarian nature of such repartitions prevented consolidation of landholdings assigned to individual households and precluded changes in cultivation methods and crop-rotation systems even where ignorance and inertia of the peasantry did not constitute an effective obstacle to such improvements.

In the long run, the scarcity of land available to the peasants in conjunction with the increase in population implied a steady deterioration in the economic position of the peasantry, despite purchases by village communes and individual peasants of gentry land and despite the formation, in the 1880s, of special institutions designed to finance such transactions.

It is true that the position of state peasants was more favorable than that of the former serfs in that their land allotments were somewhat larger and their financial burdens somewhat lighter; the so-called imperial peasants were in between the two groups. Yet these differences, particularly in the longer run, were not sufficiently large to warrant a different appraisal of the state and imperial peasantry. They too experienced the restrictive effects of the village commune, and the economic development of their farms also was restrained by the action of the government whose deliberate policy it was to bring their burdens in line with those imposed upon the former serfs.

It should be added that it would be a mistake to interpret the secular rise in land prices which characterized the period between the emancipation and the First World War as providing relief to the peasantry in the sense of reducing the real burden of their obligations. Over large areas of Europe, market values of peasant land tended to be a good deal above the capitalized yield values. But in Russia that tendency was particularly strong. Land values moved upward even when prices of agricultural products were falling. The land hunger of the peasantry, stimulated by population growth, largely accounted for this discrepancy. Thus, the rise in land values, far from relieving the peasant economy, was an expression of its precarious position.

There is little doubt that the inhibitions upon the growth of output of the peasant economy and the consequent limitations upon the peasants' purchasing power for industrial products were a serious obstacle to the industrialization of the country. They made it improbable from the outset that peasant demand for industrial goods could exercise a strong pull on industrial growth. This was clearly seen by a large number of populist writers. Their conclusion was that industrial development in Russia was unlikely to start and, if started, was bound to founder in the shallowness of the "internal market."

This prospect left the populists undismayed because of their aversion to industrialization and their fears of its social consequences. Yet the predictions did not come true. By 1914, Russia had taken very long strides along the road of industrial development. What had vitiated the populists' predictions was their failure to see the manifold flexibilities and adjustabilities which are inherent in processes of economic development. The growing purchasing power of the peasant economy can indeed be important as a motive of industrialization. Yet it is but one among a number of possible alternatives.

Economic development in a backward country such as Russia can be viewed as a series of attempts to find — or to create — substitutes for those factors which in more advanced countries had substantially facilitated economic development, but which were lacking in conditions of Russian backwardness. Such substitutions are the key to an understanding of the way in which the original disabilities were overcome and a process of sustained industrial growth was started. It is these acts of substitution that came to determine the specific pattern of industrial development in Russia.

But the process of industrialization is also a process of diminishing backwardness. In its course, factors that were lacking formerly tend to become evident and acquire increasing importance within the body economic. What was once in vain looked for to serve as a "prerequisite" or a "cause" of industrial development comes into being as its effect. It is a fascinating pursuit in the history of modern industrialization to see to what extent the original substitutes were thereby rendered obsolete and disappeared after having fulfilled their function; and to what extent they were preserved and continued to dominate the pattern of development in its subsequent stages, even though the special need for them no longer existed.

The present assignment requires this writer to supply, within the scope of a few pages, a background chapter on the last hundred years of Russian economic history — a period of unprecedented economic change. Obviously, no more can be done than to select for discussion some significant aspects of that change. Perhaps the processes touched upon in the preceding paragraph may serve this purpose.

Over long stretches of the period under review, in manifold ways, in ever-changing forms, and at different levels, innovation and anachronism seem to coalesce and to separate, to follow and to displace each other. The remainder of this essay will be devoted to an attempt to see the peculiarities of Russian industrialization in terms of these relationships.

I

The big spurt of Russian industrialization in the prerevolutionary period largely coincided with the decade of the 1890s. Thus, almost thirty years had passed over the land before the great effort could come about. This is not surprising. The peasant reform would have had to be very different if a direct and immediate impact upon industrial growth could have been expected from it. Moreover, even if the reform had been deliberately designed to favor industrialization rather than to obstruct it, a certain preparatory period of slow growth was almost inevitable. The judicial and administrative reforms which came in the wake of the emancipation were essential in creating a framework for modern business activity. But other changes, at least equally significant, were much slower in coming. Certainly a radical improvement in communications was crucial. One does not have to conjure up the dramatic and pathetic vision of a huge boiler being dragged by teams of oxen through the deep mud of the Ukrainian steppes on its way to the construction site of the first blast furnace in the Donbas in order to understand that some railroad building had to antedate the period of rapid industrialization. Railroads were indispensable to sustain a level of exports consonant with the needs of an industrializing economy. Railroad materials had to be imported from abroad, which in turn meant pursuit of a liberal foreign-trade policy with only a modicum of encouragement to domestic industry. Besides, a period of rapid growth does not materialize overnight simply because an institutional barrier to industrialization has disappeared. Such a period requires a simultaneous development of complementary efforts in many directions. The component elements of growth in the individual industrial branches must be adjusted to each other, and only when a number of such "development blocks," to use Erik Dahmén's felicitous phrase, has been created is the stage set for the initiation of the great spurt.

There is little doubt that the decades following the emancipation can be conceived as such a period of preparation. And yet it is only in retrospect that they can be so viewed. The deficiency of the internal market, so untiringly stressed by the populist writers, might have postponed the period of rapid growth until a far and indefinite future. The strategic factor in the great industrial upsurge of the 1890s must be seen in the changed policy of the government. The fear of industrialization, so much in evidence in the 1860s, was gone. Industrial development became an accepted and in fact the central goal. Once this happened, the problem of peasant demand lost its previous significance, and its relation to industrialization was thoroughly reversed. It was as though a rotating stage had moved, revealing an entirely new scene. The growth of peasant demand for industrial goods no longer was a prerequisite of successful industrialization. On the contrary, its curtailment became the objective. To reduce peasant consumption meant increasing the share of national output available for investment. It meant increased exports, stability of the currency, chances for larger and cheaper loans from abroad, and the availability of foreign exchange needed to service foreign loans.

The Russian state under Vyshnegradski and Witte put the peasantry under very considerable fiscal pressure. It left the agricultural economy of the country to its own devices, satisfied that conversion of pastures into grain lands and some modest rise in productivity on those estates which were cultivated as such rather than leased to the peasants were sufficient to support the process of industrialization. The population of course was growing rapidly. In the closing years of the 1890s, Russian agriculture produced less breadgrains per capita of the population than had been the case three decades earlier. If the increased exports are taken into consideration, the domestic availabilities were still smaller. A central principle of governmental policy was to impound a larger share of the peasants' output rather than to take active steps to raise that output.

Thus, the government's budgetary policy was effectively *substituted* for the deficient internal market. The continuation of railroad construction on a large scale throughout the 1890s provided the government with convenient machinery for the maintenance of demand for industrial products. At the same time, in multifarious ways the government either supplied investment funds to industry directly or encouraged and facilitated investment in industry. Government action took the place of what in other countries was achieved through the pull of a growing free market, or through forced savings generated either by credit creation or by the impact upon current income of previously accumulated claims.

Those, however, were not the only processes of substitution that were taking place during the period. The Russian government, far from favoring all branches of industrial endeavor indiscriminately, concentrated its primary attention on the output of the iron and steel and the machinery industries. The strategic interest in railroads and general political considerations certainly prompted the government in that direction. But, as may be deduced from comparisons with other countries, this cannot be more than a part of the story. In a sense, this concentration upon certain branches of industry also was an emanation of substitutive processes.

Russia on the eve of its great industrial spurt suffered from many disabilities. Its entrepreneurs were far too few; their time horizon was often limited, their commercial customs backward, and their standards of honesty none too high. The influx of labor to industry was inadequate because of the institutional framework that had been imposed upon agriculture. Such labor as was available was uneducated, restless and fitful in its habits, often trying to submerge the sense of frustration and loneliness in alcoholic excesses with consequent absenteeism, low productivity, and rebellion against the rules of factory discipline. One of the few advantages that Russia, as many other backward countries in similar conditions, possessed was the possibility of borrowing technology from more advanced and more experienced industrial countries. In this field alone, Russia could equal, if not excel, them. It could concentrate on modern technology so that its factory equipment, though much smaller in the aggregate, could be much more up-to-date in its average composition. But the introduction on a large scale of technology from advanced countries, by its very nature, also meant a substitution of capital for labor. Far from being irrational in conditions of a backward country, it was the modern Western technology which enabled the Russian entrepreneurs to overcome the disability of an inadequate labor supply and very frequently also the inferior quality of that labor.

This is not to say that lack of suitable industrial labor in itself was not a hindrance to Russian industrialization. Introduction of a labor-saving process may mean lower cost per unit of the product; and still the entrepreneur may find the resulting saving insufficient to justify the effort of plant reorganization and modernization. His decision may be positive only if he feels that cost reductions will lead to a great expansion of output, thus increasing total profits very considerably. But a sizable expansion of output, even though the innovation is labor-saving, will require a large increase in the labor force; accordingly, the decision may still fall against the innovation, unless the needed labor is expected to come forth without too great a rise in wage rates. The point, therefore, is not that the difficulties which Russia experienced with the formation of an industrial proletariat were not a bothersome obstacle. The point rather is that the assurance of government demand for a considerable portion of the growing output in conjunction with the introduction of modern technology created a situation in which the quantitative and qualitative inadequacy of the labor supply could be neutralized to an extent that still permitted a relatively high rate of industrial growth.

A historian of the period cannot fail to be impressed by two aspects of this process of assimilation of foreign technology. It may be taken for granted that, throughout the nineteenth century, technology tended to become more and more labor-saving. This was true of the individual industrial branches, and even more so of industrial economies as a whole, because of the increasing share of those industries where technological progress led to particularly rapid increases in the capital-labor ratios. It is true of course that, broadly speaking, Russian entrepreneurs had to accept Western technology as it was. But if they had wanted to keep down the capital-labor ratios, they might well have tried to obtain secondhand equipment built in earlier phases of Western industrialization. The least they could do was to import technology from those countries where technological progress had been less rapid. In fact, the opposite was true. During the great spurt of the nineties, it was no longer the English technology but the more progressive German technology that came to dominate Russian imports; and increasingly the eyes of engineers and factory managers turned toward the United States whence even more capital-intensive equipment was brought into the country. Thus alternatives were available, and there is no reason to assume that the choices made were not the rational ones.

On the other hand, it would be wrong to see the process of technological acquisition as one of mere imitation. True, in the last decade of the nineteenth century, the Russians had as yet very little opportunity for producing equipment which combined certain features of, say, American and German machinery (as began to happen several decades later). But they exercised discretion in the processes that were modernized and those that were left unchanged, often within the same plant. While the Russian blast furnaces were rapidly becoming bigger and technically more advanced, the processes of introducing the charge into the furnaces remained untouched by this development and workers equipped with wheelbarrows still carried out the job. Where industrial work was similar to that used in agriculture and capable of being performed by an unskilled and fluctuating labor force, it was allowed to continue to do so.

Finally, there is the problem of bigness. Bigness, in a broad sense, is of course inherent in the concept of a great spurt. But the industrialization in Russia, as in so many other backward countries in the last century, was also characterized by bigness of both individual plant and individual enterprise. There were many reasons for this.

For one, the technology of the nineteenth century typically favored large plants, and to accept the most advanced technology also meant accepting larger and larger plants. The state in its promotion of industrial establishments, for good and not so good reasons, showed remarkably little interest in small businesses. Large enterprises were a much more lucrative source of graft; and the corruption of the bureaucracy tended to reinforce a tendency that was already present for weighty economic reasons. Similarly, the Russian government did little to check the strong cartelization movement within industry that acquired momentum after the great spurt of the nineties. But what is of interest here is that the bigness of plant and enterprise must also be viewed as a specific substitution process. The lack of managerial and entrepreneurial personnel was compensated for by a scale of plant which made it possible to spread the thin layer of available talent over a large part of the industrial economy.

What were the results and the aftermath of these developments? In purely quantitative terms, in terms of growth of industrial output, the spurt was truly a great one. The average annual rate of industrial growth during the nineties was around 8 percent, and it was even better than that in the last years of the decade. None of the major countries in Western Europe had experienced a comparably high rate of change. The very rapidity of the transformation, however, made for maladjustments of various kinds. The discrepancy between the advancing industrial segment of the economy and the relatively stagnant agricultural segment was perhaps the most crucial among those lags and tensions. But others were by no means unimportant.

The specific processes of substitution tended to reinforce the heterogeneous character of the resulting economic structure. Contrasts between the new and the old appeared within the industrial group itself and within the individual plants and enterprises. Technology as a strategic factor in the industrial spurt implied modernization of some industrial branches and not of others. Within an industrial plant age-old processes based on tools used in the construction of the Pyramids were carried on side by side with methods representing the last word of the inventive genius of the nineteenth century. This inevitably was reflected in human contrasts within the labor force.

But the contrasts obviously transcended labor; they extended into the managerial group. The technical director, as the chief engineer frequently was called in a Russian factory, may have been indistinguishable from his Western counterpart. The commercial manager or the entrepreneur as likely as not was a much more complex phenomenon. He was able to understand and willing to exploit the economic advantages of the new technology, but at the same time he carried on attitudes and displayed forms of behavior which differed little, if at all, from those of preindustrial entrepreneurs in Russia. This was true of his relations to consumers, suppliers, credit institutions, and competitors. In addition, his relations with the governmental bureaucracy called for special, often very devious, actions. He had to be a different man in his way of dealing with a German firm which supplied his business firm with machinery and know-how and in dealing with an official in the Ministry of Finance whence he obtained both subsidies and orders for deliveries. The great spurt in conditions of Russian backwardness could not fail to give rise to manifold stresses, tensions, and incongruities. Sociological research which would view those tensions against the economic background of the mechanics of backwardness should discover a rich field for empirical findings and analytical comprehension.

All these disparities, created almost inevitably in the course of the great spurt, can be seen as problems for the phase of Russian industrial development that followed. However, overriding all of them in importance was the problem which the emancipation of the peasantry did not solve and the gravity of which was enhanced precisely by the policy of rapid industrialization. Industrialization required political stability, but industrialization, the cost of which was largely defrayed by the peasantry, was in itself a threat to political stability and hence to the continuation of the policy of industrialization. The immediate effect of the basic substitution of the government's budgetary policies for the deficiency of the internal market was growth of industrial output. In the longer run, the effects were more complex.

II

What happened in Russia in the nineties of the last century was the great upsurge of modern industrialization. Nevertheless, certain aspects of it were not modern at all. Several times before in the course of Russian history, economic development seemed to follow a curious pattern: the military interests of the state induced the government to bring about a rapid spurt of economic growth. In the process, heavy burdens were imposed upon the peasant population of the country, the enserfment of the Russian peasantry having been inextricably connected with the policies of economic development. So great were the burdens, and so heavy the pressure, that after a number of years the spurt tended to peter out, leaving an exhausted population to recover slowly from the stress and the strain that had been imposed upon it.

There is little doubt that military considerations had a good deal to do with the Russian government's conversion to a policy of rapid industrialization. True, no immediate military discomfiture preceded the initiation of the new policy. But the war of 1877 against the Turks was won on the battlefields in the Danube Valley and the Balkan Mountains, only to be lost in Berlin against the British and probably the Germans as well. In the course of the Berlin congress, particularly during its dramatic moments, the Russian government had much opportunity and reason to reflect that it was not much better prepared for any military conflict with a Western power than it had been a quarter of a century earlier on the eve of the Crimean War. In the short run, Russian reaction consisted in shifting the direction of its expansionist policy away from Europe to Central Asia and the Far East. Taking a somewhat longer view and further prompted by the formation of military alliances in Central Europe, the government turned toward the goal of a drastic increase in the economic potential of the country.

In the 1890s, a renewed enserfment of the peasantry was, of course, not in the realm of practical politics. Nor was there any need for such a measure. The reforms of rural administration which had been introduced with the advent of reaction under Alexander III gave the central bureaucracy sufficient tax-exacting power over the peasantry; at least for some time it was possible to keep the peasantry in a state of docile compliance. The joint responsibility of the village commune for tax payments was helpful, though far from indispensable. The considerable shift to indirect taxation further increased the government's ability to pay for the industrialization in conditions of a relative price and currency stability. The fiscal policy of the government was able to perform the function which at an earlier age had been performed by the institution of serfdom.

The great spurt of the 1890s came to an end in 1900. The depression of that year was variously interpreted as an overproduction crisis, a financial crash, or a response to economic setbacks abroad, particularly in Central Europe. It is fairly clear, however, that below the surface phenomena lay the exhaustion of the tax-paying powers of the rural population. The patience of the peasantry was at its end. The following years were characterized by growing unrest in the villages until the folly of the war with Japan fanned the isolated fires into the flame of a widespread peasant rebellion during the 1905 Revolution. All this was very much like the consummation of the traditional pattern of Russian economic development: a quick upsurge compressed within a relatively short period and ending in years of stagnation. But there was a great deal more to the industrial spurt of the 1890s than simply a repetition of previous sequences of economic development. It would seem more plausible to view those similarities as the last emanations in prerevolutionary Russia of the traditional pattern. For the differences were fully as important as the similarities. Also, in this broad sense, the new and the old appeared curiously commingled. Along with the resurrection of a specifically Russian past, there was also the assimilation of Russian economic development into a graduated but still general pattern of European industrialization.

Two, and perhaps three, factors stand out in distinguishing the upswing of the 1890s from similar episodes in the more remote past. One of them has just been mentioned. During the decade of the 1890s, the Russian government abstained from introducing for the sake of the industrialization any far-reaching institutional change which, while aiding the process in the short run, would have become a serious obstacle to its continuation in the long run. Neither the institution of the *zemskii nachal'nik* nor the additional steps taken in the 1890s to preserve and protect the village commune could of course compare in any way with the enserfment of the peasantry. That a government firmly committed to the policy of industrialization went out of its way to safeguard the obshchina seemed paradoxical. But, apart from the fiscal value of the arrangement, it was felt that its existence contributed to political stability within the country. Neither reason was persuasive. Satisfactory substitutes for joint responsibility for tax payments could easily have been found; and the events of the subsequent years showed clearly that the village commune nursed rebellious rather than conservative sentiments. The abolition of the commune still remained a problem of industrial policies in Russia, but it was one which antedated the period of rapid industrialization.

The other factor was positive. Modern industrializations based on the creation of fixed capital of considerable durability are not followed by periods of protracted stagnation as easily as are earlier, much more labor-intensive spurts of economic development ("stagnation" of course is to be understood simply in terms of a very low or even negative rate of growth). The recuperative power of a capital-intensive economy is greatly superior to that of its historical predecessors. And, finally, a modern industrialization is characterized also by a more substantial investment in human capital. In particular, it tends to bring about, over a relatively short period, a considerable change in entrepreneurial and managerial attitudes as well as, though to a lesser extent, in those of skilled labor. All this means that the effects of Russia's great spurt reached out strongly into the future; that the process of industrialization could be resumed at diminished *faux frais* and in a form more efficient and less dependent upon the support of the state.

Such were the characteristic features of Russian industrial growth in the years between the 1905 Revolution and the outbreak of World War I. This, too, was a period of rather rapid growth (some 6 percent per year), even though the rate of change remained below that of the 1890s. During those years industrialization could no longer be the primary concern of the government. War and revolution had greatly strained budgetary capabilities. The redemption payments (as well as the institution of joint responsibility) had disappeared under the impact of the revolution. Kokovtsev, first as Minister of Finance and later as head of the Cabinet, pursued a cautious policy of thrift. Railroad building continued, but on a much reduced scale. The execution of such armament plans as were conceived was being postponed from year to year. In the eighteenth century, the death of Peter the

Great and the withdrawal of the state from an active economic policy spelled the doom of the contemporaneous economic development. But in Russia of the twentieth century, Count Witte's fall and the abandonment of his policies did not prevent a renewed outburst of industrial activity.

Nothing underscores more clearly the changed attitude of the government than the fact that its most important action in the field of economic policy was Stolypin's legislation against the obshchina. In a radical reversal of the agrarian policies pursued only a few years earlier, Stolypin's reforms of 1906 and 1910 made it possible for the peasants to sever their connection with the obshchina through a simple and advantageous procedure, permitting them to acquire personal ownership of the land and in the process often to swap the numerous strips of their former allotment for a single consolidated holding.

There is no question that many aspects of the reform were harsh and unfair to the less prosperous members of the village communes. There is also every evidence that the government's about-face was caused by political considerations, that is to say, by the impressive lesson learned from peasant uprisings during the preceding revolution. The consequences of the reform for the process of industrial development were accidental from the government's point of view, despite some liberal phraseology ("liberal" in the European sense of the term) used in defending the reforms.

Nevertheless, the potential positive effects of the reform on industrial development were indisputable. The authors of the reform, despite considerable opposition within the government, refused to accept the concept of family or household ownership; the ownership of peasants leaving the village commune was vested in the head of the household. For the first time, the road was open for an unimpaired movement to the city of peasant family members; for the first time, large groups of Russian peasants could, like their counterparts in the West, sell the land and use the proceeds for establishing themselves outside agriculture. The war of 1914 necessarily cut short the implementation of the reform, but its initial effect was considerable. Those peasants who had felt that leaving the commune would enable them to increase the productivity of their farms and those peasants who had been anxious to leave the village both hastened to avail themselves of the separation procedure. It was a considerable step on the road of Russia's westernization.

And this is the aspect of the reform that is of primary importance here. The gravity of the economic stagnation that followed the reign of Peter the Great was compounded by the legacy of serfdom. The very modernization of the state machinery under Peter meant that the government was much better equipped to enforce the serfdom condition upon the peasant and to deal effectively with fugitives from serf status. At the same time, the territorial expansion of Russia kept reducing and making more remote the frontier regions which formerly had been the sanctuary of so many peasants in their flight from oppression. It was in these conditions that the edict granting the nobility and the gentry freedom from service obligations marked the acme of the state's retirement from active guidance of the country's economic life. That act finally severed the original connection between serfdom and economic development and sealed the perpetuation of serfdom as a main obstacle to economic progress. With regard to both its historical locus and its "liberalizing" character, the Imperial Edict of Peter III (1762) bears a certain resemblance to Stolypin's reform. Yet, despite these similarities, it is the difference between the two measures which may be taken as a gauge of the contrast in historical situations. The great spurt under Peter the Great had not led to sustained growth. The traditional pattern of Russian economic development was allowed to work itself out fully. By contrast, the withdrawal of the state after the upswing of the 1890s was marked by a measure which was designed to further rather than thwart industrial progress.

The westernization of Russian industrialization between 1906 and 1914 expressed itself in a large variety of ways. To use the previously adopted terminology, one could say that the pattern of substitutions was changing rapidly. To some extent banks stepped into the vacuum left by the state. In this way, credit-creation policies and some entrepreneurial guidance by the banks continued as substitutes for the scarcity of both capital and entrepreneurship in Russia. But this mode of substitution tended to approximate the pattern prevailing in Central Europe. The credit policies of the banks were still a substitute for an autonomous internal market, but there is little doubt that one of the consequences of the industrial creations of the nineties was the gradual emergence of such a market.

It may be quite tempting to view again the change between the period under review and that of the 1890s in terms of Dahmén's dichotomy between development blocks in the state of full completion and development blocks in the beginning stage. The years 1906–1914 were characterized by the relative scarcities of coal, oil, and metals, in conjunction with the rapid forging ahead of metal-processing industries. There is a persistent and very much exaggerated tendency in current Russian historiography to present those scarcities as consequences of monopolistic policies in the basic-materials industries. It is probably more reasonable, still following Dahmén, to say that during the years preceding the First World War the structure of Russian industry was distinguished by specific disproportionalities and that once again, though on a much higher level, industry may have been passing through a period of dynamic preparation for another great spurt. Such a spurt, of course, never materialized. The point, however, is that considering the years 1906–1914 as a period of formation of new development blocks may help to explain why the rate of growth during those years was not higher than it was. It cannot explain the high growth that was actually attained in a situation where the outside aid to industry had manifestly declined to a fraction of its previous volume. It is more helpful, therefore, to regard this period as governed by the effects of diminished backwardness, and in this sense to view the whole stretch between the end of the 1880s and the outbreak of the war as consisting of two disparate and yet connected parts. The great spurt of the 1890s had prepared for the subsequent continuation of growth in changed conditions.

Many of the tensions and frictions that could be so strikingly observed during the 1890s reappeared in the second period, when at all, in a considerably modified and tempered form. There is no question that great progress had taken place with regard to entrepreneurial attitudes. Without such progress and, in particular, without the general rise in trustworthiness of Russian businessmen, the banks could never have come to play a powerful role as suppliers of long-term credit to industrial firms. The general modernization of entrepreneurial attitudes no doubt made the complex of actions and relations of the individual entrepreneurs less heterogeneous. The decline in the importance of the government as an economic agent pointed in the same direction.

The years that had passed since the second half of the 1880s considerably increased the stock of permanent industrial labor in the country. At the same time, after 1905, more tangible improvements both in real wages and in working conditions became noticeable. The reduction in the importance of foreign engineers and foremen in factories and mines also tended to diminish friction. The great pressure upon the peasantry had subsided as well. In contrast to the last decades of the nineteenth century, the quantity of breadgrain available for domestic consumption rose faster than did the population. The industrialization between 1906 and 1914 no longer offers a picture of a race against time and of progressive exhaustion, physical and mental, of the population's power to suffer and endure.

Those elements of relaxation and "normalization" in the industrial process should not, however, disguise the fact that in other respects the great spurt of the 1890s, the industrial upsurge in conditions of extreme backwardness, still dominated the course of the development in the later period. The composition of the growing industries continued to favor the same branches. As before, the stress on bigness was characteristic of both the productive and the organizational structure. The movement toward cartelization, which was mentioned earlier, must be regarded as a part of this continued emphasis on bigness. As was true in countries west of Russia, the policies of the banks tended to accelerate the process. In this sense they were the true heirs to the policies previously pursued by the bureaucracy. And, like the latter, they tended to exaggerate and accelerate the process for both good and bad reasons. Interest in small enterprises would have strained the organizational and supervisory powers of the banks, just as it had proved unmanageable for the bureaucracy. Other reasons were less respectable. Just as many a civil servant had found opportunities for personal enrichment in his official connection with large enterprises, the banks, too, very often promoted increases in capital, mergers, and mediation of monopolistic agreements because they proved a considerable source of profit, even when not required by the process of growth. Still, when everything is said and done, it was of utmost importance that the stress on large-scale business, the very essence of industrialization in conditions of backwardness and the basis for its successful implementation, could be preserved after the withdrawal of the state.

Russia before the First World War was still a relatively backward country by any quantitative criterion. The heavy weight of the agrarian sector of the economy and the low level of the national per-capita output placed it far below and behind neighboring Germany. Nevertheless, as far as the general pattern of its industrialization in the second period was concerned, Russia seemed to duplicate what had happened in Germany in the last decades of the nineteenth century. One might surmise that in the absence of the war Russia would have continued on the road of progressive westernization.

It is not entirely pointless to speculate on what might have happened in the course of such a development. Diminution of backwardness is a complex process. As has already been noted, certain paraphernalia of backwardness are shed fairly soon. Other elements are more resistant to change. Thus, the great school of industrialization tends to educate the entrepreneurs before it educates the workers; and it takes still longer before the influence of the industrial sector of the economy penetrates into the countryside and begins to affect the attitudes of the peasantry. In the latter respect, prerevolutionary Russia saw no more than the first modest traces of such an influence. Yet the likelihood that the transformation in agriculture would have gone on at an accelerated speed is very great.

In addition to the age-old attitudes which are more or less rapidly modified under the impact of economic development, there are specific institutional and economic factors which are created in the very process of industrialization, and which often appear strange and incomprehensible from the point of view of an advanced country. But they are the stuff that industrialization in backward areas is made of. Some of them disappear after they have fulfilled their mission, teleologically speaking. Thus did the Russian government leave the economic scene after the upswing of the 1890s. It is again extremely likely that the banks would not have been able to keep their ascendancy over Russian industry for very long. Diminishing scarcity of capital, further improvements in the quality of entrepreneurship, and the sheer growth of industrial enterprises in all probability would have in due time enhanced the position of industrial firms to a point where they no longer needed the banks' guidance. That is what happened in Germany after 1900, and the natural course of events might well have moved Russian industry in the same direction. Even so, if the German example has predictive value, the banks would not have necessarily been transformed into the English type of commercial bank. They would have retained their interest in long-term investments, and in this sense the Russian economy would have remained characterized by a peculiarity created in the earlier stages of its development. Even more important, the stress on bigness, the specific composition of industrial output, and the significance of cartels and trusts within the industrial structure are likely to have increased rather than diminished over the years. One of the curious aspects of the European development was that the process of assimilation of backward countries to advanced countries was by no means a onesided affair. To some extent, as the degree of backwardness was reduced, the backward country tended to become more like the advanced country. Yet precisely because in the process of its industrialization the backward country had been forced to make use of very modern technological and economic instruments, in the long run it was the advanced country that in some respects assimilated its economy to that of the backward country. A comparison of the structure of, say, the German and the English economies in 1900 and some decades later would serve to illustrate this point.

Russian industrial development around the turn of the century was frequently decried as "artificial." Count Witte used to reject the accusation with considerable vehemence as meaningless and irrelevant. For what matters is both the degree and the direction of artificiality or spontaneity in the process seen over an appropriately long time. Taking into consideration the economic conditions that prevailed in Russia prior to its great spurt of industrialization, it is difficult to deny that the Russian development fitted well into the general pattern of European industrialization, conceived, as it properly should be, in terms of a graduated rather than a uniform pattern.

The only purpose in speculating about the probable course of Russian economic development as it might have been, if not interrupted by war and revolution, is to try to cast more light on the general industrial trends that dominated the last period of industrialization in prerevolutionary Russia. Still the question remains whether war and revolution cannot be interpreted as the result of the preceding industrial development. Some Soviet historians certainly incline in that direction. If the Russian bourgeoisie could be saddled with the main responsibility for the outbreak of the war and if, in addition, it could be shown that in bringing about the war it had acted in response to the pressure of its economic interests — if, in short, the process of Russian industrialization carried in itself the seeds of the coming military conflict — then to abstract the war from the process in order to elucidate the course and prospects of Russian industrialization would mean to abstract the process as well. Some Russian manufacturers indeed may have welcomed the wartime orders for their products. Yet the precise mechanism through which such interests of the bourgeoisie were in fact translated into the decisions reached by the emperor and his government has remained altogether obscure.

The view just described seems to magnify the political significance of the Russian bourgeoisie out of all proportion and to substitute suppositions of various degrees of plausibility for historical evidence. It might be more persuasive to argue that the government saw a relatively short and victorious war as a chance to solidify the regime and to avert the danger of revolution. And the question then would be to what extent the preceding industrial development may be said to have been leading to another revolutionary cataclysm.

It is true, of course, that the social and political structure of the empire was shot through with manifold serious weaknesses. Opposition to the regime was nearly universal among the intelligentsia and certainly widespread among the industrial and mercantile groups. Since 1912, the year of the terrible massacre in the Lena goldfields, the strike movement of the workers was again gaining momentum. And at the bottom of the social edifice there was the old resentment of the peasants who had never accepted the rightfulness of the gentry's ownership rights over the land. The peasantry's land hunger was a steady source of ferment. The sentiment in the villages was no doubt further exacerbated by the blows struck against the village commune and the threat of its dissolution. A new outbreak of revolutionary violence at some point was far from being altogether improbable.

And yet, as one compares the situation in the years before 1914 with that of the nineties, striking differences are obvious. In the earlier period, the very process of industrialization with its powerful confiscatory pressures upon the peasantry kept adding, year in and year out, to the feelings of resentment and discontent until the outbreak of large-scale disorders became almost inevitable. The industrial prosperity of the following period had no comparable effects, however. Modest as the improvements in the situation of the peasants were, they were undeniable and widely diffused. Those improvements followed rather than preceded a revolution and accordingly tended to contribute to a relaxation of tension. Stolypin's reforms certainly were an irritant, but after the initial upsurge their implementation was bound to proceed in a much more gradual fashion.

Similarly, the economic position of labor was clearly improving. In the resurgence of the strike movement economic problems seemed to predominate. It is true, of course, that in the specific conditions of the period any wage conflict tended to assume a political character because of the ready interventions of police and military forces on behalf of management. But this did not mean that the climate of opinion and emotion within the labor movement was becoming more revolutionary; as is shown by the history of European countries (such as Austria or Belgium), sharp political struggles marked the period of formation of labor movements that in actual fact, though not always in the language used, were committed to reform. There is little doubt that the Russian labor movement of those years was slowly turning toward revisionist and trade-unionist lines. As was true in the West, the struggles for general and equal franchise to the Duma and for a cabinet responsible to the Duma, which probably would have occurred sooner or later, may well have further accentuated this development. To repeat, I do not mean to deny that there was much political instability in the country. There clearly was. What matters here is that, from the point of view of the industrial development of the country, war, revolution, or the threat thereof may reasonably be seen as extraneous phenomena. In this sense, it seems plausible to say that Russia on the eve of the war was well on the way toward a westernization or, perhaps more precisely, a Germanization of its industrial growth. The "old" in the Russian economic system was definitely giving way to the "new." It was left to the regime that finally emerged from the 1917 Revolution, generated in the misery of the war and the shame of defeats, to create a different set of novelties and to mix them with old ingredients of Russian economic history into the strange and powerful infusion of Soviet industrialism.

III

The 1917 Revolution redeemed the ancient hopes of the Russian peasantry by letting them seize the lands of the gentry. In addition, after the end of the Civil War, when the NEP compromise was put into operation, the peasants found themselves greatly relieved of obligations toward the state as compared with the prewar years. At length, the "internal market" of the populists seemed to have become a reality.

If the revolution had effected nothing else but a change in the position of the peasantry, one might perhaps have envisaged a slow but steady growth in agricultural output and a rate of growth in industry perhaps slightly exceeding that of agriculture, if for no other reason because of a sustained shift of many industrial activities from the farms to urban industries. The increased strength of peasant demand was bound to effect a change in the composition of Russian industry in the direction of greater stress upon "light" industries. Presumably, the rate of investment would have been lowered and the over-all rate of growth of industrial output slowed down thereby. It was apparently in these terms that Stalin, during the twenties, envisaged the course of the country's industrial development.

Yet, in addition to the new role of the peasantry, the revolution also established a dictatorial government controlling large-scale industry. Instead of asserting itself through a market mechanism, the peasant demand, if it was effectively to change the structure of relative prices and the composition of industry, had to be reflected in governmental decisions. These decisions, however, might or might not be the appropriate ones. During the NEP period, the problem expressed itself largely in the so-called scissors crisis: in the fact that the government-dominated industry had insisted upon terms of trade that were unfavorable to agriculture. Nor was any shift toward greater stress on consumer-goods industries visible. If anything, toward the end of the NEP the share of heavy industries in total output was somewhat larger than before the war.

It is true that through most of the NEP period the high rate of industrial growth overshadowed the difficulties and prevented them from becoming overpowering. As long as the problem was to rebuild the prewar industry, largely using prewar equipment and prewar labor and technicians, the incremental capital-output ratios were very low and the rapid increases in the supply of consumers' goods kept discontent at bay. The situation was bound to change as the prewar capacity of Russian factories was being reached and further increases in output began to require much more sizable investment funds.

This, no doubt, was a crucial and critical moment in the economic history of Soviet Russia. The adjustment to a lower rate of industrial growth would have been difficult in any circumstances. In the specific Soviet conditions of the later twenties it was aggravated by political factors. To prevent too deep and too sudden a fall in the rate of industrial growth, either voluntary or politically enforced savings were necessary. But the savings of the peasant economy were small since, despite all improvements, the absolute levels of peasant incomes still were very low. To increase the rate of taxation carried the threat of resistance; and a rise in industrial prices charged to the peasants after the experience of the scissors crisis, when such prices had to be *lowered* in relation to farm prices, was hardly within the range of practical politics. The legacy of the NEP policies, with their low taxes, downward pressure upon the industrial terms of trade, and failure to provide in time for a shift in the composition of industrial output in favor of consumers' goods, expressed itself in a situation of inflationary pressures where too large a volume of purchasing power of the peasantry pressed upon too small a volume of available consumers' goods.

The internal market supported by the peasantry had been regarded for decades as the natural and spontaneous form of industrialization. After what has been said above, it may be doubtful whether in conditions of still considerable backwardness the peasants' demand alone would have sustained any reasonable rate of increase in industrial output. Too low a rate of increase in demand may have proved insufficient to solve the problem of indivisibilities and complementarities inherent in the process of development. Without a strong flow of external economies (in the broad sense of the word), the nascent industrial enterprises might have found themselves burdened with costs of production that were too high for successful operation. Paradoxical as it may sound, industry might have been better able to satisfy a strong rather than a weak increase in demand.

The immediate problem, however, was different. The change in the economic position of the peasantry greatly increased the flexibility of Russian agriculture. In certain circumstances, higher outputs per farming household will lead to an increase in the peasants' demand for industrial goods — whether adequate or not from industry's point of view. In different and less favorable circumstances, the peasant economy can reduce the extent of its connections with outside markets by diverting cereals into converted products for its own consumption, and by assigning a larger portion of the land to fibrous crops for home spinning and weaving. For the Russian peasantry with its weak marketing tradition the escape into greater self-sufficiency suggested itself as an easy and natural response to the economic conditions which prevailed in the second half of the 1920s. As the marketings of grain began to fall off, the inevitable adjustment to a lower rate of industrial growth seemed to turn into the threat of a negative rate of growth, of deurbanization and agrarianization of the country.

The economic crisis that thus marked the end of the NEP period was at the same time a political crisis of first magnitude. Inability to maintain the food supplies to the cities and the growing resistance of the millions of peasants, strong in their intangible diffusion, seemed to spell the doom of the Soviet dictatorship. To be sure, a change in the political system of the country would not have in itself solved the economic problem. The inflationary pressures still would have called for a solution. It is possible that a government truly representing the peasants might have been able to raise taxes and by so doing to establish the equilibrium between rural purchasing power and the volume of industrial consumers' goods available, at the same time reversing the declining trend in agricultural marketings. Such a government might have sought and found foreign credits and used the proceeds for importation of consumers' goods from abroad — thereby making the increases in taxation less unpalatable. The immediate problem might have been solved in this fashion, but the question of industrial growth would have been another matter. Barring further fundamental changes in the economic structure of the country, the conditions for resumption of industrial growth would seem to have been rather unfavorable.

In retrospect, the threat to the continuation in power of the Soviet regime appears blurred by the indubitable successes achieved subsequently. But it was real indeed. It was under the pressure of that threat that Stalin underwent a radical change of mind and embarked upon the gamble of the First Five Year Plan. Viewed as a short-run measure, the purpose of the First Five Year Plan was to break the disequilibrium through increase in consumer-goods output based on increase in plant capacity. It was a daring scheme if one considers that its coming to fruition presupposed a further, though temporary, deterioration in the situation as a result of deflecting a larger share of national income into investment and away from consumption. Again, in the best Russian tradition, it was to be a race against time. If the Soviet government could keep peasant resistance within bounds for the relatively short period of a few years, it might be able to offer sufficient quantities of consumers' goods to the peasants at terms of trade not too unfavorable to them, and thus it could eliminate the dangers and place the relations between village and city on a new and sounder basis.

Not unlike the Imperial government after the revolution of 1905, the Soviet government was keenly aware of the peasants' hostility to it. In a very similar fashion it was anxious to find or to create at least some points of support in the villages which might facilitate its task during the difficult years to come. Stolypin had gambled on the "strong and the sober," expecting the prosperous peasant outside the village commune to neutralize in some measure the antagonism of the majority. After certain adjustments, the collective farms were originally supposed to perform the same function. They were con ceived as limited injections of communal vaccine into the individualistic climate of the villages. As long as the number of collective farms was kept small, it would be possible to provide them with sufficient state aid, so that membership in the collective farms would carry real advantages.

The plans, however, did not succeed; alternatively, they succeeded only too well. The resistance of the peasants proved much greater than had been expected. The peasantry which had emerged victorious from the revolution and the civil war was very different from the docile masses of the Imperial period. The bitter struggles that followed developed a logic of their own. In the course of the "revolution from above," as Stalin termed it and which more justly might be called a "counterrevolution from above," the original plans of the Soviet government were quickly rendered obsolete. The dogged defense by the peasants of the revolutionary land seizures evoked an all-out offensive by the government. The peasants went down in defeat and a complete, or nearly complete, collectivization was the result.

The collectivization supplied an unexpected solution to the besetting problem of disequilibrium, the actual starting point of the great change in Soviet economic policies. But it also affected profoundly the character of the government's plans with regard to industrialization. Once the peasantry had been successfully forced into the machinery of collective farms, once it became possible to extract a large share of agricultural output in the form of "compulsory deliveries" without bothering much about the *quid pro quo* in the form of industrial consumers' goods, the difficulties of the late twenties were overcome. The hands of the government were untied. There was no longer any reason to regard the First Five Year Plan as a self-contained brief period of rapid industrialization, and the purpose of the industrialization no longer was to relieve the shortage of consumers' goods. A program of perpetual industrialization through a series of five-year plans was now on the agenda. What was originally conceived of as a brief spell became the initial stage in a new great spurt of industrialization, the greatest and the longest in the history of the country's industrial development.

Any historical contemplation of Soviet industrial history must begin with a description of the proximate chain of causations which connects the period of the NEP with that of superindustrialization under the five-year plans. Such a description brings out and explains the precise timing of the change that took place. The discussion must be in terms of the answers found by the Soviet government to the pressures and exigencies of a given situation. Yet to place the whole weight of emphasis upon those aspects of the evolution may not be sufficient. Other forces, perhaps less clearly visible, may have been at work determining the course of development and its outcome. Much of what happened at the turn of the third and fourth decades of the century was the product of that specific historical moment; but however great the change, and however drastic the momentary discontinuity in the process, the deep historical roots and its broad continuity must not elude the historian.

If Peter the Great had been called back to life and asked to take a good look at Russia, say, in the second half of the thirties, he might have had some initial difficulties because of changes in language and technology; he might have found the purge trials unnecessarily cumbersome and verbose; and he might have upbraided Stalin for the unmanly refusal to participate physically in the act of conveying the modern *Strel'tsy* from life to death. Yet it should not have taken him long to understand the essentials of the situation. For the resemblance between Soviet and Petrine Russia was striking indeed.

Nothing has been said so far about the role of foreign policy in molding Soviet economic decisions. Yet it must not be forgotten that the smashing defeat of the country by Germany stood at the very cradle of the Soviet regime. Foreign intervention in the Civil War, however halfhearted, certainly left memories that were long in fading. The 1920s witnessed a gradual improvement in Soviet diplomatic and commercial relations with foreign countries. But tensions were ever-recurring, and in 1927 there was much talk of military dangers in the course of the diplomatic conflict with England. Germany, despite the Russian aid to the *Reichswehr*, was still the military vacuum of Europe. After 1930, with the beginning disintegration of the Weimar Republic, both Russian fears and Russian ambitions were increasingly concentrated on Germany; until after Hitler's advent to power the ambitions were frustrated and the threat of a military attack began to loom larger and larger each year. There is very little doubt that, as so often before, Russian industrialization in the Soviet period was a function of the country's foreign and military policies. If this is so, however, one might argue that there was more instability in the second half of the NEP period than that stemming from inflationary pressures alone. If, as has been indicated above, the continuation of NEP policies even after a successful removal of monetary disequilibria was unlikely to lead to a period of rapid industrialization, pressures for a revision of those policies might well have materialized in any case.

A resurrected Peter the Great would have found sufficient operational resemblance between Charles XII and Adolf Hitler, however much he might have preferred his civilized contemporary to the twentieth-century barbarian. Nor would the great transformation in rural Russia have caused him much trouble. He would have quickly recognized the functional resemblance between collectivization and the serfdom of his days, and he would have praised collectivization as the much more efficient and effective system to achieve the same goals — to feed gratis the nonagricultural segments of the economy and at the same time provide a flow of labor for the public works of the government, which the Soviet regime accomplished by the institution of special contracts between the factories and the collective farms. He would no doubt have acquiesced in the tremendous human cost of the collectivization struggles, once it had been explained to him that the quantitative difference between the Soviet period and his own time in this respect was largely the result of the colossal growth in population in the two intervening centuries. And while regretting the loss of animal draft power in Russian agriculture, he may have even understood that the reduction in cattle herds in the course of the "great slaughter" actually facilitated the task of industrialization inasmuch as the amount of calories per unit of land available for the feeding of the population was greatly increased as a result. Neither the formidable stress on technology in the earlier portions of the period of industrialization nor the resolute concentration upon heavy industries would have evoked the visitor's astonishment. True, at times Peter the Great was given to flights of fancy and attempted to launch in Russia production of Venetian mirrors and French Gobelins, but the great line of his policy, so different from that of French mercantilism, was essentially devoted to the increase of the country's military power.

Thus a pattern of economic development which before the First World War seemed to have been relegated to the role of a historical museum piece was reenacted in Soviet Russia. The anachronistic — or rather parachronistic — character of the Soviet experiment in rapid industrialization did not, however, prevent it from attaining a very high measure of success. On the contrary, the combination of ancient measures of oppression with modern technology and organization proved immensely effective. All the advantages of industrialization in conditions of backwardness were utilized to the hilt: adoption of the fruits of Western technological progress and concentration on those branches of industrial activity where foreign technology had the most to offer; huge size of plant and the simultaneity of industrialization along a broad front assuring large flows of external economies.

To be sure, the tendency to exaggerate and overdo was ever-present. In many cases, smaller plant size would have been more rational. In addition, the very breadth of the effort kept creating and recreating bottlenecks; and the excessive bureaucratization of the economy absorbed an undue share of the available manpower. Yet when everything is said and done, the result in terms of growth of industrial output were unprecedented in the history of modern industrialization in Russia. True, the Soviet official index exaggerated the speed of growth. The rates of 20 and more percent a year that were claimed never materialized in reality. It is, however, now possible on the basis of the computations performed by American economists and statisticians to conclude that the average annual rate of industrial growth in Russia throughout the first ten years after the initiation of the First Five Year Plan was somewhere between 12 and 14 percent; the rate fell in the years immediately preceding the outbreak of the Second World War but rose again after 1945. Its high level was maintained far beyond the period of reconstruction from war damages. In the first half of the fifties, industrial output still kept increasing at some 13 percent a year. And it was only in the second half of the decade that the rate of growth began to decline, though

149

very gradually. One has only to compare these rates with the high rate attained under Witte in the nineties (8 percent) in order to gauge the magnitude of the Soviet industrialization effort.

The success of the Soviet experiment is frequently described as a proof of the efficiency of a "socialist" system. That is how the leaders of Soviet Russia like to refer to their achievements. On the other hand, there is a good deal of unwillingness to accept the fact of rapid growth of Soviet industry because of the prevailing assumption of the fundamental inefficiency of socialism. Much of it is a question of semantics. It is at the least doubtful, for instance, whether Stalin's Russia could be described as a socialist country in terms of Anatole France's definition of socialism: *Le socialisme c'est la bonté et la justice.* A historian has little reason to get enmeshed in these discussions since he may find himself discussing the problem of whether or not Peter the Great was a socialist. Nor is this the place to explain why in the opinion of the present writer Marxian ideology, or any socialist ideology for that matter, has had a very remote, if any, relation to the great industrial transformation engineered by the Soviet government.

What matters much more is the specific nature of the Soviet spurt and the economic mechanism which sustained it. The essential juxtaposition is between an approximate sixfold increase in the volume of industrial output, on the one hand, and, on the other, a level of real wages which in the early fifties was still substantially below that of 1928, with the peasants' real income probably registering an even greater decline in comparison to 1928. By holding down forcibly the consumption of the population and by letting the area of consumer-goods output take the brunt of errors and miscalculations that occurred in the process of planning, the Soviet government succeeded in channeling capital and human resources into capital formation, thus assuring the rapid growth of the only segment of the economy in which it was interested. The Soviet leaders have kept asserting, and the Soviet economists have kept repeating after them, that according to Marx the rate of growth of investment-goods output must necessarily be higher than that of consumer-goods output. The reference to Marx is hardly meaningful within the context of the Soviet economy, which has no specific marketing problems with regard to consumers' goods. Nevertheless, the assertion is quite correct as a description of the actual policy pursued by the Soviet government, pursued not by force of economic necessity but by virtue of *political choice*. It means implicitly that, as the volume of output grows, so does the rate of investment in expanding output; in other words, a larger and larger portion of national output is allocated to the production of nonconsumable goods. It is these relationships that are the essence of Soviet industrial development. This has been the strategic lever that permitted the Soviet government to make use of every advantage of backwardness to a degree unknown to all its predecessors.

7

Economic Development in Russian Intellectual History of the Nineteenth Century

THE assigned title of this essay promises much more than can possibly be redeemed by its contents. All that can be done here is to find some significant yardstick and try to apply it to selected portions of the material, in the hope that in this way an interesting problem might be posed for discussion. This, of course, is a highly arbitrary procedure, involving a number of decisions which should be made explicit.

First of all, what is Russian intellectual history? The concept is a vague one, but thus are we wont to translate what, in literal rendition, went in Russia under the alternative names (or misnomers) of "history of Russian intelligentsia" and "history of Russian social thought." Let us accept the term in this sense, but let us also be clear that by so doing we have implicitly decided to deal primarily with those Olympian figures who, in the parlance of the nineteenth century, provided the Russian intellectuals with "nourishment for heart and mind." It is indeed attractive to analyze the caloric content of that diet from a specific economic point of view and to try to see how much light, in addition to heat, was generated in the process. Yet it should be clear that thereby the accent is shifted away from those writers who, for one reason or another, remained excluded from the intelligentsia's pantheon, even though, on substantive grounds, those ordinary mortals may have acquired as strong or stronger claims to our attention. Were this an essay on Russian economic development or Russian economic thought during the past century, such a distribution of emphasis would be patently inadequate. It seems justified within the framework of a conference devoted to Russian intellectual history. Even when so confined, the subject remains much too vast for treatment here. The intelligentsia's Olympus was even more populous than Homer's. How much of our attention can be devoted to its individual deities must needs depend on their importance for the problem at hand.

The problem at hand! It is to be conceived here as a confrontation between the actual flow of Russian economic history and the direction of Russia's economic development which our authors considered desirable, or likely, or even inevitable. This, no doubt, is a very narrow approach. Still, an evaluation of the closeness between thought and event, between idea and reality, may contribute in some measure to an appraisal of the degree of vitality that was encased in Russian intellectual history of the period. We shall begin, therefore, with a brief and necessarily schematic sketch of Russia's economic development and thereafter turn to a discussion of the relevant writings.

I

The period of Russian mercantilism, culminating in the policies of Peter the Great, had marked a period of relatively rapid industrial development. Viewed for Europe as a whole, it is difficult to conceive of mercantilistic policies as of an altogether consistent phenomenon. But Russian mercantilism with its close connection between power policies and economic development, its clear stress on industrialization and disregard for agriculture, and but a modicum of interest in consumer-goods industries proper is much more clearly discernible as a unified system of policy than are its Western counterparts. The reasons for that presumably lay first in the magnitude of the discrepancy between policies of the government on the one hand and levels of output and economic skills in the country on the other and, second, in the absence of both developed vested interests and theoretical thought. In other words, the backwardness of the country was primarily responsible for the character of Russian mercantilism. But at the same time it was the backwardness of the country that accounted for still another difference between Russia and the West. Mercantilist policies in the West were pursued in an environment in which, by and large, serfdom either had disappeared or was in a state of disintegration. In Russia peasant serfdom became an essential wheel in the mechanism of mercantilist policies. When these policies came to an end, serfdom lost its connection with economic development of the country and emerged, more firmly established than ever, as the main force retarding the economic growth of the country.

The question of whether Russia under Catherine the Great was a backward country has been under discussion for more than four decades, and contemporary Soviet historiography tends to answer the question in the negative. It is less important for the purposes of the presentation that this view ignores matters like the near constancy of the city population over long decades of the eighteenth century, or the absence in Russia of skills and standards of commercial honesty comparable to those in the West, or the lack of wide markets for industrial products which, for instance, led to exports of a large fraction of the pig iron produced. What does matter is that in the last quarter of the eighteenth century England experienced a great upsurge in the rate of industrial growth, that postrevolutionary France went through a period of rapid industrial development, even though the speed of that development could not be sustained after 1815. At the same time, the territorial spread of serfdom under Catherine, the rapid deterioration of the serfs' juridical position, and the government's withdrawal from mercantilist policies not only perpetuated serfdom, but also imparted to it an extent and a severity which it had not possessed before. Whatever the actual degree of economic backwardness in Russia in the last decades of the century, dynamically seen, it is in that period that the basis was laid for the growing backwardness of the Russian economy throughout the first half of the nineteenth century.

The rate of growth of Russian industry during that period cannot be ascertained with high statistical accuracy, but there is little doubt that, by and large, it was very low. To be sure, the development was somewhat faster in certain branches of the textile industry, but progress was almost imperceptible in other fields, particularly in the iron industry, the output of which hardly kept up with the increase of the population. As a general proposition the statement may be hazarded that the relative economic backwardness of the country increased not inconsiderably during the first half of the century.

Once a country experiences such a process of increasing lags, it is not unreasonable to expect — in conditions of the past century and within the sphere of European civilization — that at some point the specific mechanism of economic backwardness would come into play, so that, depending on the degree of the country's backwardness, one of the usual patterns of economic development in such conditions will reproduce itself. To repeat what has been said elsewhere,[1] the situation in a backward country may be conceived of as a state of tension between its actualities and potentialities. For, *pari passu* with the increase in a country's backwardness, there is an increase in potential advantages that can be reaped by a sustained effort to overcome that backwardness. The reason essentially lies in the fact that postponed economic development implies the opportunity for borrowing highly developed foreign technology while deriving additional benefits from the process of capital cheapening that has occurred outside a country's borders. As the tension mounts, it becomes more and more likely that a point will be reached at which the advantages implied in rapid development will more than offset those obstacles to progress which are inherent in the state of economic backwardness. Clearly, the tension can be artificially increased from two sides, both by deliberate abolition of such obstacles and by creating deliberate inducements to economic development. The process is to some extent a discontinuous one and this not only because of the suddenness of deliberate actions just referred to, but also because *in conditions of the nineteenth century* the advantages inherent in "bigness" were particularly telling. Thus, economic development either took place as a rapid spurt of industrialization fully utilizing economies of scale of plant and economies inherent in "balanced growth" — that is, simultaneous development of a considerable number of industrial branches — or else it did not take place at all. It can also be argued that the more delayed was the industrialization process in conditions of secularly growing capital intensity of output, the more rapid the spurt of sudden growth which was required to break through the trammels of routine and stagnation.

[1] See Chapter 1 of this volume.

In other words, the tension of which we spoke before had in such conditions to become particularly large.

Schematic as the foregoing presentation has been, it seems that it contains a generalized view of how economic backwardness was overcome in a number of European countries of the nineteenth century (such as France, Germany, and Austria). But the same pattern essentially applies to the economic development of Russia.

The emancipation of the peasantry was no doubt a decisive step in widening the tension and thereby facilitating subsequent economic development. That it did not lead immediately to a period of rapid industrialization must be explained first in terms of the way in which the abolition of serfdom was carried out. Moreover, in conditions of very considerable backwardness, provision of capital by the state was an indispensable part of the industrialization process and accordingly the process could not begin until the beginning of the deliberate industrialization policies by the government in the middle eighties, leading to the magnificent spurt of industrial growth in the 1890s. In conditions of backwardness far greater than that of countries in Western Europe, supply of capital by dint of investment banking was hardly feasible and the functions performed by the latter to a considerable extent were performed in Russia by the state.

These similarities in policies pursued by the respective institutions denote the existence of a common pattern of economic development in conditions of backwardness; differences in the role of institutional instruments applied denote variations in the degree of relative backwardness. Viewed over a sufficiently long period, the differences tend to disappear as diminishing backwardness makes possible — and did make possible in Russia — gradual transition from the use of government finance to that of investment banking.

The use of either instrument implies temporary reduction in the levels of consumption of the population. The purpose in both cases is to achieve a rate of investment higher than would emerge in the absence of intervention by government or banks. Forced saving (inflation) and taxation perform the same service in achieving a temporary redistribution of income. The Russian experience illustrates the sequence with great clarity. Both the period of the nineties and the period preceding the outbreak of the First World War were periods of high rates of growth, but, whereas the former period was one of considerable pressure upon consumption levels, improvements in standards of living were clearly discernible during the latter period.

To sum up, it may be said that the main drift of Russian economic history reproduced a series of sequences which were familiar from the economic history of the West, and that such deviations from those sequences as could be observed fitted well into a general continental pattern of development adjusted to gradations of backwardness. The outstanding feature of the process was the utilization in Russia, as elsewhere, of the advantages which are inherent in delayed economic development.

There is no intention in the foregoing sketch to imply that Russian economic development proceeded *necessarily* as it did in faithful obedience to some iron law of evolution. What is implied is that the actual development seems to conform to a certain pattern and that such conformities and uniformities as can be observed do help us understand the course of events. In fact, historical understanding essentially consists in the formulation of such patterns. That the development followed a certain course does not preclude the possibility of alternative routes, but it does suggest that the forces which propelled the Russian economy along its actual course must have been strong indeed. It appears justifiable, therefore, to raise the question to what extent an awareness of these forces and, more specifically, of the individual elements which combined to produce the actual pattern of Russian economic development can be discerned in the writings of men who figured so prominently in Russia's intellectual history of the nineteenth century. It is to the discussion of this question that the next section is devoted.

II

Russian writers were fond of describing Radishchev as the "first Russian *intelligent*." What they had in mind no doubt was his adherence to the two principal articles in the intelligentsia's creed: hatred of slavery and deep concern for the well-being of the peasantry (*narod*). Whatever the strict validity of Radishchev's claim to seniority, a striking change in attitude had taken place over the short period of some seven decades which separate his *Puteshestvie iz Peter-*

burga v Moskvu (A Journey from Petersburg to Moscow; 1790) from Pososhkov's *Kniga o skudosti i bogatstve* (The Book on Scarcity and Wealth; 1724). It is almost difficult to believe that Pososhkov and Radishchev sprang from the same soil.

Pososhkov's interests turn essentially around one thing — the economic development of the country. His was an altogether dynamic philosophy in the sense that what concerned him was the *change* in the given data of the Russian economy. His main attention was devoted to increases in the technical and commercial proficiency of that economy. Introduction of new industries and their placement in economically rational locations; organization of geological expeditions; reform of Russian handicraft by adapting the Western craft-guild framework with well-regulated apprenticeship; promotion of innovations by adoption of patent laws; attraction of foreign skills and foreign technology; encouragement of thrift; measures to increase the quality of output and to raise the standards of honesty in commercial dealings; putting children to work; forced measures to turn the beggar population to productive employment — all these reflected a mind bent upon rapid changes in economic structure and willing to consider most social and economic problems from that one point of view.[2] Accordingly, a problem like the judicial reform was treated largely from the point of view of its effects upon the taxpaying capacity of the population and its propensity to escape abroad or into frontier regions. Similarly, peasant serfdom did not interest Pososhkov directly. It is difficult indeed to regard him as opposed to the system of serfdom. He was much more concerned with legal steps which would prevent large serf owners from appropriating the serfs of the poorer gentry. And beyond this he recognized that the nobility and the gentry and the government competed with each other for the labor or the produce of the serf. It would indeed strain the imagination to see in Pososhkov's famous phrase, "The lords are not permanent possessors of the peasants,"[3] an attack upon peasant serfdom. It was rather a threat to replace serfdom to the *pomeshchik* by serfdom to the state, should the system be used to

[2] I. I. Pososhkov, *Kniga o skudosti i bogatstve* (Moscow, 1951), pp. 150, 148–149, 146, 142–143, 140, 128, 117–118, 110.
[3] *Ibid.*, pp. 178, 182.

the detriment of the government's interest in economic development. And, analogously, his interest in the well-being of the peasants was largely expressible in terms of the fiscal needs of the government and its desire to increase the productivity of the economy.[4] It seems a fair guess that Pososhkov's statements in this respect would have turned out to be even more unambiguous had he not been writing in the later years of the reign of Peter I, when the disastrous effects of his policy upon the peasantry had become quite obvious.

How different is Radishchev's case against serfdom. Moral indignation against ownership of man by man is coupled with deep compassion for the misery of the peasant. He finds burning words to describe the grain stored up by the nobility: it has been produced by labor services; it embodies the sorrow and despair of the peasantry and carries upon it the curse of the Almighty.[5] Even more important than what is said by Radishchev is what he does not mention. Gone is the concern with economic development, the concern with levels of output and economic skills. The people's well-being is no longer a means to an end; it is an end, in fact, a supreme end in itself. "Can the citizens be happy if the granaries are full but the stomachs empty?" [6] At the same time, references to economic progress have been reduced to an occasional phrase concerning "flourishing of trade" and to the brief remark in the "Letter on China Trade" that imports of textiles from China would regrettably reduce Siberian consumption of domestic textiles.[7]

In this sense, Radishchev does appear as an ancestor of several generations of Russian intellectuals. In the field of economic policy, deep interest in the conditions of the peasantry and lack of interest for Russian industrial development seem to be characteristic of a long stretch of Russia's intellectual history. Pososhkov's harshness and his worship of the state had given way to a humanitarian view. That for quite some time the change that had occurred remained almost unrecognized or at least was not seen as a problem may be explicable by a number of reasons, but perhaps the most important

[4] *Ibid.*, pp. 182–183.
[5] A. N. Radishchev, *Polnoe sobranie sochinenii* (Complete Collection of Works) (St. Petersburg, 1907) I, 159.
[6] *Ibid.*, I, 161.
[7] *Ibid.*, II, 240.

one was that after the reign of Catherine the Great abolition of serf-dom had become a necessary precondition of economic development. Presumably, Peter the Great had civilized Russia to the point at which a return to his own methods of industrialization no longer was in the stars of practical policies. It required, in our time, a collapse of civilization through an unprecedented war and the establishment of the Bolshevik dictatorship to bring about such a return. In principle, at least, to advocate the emancipation of the peasantry was not to predetermine the direction of further economic development. In reality, however, Russian intellectual history in many instances went beyond such a noncommittal attitude, and the Decembrists, the "crowd of noblemen" who were expected to become the "liberators of the peasantry," to use Pushkin's words, provide the first case in point.

With Pestel and N. I. Turgenev, Radishchev's indifference toward industrial development seems to give way to an attitude of opposition. This may seem strange, particularly for Turgenev, who is perhaps the most emphatic "Westerner" of the century. "Si l'on se demande dans quel sense le peuple russe est destiné à marcher, je dirai la question est déjà résolue par le fait; il doit marcher vers la civilisation européenne." [8] But did this mean that marching toward European civilization implied industrialization of the country? One might have expected so from a man who was primarily an economist and from a book which was published as late as 1847. But beyond an occasional statement (such as that industry and commerce in Russia failed to show much progress in the last twenty-five years [9]), one would look in vain for any sign of appreciation of industrial progress. It is true that in dealing with the ill effects of serfdom upon the country Turgenev does not forget its retarding impact upon develop-ment of industry: "Quant aux fabriques et aux manufactures, l'existence de l'esclavage agit sur elles d'une manière plus fâcheuse encore que sur l'agriculture; il leur est non moins impossible de prospérer là où le travail n'est pas libre." [10] But the author catches himself in midparagraph for he continues:

[8] N. I. Turgenev, *La Russie et les Russes* (Paris, 1847), III, 4.
[9] *Ibid.*, III, 20.
[10] *Ibid.*, II, 167.

D'ailleurs, lors même que l'esclavage n'existerait plus, la grande étendue des terrains susceptible de défrichement et de culture empêcherait l'industrie manufacturière de prendre une grande extension: car les ouvriers n'iront pas s'enfermer dans les fabriques tant qu'il y aura pour eux d'autres travaux, tant que la terre leur offrira des resources plus faciles.[11]

Should someone feel that the sentence just quoted carries some sense of regret about the fact that availability of free land constitutes an obstacle to industrial development because it limits the labor supply to manufacturing plants, he is quickly disabused. For the very next paragraph reads: "Cependant le gouvernement russe, comme tous les gouvernements, veut à toute force des fabriques et des manufactures, et lui aussi il en encourage l'établissement *aux dépens des véritables intérêts de la nation.*" [12]

It is of less interest here that among the many accusations that could have been, and were, leveled against the regime of Nicholas I this particular one was least deserved. What does matter is that in Turgenev's view even the modicum of attention which the government of the period devoted to industry is regarded as being in conflict with the "true interests of the nation."

Pestel's views on the subject are at times less easy to state succinctly, since in some respects they were in a state of flux. In particular, certain discrepancies between his *Russkaya Pravda* (Russian Law) and the earlier *Prakticheskie nachala ekonomii* (Practical Principles of Economics) are fairly obvious. Still, the affinity between the views of Turgenev and Pestel is undeniable. Like Turgenev, Pestel accepts the principle of the greater efficiency of free labor as against slave labor, even though the actual liberation of serfs, it is said, had best be gradual rather than instantaneous. This position is taken in the *Nachala* and reiterated in *Russkaya Pravda.*[13]

The stress on gradualness should not be taken as denoting a more friendly attitude on Pestel's part toward serfdom as such. Quite the contrary, the passage dealing with the subject of serfdom is almost the only one in *Russkaya Pravda* where the matter-of-fact style of

[11] *Ibid.*, II, 167–168.

[12] *Ibid.*, II, 168.

[13] See P. I. Pestel, in *Izbrannye sotsial'no-politicheskie i filosofskie proizvedeniya dekabristov* (Selected Sociopolitical and Philosophical Works of the Decembrists) (Moscow, 1951), II, 16–18, 119–120.

the document is suddenly relinquished and the dry Pestel almost reaches Radishchev's feverish eloquence. It seems correct to say that the Decembrists were unanimous in this rejection of serfdom on both moral and economic grounds.[14] But what about the stage beyond the abolition? The author of the *Nachala* is of two minds on the subject.

First, he produces some statements on development of manufacturing which might be taken as suggesting genuine interest in the subject. In particular, he pleads for the introduction of craft guilds in order to ensure technical skills and high quality of the product. This paragraph sounds almost like a return to Pososhkov. So does the proposal of market controls by government organs to prevent sales of shoddy goods. And it is at this point that a direct reference is made to the backwardness of the country and the need of educational measures by the government in countries where "factories and mills are in an embryonic state" and the ignorance of the entrepreneurs is great. Just one step seems to separate Pestel at this point from developing an infant-industry argument comparable to that of Hamilton and List, and in this way stating at least one aspect of economic development in conditions of economic backwardness. But the step is never taken. In fact, in a different passage of the essay (which, incidentally, like *Russkaya Pravda,* remained a fragment) we find an altogether different attitude. Introduction of machinery is said to be irrational where labor is cheap, so that only rich countries can afford mechanization of production. Pestel is not quite aware that he uses two distinct, though related, arguments — relative scarcity of factors *and* the inability to sustain a high rate of investment — but it is clear that, to his mind, industrial development in Russia is impractical. Indeed, after having referred to difficulties which, according to J. B. Say, were experienced with the introduction of machinery in France, he describes such a policy for Russia as "fantastic." [15] Thereafter, the classical argument of international division of labor is applied and is finally buttressed by the surmise that agrarian countries enjoy greater independence than industrial countries.[16]

[14] See the summary given by M. V. Dovnar-Zapol'skii, *Idealy Dekabristov* (The Ideals of the Decembrists) (Moscow, 1907), pp. 156f.

[15] Pestel, in *Izbrannye*, pp. 28, 65, 66, 68.

[16] *Ibid.*, pp. 63, 64.

Russkaya Pravda reflects this attitude in a rather consistent fashion. The interest in governmental concern for quality of output and development of skills is eliminated and craft guilds are rejected as useless and inequitable. Alongside private-land property, the inalienable right of *every* Russian citizen to land allotment is to be regarded as a fundamental provision of the new order, thus not only incorporating into it a form of the obshchina but also introducing a specific institutional barrier to industrial development by placing a premium upon the flight *from* the city. Finally, Pestel finds strong words against aristocracy of wealth which is "much more harmful than feudal aristocracy." The government must beware lest such an "estate" establish itself spontaneously and must destroy it where it exists. This attack upon the bourgeoisie shows perhaps more clearly than the other provisions Pestel's aversion to an industrial society.[17]

It would not be difficult to trace some of the economic argument of the Decembrists to Adam Smith and J. B. Say, and even more directly to the German economists who taught in Russia, most notably H. Storch and F. B. W. Hermann. The influence of Storch's teachings is particularly conspicuous. Also Storch easily combined statements that manufactures cannot thrive in Russia in conditions of serfdom [18] with the emphatic view that Russia should not be tempted upon the road of industrialization, all the more so since the "monopoly position" of an industrial country is temporary while that of an agricultural country is "permanent." [19] To pursue any other policy would mean to relapse into the errors of mercantilism which gave precedence to industry over agriculture.[20]

It is not claimed here that the influence of classical economics was the only determining influence upon the views of Turgenev and Pestel. Rather what is interesting to note here is (1) that by his concern with the creation of *obstacles* to industrial development Pestel went far beyond what he may have learned from Storch and Hermann and (2) that by adopting this position he also moved a

[17] *Ibid.*, pp. 98, 108, 110, 134, 141.
[18] H. Storch, *Cours d'économie politique* (Paris, 1823), IV, 264, and III, 184.
[19] *Ibid.*, III, 79, 82.
[20] *Ibid.*, III, 214.

good deal beyond Radishchev. The stress on agrarianism, the aversion to the bourgeoisie, the desire to hamper the formation of a permanent industrial labor force — this is the legacy of the Decembrists to the next stages of Russia's intellectual history. The discrepancy between what was considered desirable and what actually happened became very large indeed.

If in some sense Radishchev and the Decembrists were the beginning of an era, in a different sense the Decembrists also closed a period. While opening up the intellectual history of the nineteenth century, they were the last link in the series of *coups d'état* of the eighteenth century. To them, seizure of power and reorganization of the country were immediate practical tasks. As a result, their proposals included elements which would have been quite unacceptable to most, though not all, of their successors. The establishment of a ubiquitous secret police proposed by Pestel under the high-sounding name of "Vyshnee Blagochinie" (Superior Decency) and the explicit approbation of spying and secret investigations is an extreme case in point.[21] At the same time, the feeling that what they proposed was not just gray theory, but measures that might be put into effect shortly, certainly induced them to consider problems which were of much less importance to men of pure thought. The gradualness of the abolition of serfdom may have reflected the necessity to secure the support, or at least reduce the opposition, of the nobility to the reforms; but presumably it also reflected the recognition of the fact that a sudden cutting of the Gordian knot in conditions where the gentry economy and the peasant economy were intertwined through labor, capital, and perhaps entrepreneurship would have resulted in an economic crisis, if not catastrophe. With the smashing of the Decembrist uprising and the establishment of the regime of Nicholas I, Russian intellectuals were freed from paying too close attention to the exigencies of reality. At least for the immediately following decades, the change was not favorable for a preoccupation with problems of economic development. Economic treatises began to disappear from the "must" reading lists of Russian intellectuals. If the "younger brother" of the Decembrists, as Kliuchevski once called Eugene Onegin, still liked to flaunt his knowledge of Adam Smith,

[21] P. I. Pestel', *Russkaya Pravda* (St. Petersburg, 1906), pp. 110–112.

the "children of the Decembrists," to use Ogarev's phrase, primarily had other interests. To be sure, metaphysics and aesthetics, even when not combined with Saint-Simonism, in many respects were just the mold within which discussion of social problems was cast. But the debate concentrated on fields other than economics, and it was not until Chernyshevski's time that Hegelian propositions were deliberately used for elucidation — or obfuscation — of problems of economic development. At any rate, it was only in the second half of the forties that such problems were taken up again.

Belinski, the dominating figure of the period, reflects this change. His Westernism as a rule does not descend into the low plains of economic interests. Belinski is, of course, quite willing to discuss serfdom from the humanitarian and moral point of view, but its economic implications, let alone the problems of its aftermath, are well outside his purview. For that reason a certain exception to the rule is all the more interesting. The reference is to Belinski's participation in 1847–48 in the debates between Botkin and Annenkov on the one hand and Herzen on the other. The subject of this discussion was Herzen's *Letters from Avenue Marigny* and specifically the attitude toward the bourgeoisie. The respective positions were succinctly expressed in the two prayers of the antagonists — Herzen's "God save Russia from the bourgeoisie"; [22] Botkin's "God give Russia a bourgeoisie." [23] A reflection of Belinski's attitude is even contained in a published article, the last written — or rather dictated — by him before his death.[24] There he takes mild exception to Herzen's negative view. But the uncensored letters show how seriously Belinski — in the last months of his life — struggled with the problem. The letter to Botkin written in December 1847 reflects these struggles. Hesitant to break away altogether from Herzen's position, Belinski seeks to define and redefine the concept of bourgeoisie, distinguishes between rich capitalists and bourgeoisie, explodes in a diatribe against the trader, and yet ends on a very different note: "I do not belong to people who take it for an axiom that the bour-

[22] P. V. Annenkov, *P. V. Annenkov i ego druz'ya* (P. V. Annenkov and His Friends) (St. Petersburg, 1892), p. 611.

[23] *Ibid.*, p. 551.

[24] V. G. Belinskii, *Sobranie sochinenii v trekh tomakh* (Collected Works in Three Volumes) (Moscow, 1948), III, 840.

geoisie is an evil . . . I shall not agree to that before I have been shown in real life a country which prospers without a middle class; so far all I have seen is that countries without a middle class are doomed to eternal insignificance." [25] But in the letter to Annenkov, written only two months later, an even firmer position is taken:

My never-doubting friend [Herzen] and our Slavophiles have helped me much to shed the mystical faith in the people. Where and when did ever the people liberate itself? Everything is always done by individuals. When in our debates on the bourgeoisie I called you a conservative I was an ass to the second power while you knew what you were talking about. When in the presence of my never-doubting friend I said that Russia needs a new Peter the Great, he attacked my view as a heresy and said that the people itself must do all for itself . . . And now it is clear that the internal process of civil development in Russia will not start before . . . the Russian gentry has been transformed into a bourgeoisie.[26]

In many respects, this is a unique statement. Acceptance of the bourgeoisie with its implied stress on industry; prayer in the same connection for a new Peter the Great which can only mean revival of industrialization policies — these views denote not only an abandonment of the agrarian position of the Decembrists but a recognition of special governmental policies in the process of industrialization.

To be sure, this statement also implies complete lack of hope that a Russian bourgeoisie may emerge alongside the gentry rather than from the ranks of that group, a sentiment, incidentally, shared by Botkin.[27] Nor would it be wise to overlook entirely the fervor of the denunciation of the merchant in Belinski's letter to Botkin — "the base, despicable, vulgar creature who serves Plutus and Plutus alone." [28] But when all is said and done, it seems fair to say that the "Furious Vissarion" came closer than anybody else among the great figures in Russian intellectual life of the time to an industrial vision, one might perhaps say a correct prevision of the country's economic development.

It is tempting to speculate whether Russia's intellectual life was

[25] *Izbrannye filosofskie sochineniya* (Selected Philosophical Works) (Moscow, 1948), II, 550.

[26] *P. V. Annenkov i ego druz'ya*, p. 611.

[27] *Ibid.*, p. 523.

[28] *Pis'ma* (Letters) (St. Petersburg, 1914), III, 329.

not at the crossroads in these months before the outbreak of the European revolutions. Belinski's death, the wave of suppression which passed over Russia after the February revolution in Paris, the effect of the course of that revolution upon Herzen himself in greatly reinforcing his still inchoate adverse views on the West — all these factors served to decide the disagreement between Belinski and Herzen in favor of the latter. The "child of the Decembrists" took up their tradition and transformed it into populist socialism. The brief moment of deep doubt in the value of that tradition passed unnoticed. But its existence is important and, in any attempt to go beyond the mere report of views held to an interpretation of the reasons for their emergence and persistence, Belinski's heretical stand deserves much attention.

Turning to Herzen, it is neither possible nor necessary within the scope of this essay to do more than explore his relation to his predecessors and indicate his general position on the subject of Russian economic development. To say that the struggle against serfdom unites Herzen with Radishchev and Pestel is of course a flat truism. The problem is what in Herzen's mind was to follow the abolition of serfdom. The espousal of the obshchina as the ideal form of organization of agriculture, the view of an economy organized in obshchinas freed from the power of the *pomeshchik*, does indeed constitute a vision of Russian economic development, the specific vision of Russian agrarian socialism. But what was new in the vision? Pestel had in fact, though not in name, incorporated the obshchina into the program of his *Russkaya Pravda*. That Herzen's ideas on the subject came from Haxthausen and the slavophiles while Pestel's work was unknown to him is, of course, true; but it is immaterial from a point of view which is concerned with the basic trends of intellectual development rather than with the question of specific influences, let alone priorities.

Something else was new in Herzen. The question of Russia's pursuing a road of economic development different from that of the West did not explicitly arise for Pestel. That Russia would essentially remain an agricultural country was basically the result of general economic laws concerning the international division of labor — valid for both the Orient and the Occident. It is true that Pestel, as we have seen, envisaged special legal measures designed to reinforce and preserve the agrarian character of the Russian economy, but in a sense this was no more than an attempt to buttress the operation of an economic law common to both Russia and the West. By contrast, Herzen's views contain a deliberate rejection of the road traveled by the West. The Russian past was different from that of the West; accordingly also the Russian future need not follow the road traveled by the West. The following sentences present this view in a most concise form. Addressing himself to "the West" Herzen said:

> Nothing in Russia . . . bears the stamp of routine, stagnation, and finality which we encounter with nations which, through long labors, have created for themselves forms of life which to some extent correspond to their ideas.
>
> Do not forget that in addition Russia remained ignorant of the three scourges which retarded the development of the West: Catholicism, Roman law, and the rule of the bourgeoisie [*meshchane*]. This much simplifies the problem. We shall unite with you in the coming revolution. [But] for that we need not pass through those swamps which you have crossed; we need not exhaust our forces in the twilight of [your] political forms . . . We have no reason to repeat the epic story of your emancipation, in the course of which your road has become so encumbered by the monuments of the past that you hardly are able to take one single step ahead. Your labors and your sufferings are our lessons. History is very unjust. *The latecomers receive instead of gnawed bones the [right of] precedence [at the table] of experience. All development of mankind is nothing else but [an expression of] that chronological ingratitude.*[29]

This is a remarkable passage. There is no need to ask whether Russia of mid-century was an appropriate vantage point from which to accuse the Europe of industrial revolutions of routine and stagnation, nor need one pause to marvel at the hubris which such an accusation reflects. In a sense, not even the rejection of the Western course of development for Russia is so striking; though an innovation in relation to Pestel, it was, at least in principle, none in relation to earlier slavophile thought.[30] What is so surprising is the clarity with

---

[29] A. I. Gertsen, *Polnoe sobranie sochinenii i pisem* (Complete Collection of Works and Letters), ed. M. K. Lemke (Petrograd, 1919–1925), VIII (1854–1887), 151. My italics.

[30] Herzen's triad in the preceding quotation (Catholicism, Roman law, and the bourgeoisie) is rather curiously paralleled by Ivan Kireyevski's triad (Roman Church,

which Herzen here recognizes the importance of what was to become an essential element of Russian economic development; the advantages of backwardness, which are elevated to the rank of a ubiquitous law, or at least of a ubiquitous phenomenon, of human history. Again, just one step seems to separate Herzen from asking the question of how the industrial development of Russia might differ from that of the West because of her latecomer's position. But the question is never asked; the hatred of the bourgeoisie and the horror of a proletariat (which as often as not is conceived by Herzen as an agricultural labor force [31]) preclude any serious consideration of Russia's industrial possibilities. The vision remains riveted to the obshchina; the "advantages of backwardness" are applied not to the mode of industrial development but to the opportunity to pass from the age of serfdom into the age of socialism, and as a result the preservation of the old rather than the easy introduction of the new comes to be considered the essence of a latecomer's position. When Chernyshevski adapted Herzen's view and faithfully repeated the operation of holding the key to the understanding of Russia's economic development in his hands only to turn it the wrong way, it required a good deal of strenuous dialectical reasoning to explain that the new and the old were really one and the same thing. But before we look at Chernyshevski's treatment of the problem, a few preliminary remarks may be in order.

There is little doubt that Herzen's thought after 1848 is representative of much in the views of his former antagonists, the slavophiles. True, most important differences remained with regard to orthodoxy, humility, peasant violence, foreign policies, and so forth; but with regard to the problem at hand the differences are imperceptible. Khomyakov, too, understood the advantages of backwardness and, in fact, was willing to apply them to phenomena much more concrete than the advent of agrarian socialism. As early as 1845 he wrote: "With regard to railroads, as in many other things, we are particularly fortunate; we did not have to expend energy on experi-

---

Roman culture, and a state established by violence). See I. V. Kireyevskii, *Polnoe sobranie sochinenii v dvukh tomakh* (Complete Collection of Works in Two Volumes), ed. M. Gershenson (Moscow, 1911), I, 184.

[31] Herzen, *Polnoe*, VII (1852–1854), 276.

ments and to strain our imagination; we can and shall reap the fruits of others' labor." [32] And he becomes even more specific: the advantage of easy technological borrowings, he says, is complemented by the advantage of not being hampered by the immediately preceding stage of technical development, the network of comfortable roads.[33] He continues:

We have been imitating Europe for nearly a century and a half, and we shall continue to do so, and for a long time shall utilize European inventions. Possibly, the time might come when we, too, shall serve in many respects as a model for Europe, but it is impossible for her intellectual achievements ever to become completely useless to us.[34]

It is not unlikely that Khomyakov's personal interest in technology explains his views to some extent. After all, he was himself the inventor of a "silent steam engine" which, incidentally, when sent to the World Exhibition in London, is said to have caused the inhabitants of the surrounding district to consider petitioning the government because of its insufferable noise.[35] Probably much more important is Khomyakov's awareness of the military importance of railroads. "When all other countries are crisscrossed by railroads and are able rapidly to concentrate and to shift their armed forces, Russia necessarily must be able to do the same. It is difficult, it is expensive, but, alas, inevitable." [36] The slavophiles were better equipped than any other group of the Russian intelligentsia to appreciate the significance of national power interests and power policies. It is true that their views on Peter the Great did not reveal such an appreciation. But there is always a great difference between appraisals of history and of current problems. And to the extent that power policies in fact cannot be easily disassociated from the causes of Russian economic development in the second half of the nineteenth century, the slavophiles actually probed more deeply than Herzen. It should not be surprising, therefore, that Khomyakov has much more to say on railroads, a prerequisite of later industrial upsurge, than does Herzen

[32] A. S. Khomyakov, *Polnoe sobranie sochinenii* (Complete Collection of Works) (Moscow, 1861), I, 420.

[33] *Ibid.*, p. 424.

[34] *Ibid.*

[35] B. S. Zavitnevich, *Aleksei Stepanovich Khomyakov* (Kiev, 1902), I, 243.

[36] Khomyakov, *Polnoe*, I, 420.

or Ogarev, Herzen's economic expert, who confines himself to a passing and perhaps half-ironical word of approval of governmental programs of railroad building.[37]

For the rest, however, the difference between Khomyakov and Herzen is almost imperceptible, and, though Khomyakov does not consider himself a socialist, he is happy to point out the similarities between Russian artels and Fourier's *phalanstères*.[38]

Two honorific titles have been conferred upon Chernyshevski in Soviet hagiology. He is a "great revolutionary democrat" and, in addition, the "great Russian economist." The second title is both more distinctive and more dubious than the first. It is not clear at all that Chernyshevski made any independent contribution to economic analysis. But at the same time it is true that by his knowledge of economic literature and by his interest in empirical economic problems he stands out in the line of writers with whom this essay is concerned. There is in particular no doubt that his economic erudition and his comprehension of economic problems is infinitely superior to that of Ogarev, the man who in the preceding generation devoted the most attention to economics. And yet, with regard to the problem of economic development, Chernyshevski appears to be hardly more than a continuation of Herzen.

Chernyshevski does not simply ignore industrial developments. He returns many times to the themes of accumulation of capital and of mechanization of productive processes.

Russia enters upon that stage of economic development in which capital is being applied to economic production.[39]

We must not conceal from ourselves that Russia, which so far has taken little part in economic development, is being rapidly drawn into it; our economic life, which up till now has remained almost entirely outside the influence of those economic laws which reveal their power only when economic and commercial activities have been enhanced, begins to fall rapidly under the sway of those laws. Possibly we, too, will soon enter the sphere within which the law of competition is fully valid.[40]

[37] N. P. Ogarev, in *Izbrannye sotsial'no-politicheskie i filosofskie proizvedenya* (Selected Sociopolitical and Philosophical Works) (Moscow, 1952), I, 135.

[38] Zavitnevich, *Khomyakov*, I, 300.

[39] *Izbrannye ekonomicheskie proizvedeniya* (Selected Economic Works) (Moscow, 1948), I, 148.

[40] *Ibid.*, p. 108.

In the era of railroads it seemed impossible to ignore the change that was in the making. It was perfectly clear to Chernyshevski that Russian peasants would be profoundly affected by the growth of the railroad network, the consequent increases in grain prices, and the volume of foreign trade. Factory cloth would enter the huts of the peasants, but:

Whatever those changes, let us not dare touch on the sacred and saving custom that we have inherited from our past, all the misery of which is redeemed by one invaluable legacy — let us not dare assault the common use of land — the great bounty on the introduction of which depends now the welfare of land-tilling classes in Western Europe. May their example be a lesson to us.[41]

The obshchina must be saved despite the coming great transformation. No one can read Chernyshevski's statements on the latter without receiving the sense of an impersonal, almost elemental process. How can the obshchina, the very symbol of everything that is traditional, be preserved when past traditions rapidly give way to innovation? Hegelian dialectics provide the answer: "In its form, the highest stage of development is similar to the initial stage."[42] A long stream of analogies from geology, zoology, philology, military history, history of economic protectionism, history of fashions, and so on, is marshaled to illustrate that "axiom." Languages uninflected in the early stages became inflected, only to drop the inflections later; savages do not protect domestic industries, but after a mercantilistic period of protectionism the period of free trade returns mankind to the starting point. And if the evolution of the "whole material and moral world is subordinated to that law, is it likely that the area of landownership should remain the lonely exception?"[43] The obshchina thus is not an anachronistic survival; it is the inevitable end of development. True, Russia had never known the intermediary stage, which, after all, is an essential link in Hegel's "axiom" or "law." But this is precisely the point. Russia, because of her very backwardness, is able to skip the intermediary stage. Example after example is adduced showing both the gradualness of technological progress and

[41] *Ibid.*
[42] *Ibid.*, p. 697.
[43] *Ibid.*, p. 715.

the ability of backward nations to borrow its most recent, most perfect form. After having thus elaborated on Herzen's advantages of backwardness, Chernyshevski ends by paraphrasing Herzen's words: "History is like a grandmother; it loves the younger grandchildren. To the latecomers *(tarde venientibus)* it gives not the bones *(ossa)* but the marrow of the bones *(medullam ossium)*, while Western Europe had hurt her fingers badly in her attempts to break the bones." [44]

Like Herzen, Chernyshevski stood on the threshold of an understanding of important aspects and, like Herzen, he chose to turn away. To do so was in many respects more difficult for him than it had been for his predecessor. Herzen never concerned himself much with any aspect of technological progress. Chernyshevski introduced technological change into the very reasoning designed to prove that in Russia advantages of backwardness consisted in the opportunity to preserve the obshchina. To overlook the obvious required a considerable effort, and Chernyshevski carefully avoided use of examples pertaining to modern industrial machinery and preferred to choose his illustrations from the instruction of savages in the use of matches and Latin script.

Though in the crucial respect Chernyshevski follows Herzen, the difference between the two writers need not be blurred. The obshchina for Chernyshevski is more than a form of land tenure. He likes to think of it as a form of reorganized production by the associated members.[45] An important consequence is that modern technology then could find its entry into the reorganized obshchina, and Chernyshevski places much stress on technological progress in agriculture.[46] That preservation of the obshchina might militate against introduction of modern technology into agriculture is strongly denied. If agriculture in the past was slow to adopt machinery, the reason does not lie in the obshchina, nor in any mental resistance on the part of the peasantry, but in the poverty of the peasant population.[47]

And what about manufacturing? It is astonishing how little the

[44] *Ibid.*, p. 727.
[45] *Ibid.*, p. 213.
[46] *Ibid.*, pp. 288f.
[47] *Ibid.*, III:2, 418.

"great Russian economist" has to say on the subject — if we abstract, as we well may, from Vera Pavlovna's dreams — beyond his agreement to the proposition that more important than the growth of factory production is the growth of output of factory wares by the domestic industry and that, concerning the "question of usefulness of direct protection of factories, one should consider not so much the relation of our factories to foreign production of similar goods as their relation to the well-being of people who find work in the factories and still more the effect of factories upon the output of the same products by domestic industries." That the latter deserve to be protected does not raise any question in the author's mind.[48]

The implications of the foregoing are clear. Governmental policies should discriminate in favor of small-scale domestic production of manufactured goods and against large-scale factory production. After having looked the other way so as not to see the advantages of backwardness in the application of very modern technology, it is only consistent to disregard the importance of large-scale factory production, through which alone, in the conditions of the nineteenth century, these advantages could be efficiently utilized. When, in addition, one remembers that Chernyshevski was inclined, in his *Annotations to J. S. Mill's Principles,* to view even Western industrialization and railroadization as a relatively short-lived process, pointing out that newly formed capital will find less and less application in trade and industry and hence will tend to turn to investments in agriculture,[49] and that at the same time large-scale units which are frowned upon in industry are favored in agriculture, the picture is completed. Russian industrialization and, by the same token, Russian economic development remain outside the scope of Chernyshevski's vision. It is not surprising, therefore, how often our author emphasizes his basic agreement with the slavophiles on questions of practical economic policies, even though he refused to side with them on the "more nebulous" problems which separated them from the Westerners. True, his early incarceration and subsequent exile severed Chernyshevski's immediate contact with Russian economic reality at a fairly early point. Had he remained in the centers of

[48] *Ibid.,* I, 142.
[49] *Ibid.,* III:1, 301.

European Russia throughout the rest of the sixties and the seventies, his views might well have undergone some changes. As it was, the discrepancy between Russian thought and actual Russian development perhaps nowhere else appears as clearly and as strikingly as in the writings of Chernyshevski.

It would be difficult, indeed, on the basis of what has been said so far, to visualize Russian intellectual development as guiding and anticipating her economic evolution. As we move on, however, an unusual and solitary figure lays claim to our attention. Pisarev, like Belinski (and unlike Chernyshevski), was, despite his interests in science and history, in the main a literary critic. Though in Russia at this time literary criticism necessarily implied concern with social problems, questions of economic development as a rule remained outside the purview of the critic. We cannot hope, therefore, to find more in Pisarev than a few disjointed remarks on our problem. But what we do find is very much worth recording here.

Coming from a line of thought which placed so much emphasis on collectivism in one form or another, and being particularly influenced by Chernyshevski, Pisarev surprises us by his attitude of strong individualism. At least, after 1863, Pisarev appears more and more as an advocate of industrial development and a defender of an enlightened capitalism. Following Russian traditions — or perhaps the general traditions of the nineteenth century — these views are presented as emanating from a general law:

There have been many revolutions in the course of history; political institutions, religious institutions disappeared, but the rule of capital over labor emerged from all these revolutions completely unimpaired. Historical experience and simple logic alike convince us that strong and intelligent people will always win over weaklings and dullards . . . Hence to wax indignant over the fact that educated and well-to-do classes rule over the toiling mass would mean to run against the indestructible and unshakable wall of a natural law . . . When we encounter an inevitable fact of this order, what is called for is not indignation, but an action which would turn this inevitable fact to the benefit of the people. The capitalist possesses intelligence and wealth. These two qualities assure his rule over labor. But whether that rule will cause damage to, or confer benefits upon, the people depends on the circumstances. Give that capitalist some sort of vague education and he will become a bloodsucker. But if you give him a complete, firm, humanitarian education — the same capitalist will become not indeed a benevolent philanthropist, but a thinking, calculating leader of people's labor, that is to say, a man a hundred times more useful than any philanthropist.[50]

These words sound indeed like an elaboration of Belinski's conviction that Russia could not prosper without a bourgeoisie. Pisarev, of course, goes far beyond Belinski. The interest in specialized disciplines was quite alien to Belinski's "Do throw away your political economy and statistics; any specialized knowledge lowers and degrades men; thought alone in its general universal sense must be the subject of man's study." [51] For Pisarev, it is the growing body of specialized knowledge that is the earnest of social and economic progress. What is wrong with Tolstoy's Nekhlyudov is precisely that he wants to help his peasants without having first acquired a practical profession.[52] Diffusion of such knowledge will solve all problems:

The time will come — and it is not far off — when all intelligent youth . . . will live a full intellectual life and its outlook will be serious and calculating. Then the young owner of an agricultural estate will organize it in European fashion; then *the young capitalist will establish the factories* which we need, and will organize them in such a way as is required by the interests of both the owner and the workers; and that is all that is needed. A good farm and *a good factory* constitute the best and the only possible school for the people.[53]

Add to the foregoing Pisarev's penetrating idea that introduction of modern methods into agriculture is extremely difficult unless done in the atmosphere of a considerable industrial development,[54] and the result is not only a picture of a man for whom industrial development is much more important than agrarian collectivism and social problems in industry, but of one who also possesses a considerable insight into eminent practical problems of economic development, something that altogether eluded Chernyshevski.

The preceding quotations from Pisarev's works could be mul-

[50] D. I. Pisarev, *Sochineniya, Polnoe sobranie v shesti tomakh* (Works, Complete Collection in Six Volumes) (St. Petersburg, 1897), IV, 132.

[51] Belinski, *Pis'ma*, I, 89.

[52] Pisarev, *Sochineniya*, 237.

[53] *Ibid.*, III, 305. My italics.

[54] D. I. Pisarev, *Izbrannye filosofskie i obshchestvenno-politicheskie stat'i* (Selected Philosophical and Sociopolitical Essays) (Moscow, 1944), pp. 184, 212, 235.

tiplied to show the same trend of thought. It is also true that a considerable number of quotations could be gleaned that would point in a very different direction. In fact, Pisarev's inconsistencies are often staggering. It must suffice here to place on record this second brief departure from the rut of established thought and the willingness on the part of an important representative of Russia's intellectual history to accept industrial development and the philosophy of economic individualism. Pisarev's acceptance for Russia of the contents of Western economic development goes so far that there is no trace at all of any recognition that in Russia the mechanics of backwardness might have led to not inconsiderable differences in the course of industrialization. If Pisarev, in addition to his admiration for the figure of Rakhmetov, had taken over Chernyshevski's ideas on the advantages of latecoming, the result would have been remarkable indeed.

Yet Pisarev's failure to see an important aspect of Russian economic development hardly deserves any criticism in the light of subsequent intellectual history. As we approach the closing stretches of our review we encounter not a stress on the advantages but on the *disadvantages* of backwardness. From the end of the sixties on, it becomes almost impossible to ignore the fact of an important industrial development. But the prevailing attitude is to show that in the specific conditions of Russian backwardness the effects of industrialization and its very character must be particularly detrimental and that in such conditions industrial progress cannot proceed very far.

The remainder of this section will be used to illustrate this point briefly. Lavrov, while stressing the "borrowed" nature of Russian capitalism, claimed that the lateness of capitalist development in Russia implied the importation of a degenerated and debased form of capitalism:

We are passing not only through the transformation of our pre-emancipation economy into a bourgeois economy; that in itself would not be so bad; but together with the whole civilized world we are in the state of transition to the highest, that is to say, to the ugliest form of bourgeois economy. This is the stage at which the capitalists become large financiers; at which little stock-exchange kings become the rulers over the economic life of nations; at which the bourgeoisie develops into a financial aristocracy. This transition causes disastrous developments in the economic life of the masses — [it is] the true reason for the emergence of Western European socialism. But with us matters are much worse than with any other European nation. In the West, a bourgeois economy developed gradually, step by step, paralleling a process of discoveries and inventions. In some measure, the development of the bourgeois economy in the West was beneficial for the whole mass of the population . . . Only by-and-by it became clear that bourgeois economy in its very essence is hostile to the masses. That economy passed through several phases before reaching its present stage at which the inconsistency and irreconcilability of the interests of labor and capital have been revealed in their merciless nakedness . . .

With us the peasants were liberated — and accordingly a bourgeois economy became possible — when in the West it has acquired its latest form. But following the immutable law of competition of the bourgeois economy, the economy of any individual or any nation when drawn into the circle of the capitalist economy must necessarily assume the highest, the most developed, form of that economy. Thus we have passed without any intermediary stages from the economy of serfdom into the economy of stock-exchange kings, concessionaires, shady dealers, and the like. It is easy to understand that this order at once has become diametrically opposed to the interests of the whole population; that it is disadvantageous to our estate owners, our petty bourgeoisie, and the masses of the people. Only a tiny number of crooks and cheats have accumulated fabulous riches on the basis of general impoverishment and bankruptcy.[55]

Thus, because Russia appears late on the industrial scene her industrialization has only negative effects upon the economy of the country.

It would be perhaps more natural to draw for our last illustration on the writings of N. K. Mikhailovski,[56] who in many respects concludes the long chapter of intellectual history with which we have been concerned here. Nikolai –on, to whose views preference is given here, strictly speaking does not fit into the line of figures we have

---

[55] P. L. Lavrov, *Vpered*, no. 16 (September 1, 1875/August 20, 1875), pp. 491f.

[56] Perhaps a brief reference to Mikhailovski's review of Dostoyevsky's *Demons* may be in order because it so clearly illustrates the almost unbelievable extent of the Populists' anti-industrialism. Mikhailovski upbraids Dostoyevsky for fastening his attention upon the insignificant group of criminal fanatics, while Russia is being crisscrossed by railroads, factories and banks are cropping up everywhere, and the real demons, not murderous at all — *mirnye i smirnye* — take possession of the country and destroy all that is worth preserving; see *Sochineniya* (Works) (St. Petersburg, 1888), II, 309–310. Compared with these attitudes, an organization like the Junker-led *Bund der Landwirte* in Germany appears like an association for the promotion of industry.

treated so far. He, like Vorontsov, is essentially an economist rather than a general preceptor of the intelligentsia. But his writings provide an additional and important point of view concerning the specific character of Russian economic development.

What is Nikolai –on's contribution to our problem? Writing in the eighties and early nineties, he, even more than Lavrov, had to take for granted the fact of capitalist penetration, the economic history of three decades following 1861, "a highly detrimental process." But in analyzing this process he did not confine himself to remarks about the degradation of capitalism, but treated the problem essentially in terms of Marxian contradictions of capitalist development. On the one hand, as output grows, the "number of workers engaged in capitalist enterprises is bound to diminish in relation to the value of product," [57] and the share of labor income in total income produced must fall. This is the result, among other things, of increased mechanization of production. On the other hand, capitalist industry destroys the indigenous industrial activities of the peasants. The internal market shrinks. Capitalist production of necessity requires a wide and growing market outside the domestic economy. There is no need, of course, within the scope of this essay to present more than the barest skeleton of this train of thought. In one form or another, the concept of deficiency of effective demand goes through much of modern economic theory from Malthus to Keynes. In the case of Malthus, as was true in the case of Nikolai –on, the discussion bore directly on the problem of industrialization of an agrarian country. What interests us here is the specific application of those ideas to the Russian scene. Nikolai –on believed that in Russia, because of her backwardness and the suddenness of her economic development, the general problem of capitalist development appeared in a much more acute form. Capitalist production in Russia did not increase the value of total output. It merely shifted production from the peasant hut into the factory. The peasant could do nothing save increase the exploitation of the soil; he was unable, in conditions of shrinking income, to improve the techniques of agricultural production, while confronted by American competition which used virgin soil and modern tech-

[57] Nikolai –on (N. Danielson), *Ocherki nashego poreformennago khozyaistva* (Essays on Our Post-Emancipation Economy) (St. Petersburg, 1893), p. 183.

nology.[58] At the same time, the growth of the tax burden upon the peasant further reduced the capacity of the internal market. Within the framework of capitalist development, industrial exports were indeed the only way out of the impasse into which capitalism had propelled the economy. But precisely at this point the disadvantages of industrialization in conditions of economic backwardness inevitably asserted themselves. Russian industry had been built up behind the shelter of high tariff walls. It was expensive and inefficient. The advanced industrial countries had long established themselves in foreign markets. To compete with such countries Russian industry had neither the requisite knowledge nor the technological equipment.[59] Its industry was, therefore, doomed to collapse. The great famine of 1891 was the catastrophic result of the inept policy of industrialization; it was the price paid for the abandonment of a principle that had been sanctified by long centuries of Russian economic life — the obshchina.[60]

Thus, it can be seen that even a generous injection of Marxian theory did not necessarily lead to a radical change in the attitude toward the economic development of the country. A different group of people who also drew upon Marxian theories contrived to arrive at very different conclusions. A discussion of that group transcends the scope of this essay, but perhaps it is in order here to venture the surmise that the difference in conclusions followed much less from the theoretical structure used and much more from differences in response to the actual economic change that was taking place in the country. Nikolai –on's book with its extreme pessimistic forecast regarding Russia's industrial development appeared at a moment when the country stood on the threshold of a magnificent industrial upsurge. The very high rate of growth for the remainder of the nineties and the resumption of that growth after the 1905 Revolution effectively disproved the prophecy. It is perhaps not entirely inappropriate to conclude our survey with a mention of this glaring discrepancy between prognostication and event.

[58] *Ibid.*, pp. 129f, 322.
[59] *Ibid.*, p. 213.
[60] *Ibid.*, pp. 331, 375.

III

The divorce of the country's intellectual history from its economic history is curious indeed. Of course, its extent varied over the period under review. In a sense, the year 1861 provided an important dividing line. If it is true that the emancipation was a necessary prerequisite to the country's economic development, then the intelligentsia's abhorrence of serfdom entailed at least the acceptance of a long step on the road to industrialization. In addition, there is Belinski's brief flash of foresight. After 1861, there is a rapidly growing schism between idea and reality which Pisarev tried in vain to bridge. But, as the industrialization of the country gathered momentum, the process was either overlooked or viewed as transitory, and deplored withal. At the same time, the essential continuity of thought and attitude before and after 1861 cannot be gainsaid. The road of Russian economic development was rarely illuminated by the strong brilliance of prevision and prescience. Nietzsche once remarked that Hesiod's golden age and iron age actually referred to the same period, seen from two different points of view.[61] It is tempting to suggest that what must appear to those interested in literature, sociology, perhaps philosophy, as the golden age of the Russian intelligentsia appears far from brilliant to the economist. The point is not that the prophets of the intelligentsia kept revealing verities that did not materialize. For all we know, their prophecies — or wishes — *might* have materialized and there is no suggestion here that what happened was bound to happen. But they are exposed to a different charge. They proved unable to grasp the nature of the forces that were pushing the country's economy in a direction which was repulsive to them. Much as they had thought about the peculiarities of Russia's economic evolution, they remained blind to those peculiarities which so greatly increased the chances of successful industrialization. As a result, Russia's economic history appears largely incomprehensible from the point of view of its intellectual history. But it is one thing to ascertain a deep rift between idea and economic reality. It is another to try to find what caused it.

[61] Friedrich Nietzsche, *Zur Genealogie der Moral, Werke* (Leipzig, 1902), VII, 323.

To some extent, the ascendance of socialist ideas and ideals among Russian intellectuals may provide an explanation. Venturi in his monumental work on Russian populism essentially sees it as a branch of socialist thought. At least from the 1830s on, the influence of Western socialist ideas was undeniably strong. Not even Pisarev, not even Botkin, completely escaped that spell. Much of nineteenth-century socialism was characterized by two aspects: (1) strong interest in distribution as against production and (2) criticism of the results of capitalist development in the West. To accept industrial development seemed to imply deliberate acceptance of the ills of Western industrialization. Shelgunov, writing in 1861, put this attitude into clear words: "Europe has awakened; she has understood her malady. Russia too has awakened, but has she risen from slumber only in order to walk consciously the road over which Europe has passed unconsciously?" [62] To approve of industrialization, then, meant to accept deliberately the "cancer of the proletariat," as the phrase ran, to approve the destruction of the obshchina and the uprooting of a traditional way of life, and to countenance the corruption of a value system which apparently contained many elements of socialist morality, only to see it replaced by the vice and the depravity of a factory town, so vividly and so shockingly described by G. Uspenski. The cold-blooded concept of economic progress as "service for the future centuries" and not as an aid to the lowly and humiliated, scorchingly satirized in one of Konrad Lilienschwager's poems,[63] ran counter to all the ingrained ideas of Russian intellectuals. It is therefore not surprising that even a man like Kavelin, who remained free from socialist influences, was genuinely concerned with Russia's industrial development. He thought a good deal about the restrictive elements of communal landownership, but he not only shrank away from an emancipation favoring industrial progress, not only warned against an "industrial delirium tremens," but also regarded the obshchina as the "great reservoir of the people's forces," advocated its retention in a reorganized form, and, though recognizing the "miracles of in-

[62] N. V. Shelgunov, *Sochineniya* (Works) (St. Petersburg, n.d.), I, xxv.

[63] "Progress sovsem ne bogadel'nya, / On sluzhba budushchim vekam, / Ne ostanovitsya bestsel'no / On dlya posob'ya bednyakam." N. Dobrolyubov, *Stikhotvoreniya* (Poems) (Moscow, 1948), p. 138.

dustrial development" of which Europe and the United States "are so justly proud," was quick to call attention to "the unfavorable sides of the process," its social effects.[64] And it is perhaps even less surprising that Marx, much to the embarrassment of later Russian Marxians, also tended on the whole to espouse the basic attitude of Chernyshevski. Not only did Marx in 1877 explicitly refuse to grant the applicability of his theory of economic development to Russia beyond the truism that success of industrial development required transformation "of a good part of its peasants into proletarians"; but, in the drafts of his well-known letter to Vera Zasulich in 1881, he explicitly combines the discussion of the obshchina with the problem of advantages of backwardness and envisages a development and transformation of the obshchina in accordance with "the positive results of the mode of [capitalist] production." It is true that, in speaking of economic development of a backward country, Marx refers to the rapidity with which Russia introduced the modern financial institutions, while Chernyshevski preferred to escape into anthropology in order to make the same point. But this only serves to underscore the remarkable closeness between Marx and Chernyshevski.[65] Though it may make good sense to explain the attitudes taken by the Russian intellectuals by reference to their socialism and their general humanitarianism, it would hardly be reasonable to suggest that their failure to adopt the specific Marxian socialism prevented them from seeing, let alone foreseeing, the course of the country's industrial development. As the example of Nikolai –on shows and as Marx's scattered thoughts on the subject confirm, any position with regard to Russian industrialization was deducible from Marx's theoretical framework.

But to use socialism as an explanation inevitably raises a further question. Surely, there was no iron law in obedience to which the main current of Russian intellectual thought came to display socialist features. Why was it socialism that Russia borrowed from the West rather than Bentham's utilitarianism? It is again very difficult not to

[64] K. D. Kavelin, *Publitsisitka*, in *Sobranie sochinenii* (Essays on Current Themes, Collected Works) (St. Petersburg, 1898), II, 163, 164, 177, 181, 184.

[65] Karl Marx and Friedrich Engels, *The Russian Menace to Europe*, ed. P. W. Blackstock and B. F. Hoselitz (Glencoe, Ill., 1952), pp. 216–217, 222–223.

associate the peculiar bent of Russian intellectual history with the backwardness of the country, and that in several respects.

First of all, there is something like an ideological counterpart to the play of backwardness in the economic sphere. In a backward country there is a coexistence of abject material poverty and modern humanitarian ideas which to a large extent have developed elsewhere after, and on the basis of, a good deal of economic progress. A comparison between Pososhkov and Herzen may illustrate the point.

This leads directly to the second point. So far it has been possible to maintain the artificial separation of economic backwardness from political backwardness. The relation of the latter to the actual economic development in Russia is a most complex phenomenon and need not concern us here. But the retardation in the development of modern forms of government, that is to say, the preservation of the autocratic regime and the absence of a normal political arena, meant that the Russian intellectuals were forcibly excluded from active preoccupation with practical problems. Accordingly, they were pushed into abstract thought which, untempered by contact with reality, assumed the form of growing radicalism, and the radicalism in thought in turn led to radicalism in action. In the absence of political oppression, it may not have taken Belinski all his life to arrive at a positive appraisal of the role of the bourgeoisie. Pisarev's "nihilists" were men interested in the study of natural sciences. It was not the fault of the moderate, even though boisterous, Pisarev that Russia's political backwardness deflected the energies of her youth into other channels and that the nihilists, instead of being Benthamite utilitarians in thought and managers of chemical factories or steel mills in practice, actually used their scientific knowledge for the preparation of bombs to be employed in terrorist assaults upon the government.

Third, precisely because of the backwardness of the country, and the resulting absence of a significant gradual change in the value patterns of the population, Western socialism easily coalesced with the system of agrarian value orientations with its emphasis on the worth of the plowman's labor and its rejection as sinful of activities which were not directly connected with tilling the soil. Russian socialism of the period deserves its name of *narodnichestvo* because, to a great extent, it adopted the value orientations of the *narod* which placed considerable opprobrium on trading and industrial pursuits.

And, finally, the economic development of backward countries, in the conditions of the nineteenth century with its growing capital intensity of output and its stress on bigness in the sense described earlier, also implied the costliness of a big spurt of industrial development in terms of the sacrifices to be imposed upon the population. The transitory detrimental effects of industrialization in Russia were bound to be greater than had been the case in more advanced countries, and a comparison of the change in the levels of consumption in Russia of the 1890s and, say, England of the closing decades of the eighteenth century fully confirms the difference. To accept these sacrifices, however temporary they may be, certainly was difficult, if not impossible, for minds dominated by compassion for the misery of the peasant and eagerness to improve his position as speedily as possible.

Thus, the strength of socialist doctrine in Russia is at best only a part of the explanation for the inability to accept or even to comprehend the nature of the country's economic evolution.

Perhaps nothing shows this more clearly than the circumstance that, if they had wished to do so, Russian intellectuals could have extracted a great deal from Western socialism which would have had direct application to the country's industrial progress. Marx is the obvious, but perhaps not the most important, case in point for the period under review. The close relation between Saint-Simonian tenets and the industrial development in France, Germany, and other Western countries is a matter of historical record. There were indeed men in Russia who were attracted by that aspect of Saint-Simonian doctrines. One need only mention names like I. Vernadski, V. Bezobrazov, Tengoborski, and others. The use of investment banks for purposes of industrial development certainly appealed to their imaginations. To some extent, they may even be said to have continued a more indigenous Russian tradition because of similar ideas in Mordvinov's writings. But neither Mordvinov nor the group of men just mentioned properly belongs within the scope of what has been treated here as Russian intellectual history. Perhaps Ogarev alone reveals some traces of Saint-Simonian influence in this respect, but significantly his interest in credit institutions is confined to the sphere of agriculture rather than industry.[66] In addition, it is not even clear whether Saint-Simon or Proudhon had inspired Ogarev's ideas. Thus one cannot accuse the Russian intellectuals of wholesale blind acceptance of Western socialism. They took over what fitted into the pattern of their basic predispositions and predilections. The roots of the latter, however, were deeply imbedded in the value system of the peasantry and the general backwardness of the country.

Some conclusions might emerge from the preceding survey for the present-day problem of underdeveloped countries. It would seem that the specific Weltanschauung of Russian intellectuals, with its deep and immediate concern for the welfare of the peasantry and its unwillingness to accept industrialization, need not necessarily be confined to Russia of the nineteenth century. We have so far neglected the effects of those attitudes upon Russia's economic development. To some extent such neglect is justified. The Russian autocratic regime effectively excluded most of the intelligentsia from direct participation in political decisions. Their thought could not be translated into action. By the same token, they remained unable to influence, let alone to determine, the nature of the country's economic development. The latter was partly the result of impersonal economic forces, partly an almost accidental by-product of government decisions pursuing other goals, and partly the result of deliberate governmental policies. Even so, the attitudes of the intelligentsia could not fail to have some negative effects. While Chernyshevski could not affect policies, he could — and did — influence the attitudes of thousands of Russian university students. Their unwillingness to prepare themselves for practical industrial work, their scorn of "careerism," and their preference for pure knowledge untainted by any suggestion of monetary rewards — this "oriental" attitude was no doubt greatly reinforced by the whole tenor of the intelligentsia's general philosophy.[67]

There is no question that to some extent such attitudes served

[66] Ogarev, *Izbrannye* (n. 37), I, 740f.

[67] It is useful to read in this connection Prince Obolenski's vivid description of the criteria which he and his generation applied to the choice of profession when entering the universities; see *Ocherki minuvshego* (Sketches of Time Past) (Belgrade, 1931), pp. 82–83.

to retard the country's economic development. They belonged to the specific *disadvantages* of backwardness and tended to decrease the "tension" that has been discussed in the first section of this essay.

But the role of the intellectuals in backward countries of today is very different from what it used to be in Russia of the past century. They are no longer doomed to inactivity or confined to passive resistance. They can and they do exert a great deal of direct influence. If it is true that the ideas and attitudes of the Russian intelligentsia described here stem largely from the very backwardness of the country, we may ask whether the same patterns are not likely to reproduce themselves in today's countries and to constitute great obstructions to their industrialization. For a number of reasons, the advantages of backwardness in conditions of the twentieth century are not as strong as they were during the nineteenth century. It would augur ill for the prospects of industrial progress of backward countries of our time should it become clear that these *diminished advantages* of backwardness are coupled with *increased disadvantages* of delayed economic development.

In some sense, a belated and precarious reconciliation between intelligentsia and industrial progress was effected in Russia by the Russian Marxism of the eighties and the nineties. There is little doubt that that curious reconciliation itself fits well into the general historical pattern of industrialization in conditions of backwardness. Moreover, it has a natural bearing on the present situation in underdeveloped countries.

Realism and Utopia in Russian Economic Thought

A Review

It is not the purpose of these remarks to sum up the preceding papers.[1] This is hardly necessary; each one stands on its own feet. Still less is it intended to take issue with one or another point in the papers. If nothing else, my double role as participant and chairman would effectively bar me from following that course. The purpose rather is to point to certain general problems which are evoked by the foregoing story of ideas on economic development in Russia's intellectual history from Radishchev to Stalin and to discuss them briefly.

The problems I have in mind relate to: (1) the question of continuity and discontinuity in that intellectual history, more specifically the question of whether the changes that could be observed in the closing decades of the nineteenth century, and perhaps even in 1917, were really as far-reaching as one is tempted to assume; (2) an evaluation of the broad significance of the official ideology in Soviet Russia in its relation to the country's economic development; and (3) the general role of ideology in an economic development that proceeds in conditions of considerable backwardness.

As Solomon Schwarz has said in his paper, the Russian Marxians of the 1890s achieved an indubitable victory in their disputes with the populists. In some sense, this is an unexceptional statement. It was certainly a victory within the ideological context of the time. The swing in public opinion was unambiguous. But, viewing that victory half a century or more after the event, one cannot but wonder at its belatedness. It took the magnificent development of the nineties to open the eyes of the intelligentsia to a process that had been going on for almost four decades. Johann Nestroy's immortal "Ah, der Leim!" is indeed apposite here.

Nor was the victory won, strictly speaking, by Marxian theory. As

[1] At the Conference of the Joint Committee on Slavic Studies and the Social Science Research Council at Arden House in March 1954, on continuity and change in Russian thought, this writer reviewed papers by Solomon M. Schwarz ("Populism and Early Russian Marxism on Ways of Economic Development of Russia"), Oliver H. Radkey ("Chernov and Agrarian Socialism Before 1918"), and Alexander Erlich ("Stalin's Views on Soviet Economic Development").

I tried to show in my paper,[2] Marxism lent itself just as well to a rejection as to an acceptance of Russian industrialization. Nikolai –on operated exclusively with weapons fetched from Karl Marx's intellectual armory and Marx did not upbraid him for shooting at the wrong bird. Quite the contrary is true. We may leave open the question of how much Marx's own thoughts on the subject were influenced by the false hope of an impending seizure of power by populist revolutionaries or by his strong German nationalism. What matters here is that the populists were confounded neither by Marx's economics in the strict sense of the word nor by his materialistic conception of history, but by the hard pressure of irrefutable economic fact. That people who were willing to look at those facts a little earlier than their adversaries preferred to appeal to different aspects of Marxian theory and to call themselves Marxians or "Russian students of Marx" should not disguise what actually occurred.

Schwarz's paper aptly points up the importance of published statistics in the conversion process. And equally significant in this respect is what Oliver Radkey has stressed: how easily and how readily Chernov accepted Marxian concepts in their revisionist form for the purpose of constructing his brand of agrarian socialism. Max Weber's famous and oft-repeated phrase — which he borrowed from Schopenhauer — that Marxism is not a hansom from which the Marxians can jump off any time that a discussion of Marxism itself is at stake, inevitably comes to mind here. That Russian Marxism of the nineties was also a "reflection" can be safely asserted, except that what was reflected was not class interests but emotional preferences and predilections of intellectuals as adjusted to a "given" character of economic development in the country.

To have convinced fellow humans on the basis of more than three decades of accumulated experience that barking at the moon did not alter her course was hardly an impressive achievement. By the same token, one need not be overmuch impressed with the specific brand of verbal or conceptual magic used to make the facts palatable. But, in addition, it should also be considered that the victory which had been won remained singularly incomplete. And that seems to be so for a variety of reasons.

In many respects, Stalin, the last link in the series of figures discussed in these papers, constitutes a return to Pososhkov. It is the tragedy of today's Russia that patterns of economic behavior and trains of thought that should have remained confined to long-bygone ages have been revitalized and reproduced in contemporary Soviet reality. But at the same time there is little doubt that a good many specific elements of Russian populism were taken over by the Bolshevik wing of Russian Marxism and reincarnated in Lenin's and Stalin's thought and action.

The reference here is not only to the peasant discontent with which

[2] Included as Chapter 7 of this volume.

the revolutionary hopes of most, though not all, populists had been connected and which Lenin used so deliberately in designing the strategy of the revolution. Lenin did steal the populist thunder, and the Bolsheviks were brought to power on the crest of a peasant rebellion reaching out for the long-craved-for land of the gentry. But another fact may be equally important. The unwillingness of the populists to accept the economic development in the country in conjunction with autocratic oppression provided the background for a radicalism in thought which kept wavering uneasily between anarchism, on the one hand, and the apotheosis of the omnipotent Jacobinic state, on the other. In practice, it provided the background for the disastrous "race against time," and it created a moral climate that displayed a most complex bundle of contradictory features: the spirit of self-sacrifice, heroism, love of the people, conjoined with the idea that means justified the ends and that any method, from forged imperial manifestoes to murderous conspiracy, was justified in the struggle against the absolute evil of absolutism. That these latter aspects of populism were carried over and absorbed within the fold of Bolshevist thought and practice is undeniable. These considerations, it may be argued, are essentially political in nature, a ground an economist perhaps cannot venture upon with impunity. His only justification in doing so is that the connection between those political aspects and an either profoundly pessimistic or highly utopian view of the populists on the subject of economic development is fairly obvious.

There is, however, another aspect of the basic continuity in Russian thought that is more important from our point of view and bears more directly on our subject. Why was the vehicle of Marxism chosen in order to teach the Russian public opinion a simple lesson in empirical facts? Again Schwarz rightly remarks that as long as "Manchester liberals" or "List protectionists" preached the same simple truth, their sermons fell on deaf ears. It was different in the case of Marxism.

Radkey refers briefly to the problem and states that the intellectuals "did not wish to be caught lagging behind the West, and so could only be socialists." There is something to that explanation. Since the days of the Russian Voltairians, the desire to take over "the last word of Western thought" certainly was widespread in Russia and we have many testimonies, including that of Professor Trubetskoy, that Russian university students of the period did consider Marx "the last word of Western social science." Still, this view is but a part of the whole story. It tends to neglect the whole flow of preceding intellectual history. I do not disagree at all with Radkey when he points at the inchoate and inarticulate character of nineteenth-century populist socialism. But, such as it was, its strength and its influence in forming opinions and conditioning emotions were undeniable. It seems at least plausible to assume that an inevitable shift in public opinion assumed the form of Marxism *because* populism had been its predecessor. The violence of the literary clashes should not conceal from us the important fact of continuity in Russian intellectual development. Marxism, in preaching acquiescence in industrialization, also showed that the socialist goal need not be relinquished along with the abandonment of the obshchina.

But perhaps we may go even a step further and relate the victorious emergence of Russian Marxism to the specific stage of the country's economic development. Just because in viewing the historical processes of industrialization our eyes so often remain riveted to the case of England, there is a tendency to assume that nineteenth-century industrial development was essentially associated with the ideology of economic liberalism. This, however, is far from being the general case. It is, on the contrary, possible to hazard the opinion that the specific ideologies which accompany the process of industrialization tend to vary in accordance with the degree of backwardness in which a given country finds itself on the eve of its great economic upsurge.

I have referred in my paper to the role of Saint-Simonian doctrines in connection with the fine spurt of industrial development which France experienced after the advent to power of Napoleon III. The paradox of a vigorous capitalist development sustained by a group of great entrepreneurs who professed to be fervent adherents of a socialist creed must remain baffling, unless we assume that in a backward country a very strong ideological medicine is needed to overcome the barriers of stagnation and routine and to elicit popular support for a policy which as a rule involves some temporary material sacrifices for large groups of the population and necessarily entails losses in terms of traditional values and beliefs. In the case of Germany, which was still more backward than France, Saint-Simonian doctrines were effectively supplemented, if not supplanted, by placing nationalist ideology in the service of the industrialization process.

That in Russia, which in turn was much more backward than Germany, the same function was performed by the still more virulent doctrines of Marxism seems to fit well into a general European pattern. It is perhaps this connection rather than the long socialist tradition which helps to explain the attraction which Marxian doctrines exercised in the 1890s upon men who, like Struve (and in some sense even Milyukov), neither by temperament nor by general philosophy were predisposed to accept such doctrines. To present the costly and (for those idyllic days) in many ways ruthless process of industrialization not as a deliberate decision but as a product of iron laws of economic development obviously tended to appease the disturbed conscience of the intelligentsia, a group traditionally ridden by guilt complexes of all kinds. They all were "guilty without guilt" — *bez viny vinovatye,* as the Russian phrase goes. For all those successors of the repentant nobleman of the nineteenth century, for the repentant merchant, the repentant factory owner, and particularly the repentant intellectual, for all those guilty innocents, abroad in the stream of industrialization, Marxism provided a welcome relief. And it also appeared most convenient to those who were primarily interested in civilizing the country through the processes of industrialization as well as to those who desired industrialization for nationalistic reasons.

I have referred to the fact that, as economic backwardness was being diminished in Russia by the process of industrialization, the temporary reductions in the standard of living gave way to its improvement, and the use of government finance in industrialization tended to be replaced by the use of investment banking. In the period preceding the outbreak of World War I, the results of the great upswing of the nineties began to tell and Russia was clearly moving to a new stage in its economic development. It is perhaps not too hazardous to suggest that these gradations of backwardness in the economic and institutional spheres were, to some extent, paralleled by similar processes in the sphere of ideology.

The appearance of the *Vekhi* symposium (1909) with its broad attack upon the intelligentsia's traditional creeds is usually attributed to the general climate of reaction which followed in the wake of the defeat of the 1905 Revolution. It is true that the strictures of the symposium were not directed against Marxism alone; nor could it be said that revision of attitudes toward industrialization was the *primary* concern of the seven contributors. Still it seems reasonable to suggest that *Vekhi* reflected a fundamental fact: the sway of Marxism over the minds of the intelligentsia had been weakened as a result of the progressing industrialization of the country. Radkey suggests that Stolypin's reform imparted a severe blow to Russian agrarian socialism. If the course of the reform had not been interrupted, the blow might well have been a final one. The prospects of Marxian socialism were much less dim because the continued growth of the industrial labor force was bound to strengthen the Social Democratic Party and the trade unions. But this process was perfectly compatible with a decline in the appeal of orthodox Marxian ideas to the intelligentsia, even though the rate of that decline was not hastened by the unyielding policies of the autocracy. Thus, from two sides the foundations were being laid for the development of a nonsocialist, bourgeois ideology in Russia. For the understanding of the significance of the intellectual movements that have been discussed here, these processes deserve to be mentioned even though they were, of course, halted and reversed by the outbreak of war and revolution.

Thus, for a number of reasons, the victory of Marxism in prerevolutionary Russia was neither as complete nor as final as is often believed. But what about the reversal just mentioned? Did not the Bolshevik revolution constitute the second and this time both the complete and final victory of Marxism in Russia? This is claimed by the *communis opinio* and corroborated by the appearances. It seems to me that Alexander

Erlich's paper performs a valuable service in showing, at least indirectly, that the extent of that victory may be easily exaggerated. To say this is not to deny, of course, the obvious fact that Marxism in Soviet Russia has been elevated — or lowered — to the position of absolute monopoly. But even in this respect a somewhat more penetrating view would easily disclose that much of what goes in Soviet Russia under the name of the established doctrine has in reality little, or nothing, to do with Marxism, however generously we may conceive the term. That the Soviet government can derive considerable political advantages from evoking the image of an unchanged system of basic beliefs is clear. It should be equally clear that to accept that deliberately misleading image would be to bar ourselves from perceiving important processes of change in Soviet ideology and from understanding the relation of that ideology to political and economic decisions which in the course of nearly four decades have hewed and shaped the economy of the country.

Few would disagree that among those decisions the decision taken in the second half of the twenties to embark upon the road of rapid industrialization and collectivization of agriculture occupies the central place. In a general sense, that decision seemed to be broadly consonant with the general tenor of accepted Marxian doctrines. But as soon as we are tempted to attribute the great change that concluded the NEP period to the influence of Marxism, we are inevitably baffled by a number of facts that do not fit well into such an interpretation. The debates of the twenties in Soviet Russia with regard to the basic policies to be pursued were obviously not debates between Marxians and non-Marxians. They were conducted by people who from early youth had been bred and steeped in the tenets of Marxism. To suggest that Stalin was a better Marxian than, say, Bukharin or Preobrazhenski makes good sense within the context of a Soviet purge trial, but is meaningless without it. What Erlich has described so well in his paper is the great break in Stalin's thinking on the subject of industrialization and his attitude toward the peasants.

After having asserted the need to preserve the *smychka*, after having maintained that the rate of growth in agriculture would exceed that of industry, after having dragged out of the historical cupboard the populist skeleton of internal market, and after having accused his opponents of nursing plans to exploit the peasantry, Stalin embarked upon a policy which was contradictorily opposed to his previous views. What had caused him to change his mind? Surely not a belated remembrance of the Marxian preference for large-scale units in agriculture. Erlich rightly mentions the significance of the disastrously declining volume of grain deliveries to the cities. It is not unlikely that toward the end of the NEP period, as the prewar capacity of Russian industry was being attained and considerable inflationary pressures developed, the Russian economy was headed toward an impasse and that the traditional measures of higher prices or higher taxes were politically intolerable and could not be used to break the dead-lock. The bold idea of a large investment effort compressed within the period of a few years in order to break the deadlock from the commodity side — because it could not be broken from the money side — seems to have been the original purpose of the First Five Year Plan. Collectiviza-tion was to remain within moderate limits and its purpose — not unlike that of Stolypin — was to buttress the industrial program by creating for the regime some *points d'appui* in the villages. When the bitter resistance of the peasantry to collectivization threatened to develop into a full-fledged civil war, the nature of the collectivization policy was changed. From an infiltrating operation it evolved into a frontal attack upon the peasantry. And once the great gamble was won, once Russia's great op-portunity to rid herself of the dictatorship was lost and the peasantry was well encased in the strait jacket of the kolkhoz — once the produce of the land could be appropriated by the government, however small the *quid pro quo* in terms of industrial products — the need for a limited in-dustrialization program designed to re-establish the monetary equilibrium in the country was removed. Industrialization could and did become an end in itself or, rather, a means for further strengthening of the internal and external power of the Soviet government.

There is a certain tendency nowadays to view Soviet intellectual history from a static point of view. Such a view, probably inadequate at all times, is particularly unsatisfactory when applied to a period of very rapid social change. That an ideology is likely to undergo considerable changes as the social movement with which it is associated passes from a purely intellectual to an organizational and then to a "power" stage has been impressively shown by R. Mayreder. In this particular case, the changes have been momentous indeed. Basic tenets of Marxian ideology suffered a radical revision. One may refer alone to such pillars of the Marxian edifice as the view on the role of great men in history, the principle of internationalism, the marcescence of the state, and the idea of egalitarianism, and consider in that light the shameless idolization of Stalin, the excesses of Soviet Russian chauvinism, the hypertrophy of the Soviet state, and the deliberate policy of a far-reaching income differentia-tion. To be sure, all these have been incorporated by the Soviets into a body of ideology that still goes under the name of Marxism. A totalitarian dictatorship which monopolizes the instruments of communication need not fear the charge of inconsistency when it tries to create the false impression of ideological constancy. Stalin's clumsy but persistent attempts in his *Economic Problems of Socialism* to preserve the Marxian concept of economic law in conditions which are patently unsuitable for the concept provide a vivid illustration of the importance which the regime attributes to ideological stability. But all this should not prevent scholarly opinion from recognizing that the name of Soviet ideology has long become *Schall und Rauch,* even though — to continue Goethe's line — what is thus shrouded in fog has nothing to do with heavenly fire. No, the October Revolution did not carry with it a complete victory of Marxism. Quite the contrary, it is tempting to suggest that in a very real sense the advent of the Bolsheviks to power spelled the end of Marxian ideology in Russia.

Thus one cannot help observing the subsidiary character of the generally recognized and much advertised ideologies in their relation to economic development in Russia. The problem, of course, is not one of metaphysical choice between "idealistic" or "materialistic" factors. Also Stalin's *libido dominandi* had an ideology and a value system of its own. Without it, his reaction to the situation as it developed in the second half of the 1920s may well have been very different. What is so surprising, rather, is how little the different ideas which have dominated the visible flow of Russian intellectual history for the last hundred and fifty years can be said to have exercised a determining influence upon the sequence of economic events and the course of economic change in the country. Those who disagree with this view might wish to point to the persistent clamor — from Radishchev to 1861 — for the liberation of the peasantry. In some measure, the point would be well taken. But its validity does not extend beyond the significance which, among a large variety of competing factors, can be imputed to the attitudes of the intelligentsia as one of the forces that prompted the act of emancipation. And one must beware of overrating that significance.

Perhaps a few words on the general significance of the Russian intellectual experience may be added in conclusion. In the last section of my paper I stressed the connection between anti-industrial ideologies (anti-industrial socialism in particular) and the general conditions of economic backwardness and expressed the view that, though in Russia the retarding effect of such ideologies upon industrial development remained moderate on the whole, it is likely to be much stronger in the underdeveloped countries of our day. We can now go one step beyond what was said in the paper. If the argument in the present review is at all correct and the intelligentsia's approval of industrialization assumed the form of Marxism because of the preceding intellectual history and the specific economic backwardness of the country, then it is perhaps plausible to expect also that industrialization of backward countries of our day may similarly proceed under the auspices of a rather radical ideology. In a broad sense, this would be only a repetition of what occurred in European countries of the nineteenth century.

And yet the situation is a rather different one in important respects. As intimated before, the connection between such a radical ideology and industrialization tended to characterize just the first phase of the rapid spurt of modern economic development. Saint-Simonism was a powerful force in France of the fifties; it was dead and buried in France a quarter of a century later. The influence of Marxism was on the decline in Russia after the 1905 Revolution and in addition Marxian ideology itself was in a state of transformation through infusion of revisionist elements. There is little doubt that those changes were the effect of the very success of industrialization. Can we assume that in backward countries, too, the specific connection between industrialization and Marxian ideology will remain a temporary one? Can we take it for granted that previous patterns will faithfully reproduce themselves in contemporary conditions in backward countries? Again we must point to the differences between the twentieth and the nineteenth centuries. On the one hand, it is often claimed that the pressure for rapid increases in the levels of consumption is particularly strong in underdeveloped countries and some observers (Ragnar Nurkse, for instance) speak of the "international demonstration effect," that is, of the keen desire of underdeveloped countries to adopt quickly the full consumption pattern of the advanced countries. Considering that any sustained industrialization effort will presumably require a temporary *decline* in consumption levels, the discrepancy between wish and reality is likely to become as large as it will be painful. This consequence must be particularly strong in those underdeveloped countries where the pressure of over-population is very considerable. As an incidental by-product of this discrepancy, a good deal of credence will be lent to the theory of increasing misery, and the temporary decline in consumers' welfare will be taken as flowing irresistibly from an inevitable law of capitalist industrialization, thus reinforcing the belief in the validity of Marxian theories.

On the other hand, as has been indicated before, the intelligentsia in those countries is in a position of doing things rather than philosophizing about them. Whereas in Russia the influence of Marxism may at length have caused young men to study engineering rather than philosophy or philology, in a modern underdeveloped country ideologies of the type discussed in these papers may at least for some time become main determinants of action and, specifically, the influence of Marxism may be directly translated into practical governmental policies. Moreover, it is likely to be an altogether different brand of Marxism, strongly influenced and distorted by ideological importations from Soviet Russia. Russian Marxism began to evolve very early in a revisionist direction. What happened in Russia under the impact of the First World War may be regarded as a tragic accident brought about by extraneous circumstances. But developments in present-day backward countries may follow the Russian path as a result of a much more continuous play of internal forces.

The situation no doubt is complex and shot through with irrational elements. Increase in the levels of consumption of the people seems to be the primary concern. Slow industrialization or its absence is decried because standards of living are not raised quickly enough. But also very rapid industrialization leading to a passing reduction in standards of living is likely to arouse formidable opposition and to result in considerable radicalization of both the intelligentsia and the population. And, illogically, the establishment of a dictatorship upon the Soviet pattern, which would keep down the levels of consumption permanently, may begin to loom as a natural solution to those who fail to realize that both their genuine compassion for popular misery and the ideology of Marxism would be among the first victims of such a dictatorship.

Thus, no easy inferences can be drawn from the Russian experience for the present conditions in underdeveloped countries. Lessons from history are precarious at all times, and perhaps never more so than in this case. But to say this does not mean that the Russian experience is not suggestive of possibilities that may be worth considering.

If it is true that both rapid industrialization and its absence are pregnant with grave perils, the question should at least be raised whether or not a period of rapid industrialization, sufficiently long to turn upward the curve of per-capita consumption, may be expected to break the fatal link between industrialization and radical ideology. If it is likely at all to "normalize" the situation in terms of the historical experience of West European industrialization and to eliminate the danger of totalitarian dictatorships, then the essential problem would be to minimize the burdens which a high rate of investment must impose upon the shoulders of the populations concerned by generous injections of capital from advanced countries. To follow such a course no doubt involves great and real risks, and a historian should not be surprised if hardened statesmen refuse to act on the basis of uncertain historical analogies. It is not suggested that they should. But perhaps they may be reminded of a much broader and much more valid lesson of human history. In a situation where both action and inaction appear to threaten disaster. the statesman's choice should lie among different forms of action.

8

Some Aspects of Industrialization
in Bulgaria, 1878—1939

❦

> Un paese dove si verificano sempre
> le cause e non gli effetti. — Italo
> Calvino, *Il barone rampante*

THE following discussion of some problems that have emerged
from Bulgarian industrial development before World War II may
not prove directly pertinent to other countries of the Balkan Peninsula. It would seem, however, that the Bulgarian case may cast some
additional light on the general patterns of European industrialization
in varying conditions of economic backwardness. It is conceivable,
therefore, that by a detour, as it were, consideration of the economic
evolution in Bulgaria may yield some questions which may be useful
in studying the economic history of the whole peninsula.

The narrow scope of this essay naturally precludes any systematic treatment. It must suffice to show the results of some statistical
computations and then try to place them within a plausible interpretative framework. The essay is divided into two sections. The first
presents the statistics of industrial change and the second a historical
interpretation of that change.

I

The view is often expressed that Bulgarian economic life between
the country's liberation from the Turks and its liberation from the
Germans was essentially characterized by inertia of men and stagna-

tion of things. At the same time, it is the last quarter of the nineteenth century that is said to encompass the birth of Bulgarian "capitalism." Since the early days of Blagoev — the Bulgarian Plekhanov — Marxian writers in Bulgaria stressed what they kept describing as a momentous transformation of the country's economy. They welcomed the change as the necessary prerequisite for the establishment of socialism in Bulgaria. The concept of capitalism may be too big for any reasonable manipulation, and there will be some opportunity later on to gauge the predictive or explanatory value of Marxian concepts in an analysis of Bulgarian industrialization; in addition, something more will have to be said about Marxism as a specific industrialization ideology in conditions of economic backwardness. What matters at this point, however, is to remain undisturbed by easy generalization or conceptual grandiloquence and to establish a few appropriate empirical magnitudes through which to approach the nature of such economic evolution as may have taken place. The area of the so-called state-encouraged industry has readily suggested itself for this purpose.

Through a number of legislative measures beginning in 1894 and continuing in 1897, 1905, 1909, and 1928, Bulgaria gave an especially favored status to the leading segment of her industry (manufacturing and mining). The benefits conferred were manifold and comprised *inter alia* long-term tax exemptions and reductions, rights of duty-free imports of machinery, raw materials, and fuel, reduction of freight rates by the railroads, gratis allocation of land for factory construction, and assured preference with regard to government contracts. The quantitative importance of these measures will be touched upon later. The important point is that in this fashion the government developed a general interest in a number of industrial enterprises and placed them under obligation to supply an unusually extensive body of statistical information, including data on such magnitudes as output, cost of raw materials, fuel and power, employment and capital. The scope of the enterprises which were included in the governmental scheme of encouragement varied from amendment to amendment. Yet there seems to have been no major change of policy with regard to the relative significance of the individual branches of industry. At any rate, by excluding from consideration one or two branches of industrial endeavor (such as mines, sea-salt production, and railroad-repair shops), one can obtain series which, if not absolutely uniform over time,[1] are sufficiently homogeneous for the purposes of this essay.[2]

On the basis of the data described in the following pages, it has seemed possible to construct an index of growth of industrial output. A more detailed description of the way in which the index has been prepared will be found in Appendix II, together with tabulations of basic data and citations of the sources used. A very brief summary may be in order here:

1. It was felt that the data for the years before 1909 were too inchoate and unreliable to warrant their inclusion in the index period, which was confined to the years 1909–1937. The computation was made for the initial and terminal years of the period and also for 1929, all three years being ones of fairly high levels of employment.

2. Net value of output (at current prices) was computed by deducting from the value of product the cost of raw materials and fuel and (for 1929 and 1937) also the cost of power used. Obviously, the result represents but an approximation to value added by manufacturing (Appendix II, Tables 6, 7, 8).

3. The data were computed for ten separate branches of industry, as will be seen from some of the tables included in the text. The rather scanty Bulgarian price information was scrutinized for what might be termed the one or two strategic prices or price relatives of finished commodities or crucially important inputs for each of the ten groups. As a rule, no prices were available for 1909, and price averages for 1908–1912 had to be taken instead. If more than one price was

---

[1] The case of the flour mills in 1929 is one exception.

[2] For information on the legislative measures and particularly on the changing scope of state-encouraged industrial output, see: *Dnevnitsi (Stenograficheski) na osmoto obiknovenno Narodno Súbranie, Púrva Redovna Sessiya, XXVI Zasedanie* (Stenographic Records of the Eighth Ordinary People's Assembly, First Regular Session, 26th Meeting), November 25, 1894 (Sofia, 1895), text of the bill introduced by I. E. Geshov, p. 636; Christo T. Russeff, *Die Fortschritte der staatlich unterstuetzten Fabriksindustrie in Bulgarien* (Halle a.d.S., 1914), pp. 71–76; *Prilozheniya kúm Stenografskite Dnevnitsi na XXII obiknoveni Narodno Súbranie, Púrva Redovna Sessiya, Zakoni i resheniya,* "Zakon na nasúrdchenie na mestnata industriya" (Annex to Stenographic Records of the 22nd Ordinary People's Assembly, First Regular Session, Laws and Resolutions, "Law Concerning Encouragement of Domestic Industry"), II (Sofia, 1928), 144–149.

chosen to represent the group, some simple form of averaging was applied. Because of the nature of price data available, two price indices were computed for each of the ten groups: one for the period 1909–1929 and one for the period 1929–1937. The indices for the two groups were then spliced at their juncture in 1929 (Appendix II, Tables 10, 11, 12).

4. The resulting indices were used for deflating the net values of output at current prices for the respective groups. The deflating operation was threefold, resulting in net values of output at constant prices of the years 1909, 1929, and 1937. Summation of outputs at constant prices yielded values of total industrial output, with a price index for total output implicit in the comparisons of values at constant prices with those at current prices (Appendix II, Tables 13, 14, 15).

5. The manifold shortcomings of the procedure should be obvious. Variations in scope apart, the quality of the reporting of the basic data must have varied considerably from branch to branch of industry, depending *inter alia* on the prevailing scale of enterprise and especially on the degree of general "modernity" of the respective firms. In particular, the mode chosen for deflating output figures at current prices is far removed from the ideal of price indices in which prices of all the products within a group appear properly weighted (a) with their given-year outputs so as to yield an output index erected upon base-year weights and (b) with their base-year outputs so as to yield an output index erected upon given-year weights. All that can be said in defense of the procedure used is that in several cases the prices chosen seemed to be fairly representative of the general price movement within the group; there is some advantage to a simple and fairly transparent method as compared with an index based on a considerable number of unspecified commodities combined by an inconsistent or inappropriate system of weights. On the other hand, it must be noted that for 1929 (though not for 1937), in default of suitable price information, values of output in four branches had to be deflated by dint of the general price index. All in all, the index as computed here cannot lay claim to great precision; yet it should depict the main features of the country's industrial evolution with sufficient clarity.

Table 1. Net industrial output, state-encouraged industries (at constant prices)
(1909 = 100)

Base-weight year	1909	1929	1937
At prices of 1909	100	335	460
At prices of 1929	100	324	444
At prices of 1937	100	388	455

Note: see also Appendix II, Tables 14, 15, 16.

Table 1 shows the change in the volume of industrial output between 1909 and 1937. A glance at that table should suffice to dispel the idea of any stagnation in Bulgarian industrial output, if stagnation is to be interpreted as a rate of growth close to zero or at least not above the rate of growth of population (which was close to 1.4 percent a year for the period under review).[3] As can be seen from Table 2, the rates of growth of output implied in Table 1 were considerably above the rate at which the population grew.

Table 2. Average annual rates of industrial growth, 1909, 1929, 1937

Base-weight year	1929/1909 a	b	1937/1929	1937/1909 a	b
At prices of 1909	6.23	7.85	4.05	5.60	6.56
At prices of 1929	6.05	7.63	4.01	5.47	6.41
At prices of 1937	7.02	8.84	2.01	5.56	6.52

Note: the rates have been computed on a compound basis, using the first and the last years of the respective periods. In the two estimates marked "b," the Balkan wars of 1912–13 and World War I were arbitrarily taken into account by reducing the length of the period concerned by four years. It may be noted that in 1912–13 almost 90 percent of the Bulgarian males between the ages of twenty and sixty were called to the colors. See Walter Weiss-Bartenstein, *Bulgariens volkswirtschaftliche Verhaeltnisse* (Berlin, 1917), p. 261.

Those rates are fairly high if judged by comparison with rates in other countries, particularly if some account is taken of the disorders and retardations caused by World War I and its aftermath (to say

[3] See Glavna Direktsiya na Statistikata, *Statisticheski Godishnik na Tsarstvo Búlgariya* (Central Statistical Office, Statistical Yearbook for the Tsardom of Bulgaria), XXXI (Sofia, 1939). (Hereafter this publication will be cited as *Godishnik*, volume and year.) The rate of growth of population has been computed from data given in *Godishnik*, XXXI (1939), 21.

nothing of the Balkan wars) and of the debilitating effect of the Great Depression. On the other hand, however, it must be considered that the "state-encouraged sector" of Bulgarian industry, which alone is considered here, represents if not the very top still a very selective group among Bulgaria's industrial enterprises of the period. The rate of progress of leading enterprises is bound to be a good deal higher than the corresponding rate of industry as a whole, which must comprise a large number of lagging or stagnant enterprises. Furthermore, there is a certain presumption that the speed of industrialization in a country in its early stages is directly related to the degree of its economic backwardness. This at least seems to be the case with regard to the "initial" great spurt of industrialization. There is little doubt that Bulgaria at the beginning of the century was one of the most backward countries on the European continent. If Bulgaria had been passing, between 1909 and 1937, through *the* great upsurge of its industrial development, one could have reasonably expected such a period to be characterized by rates of growth considerably above those shown in Table 2; this should have been true for industry as a whole and particularly for the spearhead of industrial advance.

Like most historical concepts, the concept of the initial great spurt of industrial development cannot be forced into an overly precise definitional shell. Some of the features of such spurts as observed from nineteenth-century European industrial history are clearly quantitative — such as the sudden kink in the curve of industrial output denoting a considerable acceleration in the rate of growth. If the high rate of growth is maintained undiminished or virtually undiminished throughout a period of international depression, the presumption that the phenomenon is a great spurt is further enhanced. Yet it would be inadequate to define a great spurt merely in quantitative terms. From all we know from the economic history of other countries, we must expect very considerable changes in industrial structure to take place in the course of rapid industrial development and, in fact, as an integral part thereof. It is the various complementarities and indivisibilities in industrial processes that often preclude early industrial developments from following any but a discontinuous path. But it is the great advantage of sizable technological borrowings from other countries that makes such a spurt possible. This is done by concentrating upon those branches of the industrial economy where recent technical progress in the world at large had been particularly vehement and where a reservoir of innovations (of the type which do not require an excessively skillful labor force) is available for quick adoption by the backward country. The result must be a considerable change in the prevailing scarcity relations. Commodities previously produced in small quantities and sold at high prices are now produced in increasing quantities at prices which are falling as a result of the application of cost-reducing innovations. On the other hand, commodities which before the great spurt had been the mainstay of industrial output develop at much lower rates while their prices tend to rise (rise and fall of prices in both cases is to be taken in relative rather than absolute terms).

With the foregoing in mind, let us turn again to the data in Tables 1 and 2. In both tables each of the three rows refers to the price system of a different year. In other words, the measurements of output in the first row are based, for all three years, upon the prices — and that should mean scarcity relations — prevailing in 1909; the two other rows refer to the price systems of 1929 and 1937, respectively. Implied in what has been said in the preceding paragraph is the expectation that the price system stemming from the postspurt period should yield an index connoting much lower rates of growth than would an index based on prices pertaining to a period preceding the beginning of the great spurt or to its early phases. Those discrepancies in measurements are known as the index-number problem and are gall and wormwood to the statistician or theoretical economist. By contrast, their existence, magnitude, and change over time are a subject of very positive interest to the economic historian who regards them as an integral part of the processes of economic change. It is unfortunate, as said before, that the value of such comparisons has been limited here by some recourse for purposes of deflation to the general price index. This is more than just a beauty blemish. Still it does not suffice at all to explain the near absence of discrepancies among index numbers yielded by the three price systems. If great technological progress involving considerable cost reductions had taken place in Bulgaria between 1909 and 1937, the rates of growth of output at 1937 prices would have been far below those based on 1909 prices. A more detailed look at the structure of Bulgarian industry during the period under review fully confirms this point.[4]

Table 3 shows changes in the productivity of labor within the

[4] Still from the height of an aggregative bird's eye view of the industrial process in Bulgaria, yet another illustration of the same point may be offered in passing. A computation by a Bulgarian economist yielded data on gross investment in fixed industrial capital for each year between 1880 and 1939: L. Berov, "Kúm vúprosa za tempovite na kapitalisticheskata industrializatsiya na Búlgariya" (On the Question of the Rates of Capitalist Industrialization in Bulgaria), Búlgarska Akademiya na Naukite, *Izvestiya na Ikonomicheskiya Institut* (Bulgarian Academy of Sciences, Bulletin of the Economic Institute), VIII, nos. 3–4 (Sofia, 1954). These data were also presented in terms of constant prices of the year 1939. By applying to these annual investment data a depreciation rate of 25 percent per quinquennium, it was possible to obtain an estimate for the capital stock in Bulgarian industry first for 1909 and then, continuing the procedure, for 1937. It seemed tempting to relate these figures to the data for total industrial production and labor in 1937 and to an estimate of total industrial production and labor in 1909 through the use of production functions of the Cobb-Douglas type: output equals productivity factor times labor, to the power of k, times capital stock, to the power of $1-k$. Choosing a wide range of alternative magnitudes for k and solving for what with some obvious arbitrariness has been called the productivity factor, a rather striking result is obtained which can be summarized in the following tabulation (see also Appendix II, Tables 18, 19, 20, and the concluding computations).

Change in the productivity factor (F) between 1909 and 1937

$$\frac{F_{1937}}{F_{1909}} = \frac{\text{output}_{1937}}{\text{labor}_{1937}^{k}\ \text{capital}_{1937}^{1-k}} : \frac{\text{output}_{1909}}{\text{labor}_{1909}^{k}\ \text{capital}_{1909}^{1-k}}$$

	$1-k = .25$	$1-k = .35$	$1-k = .50$	$1-k = .75$
Percentage	6.85	8.47	10.90	15.12

These percentage changes of the period as a whole imply the following average annual change in percent:

	$1-k = .25$	$1-k = .35$	$1-k = .50$	$1-k = .75$
Percentage	.24	.29	.37	.50

It is easy to see that the change in the productivity factor was quite trivial. In other words, the increase in output of about four and a half times over the period was not significantly caused by factors other than increase in the quantity of labor and capital employed. Broadly speaking, this conclusion, despite the manifold shortcomings and unreliabilities of the procedure, may be taken as a confirmation of the previously formed opinion: the negligible change in the productivity factor in a production function of the Bulgarian industry corresponds well to the virtual absence of discrepancies among index numbers based on weights which pertain to the initial and terminal years of a fairly long index period.

state-encouraged segment of industry by groups of industrial enterprises. It is clear that productivity per worker within the sector of

Table 3. Net industrial output per worker, 1909 and 1937
(at constant prices of 1909)

Industry	1909 (a)	1937 (b)	(b/a) 100
Metals	1,378	1,069	77.6
Pottery	1,130	3,392	300.0
Chemicals	1,954	2,432	124.5
Flour mills	7,172	5,805	80.9
Other foodstuffs	4,334	2,408	55.6
Textiles	1,275	1,366	107.1
Woodworking	963	867	90.0
Leather	2,798	4,005	143.1
Paper	1,490	2,131	143.0
Energy	47,372	277,290	585.3
Total	2,057	2,139	104.0
Total minus energy	1,974	1,867	94.6

Note: computed from Tables 2 and 13 of Appendix II.

the *leading* industry in Bulgaria remained virtually constant over a period of almost three decades. It is true that a computation of productivity per man-hour rather than per worker would have given a somewhat more favorable result, inasmuch as the number of working hours per day was reduced from between ten to twelve in the early years of the century to about eight in the interwar period.[5] This should have implied for the majority of the labor force a decrease in the length of the working day of at least 20 percent. but since decrease in working hours itself often and very plausibly has been presented as a factor leading to increased productivity in the long run,

[5] In 1909, about 63 percent of workers in state-encouraged industries worked between ten and twelve hours a day; about 29 percent worked longer than twelve hours and about 8 percent worked less than ten hours a day. See N. Mikhailov, "Nasúrchavanata ot dúrzhavata industriya prez 1909" (Industry Encouraged by the State in 1909), *Spisanie na Búlgarskoto Ikonomichesko Druzhestvo*, XVIII, nos. 9–10 (Sofia, 1914), 586. After World War I, the eight-hour working day was introduced (June 24, 1919). See Angelo Fozarile, *Bulgaria d'oggi nei suoi aspetti sociali, economici, commerciali e finanziari* (Milan, 1929), p. 263; also Akademiya Nauk SSSR, *Istoriya Bolgarii* (Academy of Sciences of the USSR, History of Bulgaria), II (Moscow, 1955), 583.

it is not clear how much allowance, if any, should be made for the reduction in working hours.

For the rest, the data in Table 3 must be interpreted in conjunction with data on the participation of the individual industries in the output of the whole group of state-encouraged industries. Such data both at the prices of the year 1909 and at the prices of the year 1937 are given in Tables 4 and 5. First, a brief comparison of these

Table 4. The structure of state-encouraged industry, 1909 and 1937, percentage share of net output of industrial branches

(based on prices of 1909)

Industry	1909	1937
Metals	5.99	5.22
Pottery	6.38	13.56
Chemicals	4.12	6.75
Flour mills	23.08	8.87
Other foodstuffs	19.16	9.38
Textiles	25.27	35.20
Woodworking	5.31	1.05
Leather	5.43	3.66
Paper	1.10	2.20
Energy	4.15	14.11
Total	100.00	100.00

Note: computed from Appendix II, Table 13.

two tables is useful to corroborate previously received impressions. One way of expressing the economic significance of the index-number problem is to say that the application of a later price system (as against an earlier one) should result in relatively smaller percentage shares of output of those industries that might be described as "specifically new" industries. In terms of an industrial transformation in a backward country in the first half of this century, one would assume production and processing of metals as well as production of chemicals to play the role of "new" industries par excellence. It is therefore quite significant that neither metals nor chemicals constitutes a higher percentage of output in the total when expressed in 1909 prices rather than when expressed in 1937 prices.

Table 5. The structure of state-encouraged industry, 1909 and 1937, percentage share
of net output of industrial branches
(based on prices of 1937)

Industry	1909	1937
Metals	10.00	8.81
Pottery	4.87	10.47
Chemicals	5.09	8.44
Flour mills	15.85	6.16
Other foodstuffs	23.40	11.56
Textiles	25.01	35.22
Woodworking	6.23	1.25
Leather	4.51	3.08
Paper	1.60	3.21
Energy	3.44	11.80
Total	100.00	100.00

Note: computed from Appendix II, Table 15.

It is true, however, that the price bases which underlie our
output indices are rather slender; it is, furthermore, at least imaginable that "normal" price structure can be so disturbed by uneven
incidence of monopolistic compacts as to disguise the technical
progress that did take place. But any misgivings on this score are
effectively dispelled by a glance at the percentage shares of the
industries concerned. Whether one compares the data for metals and
chemicals within each of the two tables or whether the comparison is
at current prices (comparing the first column in Table 4 with the
second column in Table 5), the conclusion is inescapable that no significant advance in relation to total output had taken place in either
industry. They were relatively small to start with and they remained relatively small throughout the period under review. The
only two industries which registered very considerable advances in
productivity of labor and certain increase in their relative importance
within the total are potteries and production of energy. At 1937
prices, the two industries together amounted in 1937 to one quarter
of total output; at 1909 prices their share in the total was even a little
higher. Yet the significance of this development should not be
overestimated. It would seem that it is entirely overshadowed by
the evolution of the textile industry. That "specifically old" industry
as a rule has played a diminishing role in all spurts of industrialization

in backward countries. In fact, one is almost tempted to argue that the more backward a country, the more appropriate it is to define its spurt of industrial development as a process during which the textile industry was divested of its dominant position. If any industry lost out in the course of Bulgarian industrialization, it was the foodstuff-producing industry and particularly the flour mills which alone, in 1909, occupied nearly one quarter of total output.[6]

To complete the picture of Bulgarian industrialization some data on the average size of industrial enterprises may be adduced. Table 6 shows the percentage change in the number of workers per enterprise that occurred between 1909 and 1937. The number of

Table 6. Change in the number of workers per enterprise, 1909–1937

(1909 = 100)

Industry	Percentage change
Metals	80.2
Pottery	37.4
Woodworking	39.7
Textiles	185.3
Leather	103.9
Flour mills	86.8
Other foodstuffs	130.1
Chemicals	157.9
Paper	479.7
Energy	161.1
Total	126.0
Total without energy	130.1

Note: computed from *Godishnik*, II (1910), 253, 255; *Godishnik*, XXXI (1939), 384–389; see also Appendix II, Table 4.

[6] The original importance of flour mills in Bulgarian industry reveals an interesting aspect of processes of early industrialization in backward countries. It is usually assumed that capital-output ratios will tend to rise in the early phases. To the extent that such an industrialization implies transition from a textile age, with its relatively low capital-output ratios, to a railroad age, with its relatively high capital-output ratios, such an expectation would seem quite reasonable. In cases, however, where the mill industry has been allowed to dominate the industrial scene until the very initiation of *modern* industrialization, the latter will reduce the weight of the mill industry and by the same token probably will tend to reduce the average capital-output for the industry as a whole. For the capital-output ratios in the mill industry in backward countries are inordinately high, first, because of the inefficiency of the equipment used and, second, because of the highly seasonal character of the industry (the mills being inactive for about eight months out of twelve).

enterprises in the paper industry was very small indeed so that the great increase in the number of workers per enterprise of that industry hardly affected the total picture. For the rest, such increases as did take place were quite modest, and it is again significant that, the paper industry apart, it was the textile industry which showed the strongest movement with a near doubling of the average number of workers per enterprise.

A very similar result is obtained from a comparison of the volume of output per enterprise between 1909 and 1937, in Table 7.

Table 7. Change in the volume of net ouput per enterprise, 1937, at constant prices of 1909

(1909 = 100)

Industry	Percentage change
Metals	62.2
Pottery	112.4
Chemicals	196.3
Flour mills	69.8
Other foodstuffs	72.4
Textiles	198.4
Woodworking	35.7
Leather	148.6
Paper	685.6
Energy	65.1
Total	131.0
Total without energy	123.1

Note: computed from Appendix II, Tables 13 and 1.

Despite some differences between Table 7 and Table 6, what has been said about the former essentially applies to the latter: the change in the scale of enterprise was small on the whole, and it was the textile industry — a branch not particularly conspicuous for large size of plant and enterprise in the economic climate of the twentieth century — that was the chief beneficiary of such changes as did take place.

It may be useful, in conclusion, to compare the structure of Bulgarian industry toward the end of the period under review with that of German industry after World War I. In view of what has been said in the foregoing pages, the comparison may be profitably stated in terms of the relative position of the textile industry by workers employed and horsepowers installed. For the purposes of such a comparison, the specific criteria determining the scope of the state-encouraged sector in Bulgaria are less appropriate because of the lack of counterparts in Germany. Accordingly, for both countries industrial plants ("Betriebe" in Germany, "Zavedeniya" in Bulgaria) employing more than fifty workers are used. The relevant data are not reported year in and year out but are contained in special censuses. The census of 1934 was chosen for Bulgaria and that of 1925 for Germany. The comparison is embodied in Table 8.

Table 8. Position of textile manufacturing within industry in Germany and Bulgaria (in plants with more than 50 workers)

Industry	Number of workers employed as percentage of workers in textile industry		Horsepowers installed as percentage of horsepower in textile industry	
	Bulgaria 1934	Germany 1925	Bulgaria 1934	Germany 1925
Metals	21.1	70.2	24.9	198.4
Machines and transportation equipment	39.9	109.0	31.1	113.2
Precision instruments	.6	45.5	.2	41.6
Pottery	8.1	—	54.7	—
Woodworking	5.9	29.3	3.6	23.3
Textiles	*100.0*	*100.0*	*100.0*	*100.0*
Leather	1.2	7.6	2.0	9.2
Rubber, etc.	5.1	6.6	13.2	7.7
Food, beverages, tobacco	53.5	44.2	62.2	49.1
Clothing, etc.	3.8	32.3	1.1	6.7
Chemicals	5.1	27.4	6.0	73.0
Paper	14.2	41.7	23.6	69.4
Construction	39.0	64.7	.7	27.3
Energy	1.1	11.0	133.2	25.2

Note: the data are from: *Godishnik*, XXXI (1939), 347 (the industry designated in Bulgaria as energy-producing also supplies water, ice, and gas for lighting); *Statistisches Jahrbuch fuer das Deutsche Reich*, XLIX (Berlin, 1930), 89.

It is true that 1934 is not a very appropriate year to use. That year marked the rock bottom of the depression in Bulgaria; national income, industrial output, and industrial investment — all reached their lowest point. As always, producers' goods suffered more than consumers' goods from the slump. But data from more suitable years are not readily available; and, even though some allowance for the depressed state of trade must be made, it seems quite clear that in Bulgaria the textile industry enjoyed a position of far-reaching supremacy within the body industrial of the country.[7] While in a developed country, such as Germany, metalmaking-machinery construction in the aggregate far outstripped production of textiles, and other "new" industries were substantial in relation to textiles, such an evolution was not even adumbrated in Bulgaria. This should corroborate once more the previously reached conclusion, and the material presented in the descriptive part of this essay may best be

[7] A comparison between the appropriate German figures from Table 8 and Bulgarian figures relating to the state-encouraged sector in 1937 suffers from the absence of a common minimum scale of plant in the two cases, but it avoids the difficulties associated with the choice of a depression year. For the Bulgarian data in the tabulation below, see Appendix II, Table 2.

The position of textile manufacturing within industrial enterprises employing more than 50 workers in Germany and within the state-encouraged sector of Bulgarian industry

Industry	Numbers of workers employed as percentage of workers in textile industry		Horsepowers installed as percentage of horsepowers in textile industry	
	Bulgaria 1937	Germany 1925	Bulgaria 1937	Germany 1925
Metals and machinery	18.9	179.2	30.1	311.6
Pottery	15.5	—	47.2	—
Woodworking	4.7	29.3	10.6	23.3
Textiles	*100.0*	*100.0*	*100.0*	*100.0*
Leather	3.6	7.6	11.3	9.2
Foodstuffs	21.0	44.2	142.7	49.1
Chemicals	10.8	27.4	21.1	73.0
Paper	4.0	41.7	28.6	69.4
Energy	2.9	11.0	366.5	25.2

It seems obvious that the preceding table fully corroborates the inferences drawn from Table 8 in the text, as far as the numbers of workers employed are concerned. With regard to horsepowers installed, one must refer to the previously made argument that the large horsepower employed in the foodstuff industry should be regarded as a sign of backwardness rather than progress.

summarized as follows. Between the early years of the century and the end of the interwar period, there was a fair amount of growth of industrial output in Bulgaria, but that growth did not reveal the specific qualities that are usually associated with a great spurt of industrial development in conditions of considerable backwardness. Thus it is the absence of structural change rather than the absence of growth that primarily calls for explanation and interpretation.

II

One might begin by denying the existence of the problem. And, in fact, it would be too optimistic to assume that all the readers of this essay would be willing to share with its author in the expectation of specific structural changes as a concomitant factor in processes of industrial growth. Indeed, the image of a fairly small annual addition to industrial output, stemming from factories based essentially on local raw materials, largely supplied by domestic agriculture, has a considerable suggestive power. It is not only that very high rates of growth almost invariably impose inordinate sacrifices upon the population. There is *prima facie* something "artificial" about a backward country which attempts to imitate and even to outdo the industrial structure of a developed country. On the other hand, there is "naturalness" about an evolution during which industry remains rooted in agricultural produce, while a prosperous agriculture readily absorbs the wares produced by the new factories. Unfortunately, predilections and preconceptions are a poor guide in explaining the course of events. There are very good reasons why the happy picture of a quiet industrial evolution proceeding without undue stir and thrust has been so seldom reproduced in historical reality. As a rule, a high degree of backwardness in a country is clearly associated with a high measure of "artificiality" in its industrial development. The case under review here casts indirectly a curiously refracted light upon this proposition. The point is that the consumer-goods industries in Bulgaria which accounted for most of the growth of output that did take place relied to a surprisingly small extent upon domestic raw materials, and particularly upon raw materials produced by Bulgarian agriculture. This is shown with regard to a group of state-encouraged industries in Table 9.

Table 9. Percentage share of imported raw materials and fuel in total consumption of selected state-encouraged industries, 1909, 1930, and 1937

Industry	1909		1930		1937	
	Raw materials	Fuel	Raw materials	Fuel	Raw materials	Fuel
Metals	93.1	66.6	86.9	55.2	82.5	35.8
Pottery	40.9	37.7	59.0	3.0	38.3	5.7
Chemicals	76.0	17.9	46.3	7.0	50.0	5.3
Flour mills	.1	57.2	2.6	47.4	.3	50.4
Other foodstuffs	31.5	46.4	9.1	24.5	7.9	5.1
Textiles	60.5	32.7	80.1	10.9	56.2	21.2
Woodworking	31.8	26.3	6.7	25.1	2.8	8.3
Leather	67.2	46.4	75.8	10.0	75.0	17.2
Paper	85.7	—	64.2	—	78.9	4.4

Note: data on 1909 from *Godishnik*, II (1910), 274–276; data on 1930 and 1937 from *Godishnik*, XXXI (1939), 384–385, 388–389. It would have been much better to offer figures for 1929 rather than 1930, but unfortunately the relevant data for the earlier year are not separated by origin of raw materials and fuel used.

This is an instructive table which must be read against the background of the statistical data supplied in the first section of this essay. The industries that could be expected to have relied on domestic farms for raw materials are primarily the foodstuff industry, the textile industry, and the leather industry. In addition, both the woodworking industry and the paper industry would be natural consumers for the products of domestic forestry. Flour mills indeed confined themselves exclusively to grinding home-produced grain (including some decortication of rice); for the rest of the foodstuff industry, the share of imported raw materials was not negligible in 1909, but fell to very small proportions in 1930 and 1937. Nevertheless, as shown in Tables 3, 4, and 5 above, it was precisely the foodstuff industry in which the productivity of labor declined drastically between 1909 and 1937, while the industry's share in the total output of the group was greatly reduced. The industry's average annual rate of growth over the whole period amounted to 2.0 percent for the flour mills and less than 3.0 percent for the rest of industry, as compared with the average rate of increase of 5.6 percent for the group as a whole. Even in the "spurtless" Bulgarian development the foodstuff industry clearly belonged to a premodern form of industrial endeavor. The industry which was peculiarly oriented to farm produce was on the whole a vehicle of economic retrogression rather than progress. The textile and leather industries, on the other hand, present a very different picture. The weight of imported raw materials in 1909 was high in both industries and it increased even further over the following twenty years. It is true that during the years of the Great Depression the government succeeded through extraordinary measures of balance-of-payments policy to reduce the share of imported raw materials in textile manufacturing, but even by 1937 that share still was a good deal more than 50 percent. And no less than three quarters of the leather industry's needs in raw materials was supplied from abroad. The reason for these conditions is not far to seek. It lies predominantly in the fact that agriculture in a backward country is much too backward to be able to produce materials suitable for industrial processing. The leather industry has little use for hides that have been damaged by dirt and perforated by warbles because of a lack of minimum standards of proper care in livestock raising. Similarly, the wool provided by the indigenous sheep in a backward country tends to be much too coarse for many industrial uses. It is therefore not surprising at all that in 1909 almost half of the wool used by the industry was imported from foreign countries.[8] The corresponding figure for 1912 is even more impressive.[9] And, finally, the Bulgarian woodlands (much of them in the hands of the state or communes) were uncared for and lacked adequate accesses to and through the forests. It is not surprising that they proved an inadequate basis for the paper industry. The latter, small but quite modern, preferred to rely mainly on imported materials. Only the woodworking industry, whose output grew at a very low rate of 1.58 until 1929 and then suffered a collapse which reduced it, by 1937, below the 1909 level, was able to reduce the share of imported raw materials and to confine itself almost exclusively to domestic materials.

It is not necessary to think in terms of universally valid principles. No doubt, a small country very favorably located with regard to the routes of foreign commerce leading to very absorbent markets and populated by a fairly educated, enterprising, and mod-

[8] *Godishnik*, II (1910), 276.
[9] *Godishnik*, IV (1912), 188.

erately prosperous peasantry could concentrate its economic development upon its agriculture, achieving a good deal of quality improvement in its agricultural exports and at the same time letting its industry develop gradually on the basis of materials supplied by domestic agriculture. But it seems altogether unreasonable to expect such a development in a country which is farther removed from large markets offering alternative selling opportunities; in which, to quote the Bulgarian figure, in 1910 only 28.5 percent of the rural population was able to read and write.[10] One must remember that in 1913, that is, thirty-five years after Bulgaria's liberation, nearly 80 percent of all the plows used in Bulgarian farming were most primitive wooden implements.[11] (Twenty years later, in 1934, the wooden plows were still more numerous than the iron ones.[12]) The hope that industry in a very backward country can unfold from its agriculture is hardly realistic. With an appropriate lag through indirect stimulation, agriculture indeed might be expected to have modernized as a result of a sustained process of industrialization. But first of all this sequence presupposes a *stacco*, a disengagement of industry from the agricultural environment. This conclusion would seem to be valid for a number of backward countries on the European continent around the turn of the century. It is at least probable that the economic development of Balkan countries other than Bulgaria might be profitably approached in the light of this generalization.

What has been said in the preceding paragraphs on the basis of data given in Table 9 should do no more than lend further plausibility to the interpretative problem as formulated at the end of the first section. The conventional way of answering the question as to why a certain structural change failed to materialize is to say that the specific preconditions or prerequisites for the change were missing. There is little doubt that much of the discussion of "prerequisites" of industrial development is not notable for its methodological soundness and shrewdness. It is in general very doubtful that a true concept of

[10] *Godishnik*, XXXII (1939), 35.

[11] *Spisanie na Búlgarskoto Ikonomichesko Druzhestvo*, XXVIII, April–May 1927 (Sofia), 7.

[12] Pawel Egoroff, "Eigentümlichkeiten der Organisation des landwirtschaftlichen Betriebes," Janaki St. Moloff, ed., *Die sozialökonomische Struktur der bulgarischen Landwirtschaft* (Berlin, 1936), p. 165.

prerequisite as a necessary and sufficient condition has much meaning in historical research. Much of what sails under the name of necessary preconditions of industrial development are not *pre*conditions at all, but the very thing itself: labor, capital, and entrepreneurs are not preconditions of industrialization; they are the stuff industrialization is made of. Tautology apart, what is historical necessity? And what operations could possibly be performed to establish the inevitability of a certain connection? How could we possibly isolate and gauge the sufficiency of a "precondition" which as a rule appears conjoined with a large number of other factors? What usually appears in the all too rigorous guise of a prerequisite is in reality something much less stringent: from the study of the economic development of a certain area, probably the most advanced country, models involving causal sequences are constructed and a certain degree of plausibility with regard to them is established. It is, of course, quite permissible to describe the causal factors involved in such models as "prerequisites" in a very specific sense of the word. Nor is it objectionable to approach the economic history of less advanced countries with a list of such prerequisites in mind, looking for the presence — or absence — of the factors that appear to have acted as causal forces in the advanced country. On the contrary, this is the normal way in which historical insights are gained. But the dangers are great. It is easy to transform a list of questions gleaned from previous study into a bold and confident expectation that the presence of identical prerequisites must be discoverable wherever industrialization occurs and that their absence necessarily precludes industrial development from taking place. This dogmatic belief in the absolute repetitiveness of history is unfortunate under any circumstances. It becomes particularly insufferable when it begins to blur the observer's eye and makes him falsify obvious differences into implausible similarities. Marxian analysis of Bulgarian industrial development supplies plentiful evidence for both the merits and the perils of the comparative approach.

Marxian literature first emerged in Bulgaria in the early 1890s under the strong influence of Russian Marxism. As such it was doubly imitative; it transposed to Bulgaria the Russian Marxians' insistence upon the inevitability of capitalist development and at the same time was willing to assume that the course of industrialization, as described by Marx, would essentially repeat itself in Bulgaria. The problem was by no means a merely theoretical one or even one of economic policy. It encompassed the future of socialism in the country. The position was stated unambiguously: "Whether the spread of socialism in Bulgaria will be fast or slow depends on how fast or how slowly our capitalism will develop." [13] But "the natural law which in our time governs all nations . . . is the modern capitalist production." [14] Hence "the law of natural development of present-day mankind leads us to socialism." [15] In their positive attitude toward industrialization, Bulgarian Marxians stood close to those relatively small groups of Bulgarian intelligentsia which, influenced by List, thought in terms of "national production" and "development of the nation's productive forces," and which published, in the late 1880s, the journal *Promishlenost* (Industry) and somewhat later accepted the leadership of I. E. Geshov and his policy of industrial promotion which has been referred to earlier.[16] Yet the latter's interest in industrial development seems pale and puny compared with that of the leading representative of orthodox Marxism. While Blagoev was willing to praise Geshov highly for what he had done for industry during the three years of his participation in Stoikov's cabinet (1894–97), he also criticized him severely for not going to extremes in protectionism, for refusing to support large-scale industrial enterprises in Bulgaria, and for expressing concern for the economic conditions of the Bulgarian peasantry.[17] In enthusiasm for capitalist development and in the readiness to use every tool of governmental policy to bring it about, Geshov, a mere capitalist businessman, trained in the textile mills of

[13] Dimitúr Blagoev, *Shto e sotsialism i ima li toy pochva u nas?* (What Is Socialism and Has It Possibilities in Our Country?) (Turnov, 1891); originally published under the pen name of D. Bratanov. Reprinted in *Súchineniya*, I (n.p., n.d.), 500.

[14] *Ibid.*, p. 480.

[15] *Ibid.*

[16] See D. Blagoev, *Moi vospominaniya* (My Memoirs), (Moscow-Leningrad, 1928), p. 59; Joseph Rothschild, *The Communist Party of Bulgaria* (New York, 1959), p. 16; I. E. Geshov, *Spomeni i studii* (Memoirs and Essays), Búlgarska Akademiya na Naukite (Sofia, 1928), pp. 329–339.

[17] See D. Blagoev, *Ikonomichnoto razvitie na Búlgariya, industriya ili zemedelie?* (The Economic Development of Bulgaria, Industry or Agriculture?) (Varna, 1902); reprinted in Blagoev, *Súchineniya*, VII, 425, 655–667, esp. 656–658.

Lancashire,[18] could not hope to rival the socialist Blagoev, who was a product of the revolutionary movements among Russian university students and a disciple of Plekhanov. There was much about Russian Marxism of the 1890s that was well suited to make palatable an unpopular and burdensome industrialization in a very backward country. Few things are more apt to enhance men's willingness to promote a certain course of events than the firm belief in its inevitability.[19] The natural result of that fundamental attitude was a rather unrestrained optimism in assessing the chances of, and discussing the prerequisites for, modern industrial development in Bulgaria.

The point of departure for that development was clearly stated by Blagoev: "After the Liberation [in 1878] Bulgaria became a country of exclusively small-scale production: in the towns the artisans became free of craft-guild regulations; in the villages began the destruction of the *zadruga* family and of feudal large estates [*chiflitsi*] while the land was parceled out among a very large number of small rural producers. *In this fashion, immediately after the Liberation, Bulgaria found itself in possession of the necessary condition for the development of capitalist production.*" [20]

In his polemics against the adversaries of industrialization policies in Bulgaria in the early years of the century (among those adversaries, the Chamber of Commerce of the port city of Varna was very vocal), Blagoev agreed that cheap and skilled labor, wide markets, and capital availabilities were also essential for industrialization, but he remained unperturbed. Was not Bulgarian agriculture an over-

---

[18] See Búlgarska Akademiya na Naukite, *Ivan Evstratiev Geshov, Vzgliady i deynost* (Sofia, 1926), p. 15.

[19] As Croce once remarked, "the will never feels as free as when it is known to be one with the volitions of God or the necessity of things." Benedetto Croce, *Storia d'Italia dal 1871 al 1915* (Bari, 1953), p. 161.

[20] Blagoev, *Sotsialismút i rabotnicheskiyat vúpros v Búlgariya, Kúm oborvaniyata na sotsialisma u nas* (Socialism and the Workers' Question in Bulgaria, On the Refutation of Socialism in Our Country) (Plovdiv, 1900); reprinted in Blagoev, *Súchineniya*, VI, 220 (italics added). In another study, published a few years later in 1906, Blagoev expressed this view even more strongly: "After her Liberation Bulgaria became a country of petty-bourgeois property and production, which is the point of departure and the necessary condition for the establishment of the capitalist form of production." *Prinos kúm istoriyata na sotsialisma v Búlgariya* (Contribution to the History of Socialism in Bulgaria) (Sofia, 1906); reprinted in Blagoev, *Súchineniya* (1960?), XI, 73–74.

flowing reservoir of industrial laborers? Was not industry known to create its own market in the very process of its development? And were not Russia and Japan carrying out their industrialization by recourse to capital markets in the advanced countries? [21]

It is still a somewhat undecided question to what extent a virtually independent small peasantry had emerged under the Turkish rule (*inter alia* through a Swedish-like "reversion" of the *spakhiya* fiefs to the state at the end of the eighteenth century and the reforms of the 1850s [22]) and to what extent the appropriation of Turkish-owned lands by the Bulgarian peasantry during and particularly immediately after the Russo-Turkish War was responsible for the final result.[23] But the fact that after the Liberation much of the Bulgarian land belonged to small Bulgarian peasantry is well established. In the early years of the century, 85.7 percent of all the land under cultivation in Bulgaria belonged to farms with less than seventy-five acres of land.[24]

This obviously was a rather un-English situation and a believer in the uniformity of industrial development might have drawn pessimistic conclusions from the absence, on the Bulgarian scene, of anything resembling the enclosure movement in England. This, however, was not the case. Even now, half a century after Blagoev's writings appeared, a modern and quite knowledgeable Marxian historian in Bulgaria in discussing the economic history of his country in the second half of the last century likens the Liberation itself to "the disintegration of the feudal system in England during the 14th and 15th centuries" and finds the English enclosures reproduced in the form of usury credit which, he says, tended to transform the Bulgarian

[21] Blagoev, *Ikonomichnoto razvitie na Búlgariya, Súchineniya*, VIII, 452ff.

[22] See Ivan Sakazov, *Bulgarische Wirtschaftsgeschichte* (Berlin-Leipzig, 1929), pp. 172–197; also "Zakon za zemite" (Law Concerning the Land), April 21, 1858, in Christo Gandev and Galab Salabov, eds., *Fontes Turcici Historiae Bulgariae* (Sofia, 1959), pp. 14–39.

[23] There is no doubt that the provision agreed to at the Congress of Berlin (Art. 12 of the treaty; see *Archives Diplomatiques*, deuxième série, 1882–1883, Paris, VI, 291) and designed to protect Turkish property rights was largely obstructed; an orderly state redemption procedure which was instituted later on (1880–1885) affected only a very small part of the land that once was in Turkish possession. Akademiya Nauk SSSR, *Istoriya Bolgarii*, I (Moscow, 1956), 378–379.

[24] Búlgarska Akademiya na Naukite, Kirill G. Popov, *Stopanska Búlgariya prez 1911, Statisticheski izsledvaniya* (The Economy of Bulgaria in 1911, Statistical Explorations) (Sofia, 1916).

peasants into merely fictional owners of their lands.[25] Usury then is regarded by Natan as the specific Bulgarian form of the original accumulation of capital as developed by Marx in Chapter 24 of Volume I of *Das Kapital*.[26] Indeed, Blagoev in his time did not fail to stress what seemed to him the crucial importance of this factor.[27] This is not the place to analyze the meaning and usefulness of the Marxian concept as a tool of historical research.[28] It is referred to here because it undoubtedly was an integral part of a view according to which after the year 1878 Bulgaria possessed all the important prerequisites for an impetuous industrial development. The only thing that was missing was such a development. Italo Calvino's whimsical phrase, which has been chosen as a motto for this essay, appears to be pertinent indeed: all causes were present, but the effects failed to materialize.

It is not surprising that excessive optimism was temptingly reflected in exaggerated assessments of the advance of the "capitalistic system" in Bulgaria. Even before World War I, Blagoev and Dimitrov spoke of 400,000 as the number of hired laborers *of all categories* (without their dependents).[29] This would have been impressive enough in a country with a population of 4.3 million in 1910.[30] But there is little doubt that the figure was considerably exaggerated and that, moreover, the vast majority of that large number was employed in activities that had little to do with modern industrial development and, least of all, with the strategically crucial industrial branches. Writing more than twenty years later, toward the very end of the interwar period, Oskar Anderson could not put the number of "real industrial workers in the West European sense of the word" in Bulgaria much above 40,000 to which "perhaps another 40,000 of

[25] See Zhak Natan, "Kúm vúprosa za púrvonachal'noto natruprane na kapitala v Búlgariya" (On the Question of the Original Accumulation of Capital in Bulgaria), Búlgarska Akademiya na Naukite, *Izvestiya na Ikonomicheskiya Institut* (Bulletin of the Economic Institute), nos. 1–2 (Sofia, 1954), pp. 30–33.

[26] Zhak Natan, *Stopanska isotoriya na Búlgariya* (The Economic History of Bulgaria) (Sofia, 1957), pp. 259–261.

[27] See, for example, Blagoev, *Súchineniya*, VII, 533ff.

[28] See Chapters 2 and 5 of this volume.

[29] Natan, *Stopanska istoriya na Búlgariya*, p. 362.

[30] *Godishnik*, XX (1928), 13.

seasonal labor engaged in tobacco processing could be added." [31] The desire to see the predictions vindicated in reality made it difficult to discern the progress that actually was being made and in addition obscured the specific structural problem of Bulgarian industrial growth.

For the rest, much of the contemporaneous analysis just described proved to be ill founded or exaggerated. Usury in Bulgarian villages no doubt gave cause for grave concern even before the Liberation, but particularly in the early years of the century. Certain forms of loans proved especially pernicious. Harrowing stories were rife of interest payments which over a very short time vastly exceeded the amount of the principal and still left an irresistibly rising debt.[32] Nevertheless, even before World War I, through a combined action of credit cooperatives and government aid, considerable alleviation was provided and orderly forms of mortgage credit were introduced. War and postwar inflation reduced the debt burden further. It is true that the catastrophe of the Great Depression left Bulgarian agriculture panting under the load of new indebtedness, and a long series of special legal measures proved necessary in order to stabilize the situation. But this was an altogether different historical situation, and it is interesting that in 1930 the Bulgarian peasants' debts to private persons amounted to less than 10 percent of the total burden.[33] The view that usury would lead to structural changes of ownership relations comparable to English enclosures was certainly proved wrong. The character of Bulgarian agriculture remained essentially unchanged. If anything, the share of small and medium farms in the total was even raised somewhat, partly as a result of the agrarian reform carried out by Stamboliyski and the settling of refugees from beyond the borders in the early twenties. In 1934 no more than 5.9 percent of the total area under cultivation belonged to farms owning more than 75 acres of land, as compared with 13 percent in 1897 and

---

[31] Oskar N. Anderson, *Struktur und Konjunktur der bulgarischen Volkswirtschaft*, Andreas Predoehl, ed. (Jena, 1938), p. 12.

[32] N. Konstantinov, "Likhvarstvoto" (Usury), *Spisanie na Búlgarskoto Ikonomichesko Druzhestvo*, XIV, nos. 3–4 (1910), 161–182.

[33] Assen Tschakaloff, "Die Verschuldung der bulgarischen Landwirtschaft," St. Moloff, ed. (n. 12), p. 184.

12 percent in 1903.[34] The small Bulgarian farmer still remained in undisputed possession of his farm. The expected expropriation had failed to occur.

Similarly, all the talk about the ruin of Bulgarian artisans — another much vaunted piece of evidence for original accumulation of capital in Bulgaria — did not prevent Bulgaria from having, still as late as 1936, no less than 134,932 persons engaged in 69,232 handicraft enterprises.[35] There is little doubt that the position of the Bulgarian artisans in the decades following the Liberation was a rather difficult one. But it is not at all clear that such decline of handicraft as took place in those years presaged successful industrial growth or was in any way connected with it. To a very large extent, the origin of the difficulties experienced by the Bulgarian artisans must be sought in the very act of the country's secession from the Ottoman Empire. It was one of the generally accepted notions of the nineteenth century that national self-determination and economic progress must go hand in hand. It took the economic catastrophe of the dismemberment of the Austro-Hungarian statehood to reveal the fallacious nature of a belief in which processes of unification and disintegration were unthinkingly commingled. The economic and social backwardness of the Ottoman Empire could not be doubted. Still, the importance of Constantinople and of the adjacent area as a market for the products of Bulgarian handicraft was great indeed, particularly because of deliveries to Turkish civil and military authorities. It was the loss of the latter that affected the economic conditions of Bulgarian artisans in the post-Liberation period. On the other hand, to regard that alleged "ruination" of Bulgarian handicraft as a precondition for industrial advance denotes a failure to understand the peculiar structural patterns of industrialization in backward areas.

[34] Slawtscho Zagoroff, "Die Grundesitzverhaeltnisse in Bulgarien," St. Moloff, ed., p. 90. Professor Dolinski, an eminent expert on problems of Bulgarian agriculture, gives an even lower figure of 3.6 per cent for land owned by farms with landholdings over and above seventy-five acres. N. V. Dolinski, "Strukturni promeni v búlgarskoto zemedelie" (Structural Changes in Bulgarian Agriculture), *Spisanie na Búlgarskoto Ikonomichesko Druzhestvo*, XXXVII, December 1938 (Sofia, 1939), 619.

[35] Anderson, p. 13; *Godishnik*, XXXI (1939), 73.

In an advanced country like England, where industrial transformation came largely as a modernization of the textile industry, the new factory had to break the competition of both the handicraft and the merchant-employer systems. But in more backward countries, entrepreneurs, banks, or governments preferred areas which as a rule had remained untouched by either handicraft or domestic industry. In this sense, the weakening of Bulgarian handicraft that did take place could only deflect the Bulgarian industry from the optimal path of its development. Uncritical application of English lessons is an enterprise involving much risk and uncertainty and yielding little profit. On the other hand, viewing the story of Bulgarian handicraft within a framework that is appropriate to the degree of backwardness of the country does make some — though probably minor — contribution toward explaining our problem of growth without structural change in Bulgaria.

From that parenthetical conclusion, one must return to Bulgarian agriculture in search of further illumination. The fact that the small farm retained its dominant position in Bulgarian agriculture cannot be readily taken as an indication that the supply of labor to industry was small or intermittent. However strong may be an otherwise very legitimate reticence to use the concept of "disguised unemployment," it seems to fit the Bulgarian conditions to a nicety. According to the excellent study of Pawel Egoroff, the total number of man-days actually worked in Bulgarian agriculture (in the narrow sense of the word), livestock raising, rose cultivation, fruit orchards, and vegetable gardens, amounted in 1930–34 to 355 million; but the number of *available* man-days on the basis of the gainfully employed population in Bulgarian agriculture in 1926 was about 564 million. Accordingly, about 37 percent of the country's agricultural population was redundant. In Egoroff's words: "Without disturbing the present course of the process of agricultural production and without any efforts to achieve a more rational utilization of labor on farms, at least 720,000 men whose labor now lies fallow on Bulgarian farms could be profitably employed in other occupations." [36] Egoroff assumes in his com-

[36] Pawel P. Egoroff, "Die Arbeit in der Landwirtschaft," St. Moloff, ed., pp. 151–153. The author adds that using 1934 (rather than 1926) population data would raise the number of redundant persons in agriculture above one million. On

putations a ten-hour working day and it is not quite clear what allowance, if any, he has made for the peaks of demand for labor during the harvesting season. Nor can one blandly assume that every "superfluous" laborer would have actually preferred casting aside the "disguise" and moving openly and lastingly into industrial employment. The small family farm in Bulgaria, as in other European countries, was much less efficient than a large estate in generating the *Landflucht* of its labor force. Still, when everything is said and done, the discrepancy between a figure of some 700,000 potential *Landfluechtlinge* and that of the 40,000 or so actually employed in Bulgarian modern industry is such that it is very difficult to accept the idea that labor shortage may have worked as a factor retarding the industrial development of the country.

This conclusion, however, should not be taken to mean that the specific character of the country's agriculture did not obstruct, let alone favor, industrialization. At least two connected considerations are relevant in this respect. The general backwardness of Bulgarian agriculture has been discussed in the foregoing pages. It should be added that the availability of land per capita of the population engaged in agriculture declined steadily from about 2.6 hectares in 1900 to less than 1.5 hectares in 1934; that the average size of farm by 1934 was below five hectares; that the holdings were not consolidated but lay (often widely dispersed) in strips of about .37 hectare on an average; that the yields per hectare of the major cereal crops remained almost unchanged between the beginning of the century and the 1930s; that when in the thirties it came at length to some expansion of industrial crops, that expansion was obtained primarily not at the expense of bread cereals (as would have been rational), but at the expense of fodder crops, thus reducing the basis for the output of converted products; that, finally, the income per unit of land began falling even before the outbreak of the Great Depression — in 1926 income per acre was almost 25 percent below what it had been in 1911–1915, and the decline continued thereafter. It is clear that

___

the other hand, that number should be reduced by taking into account the labor spent by the farm population outside agriculture. The original estimate of more than 700,000 persons whose contribution to the volume of agricultural output is nil may therefore remain unaltered.

an agriculture of that description not only (as shown before) was unable to serve as an efficient raw-material basis, but also could not exercise much demand pull upon the country's industrialization either with respect to consumers' goods or with respect to agricultural machinery, fertilizers, and conveyances.

Even more important is the second consideration. The economic disabilities of Bulgarian agriculture were conjoined with its political ability, exercised directly and indirectly, overtly and covertly, to deflect the government from the policy of supporting industrialization. This was the case during the three years after World War I (between March 1920 and June 1923) when the government was in the hands of radical populism in the person of Stamboliyski, the chief of the Agricultural Union. But it is no less true that no government in the country either before or after Stamboliyski could afford to pursue an economic policy that involved placing, for the sake of industrialization, major burdens upon the peasant population of the country. It was not merely the immediate economic interests of the peasantry, but their whole system of social values — the ethos of equality — that opposed itself to large-scale enterprise. One need only recall the violent attacks upon the first bill concerning encouragement of industry to get a measure of the intensity of the aversion from industry, and particularly from foreign capital. Geshov in his defense of the bill had to tread extremely carefully, pointing out that enterprises of associated artisans could also participate in the benefits of the law and, most of all, that the demand of the growing factories for agricultural raw materials was bound to raise prices of the products concerned.[37]

Given this situation, it was also natural for the government to try to encourage those industries which, at least in principle, could be defended as extensions of agricultural production. It is another matter that in practice the connection between those industries and agriculture was much more tenuous than was claimed in official pronouncements. The fact remains that the government was not a really free agent in determining the pattern of state-encouraged industry. Any overt discrimination in favor of strategically important industries was out of the question, and whatever there was by way of covert discrimination through various administrative actions had to

[37] *Dnevnitsi (Stenograficheski) na osmoto Narodno Súbranie*, pp. 637–643 (See n. 2 for translation).

favor industries that were said to be rooted in the soil of the country's peasant land. There is little doubt that those specific constraints upon government policy go a long way to explain the phenomenon of growth without structural change which has emerged as such an intriguing problem from a quantitative review of the period.

In the specific Bulgarian conditions, capital availabilities were the crucially scarce supply factor. The industries which would have brought about great structural changes within the body industrial were specifically those that were characterized by both high capital-output ratios and a relatively high threshold of initial capital requirements. Given the backwardness of the country's agriculture and the poverty of its population, voluntary savings could not be expected to provide the needed capital dispositions. It is true that some mercantile wealth had been accumulated even prior to the Liberation and continued growing after it. But the holders of that wealth were on the whole opposed to industrialization, as was shown by the strong reaction of some chambers of commerce against Geshov's policy.[38] All talk about processes of primitive or original accumulation of capital in Bulgaria could not alter the fact that such limited wealth as was available did not pass into the hands of industrial entrepreneurs. The task of a modern industrialization in Bulgaria could not be solved by methods peculiar to very advanced countries. If the story of industrial development in other backward countries can serve as "lessons" or at least as guiding beacons in understanding the industrial history of Bulgaria, the problem may be formulated as follows: the lack in a backward country of many things that could be reasonably regarded as "prerequisites" of industrial development in more advanced countries is an obvious fact. But it is just as obvious that in many important cases the lack of those prerequisites did not prevent the industrial development from taking place. For the prerequisites were not prerequisites in an absolute sense of the word. In other words, it proved possible to find substitutions for the missing factors, appropriately varying them with the degree of backwardness and a number of special conditions. As a result, as the observer moves from country to country, whole patterns of substitutions become discernible across the graduated scale of economic backwardness. The problem of Bulgarian industrialization, therefore, may be essentially stated as the

[38] Blagoev, *Ikonomichnoto razvitie na Búlgariya*, pp. 430f.

country's inability to discover patterns of substitutions suitable to its particular situation.

When previously accumulated wealth could not be passed on to industrial entrepreneurs for conversion into claims upon current national income so that factors of production could be lured away from consumer-goods industries into producer-goods industries, it was recourse to foreign loans, to credit-creating activities of specially organized banks, or to the budgetary mechanism of the state (or a combination in varying degrees of all three factors) that was used as a substitute. It is probably correct to say that the more backward a country was, the more likely it would have been to emphasize the role of the state as against that of investment banks. In the light of these generalizations, what the Bulgarian government did and what it failed to do for the industrialization of the country may be assumed to have been of fundamental importance.

Table 10. State aid to industry in 1912 in relation to capital stock
(1,000 leva)

| Industry | Capital (a) | State aid | | | |
		Through tariff duty and freight reductions (b)	Through tax reductions (c)	Total (d)	(d/a) 100
Mines	2,600	27	42	68	2.6
Metals	3,260	119	82	201	6.2
Pottery	7,600	25	166	191	2.5
Chemicals	4,000	345	88	433	10.8
Sugar	5,900	206	111	317	5.4
Beer	9,000	63	70	133	1.5
Textile	16,000	986	323	1,309	8.1
Woodworking	4,200	32	43	75	1.8
Leather	2,750	311	70	381	13.9
Flour mills	16,500	49	430	479	2.9
Other foodstuffs	5,200	10	30	40	0.8
Energy	6,500	—	28	28	.4
Total	85,610	2,209	1,501	3,710	4.3

Source: D. Kh. Dimov, "Kakvo e poluchila mestnata industriya prez 1912 god ot dúrzhavata i obshtestvennite uchrezhdeniya?" (How Much Did Domestic Industry Receive in 1912 from the State and other Institutions?), *Spisanie na Búlgarskoto Ikonomichesko Druzhestvo*, XVIII, nos. 9–10 (Sofia, 1914), 547.

The Bulgarian program of government encouragement to industry, as described in section one of this essay, taking its leaf from Rumanian and Hungarian statute books, was no doubt a very respectable attempt to deal with a very difficult problem. But the aid actually provided to industry was more notable for the multifariousness of the ways in which it was proffered than for its magnitude. A Bulgarian economist once computed the total value of state aid supplied under the pertinent act in 1912 and related it to the capital stock of the industries concerned. His results are shown in Table 10. The capital-stock data are admittedly uncertain; yet a very similar result obtains if the benefits received are related to the value of product of industrial enterprises. This is shown in Table 11. It is

Table 11. State aid to industry in relation to the value of product, 1912
(1,000 leva)

Industry	Value of product (a)	Total state aid (b)	(b/a) 100
Mines	1,667	68	4.1
Metals	3,399	201	5.9
Pottery	4,139	191	4.6
Chemicals	3,436	433	12.6
Sugar	3,149	317	10.0
Beer	5,429	133	2.4
Textile	22,767	1,390	5.7
Woodworking	1,292	75	5.8
Leather	6,235	381	6.1
Paper	772	56	7.2
Flour mills	49,226	479	1.0
Other foodstuffs	3.249	40	1.2
Energy	1,377	28	2.0
Total	106,137	3,711	3.5
Total without flour mills	56,911	3,232	5.7

Source: *Godishnik*, IV (1912), 187–188.

clear that the volume of state aid extended to Bulgarian industry was held within fairly modest limits. In particular, the benefits enjoyed by the industry producing and processing metals were small indeed.

It would exceed the scope of this essay to enter into a full discussion of the Bulgarian tariff policy. Suffice it to note that it took the country almost three decades before it could pass from the original restraints of Article 8 of the Berlin Treaty [39] via uniform *ad valorem* duties first of 8 and then of 14 percent to the right to produce specific import duties, which was finally obtained through the treaties of commerce concluded in 1905. Yet one would search the Bulgarian tariff in vain for any indication that its structure was influenced by the desire to achieve major changes within the sphere of protected industry. The contrary was true. Increased protection for the foodstuff, textile, and leather industries was paralleled by decreased protection for machinery production.[40] Thus the contribution of the Bulgarian state to the country's industrialization was modest, to say the least. The very considerable task of constructing, before the outbreak of the Balkan wars, a railroad network of almost 2,000 kilometers at the cost of more than a quarter of a billion leva,[41] and of acquiring a rolling stock worth some 36 million leva,[42] was accomplished by the government without utilizing the period of railroad construction for the specific promotion of industrial activities. The amount of foreign loans (in terms of net proceeds) received by the Bulgarian government over the same period exceeded the cost of railroad construction by about two and a half times.[43] The amounts actually used for industrial encouragement are quite trivial by comparison, as may be seen from another glance at Table 11. There is little doubt that concentration upon foreign and military policy effectively obstructed serious preoccupation with the industrial development of the country.

The sector of state-encouraged industry was not altogether unsuccessful in attracting foreign capital. Data which are available for the initial year of our index period show that, in 1909, fixed capital invested in those industrial branches amounted to 64.4 million leva.[44] If working capital is included, the total amount may be estimated at

[39] *Archives Diplomatiques*, p. 291.
[40] Walter Weiss-Bartenstein, *Bulgariens volkswirtschaftliche Verhaeltnisse* (Berlin, 1917), pp. 168–202; see esp. the table on p. 191.
[41] Popov, p. 376.
[42] *Ibid.*, p. 377.
[43] Leo Pazvolsky, *Bulgaria's Economic Position* (Washington, 1930), p. 36.
[44] *Godishnik*, II (1910).

about 72 million leva.[45] Of this amount, 14.6 million leva, or one fifth, was supplied from abroad. Belgian capital dominated the scene, amounting to 70 percent of foreign direct investment. Perhaps more important than the total magnitude of that investment is its distribution. In those years, Belgian capital and Belgian engineers were constructing public-utility plants over wide areas of eastern and southeastern Europe, and most of their investment in Bulgaria had been engaged in the production of electric energy. For the rest, it was the foodstuff industry and — at a much lower level — the textile industry which received most of the foreign capital.[46] Twelve years later, when the smoke of World War I began to clear away, it was the foodstuff-producing industries in which 73 percent of foreign direct investment (not including energy production) was placed.[47] Foreign capital's interest in the other branches of Bulgarian industry was either negligible or nonexistent. There is no indication that there was any significant change in this situation in the immediately following years. Foreign banks had appeared on the Bulgarian scene fairly early. In 1905–06 three important institutions were established by German, French, and Austrian banks, respectively. Among them, the Credit Bank, which stood under the leadership of the Disconto-Gesellschaft, may have seemed fairly promising for the country's industrial development. After World War I the establishment of the Sofia branch of the Deutsche Bank (1922) should be mentioned. Over the same period, there was undoubted growth in indigenous Bulgarian banking. Both foreign and domestic banks showed some interest in industrial enterprises, but the promise came to nought. Neither the one group nor the other betrayed any trace of the entrepreneurial vigor and financial broadmindedness which, for instance, the German banks had so conspicuously displayed in pre-1914 Italy. In particular, the traditional interest of the latter in new indus-

---

[45] According to N. Mikhailov, "Nasúrchavanata ot dúrzhavata industriya prez 1909" (See n. 5 above), p. 589, working capital amounted to about 12.7 percent of fixed capital. It may be noted, however, that Mikhailov's absolute figures do not quite check with those given in the text above.

[46] Godishnik, II (1910), 261.

[47] Luiven Georgiev, "Pronikvaneto na chuzhdiya finansov kapital v Búlgariya" (Penetration of Foreign Finance Capital into Bulgaria), Búlgarska Akademiya na Naukite, Ikonomicheska Misúl, I, no. 2 (Sofia, 1956), 120.

tries offering a wide field for technological change did not manifest itself in Bulgaria.

By way of summary of what has been said in the preceding pages and partly by way of amplification, one may try to state a few tentative answers to the question posed at the end of section one of this essay.

1. The poverty and economic backwardness of the country effectively precluded its industrial development upon the pattern of more advanced countries.

2. For this reason, the discussion of factors such as the process of the so-called original accumulation of capital in Bulgaria was hardly realistic.

3. In the specific Bulgarian conditions, such decline of handicraft as took place in the last quarter of the nineteenth century, instead of freeing the road for the factory system, may well have tended to deflect industrial endeavor from entering into the most promising channels.

4. Despite all predictions to the contrary, over the period under review the small-family-farm character of Bulgarian agriculture became even more pronounced. Being poor, stagnant, and inefficient, agriculture could serve neither as an adequate raw-material basis for industry nor as a source of effective and growing demand for industrial products, although, given the very low degree of utilization of labor on the farms, industry could rely on agriculture to satisfy its needs in manpower.

5. In such conditions the problem of capital supply and the problem of a sustained and growing demand for industrial products became the crucial problems in launching a great spurt of industrial development.

6. Banks, organized as "investment banks" and connected with corresponding institutions abroad, may well have participated through attracting foreign loans and through processes of credit creation in the provision of capital to Bulgarian industry. It was unlikely, however, that in conditions of extreme backwardness such as prevailed in Bulgaria they would have been able to raise the needed capital and, above all, to find investment opportunities that would prove profitable within a reasonable period of time.

7. It was the state, therefore, which should have shouldered the

twin task of covering the balance of capital needs and providing, for a number of years, the demand for the products of the new industries. On the other hand, because of the specific all-or-nothing (or, at least, all-or-much-less) nature of industrial spurts in backward countries, absence of sufficient state aid made the banks very reticent to do their part in industrial engagements.

8. It is very likely that the turn of the century was a most propitious moment for launching a policy of rapid industrialization on a considerable scale. Railroad building was still far from completed and the needs of railroad construction would have provided a widely ramified network of persistent demand for the products of the new industries. The capital markets abroad were plentifully supplied and the risk premiums astonishingly low. At the very same time, the German banks found the area of their activities in Germany curtailed by the growing independence of German industry and were ready to export their accumulated experience in promoting industrial enterprises to other areas.

9. The Bulgarian government let that opportunity pass unused. The curious combination of economic backwardness with a rather advanced system of constitutional government; the peasants' aversion to industry and capital, most notably to foreign capital; the ideology of militant nationalism amplified by the clamors of a violent irredenta in Macedonia and Thrace; greed, anxieties, the rivalries of governments and populace, as well as the ambition of a shrewd but irresponsible ruler to imitate and to reproduce within the confines of the peninsula the game of grand diplomacy; the pressures of similar motivations on the part of other Balkan nations — all these, in varying degrees, may have conspired to determine the actual political choices of the Bulgarian government. In the light of the record, those choices do not seem to have been particularly felicitous. A historical accident happened to place them within a sharp personal focus. It was a tragic fate that caused Geshov, once a great advocate and effective engineer of the country's economic development, to lay during his premiership the groundwork for the military attack upon the Turks in 1912; he felt, in his own words, "responsible to History for the conclusion of the Balkan Alliance." [48] But all this is somewhat beside the point. It

[48] Geshov, or Gueshoff in the accepted transliteration of the period, resigned, however, in May 1913 so as to dissociate himself from the "criminal insanity" of

is important to understand the decisions that have been taken against the background of foregone choices. There is, however, no intention to explain what the Bulgarians should have done. It is useful indeed to think of industrial development in terms of graduated patterns of substitution for "missing prerequisites." It is useful to delineate the contours of such a substitution that might plausibly have taken place in Bulgaria. Yet it is one thing to expect that, had a great spurt of industrial development occurred in Bulgaria, it would have in all likelihood proceeded under the strong tutelage of the state. It is quite another to assume that the great spurt was "bound" to occur. The case of Bulgarian industrialization should not only cast some additional light upon the concept of the great spurt; it may also serve as a salutary reminder of the very conditional nature of our insights into the processes of economic change.

Its illuminating aspects apart, the story of Bulgarian industrialization is not a happy one. Instead of bending upon a relatively brief concerted effort, the little country on the Danube preferred, like the great Danubian Monarchy in the words of its poet,

> auf halben Wegen und zu halber Tat,
> mit halben Mitteln zauderhaft zu streben.[49]

Thereby, Bulgarian statesmanship left the task of economic development to a much less favorable situation and to a regime which, unperturbed by such changes as may have taken place in technological determinants, was willing to do the job without counting the price or weighing the burden it imposed upon the people and without envisaging an end to the years of sacrifice and deprivation; as though desirous of illustrating Voltaire's melancholy conclusion that *tout vient trop tard.*[50]

---

the impending Bulgarian aggression against Serbia. See I. E. Gueshoff, *The Balkan League* (London, 1951), pp. 91, 94; also, I. E. Geshov, *Prestupnoto bezumie* (Criminal Insanity) (Sofia, 1914), p. 143.

[49] Franz Grillparzer, *Ein Bruderzwist in Habsburg*, Act II, lines 922–923.

[50] Voltaire, *Histoire de l'Empire de Russie sous Pierre le Grand* (London, 1830), p. 378.

9

Soviet Heavy Industry: A Dollar Index
of Output, 1927–1937

⁂

THE purpose of this essay is to communicate in summary form the results of an attempt to measure the growth of output in Soviet heavy industry.[1] The study has been conducted at Harvard in the years 1949–54 under the auspices of the RAND Corporation of Santa Monica, California. While the title chosen for this summary appeals to the author's ego, it is somewhat misleading. The underlying research did *not* cover the *whole* range of Soviet heavy industry. Most notably, production of heavy chemicals and of nonferrous metals has been entirely omitted. The investigation in its present form embraces the following five branches of industry: (1) machine building, (2) iron and steel, (3) petroleum, (4) coal, and (5) electric power.

Granted these limitations, it should be clear that the industries just mentioned, during the period under review, must have accounted for most of the heavy industrial output in Soviet Russia. It should be remembered in particular that the concept of machinery used here is comprehensive indeed. In addition to industrial machinery proper, it includes railroad rolling stock, automotive production, and agricultural and road-building machinery.

[1] I am indebted to Joseph A. Kershaw and Norman Kaplan for valuable comments and suggestions. I should like to thank Alexander Erlich, Nancy Nimitz, and Elizabeth Marbury for their participation in this project.

235

I

The initial motivation for the construction of a series of dollar indices of Soviet industrial output was provided by the grave shortcomings of the official Soviet index, which was weighted by the allegedly constant prices of the harvest year 1926/27. During the past decade, the deficiencies of that index have been widely discussed in Western literature.[2] The main trouble was with respect to commodities not produced in the base year 1926/27. In brief, the Soviet procedure was as follows: those commodities were introduced into the index at prices which prevailed during the first year of large-scale production. Since a considerable price inflation occurred during the period of the 1930s, this procedure of necessity imparted an upward bias to the index. As the share of "new" commodities in total industrial output grew, the bias of the index kept increasing. In this way, the index was affected both by past and current inflation and failed to satisfy the elementary requirement of any index of physical output, that is to say, imperviousness to changes in the value of money.

It might be added that Soviet writers themselves stressed the inadequacy of the index, although they took care not to state explicitly that the resulting bias was in an upward direction. As a rule, they argued that the direction of the bias was a moot question. In the mid-thirties, the Soviet government introduced some improvements, which, however, failed to alter the nature of the index in any radical way.[3]

The official Soviet yardstick of industrial growth was thus quite unreliable. At the same time, it was realized that the rapid development of Russian industry in the 1930s was of focal significance for the understanding of the Soviet economic history of the period and, furthermore, that any appraisal of present and future retardations — or accelerations, as the case may be — of Soviet industrial growth must be based almost inevitably on comparisons with the economic development in the 1930s. For these and other reasons, construction of inde-

[2] Among many others, the present writer commented on the problem in "The Soviet Indices of Industrial Production," *Review of Economics and Statistics*, XXIX (November 1947).

[3] For an account of this, see Alexander Gerschenkron, assisted by Alexander Erlich, *A Dollar Index of Soviet Machinery Output* (Santa Monica, 1951), pp. 1–12.

pendent gauges of Russian industrial growth over the period concerned appeared most desirable.

Such attempts have been undertaken and carried out by Naum Jasny and Donald R. Hodgman. Jasny constructed Soviet price indices by which he deflated computed values of industrial output at current prices. Hodgman's contribution was an index of Soviet industrial output, weighted by payroll data in the individual branches and subbranches of Soviet industry in 1934.[4]

The approach adopted in the present study follows a different method. The common feature of Jasny's and Hodgman's indices was the use of indigenous magnitudes for weights in the respective indices. In this study, on the other hand, U.S. dollar prices of the year 1939 were used. It is not necessary to examine in detail these two approaches. Suffice it to say that the advantage of a recomputation of Soviet industrial output in dollar prices is twofold. First, it makes it possible to cut the Gordian knot of the Soviet price system. The best that can be said for that price system is that it tends to reflect changes in average cost of production. For this reason, output indices weighted by Soviet prices seem to respond fairly well to certain pragmatic index-number tests involving changes in weighting base years.[5] Beyond this, however, the meaning of the price system is far from clear. Accordingly, an index based on Soviet weights must remain an uncertain proposition, at least to some degree. It is not suggested that the American prices of 1939 in each individual case are a faithful reflection of opportunity cost. Of course they are not. But there is little doubt that there is an immense difference between the two price systems in this respect.

The second advantage of computing Soviet output in terms of dollars is that it makes possible direct comparisons of Soviet and American outputs. But to mention the advantages is not in the least to disguise the very real shortcomings of a dollar index of Soviet output. The use of dollar weights means choosing a very remote

---

[4] N. Jasny, *The Soviet Economy During the Plan Era*; *The Soviet Price System*; *Soviet Prices of Producers' Goods* (Stanford, 1951 and 1952); Donald R. Hodgman, *Soviet Industrial Production, 1928–1951* (Cambridge, Mass., 1954).

[5] See G. Grossman, "National Income," and "Comments" by Alexander Gerschenkron in *Soviet Economic Growth*, ed. A. Bergson (Evanston, 1953), pp. 6–9, 23–24.

vantage point from which to view Soviet industrial developments. Something more will be said on the subject in the concluding section of this essay. All that need be mentioned at this point is that the results of the present study are not directly comparable, let alone interchangeable, with those obtained by either Jasny or Hodgman.

At the same time, it may be noted that the remoteness of the vantage point is at least to some extent compensated for by the availability of statistics in the United States. Whatever extraneous weighting system is chosen, ideally it should be from a country as similar as possible to Russia in its stage of economic development and one with a comparable range of measurable output. The choice of the dollar system fully satisfies the second requirement, but it does so at the expense of the first.

It is very likely that experimentation with other price systems might lead to more meaningful results. For example, expressing Soviet output in Japanese prices would seem very promising. Furthermore, by shedding light on the significance of the index-number problem in different historical industrializations, such experiments would contribute to better understanding of the measurement problem in economic development and thereby to better understanding of economic development itself. Be that as it may, the highly relative character of the present investigation must be clearly understood.

II

In principle, the way in which the present index has been prepared is exceedingly simple. For each of the five industries concerned, the first task was to obtain as complete a breakdown as possible of data on physical quantities of output for the years 1927–37. In practice, this was not simple at all. Because of the fragmentary nature of Soviet information and its tendency to decline in volume after the mid-thirties, the tabulations showed many gaps. All these gaps had to be eliminated by a series of extrapolations and interpolations. The methods used in this respect varied from case to case. Sometimes the rate of growth in the preceding years was applied; sometimes the rate of growth of related and, if possible, complementary commodities was selected. Wherever feasible, general information on output of the commodities concerned was utilized. In this fashion, complete quantitative tabulations for all the years of the decade were obtained.

The next task consisted in ascertaining the appropriate American price prevailing in 1939 for each item in these tabulations. Clearly, to obtain such a price it was necessary first to match the individual Soviet product with an identical or similar American product. This done, the U.S. 1939 price of the Soviet product was estimated, taking account of such differences as existed between the two products. Here lay the real core of the study. Neither the matching process nor the price determination could have been carried out without extensive recourse to those members of the American business community who had acquired an extensive knowledge of the relevant Soviet products either through their business activities or their personal experience (as experts, technical assistants, and so on). Wherever possible, the consultants were given the specifications or even photographic reproductions of the Soviet models. Even so, the matching process presented considerable difficulties, which were greatest in the field of machinery.

The foregoing, however, is a somewhat idealized picture of the process. In a number of cases, the consultants were unable to provide the price information, and the computed unit values of the 1939 *U.S. Census of Manufactures* had to be used instead, an obviously crude and unreliable procedure. Nevertheless, it is fair to say that the vast majority of prices was determined through the consultation process. It is only with regard to electric power that prices obtained from the *Census* prevailed. All prices arrived at by consultation were estimates of the 1939 dealer's cash price f.o.b. factory and thus conceptually comparable with unit values derived from the *Census*.

In the case of machinery, it proved impossible either through consultation or recourse to the *Census* to assign prices to all the items for which data on physical quantities were available. Out of a total of 315 commodities, for which data on quantity of output were on hand at least for some portions of the index period, only 128 items could be priced. For the remaining 187 items, available specifications were insufficient for price assignments. In many cases the matching process also involved considerable readjustments of the original physical data. Thus, where such data were given in terms of units of output but a meaningful price could not be stated except in terms of power capacity, some method for the conversion of the original data had to be devised. In many instances, the ratio of horsepower per unit was given for only a few years of the period, and the ratios for the remaining years had to be interpolated or extrapolated. If a justifiable conversion method could not be found, the commodity had to be omitted from the index.[6]

All this means that the index of machinery output does not comprise all the subgroups of this branch of Soviet heavy industry, and this raises a problem in aggregating the individual indices. Some adjustments for differential rates of growth in the omitted subgroups will be mentioned later. At present, it is important to point out that *no* similar problem of coverage existed for the remaining four industries. The output of *all* (or virtually all) the products of these was obtained and valued in dollars. This is not to say, of course, that no problems were encountered in the work on the four industries other than machinery. Many gaps of information had to be filled by estimates of various kinds. As was also true of many machinery items, there were numerous cases of conflicting information that had to be reconciled. Considerable difficulties were encountered in the matching process for coal, iron and steel, and petroleum products. In all such instances, the official Soviet standards were used for the basic identification of the individual products. Consultations with displaced persons who had served in one or another of the Soviet industries concerned were necessary in order to obtain some immediate impression of the degree of likely deviations between the standards and the actual products. As was true for machinery, expert advice on prices was of crucial importance. Thus, for petroleum products, the American prices selected were based on the *Oil Price Handbook*[7] and referred to the major American export market, the Gulf Coast market; but without the aid of expert information it would have been impossible to adjust these prices to allow for the differences in quality between the American and the Soviet products. And least of all would it have been possible to establish a reasonable price for those

---

[6] For a more complete description, see Gerschenkron, *A Dollar Index of Soviet Machinery Output.*

[7] National Petroleum Publishing Company, *Oil Price Handbook for 1939* (Cleveland, 1940).

Soviet products for which comparable American products could not be located.

It is not within the scope of this essay to do more than indicate the general nature of the problems that had to be faced. For remarks on certain specific aspects, such as the effects of the basing-point system on pricing Soviet steel products or the effect of regional variation in American coal prices on selecting the "correct" dollar price for Soviet coal, the interested reader must consult the individual studies. He will also find there full discussion of the innumerable minute problems of estimation and selection which so often had to be resolved by arbitrary decisions. It was felt that, in a field where the basic data are scarce and unreliable and so many adjustments are necessary for obtaining a set of consistent figures, the reader must be given full opportunity to check every step and to form his own opinion as to the worth and validity of the results. Accordingly, in each of the five studies, it is the detailed appendices that constitute the heart of the inquiry. In a sense, the text, containing the results and the general conclusions, is appended to the mass of detailed tabulation and comment in the appendices rather than the other way round.[8]

III

The dollar values of output yielded by the five studies are presented in Table 1. The corresponding indices are shown in Table 2.

The problem of aggregating the foregoing tabulations is not an easy one. The trouble with simply adding up the rows in Table 1 is twofold: first, as mentioned before, the dollar value of the machinery output refers only to a portion of total machinery output. Thus a simple addition gives too low a weight to that branch of Soviet heavy industry. An even more serious difficulty stems from the fact that the data in Table 1 are based on gross values of output, corres-

[8] In addition to the previously cited study on machinery output, the references are as follows: Alexander Gerschenkron and Nancy Nimitz, *A Dollar Index of Soviet Petroleum Output* (Santa Monica, 1952); Nancy Nimitz (under the supervision of Alexander Gerschenkron), *A Dollar Index of Soviet Coal Output* (Santa Monica, 1953); Alexander Gerschenkron and Nancy Nimitz, *A Dollar Index of Soviet Iron and Steel Output* (Santa Monica, 1953); Alexander Gerschenkron, assisted by Elizabeth Marbury, *A Dollar Index of Soviet Electrical Power Output* (Santa Monica, 1954).

Table 1. Value of Soviet output, 1927/28–1937
(in millions of U.S. dollars at 1939 prices)

Year	Machinery	Iron and steel	Coal	Petroleum products	Electric power
1927/28	203	184	87	119	69
1928/29	288	218	100	145	85
1929/30	427	263	119	199	111
1931	532	268	141	247	137
1932	535	308	161	237	171
1933	603	353	188	251	207
1934	734	489	230	290	259
1935	926	632	264	301	316
1936	993	822	302	336	395
1937	1065	869	304	355	441

Table 2. Indices of value of Soviet output, 1927/28–1937
(weighted by U.S. dollars at 1939 prices; 1927/28 = 100)

Year	Machinery	Iron and steel	Coal	Petroleum products	Electric power
1927/28	100	100	100	100	100
1928/29	142	118	115	122	123
1929/30	211	143	137	167	160
1931	263	146	162	207	197
1932	264	167	185	200	246
1933	298	192	216	211	298
1934	361	266	264	244	374
1935	457	343	303	253	456
1936	490	447	347	282	569
1937	525	472	349	298	635

ponding in a general way to the "value of products" in American *Census* statistics. Each figure is the sum of the products of quantity and price. These values of output include, therefore, the value of raw materials, semifabricates, power, and fuel consumed as well as produced by the branch of industry for which the computations have been made. What is needed ideally is the reduction of the gross values to value added by manufacturing of the products concerned.

Some adjustments have been made to take account of the two difficulties just described, but they are so rough and incomplete that the reader may prefer the unadjusted results. They are given below.

Let us first see how far it is possible to move in the direction of value added.

In an earlier study of Soviet machinery output, a set of value-added data at 1939 dollars was obtained by applying to the gross value figures for each individual item the ratio of value added to gross value as given for the commodity group to which the item belonged in the 1939 *U.S. Census of Manufactures.*[9] It is clear that such a procedure involved rather drastic assumptions. This is not simply because of the implied acceptance of American ratios of value-added components to the other components of gross value. Such an acceptance is quite consistent with, and in fact derives from, the basic decision to use American prices as weights in an index of Soviet output. What renders application of American ratios so questionable are rather the great differences in the respective structures (such as differences in the degree of vertical integration) of the American and the Russian industries. What appears as value added in a given American industry need not appear as such in its Russian counterpart, and vice versa. Still it might have been useful to pursue this method throughout the five industries under review if practical difficulties had not stood in the way. Unfortunately, when it comes to branches of industry other than machinery, the U.S. *Census* provides either an inadequate number of subgroups or only *one* over-all ratio for the industry as a whole rather than for the individual products or subgroups of products. Obviously, application of such an over-all ratio, say for the petroleum industry, cannot change the index for that particular industry, although it would affect the aggregate index. In addition, differences in the *composition* of output in any given industry (as distinguished from subgroups) in the United States and Russia make the application of such an over-all ratio altogether too crude a device.

It might be possible to estimate and to apply Soviet rates of value added to gross value in the individual industries concerned, but clearly the introduction of Soviet weights into a study the very purpose of which is to break away from Soviet valuations could not be considered.

For these reasons, a different method has been adopted here for aggregating the five indices. It consists essentially of an attempt to

[9] See Gerschenkron, *A Dollar Index of Soviet Machinery Output*, table 38, pp. 80–84.

eliminate some of the double counting which results from the fact that products of one industry (such as steel) are used as inputs in the production process of another industry (such as machinery).

The adjustments made can be summarized as follows:

1. The dollar value of coal consumed by the steel industry in the form of coke has been deducted from the gross dollar value of the iron and steel output.

2. The dollar value of steel products and foundry iron consumed by the machinery industry has been deducted from the gross dollar value of machinery output.

3. The gross dollar value of output of four industries (machinery, iron and steel, coal, and petroleum) has been diminished by the aggregate value of electric power consumed by these industries. It may be added that the amount deducted was somewhat excessive because the available data on power consumption referred to the metalworking industry as a whole rather than to the machinery industry proper. Since the latter is a huge segment of the former and undoubtedly consumes much more power per dollar of output, the error involved must be assumed to be small.

No similar adjustments could be made for the values of coal and petroleum consumed by the other industries, nor for the value of steel consumed by industries other than machinery. At the same time, it is believed that the amount of double counting within each industry is confined within rather narrow limits. The error stemming from that particular source cannot be very large within the machinery group. The 128 items of that group, for which the dollar value of output has been computed, are essentially in the nature of finished goods. Therefore, hardly any of these commodities enters the value of output of any other commodity within the group. Since what was valued in the other industries was likewise the final product, and since the values of crude oil, conversion iron, and raw steel were excluded from the computations, the error of double counting is unlikely to be very large in those industries.

It cannot, of course, be claimed that these adjustments have resulted in an unambiguous concept of net value. Only the most obvious cases of double counting have been eliminated. But *pro tanto* some approximation to net values has been attained. Nor have the deductions been quantitatively insignificant. In the case of machinery, the more than one quarter of gross value eliminated may amount to as much as 50 percent of what ideally should be deducted. It is true that some further adjustments may have been possible. But they would have introduced still greater uncertainties and might well have detracted from, rather than added to, the reliability and meaningfulness of the results.

As mentioned before, another problem to be faced in the aggregation process derived from the incompleteness of the coverage of machinery output. Giving too low a weight to machinery output in turn would have imparted a downward bias to the series as a whole, first, because the computed output of the machinery group developed at a relatively high rate and, second, because the output of machinery items not included in the computed output must be presumed to have developed at a faster rate than the output of the computed group. Taking into account *inter alia* the estimated value of electric-power equipment (which had been computed indirectly and was not included in the total of the computed machinery output [10]) as well as crude estimates of the aggregate dollar value of output of about one hundred of those machinery items also excluded from the computed series, it seemed reasonable to assume that in 1928/29 the computed machinery output comprised 75 percent of total machinery output and that by 1937 this ratio had fallen to 65 percent.[11]

It will be noticed that the first of the years just mentioned is 1928/29 rather than 1927/28, the first year of the dollar-index period. This change is unfortunate, but it was unavoidable because the material needed for adjustment purposes, in particular the data on steel consumption by the machinery industry, was not available for the years preceding 1928/29.

The results of the aggregation process are given in Tables 3–8. They are in three stages: (1) summation of unadjusted output values, (2) summation of output values adjusted for the incomplete coverage of machinery output, and (3) summation of output values adjusted

---

[10] Gerschenkron, *A Dollar Index of Machinery Output*, appendix 9.

[11] Accordingly, the unadjusted values of machinery output for 1928/29 were divided by 75 and multiplied by 100; the unadjusted values for 1937 were divided by 65 and multiplied by 100.

Table 3. Dollar value of output of Soviet heavy industry, 1928/29 and 1937
(unadjusted gross values, millions of 1939 dollars)

Year	Machinery	Iron and steel	Coal	Petroleum products	Electric power	Total
1928/29	288	218	100	145	85	836
1937	1065	869	304	355	441	3034

Table 4. Index of dollar value of output of Soviet heavy industry, 1928/29 and 1937
(based on unadjusted gross values, millions of 1939 dollars)

Year	Machinery	Iron and steel	Coal	Petroleum products	Electric power	Total
1928/29	100	100	100	100	100	100
1937	370	399	304	245	519	363

Table 5. Dollar value of output of Soviet heavy industry, 1928/29 and 1937
(gross values adjusted for incomplete coverage of machinery output, millions of
1939 dollars)

Year	Machinery	Iron and steel	Coal	Petroleum products	Electric power	Total
1928/29	384	218	100	145	85	932
1937	1638	869	304	355	441	3607

Table 6. Index of dollar value of output of Soviet heavy industry, 1928/29 and 1937
(based on gross values adjusted for incomplete coverage of machinery output, millions
of 1939 dollars)

Year	Machinery	Iron and steel	Coal	Petroleum products	Electric power	Total
1928/29	100	100	100	100	100	100
1937	428	399	304	245	519	387

Table 7. Dollar value of output of Soviet heavy industry, 1928/29 and 1937
(gross values adjusted as in Table 5 and for double-counting, millions of 1939 dollars)

Year	Machinery	Iron and steel	Coal	Petroleum products	Electric power	Total
1928/29	286	197	95	142	85	803
1937	1138	768	283	345	441	2975

Note: for the computations on which this table is based, see *A Dollar Index of Soviet Iron and Steel Output*, appendix 11, and *A Dollar Index of Soviet Electric Power Output*.

Table 8. Index of dollar value of output of Soviet heavy industry, 1928/29 and 1937 (based on gross values adjusted as in Table 5 and for double counting, millions of 1939 dollars)

Year	Machinery	Iron and steel	Coal	Petroleum products	Electric power	Total
1928/29	100	100	100	100	100	100
1937	398	389	298	243	519	370

Note: for the computations on which this table is based, see *A Dollar Index of Soviet Iron and Steel Output*, appendix 11, and *A Dollar Index of Soviet Electric Power Output*.

both for the incomplete coverage of machinery output and double counting as described in the preceding paragraphs.

The annual average rates of growth which are implied in Tables 7 and 8 are shown in Table 9.

Table 9. Average annual rates of growth in Soviet heavy industry, 1928/29 to 1937

Machinery	Iron and steel	Coal	Petroleum products	Electric power	Total
18.9	18.5	14.6	11.7	22.8	17.8

The rate of growth of total heavy industry output based on unadjusted figures (Tables 3 and 4) amounted to 17.5 percent; the rate of growth of total heavy industry output based on partially adjusted figures (Tables 5 and 6) amounted to 18.4 percent. Thus the adjustments do not radically affect the order of magnitude of the rate of growth. This is so partly because the two adjustments tend to offset each other. As far as it goes, this is a comforting result from the point of view of an index study based on gross values of output.

IV

The five industries discussed stood at the very center of the Soviet industrialization effort to the relative neglect of all or nearly all other branches of the Soviet economy. Consumer-goods industries, agriculture, railroads, housing — all were the stepchildren of Soviet economic policies. Their output at best was maintained and allowed to grow only to an extent compatible with, or required by, the interests of the favorite children. Even so, few would deny that an annual average rate of growth of nearly 18 percent sustained over a period of nine years must be considered very high indeed. This seems to be the first conclusion that emerges from the aggregation of the five indices.

On the other hand, it would seem equally clear that the official Soviet index grossly exaggerated the course of actual attainments. It is true that comparisons are not easy. Values of output in rubles for the terminal year of the index period (1937) are scarce. Still, with a good deal of estimation, it has been possible to obtain roughly comparable figures for three of the five industries studied: machinery, iron and steel, and electric power. The results of the comparison are summarized in Tables 10, 11, and 12.

Table 10. Output of machinery, iron and steel, and electric power, 1928/29 and 1937
(in millions of 1926/27 rubles)

Year	Machinery	Iron and steel	Electric power	Total
1928/29	2,412	901	243	3,556
1937	25,473	3,750	1,800	31,023

Note: Machinery. Data on output in 1928/29 and 1937 at 1926/27 ruble prices are available for large-scale industry only. In order to obtain data for "all industry" the figure for the earlier year (2,193 million rubles) has been increased by 10 percent, and the figure for the later year (24,260 million rubles) has been increased by 5 percent.
Power. The 1928/29 figure for the value of output at 1926/27 rubles has been obtained by adding 25 percent of the figure for 1928 (181 million rubles) to 75 percent of the figure for 1929 (263 million rubles); the 1937 figure for the value of output at 1926/27 rubles has been interpolated between the values of output in 1936 (1,485.3 million rubles) and 1938 (2,262 million rubles).
Steel. The figure for the value of output in 1937 at 1926/27 rubles has been interpolated between the values of output in 1936 (3,482 million rubles) and 1938 (4,023 million rubles).

Table 11. Output of machinery, iron and steel, and electric power, 1928/29 and 1937
(in millions of 1939 dollars)

Year	Machinery	Iron and steel	Electric power	Total
1928/29	286	197	85	568
1937	1,138	768	441	2,347

Table 12. Dollar and ruble indices of output of machinery, iron, steel, and electric power, 1928/29 and 1937
(weighted with 1926/27 rubles (R) and 1939 dollars ($))

Year	Machinery		Iron and steel		Electric power		Total	
	R	$	R	$	R	$	R	$
1928/29	100	100	100	100	100	100	100	100
1937	1056	398	416	389	740	519	872	413

The corresponding dollar figures as extracted from Table 7 above are given in Table 11. Put in index form, the two preceding tables (10 and 11) are compared in Table 12. A comparison of the rates of growth implied in Table 12 follows in Table 13.

Table 13. Average annual rates of growth of output of machinery, iron and steel, and electric power, Soviet index and dollar index, 1928/29 to 1937

Index	Machinery	Iron and steel	Electric Power	Total
Soviet	34.0	19.5	28.5	31.0
Dollar	18.9	18.5	22.8	19.0

The differences are striking indeed. Over a period of just nine years, the Soviet index has reached a point more than twice as high as that shown by the dollar index (Table 12). The crux, of course, is the evaluation of machinery output. The share of machinery output in the total output of the three industries is altogether different in the two computations. In 1937, the value of machinery output in rubles constituted 82 percent of the three-industry total. The corresponding figure for the dollar values is 48 percent. The exorbitant weight of machinery in the Soviet index is primarily responsible for the rate of growth of 31 percent per year shown by that index. Since it was in the machinery industry that the "new" commodities were concentrated, this stupendous rate of growth must be regarded essentially as the result of price inflation, which was allowed to affect large portions of the index.

The comparison of the two indices, however, must not be pushed too far. With regard to such a comparison — and far beyond it — no useful purpose can be served in disregarding the index-number problem implicit in the use of varying weights. Up to a point, the index-number problem is not dissimilar to problems encountered in descriptive geometry. In either case, the attempt is to define an object by its projection; in either case, the result varies with the direction of the projection or the position of the observer. What is seen as a square in one perspective appears as a triangle in another. Index numbers of output are essentially projections of changes in physical quantities against the screens of weights. Beyond this, however, the geometric analogy fails. Unlike the case in geometry, the individual projections cannot be meaningfully combined to reveal the "true" shape of the object of study. Nor can we walk around the pyramid of output and measure its base and sides directly. This is so because the *aggregation* of output has no independent existence except in terms of the *individual* projections. Moreover, we are not even free to erect our own screens wherever we please. We must take them as we find them, even though we may be able to choose among those we find.

Translated into more concrete terms and applied to the problem at hand, this means that in using American prices as weights a specific basic question is raised. Assuming constant cost in the sense that differences in the size of output of individual commodities as between Russia and the United States would not have affected the structure of relative prices in the United States, what would have been the aggregate value of output in five important branches of Soviet heavy industry if the commodities concerned had been produced not in Russia but in the United States in 1939? What has been called in the preceding pages "value of Soviet output in U.S. dollars of 1939 purchasing power" is an answer to that specific question and must be judged solely in its terms.

But what is the presumable effect of projecting the output of a relatively backward country across a continent and an ocean upon a screen erected in the economically most advanced country in the world? To repeat briefly what has been said at some length elsewhere,[12] the effect is likely to be a rate of growth *lower* than that resulting from the use of indigenous weights of the backward country. Industrialization may be defined as a process of changing scarcity relations. The quantity of highly fabricated goods is likely to increase

[12] Gerschenkron, *A Dollar Index of Soviet Machinery Output.*

2 5 0

more rapidly than that of goods of low fabrication, and the former tend continually to become cheaper in terms of the latter. This implies that, in using the weights of a less advanced country, a relatively high weight is imputed to the more rapidly expanding component of total output. Conversely, using the weights of a more advanced country means imputing a relatively low weight to the more rapidly expanding component of total output.

An attempt was made in the study on machinery output to test this hypothesis by gauging the effect of varying weights in U.S. machinery output over a considerable period of time. This was done on the assumption that the spatial aspect of the index-number problem was akin to its temporal aspect. The result of pricing selected portions of the American machinery output alternatively at prices of the years 1899 and 1939, 1899 and 1923, 1909 and 1939, and 1909 and 1923 revealed a very consistent pattern: at all times the *higher* rates of growth were associated with the use of weights pertaining to *earlier* periods of industrialization. In addition, the magnitude of the differentials was surprisingly high. Thus, the index of output in 1923 of American machinery (selected items) weighted by prices of 1909 was no less than 2.3 times higher than the index of output of the same items weighted by prices of 1923. The corresponding figure for the years 1899 and 1923 was 3.6. The comparison of 1909 and 1939 yielded a coefficient of 3.8. Finally, when American machinery output in 1899 and 1939 — the forty-year period — was alternatively weighted by prices of the two years, the index weighted by prices of 1899 stood in 1939 at a point 7.8 times higher than the index over the same period weighted by prices of 1939.

The size of these differentials makes it quite impossible to shrug off the index-number problem as is so often done. It must be assumed that to some extent the differences between the official Soviet index and the dollar index are due in part to a choice of weights that reflect very different stages of economic development in the two countries and not simply to the upward bias inherent in the Soviet index. If we assume a continuous development, the size of the differentials due to varying weights is a function of both the length of the index period and the rate of growth achieved during its course. Although a period of nine years is relatively short, the high rates of growth during

251

those years must have led to a considerable discrepancy between the two indices.

On the other hand, however, it must be mentioned that the actual seat of such differentials in periods of modern industrialization tends to be confined to the machinery industry in the broad sense of the word. Scott's study showed that in the United States temporal changes in weighting systems did not at all affect indices of output of a wide range of industrial consumer goods (other than automobiles).[13] Perhaps more important in the present connection is the fact that a similar study undertaken for the indices of petroleum products in the United States over the period 1899 to 1939 (and three subperiods) revealed but trifling differentials resulting from the use of varying weights.[14] The introduction of the cracking process radically changed the composition of the industry's output, and yet the use of different weights did not affect the index in any perceptible way. It is not likely that coal, iron and steel, or electric-power indices would react violently to changes in weights. The conclusion we may draw is that such index-number effect as is undoubtedly present in the dollar index of Soviet heavy industry is essentially confined to its machinery component and must appear rather diffused in the aggregation of the five indices.

This, however, is far from being an unambiguous answer. It is impossible to state clearly to what extent the differences between the Soviet and the dollar indices are due to the inadequacies of Russian statistical methods and to what extent they are due to disparate weights. It would seem more useful to consider the dollar index as something *sui generis*, as one special way of measuring Soviet output. Even when so regarded, the dollar index has obvious shortcomings. The number of arbitrary decisions and of estimates of widely varying degrees of reliability is undoubtedly considerable. The choice of prices has not always been a happy one. No one can realize these deficiencies better than the writer himself, and the reader of the underlying studies will find them unconcealed.

But, at the same time, the merits of the dollar index ought not to be overlooked. The distinguishing characteristic of the dollar index

[13] Ira O. Scott, Jr., "The Gerschenkron Hypothesis of Index Number Bias," *Review of Economics and Statistics*, XXXIV (November 1952), 386–387.
[14] See *A Dollar Index of Soviet Petroleum Output*.

is that a serious and sustained effort has been made to obtain appropriate dollar prices for a long list of machinery items and for all — or nearly all — the products of the four other industries and that painstaking adjustments have been made in order to match the Soviet product with its American counterpart. While there is nothing sensational about the methods used, the formidable amount of detailed work that went into the preparation of the index may justify some claim to novelty. And it may be added that the mass of specific information assembled may prove usable for purposes other than the one directly pursued. In particular, these materials are likely to be, and to some extent already have been, of some service in comparative studies of the productivity of Soviet labor. The comprehensive tabulations of output in physical terms are likely to stand on their own feet in any case.

Finally, the work on the dollar index may provide some stimulus to research transcending the narrow field of the Soviet economy, particularly for the much neglected empirical study of the index-number problem. What is needed is a better understanding of the behavior of output indices in different historical situations. It may throw light on some important problems of economic development: the changes in relative price structure, the type and role of the dominant industry at various stages of economic progress, and particularly the time-space relationship, that is, the relationship between the economic process over time in one area and the economic *situation* at a given moment in different areas. The bland assumption made about this problem in the foregoing pages and in the underlying studies can bear further investigation. The assumed affinity between the temporal and spatial aspects of the index-number problem implies that backward countries follow in their development the course charted by the more advanced countries. This is only a half truth at best. It is but halfheartedly asserted here because it is certainly at variance with this writer's general approach to modern industrial history where attention is focused upon diversity rather than similarities in the processes of economic development in individual countries. Thus, further study of the index-number problem may prove to be of considerable importance for a better grasp of the problem of industrialization under diverse conditions and at varying levels of economic backwardness.

2 5 3

10

Notes on the Rate of Industrial Growth in Soviet Russia

⚹

THE speed at which industrial output increases is an essential characteristic in the process of industrialization because it appears to be correlated — positively or negatively, as the case may be — with a number of other important economic elements of that process. It offers a natural avenue of approach to the understanding of Soviet economic history. It is obvious, furthermore, that the rate of industrial growth in Soviet Russia is, at the same time, a burning political problem. Within and without the country, it is presented not only as a measure of Soviet economic attainments, but also as a gauge of the Soviet power position in a bipolar world.[1] It should be in order therefore to review briefly the relevant statistical data and the main accelerating and decelerating factors whose play and interplay has determined the rate of industrial growth in the past and is likely to continue to do so in the future.

I

Table 1 shows the index of industrial output between 1928 and 1960 as given in recent Soviet statistics. The rates of growth implied

---

[1] It is another matter that after the Twenty-second Congress of the Communist Party in Moscow (1961) the transformation of a bipolar world into a "tripolar" world begins to look like a practical possibility. The reference, of course, is *not* to the so-called uncommitted nations.

Table 1. An official index of Soviet industrial output, 1928–1960

Year	All industry	Producers' goods	Consumers' goods
1928	84	76	88
1929	100	100	100
1932	169	212	136
1937	353	507	272
1939	483	677	338
1940	539	777	363
1946	413	641	244
1947	503	783	296
1948	634	1,010	358
1949	761	1,265	388
1950	934	1,592	447
1951	1,087	1,857	519
1952	1,213	2,083	573
1953	1,356	2,323	644
1954	1,537	2,639	727
1955	1,727	3,027	787
1956	1,910	3,369	861
1957	2,101	3,739	931
1958	2,317	4,166	1,006
1959	2,582	4,675	1,105
1960	2,848	5,150	1,168

Source: *Narodnoye khozyaystvo SSSR v 1960 godu, Statisticheskii yezhegodnik* (The Economy of the USSR, A Statistical Yearbook) (Moscow, 1961), p. 219. Base year changed to 1929.

in Table 1 are shown in Table 2 for four significant subperiods of the time span 1928–1960.

Table 2. Average annual rates of growth of Soviet industrial output, 1928–1960

Period	All industry	Producers' goods	Consumers' goods
1928–1940	18.41	23.53	13.76
1946–1950	22.61	25.49	16.31
1950–1955	13.06	13.19	11.97
1955–1960	10.52	11.72	8.22

Note: the rates have been computed from data in Table 1 on the assumption of an even geometric growth between the initial and terminal years of the periods concerned.

The figures in Table 2 seem to tell a clear and simple story: the war years apart, 1950 appears to have been the great dividing line, marking the beginning of a very considerable slowing down in the speed of Soviet industrialization. This conclusion may seem obvious, but it must not be drawn. For, as has often been explained,[2] the official Soviet index of industrial output before 1951 contained a strong upward bias, because a large and steadily growing part of that output was valued not at allegedly "constant 1926–27 prices," but at the inappropriately high current prices. It is true, of course, that any rapid economic change, involving aggregations, creates difficult problems of measurement. But in Russia those difficulties were compounded by the stubborn use — and shameless exploitation for propaganda purposes — of an altogether untrue yardstick. It was only in 1951, almost a quarter of a century after its initiation, that the index was finally abandoned. Even then its fatal shortcomings remained unadmitted in Soviet Russia, except for an uncommented-upon small downward adjustment of the index for the thirties. The index number for 1939 (with 1929 equal to 100) used to stand at 552;[3] now, as can be seen from Table 1, it has been reduced to 483, which implies a diminution in the claimed average annual rate of growth for the period by about 1.5 percent.[4]

The new official index was uniformly based on prices which were in effect on January 1, 1952, and were wholesale prices, f.o.b. factory and net of turnover tax. The exclusion from the prices of the tax, imposed on consumers' goods, was natural because otherwise the weight of those goods in total output would have been greatly increased. This in turn would have caused a relative understatement of the rate of growth in the years to come. At the same time, quite reasonable provisions were made for valuation and subsequent readjustment of new commodities for which no 1952 prices were available, as well as for new shifts of the weighting year to be carried out at later

[2] See Chapter 9 of this volume.

[3] See, for example, Malenkov's speech at the Nineteenth Congress: G. M. Malenkov, "Otchetny Doklad XIX s'ezdu Partii o rabote Tsentral'nogo Komiteta VKP (b)" (Report to the Nineteenth Party Congress Concerning the Work of the Central Committee of the All-Union Communist Party), Bol'shevik no. 19 (October 1952), p. 6.

[4] The change was carried out sometime in the second half of the 1950s. See Promyshlennost' SSSR, Statisticheskii sbornik (The Industry of the USSR, Collected Statistics) (Moscow, 1957), p. 9.

dates.[5] In fact, after the index was based on the 1952 prices during the years 1951–1955, it was again revised, the prices of July 1, 1955, being used as weights for the years 1956 to date.[6]

There is little doubt that the new index is a great improvement. It is free from the hybrid elements which had vitiated its predecessor. To be sure, many a problem still remains. There is the perennial question as to the meaningfulness of the Soviet price system and consequently of any measure that is built upon it.[7] No fully satisfactory answer to that question is possible. But it may be said that it is the Soviet index itself and the broadly predictable way in which it reacts to changes in weights that offers some assurance: the index does seem to reflect the specific changes in scarcity relations which are engendered by industrialization.

On the other hand, it must be said that the new index does not respond much better than did the old one to certain tests of internal consistency. The Soviet statistics now provide data on the share of producers' goods and consumers' goods in total output. It is interesting to confront those data with the shares of the two groups as they can be calculated from the index data in Table 1 by constructing an equation with two unknowns.[8] This is done in Table 3 for a number of selected years.

Except for 1940, the discrepancies are considerable and, if anything, they are larger for the new index than for the old one. While there is a large number of conceivable causes for the discrepancy,[9] the most likely seems to be that the index series for consumers' goods has been tampered with in order to indicate a rise in output faster than what actually occurred. This is suggested by the constant direction of

[5] For a description of the new index, see S. Genin, "Ob otsenke valovoy produktsii v sopostavimykh optovykh tsenakh" (On Valuation of Gross Output at Comparable Wholesale Prices), *Vestnik statistiki*, no. 2 (1952), pp. 31f.

[6] See *Narodnoye khozyaystvo*, 1960, p. 877.

[7] This is one of the reasons for which construction of an index based on dollar prices was undertaken. See Chapter 9 of this volume.

[8] To give an example, the index numbers for 1955 (1950 = 100) were as follows: all industry = 185; producers' goods (A) = 190; consumers' goods (B) = 176. Hence: $190A + 176B = 185 (A + B)$ and B (in 1950) = $5/9$ A.

[9] It should be noted, however, that a change in the weighting system, such as occurred in 1956, in all likelihood has nothing to do with the discrepancy as is evidenced by the respective 1955/1952 and 1959/1956 comparisons.

Table 3. Percentage share of producers' and consumers' goods in total industrial output

Year	Total industry	Producers' goods		Consumers' goods	
		as given	as computed	as given	as computed
1928 (computed vs. 1932)	100.0	39.5	32.0	60.5	68.0
1932 (computed vs. 1940)	100.0	53.4	52.0	46.6	48.0
1940 (computed vs. 1950)	100.0	61.2	61.7	38.8	38.2
1950 (computed vs. 1955)	100.0	68.8	64.3	31.2	35.7
1952 (computed vs. 1955)	100.0	69.2	63.7	30.8	36.3
1956 (computed vs. 1959)	100.0	70.8	65.7	29.2	34.2

Note: for data on percentage shares, see *Narodnoye khozyaystvo*, 1960, p. 224.

the discrepancy and is quite plausible in terms of Soviet propagandistic ambitions.

Moreover, the new index is still based on simple aggregations of values of product of the individual industrial enterprises. As a result, the index is affected by changes in the enterprise structure of the economy which are irrelevant for the task of measurement of output. In addition, the fact that outputs of earlier stages of production are counted several times over will influence the rate of growth, except in the historically quite unlikely case of even growth of output at all stages of production. If one assumes that in the advanced process of industrialization the value of output of finished goods grows faster than that of intermediate goods, then a gross index of the Soviet type will show a *lower* rate of growth as compared with an index based on value added of output — provided, however, that due care has been taken in constructing the latter index to make proper allowance for the increase over time in the share of value added in total output.[10]

[10] If such an allowance was not made, as is unfortunately true of most of our indices of output in which quantity relatives are weighted with *constant* amounts of value added, then a gross index of the Soviet type in all likelihood will show a *higher* rate of growth as compared with a net value index.

Finally, there is the problem of the effects upon the reliability of Soviet statistics of the decentralization of industrial organization.[11] It is most likely that after 1957 the ability of the central authorities to secure trustworthy data on industrial output and related matters has been diminished to some extent. It is a moot question whether as a result an upward or downward bias has been imparted to the data,[12] even though on balance an overstatement would seem more probable.

Thus, for a number of reasons, even the new index is far from being an ideal measure of industrial growth. Still, this writer feels that insofar as total output is concerned (as distinguished from the subgroups) the new index can be taken as a fair picture of the changes in the volume of output. This conclusion would seem reinforced by comparisons of the index of industrial output with the changes in output of a number of basic industrial commodities, taking into account the fact that in the present stage of Soviet economic development aggregate output may be expected to develop faster than its basic components.[13]

By contrast, it is clear that the old pre-1951 official index of industrial output cannot be accepted at all. Fortunately, there is no need to do so. Thanks to the work of American scholars over the past fifteen years or so, there is now available a number of independent constructions of Soviet industrial output in the 1930s. For the purposes at hand, it should be sufficient to select those of Jasny and Hodgman. Jasny comes to the conclusion that the average annual rate of change of Soviet industrial output between 1928 and 1937 amounted to about 12.5 percent. Hodgman's careful and significant computations result

---

[11] See Chapter 11 of this volume.

[12] See Alexander Gerschenkron, "Reliability of Soviet Industrial and National Income Statistics," *The American Statistician*, VII, no. 2.

[13] Thus, for example, for 1950–1955 the average annual rates of growth (in percent) would compare as follows:

Total industrial output	13.1
Pig iron	12.0
Steel	10.1
Coal	7.4
Oil	12.9
Electric power	12.5

Computed from Table 1 above; Economic Commission for Europe, *Economic Survey of Europe in 1951*, pp. 52–53; *Narodnoye khozyaystvo*, 1960, p. 235.

in a figure that is one or two percentage points higher. On the other hand, the computations of Kaplan and Moorsteen yield for the same period a lower rate of growth of only 10.6 percent.[14] It would seem on the whole that one cannot go far wrong in assuming that over a large part of the thirties the rate of increase of industrial output was somewhere in the vicinity of 12 to 13 percent per year. With the help of this conclusion, one can proceed now to a discussion of some of the problems inherent in a comparison of the rate of industrial growth in Russia in the 1930s and the 1950s.

II

On the basis of the old (and unadjusted) official index, the Soviet government claimed an average annual rate of growth of some 19 percent. Those claims did not stand up under investigation. There is no doubt, however, that an annual increase of some 12 to 13 percent, maintained for a considerable number of years, must be regarded as a very unusual achievement. Whether previous history of Russia herself is taken as a *tertium comparationis*, or whether one has recourse to the industrial history of other countries, similar speeds in the growth of industrial output for any significant period are not easily discovered.

The record-breaking result was achieved because a ruthless dictatorial government succeeded in placing the Russian peasants, then the great majority of the Russian people, into the strait jacket of collective farms. Once this was done, it became possible (1) to obtain agricultural produce for the growing population of the cities at a minimum of *quid pro quo* in terms of industrial consumers' goods while at the same time enforcing the transfer of large numbers of peasants to urban occupations; and (2) to dedicate all efforts to the goal of rapid growth of heavy industry, undeterred by the resulting formidable pressures upon the standard of living of the population.

Such no doubt was the quintessence of Soviet economic policies from the end of the 1920s until the German invasion of Russia in

---

[14] N. Jasny, *The Soviet Economy during the Plan Era* (Stanford, 1951), p. 22; Donald Hodgman, *Soviet Industrial Production, 1928–1951* (Cambridge, Mass., 1954); N. M. Kaplan and R. Moorsteen, "An Index of Soviet Industrial Output," *American Economic Review*, no. 3 (1960), p. 301.

1941. As the Second World War was drawing to its close, there was a good deal of speculation in the United States and elsewhere in the world regarding the shape of Russia's postwar economic policies. It may be instructive to review some of the thoughts expressed in those days, to restate the conclusion reached, and to compare it with the actual course of the development.

The problem at issue was twofold: first, whether, after the war, Russia would resume its prewar policies and, second, whether comparably high rates of growth would be achieved.[15] For some time there was hesitation to answer the first question in the affirmative. The possibility could not be excluded that, with the danger of German aggression gone, Russia might settle down to a policy of favoring rapid improvements in standards of living with concomitant substantial increases in the volume of its international trade.[16] The minds of those who entertained such ideas were, however, soon disabused. When Stalin, in February 1946, introduced the Fourth Five Year Plan, it became clear that the commitment to the policy of rapid industrialization with the implied priorities to heavy industry was to continue unabated.

But the second question still remained. Granting the Russian government's willingness to return to the status quo — or rather to the *motio quo ante bellum* — it was still not clear that it would have the ability to do so. In other words, comparing the period of the thirties with the prospective postwar period, could one assume that the forces favoring the high rate of growth in the earlier period would still be at work, their vigor and effectiveness unreduced? As one considered one after the other some of the relevant factors, it seemed difficult to answer the question in the affirmative.

First of all, there was the *technological* factor. In those pre-Sputnik days there was a certain tendency to infer from the existence of a dictatorial system the impossibility of any independent technological inventiveness in Soviet Russia. Syllogistic exercises of this sort were no less absurd than is the post-Sputnik belief in the absolute

[15] It may be noted that by the middle of the 1940s the deficiencies of the Soviet index of industrial output had become clear, but the extent of the upward bias was somewhat underrated.

[16] See Alexander Gerschenkron, *Economic Relations with the U.S.S.R.* (New York, 1945).

superiority of Russian technology. But even those who fully accepted for Soviet Russia the historical lesson that in any industrializing country the imitative technology gradually merges with, and finally gives way to, autochthonous innovations felt that the specific advantages which Russia had enjoyed in the years before 1941 could not be expected to recur after the war. Indeed, the situation prevailing in the thirties when numerous new industries were being created and equipped with the latest Western technology had been a unique phenomenon. It could not be reproduced even if Soviet hostility to the West had not impaired Soviet access to Western technology. It seemed clear that technology must be put down as a retarding factor, making, that is, for conditions that were less favorable than had been the case before the war.

Second, one had to consider the contingency of *diminishing returns* in certain basic industries. When engaged in general theorizing, Soviet economists like to view diminishing returns as a malicious bourgeois invention. The concept in every form is at variance with the Soviet ethos of continuous economic development. Nevertheless, the Soviets did not hesitate to attack oversized plants under the label of "gigantomania." Nor have they been unwilling in concrete cases to discuss problems of depletion and deterioration of natural resources, such as the diminution of the iron content of iron ores.[17] Production of basic industrial materials being a relatively small and declining portion of the total industrial establishment, the aggregate effect of diminishing returns in those branches could not be expected to bulk very large. Still, higher cost of extraction, investment in enrichment plants, the cost of operating those plants, and similar outlays meant that some resources otherwise available for the expansion of output would have to be used for maintaining previously reached levels of output. Again, it was clear that also in this respect the situation would be less favorable than in the thirties.

Third, one had to consider the impact of *investments in other than industrial branches* of the economy. Just as the Soviet government in the thirties derived great benefits from borrowing technology from abroad, it also enjoyed the advantage of having inherited from

[17] I. P. Bardin and N. P. Banny, *Chernaya metallurgiya v novoy pyatiletke* (Ferrous Metals in the New Five Year Plan) (Moscow, 1947), pp. 36, 53.

the prerevolutionary period considerable unutilized capacities in capital-intensive areas, such as railroads and housing. This meant that in the thirties less capital had to be invested in railroad lines and urban housing. But those advantages were exhausted by the end of the period. In particular, the crowding of the urban population into narrow "living space" had reached an absolute maximum, which was hardly compatible with proper health standards, to say nothing of human dignity and elementary comforts. Even in the absence of war destruction, capital needs for housing would have competed effectively with the claims of the expanding industry; and the same was true of the demand for capital on the part of transportation enterprises. It was difficult not to conclude that in time a smaller share of total net investment would be available for placement in industry and that thereby the prospects for industrial growth would be further limited.

Finally, along with the problem of capital availabilities, there was that of *labor supply*. Again, the end of the twenties and the thirties was an exceptional period in this respect. During the First Five Year Plan (1928–1932) the annual movement of labor into heavy industry amounted to no less than 20 percent. The rate of growth of the total industrial labor force in the Second Five Year Plan (1933–1937) amounted to 4.8 percent per year, the heavy industry doubtless showing a somewhat higher rate. The comparable rate of growth for the labor force in all industry during the Third Five Year Plan (1938–1942) was scheduled to amount to 3.3 percent.[18] Thus considerable reduction in the flow of labor to industry had taken place in the thirties. But the average annual increase between 1928 and 1940 amounted to about 10 percent, and there could be no doubt that the initial powerful injection of manpower into industry influenced the character of the whole period. It seemed extremely unlikely that any similar accretions to the labor force could be expected after the war

[18] The rates of increase of labor force have been computed from the following sources: *Sotsialisticheskoye stroitel'stvo, Statisticheskii yezhegodnik* (Socialist Construction, A Statistical Yearbook) (Moscow, 1936), p. 508; *Sotsialisticheskoye stroitel'stvo Soyuza SSR* (Socialist Construction of the USSR), 1933–1938 (Moscow-Leningrad, 1939), p. 138; Gosplan SSSR, *Treti pyatiletni plan razvitiya narodnogo khozyaystva Soyuza SSR* (The Third Five Year Plan of the USSR), 1938–1942 (Moscow, 1939), p. 199.

because thenceforth for any man taken out of agriculture some mechanical substitution had to be provided; while for any man brought into urban industry an increased accommodating investment in housing and in some municipal services was necessary. It was felt therefore that after the war the flow of labor to industry would not be very much in excess of the natural increase of population of the appropriate age groups.

It was clear at all times that the four factors discussed in the preceding pages did not tell the whole story. Along with the decelerating forces, forces working in the opposite direction could be discerned. Yet the aggregate effect of the "retarding block" seemed to be so overwhelming as to justify the prediction that the rate of industrial growth in Russia would decline very considerably after the war.

As we know now, that prediction has not been borne out by the facts. To be sure, it was not meant to apply to the years of reconstruction after the war. Very high rates naturally could be expected then. But a rate of 12 or even 13 percent for the first half of the 1950s is clearly at variance with the prediction: referring once more to the calculations of Hodgman and Jasny, one must conclude that the level of the Soviet rate of industrial growth experienced no change at all between the thirties and the first half of the fifties. It is true that the rate was somewhat lower in the second half of that decade. Considering, however, that the reorganization of industry fell into the later period and that the Sixth Five Year Plan was abandoned in favor of the Seven Year Plan, no long-term factors need be called upon to explain the decline. At any rate, it is fair to say that if this writer had been asked, in 1945 or 1946, to guess the rate of industrial growth in Russia in the last years of the century's sixth decade, he almost certainly would have named a figure considerably below the 10.5 percent that was actually attained.

III

Why did the prediction fail to materialize? It is likely that only part of the fault lay in the selection or overestimation of the retarding factors. Thus the increases in the numbers of industrial manpower were far from negligible and were significantly in excess of the rate of growth of population. But even the high average rate of growth

of the industrial labor force of 5.4 percent per year which was registered between 1955 and 1960 [19] remained almost 50 percent below
the average level of the thirties. A serious study of the economic
aspects of Soviet technology is still searching for its author or authors,
but it is very plausible to assume that the technological progress of the
fifties did not rival that of the thirties. Nor had it been wrong to
assume that investment in railroads or housing would deflect capital
from industry, although it is probably true that for some time and to
some extent investment in housing was increased at the expense of
other investments in the municipal budgets. It is more reasonable to
assume that much more weight should have been attributed to accelerating factors of which at least two deserve to be mentioned here.

First, it was obviously insufficient to consider prospective changes
in the quantity of labor without paying proper attention to changes in
its *quality*. The masses of laborers who in the thirties were transferred
from the farms to the factories were either used as unskilled labor and
occupied in multifarious auxiliary operations or else they were given
a brief training designed to enable them to perform certain recurring
operations on a given machine without providing any broader instruction. The result was a force of specialists in a distressingly narrow
sense of the word. In particular, the individual worker's inability to
understand his machine and to take care of simple repairs no doubt
was responsible for many a hitch and snag in Soviet factories of which
the thirties offer such a rich record.

In the second half of the forties, the Soviet government made a
sustained effort to remedy the situation. In fact, the first steps were
taken before the war, in the fall of 1940, when a compulsory "labor
reserve" was established designed to equip Soviet youth with the
rudiments of technical training through attendance of special schools
and apprenticeship in factories. After the war the system of labor
reserves was reinforced by adoption of special measures for professional training of young workers on the job and most notably for
increasing the skills of the older members of the labor force. Under
the provisions of the Fourth Five Year Plan no less than 13.9 million
workers were supposed to benefit from such additional training.[20] The

---

[19] Computed from *Narodnoye khozyaystvo*, 1960, p. 217.
[20] G. R. Barker, "Soviet Labor," *Bulletins on Soviet Economic Development*
(Birmingham, June 1951), p. 16.

deliberate purpose was to impart to the Russian industrial laborer some general technical education and to make him more mechanically minded. The program was pushed with great energy and appears to have provoked a good deal of resistance, some traces of which even penetrated into Soviet belles-lettres.[21] The old workers seem to have stressed the dangers of raising a generation of jacks of all trades and masters of none. But the protests remained unheeded, and there can be little doubt that the program of retraining had a considerable positive impact upon the nature of the Soviet labor force. In particular, it greatly increased its flexibility and adaptability to new conditions. It must be considered to have had a major accelerating effect upon the rate of industrial growth. Naturally, the quality of the labor force will continue rising in the future. But the big discontinuous leap ahead implied in the delayed retraining of millions must remain a once-over affair.

The other accelerating factor is likely to be of even greater importance. Growth of output at all times creates the problem of the utilization of the increments of goods produced. Roughly speaking, those goods can be either consumed or invested — the investment being either unproductive, such as stock piling, or productive, such as machinery in plants. If the rates of consumption and investment in national income remain constant over time, the increment will be always divided in the same proportion. It is possible, however, to pursue a different policy. One could, for instance, try to keep the consumption per capita of the population constant and devote the rest of the increment to investment. To give an arbitrary example, let us assume that Soviet national income increased at, say, 6 percent per year, while the annual rate of growth of population amounted to 1.5 percent and the rate of consumption and investment to 80 and 20 percent per year respectively. It would be possible then at the end of the first year to take out one fifth (1.2) of the increment (80 × 1.015 = 81.2) in order to safeguard the consumption of the current additions to the population, while the rest of 4.8 percent (6−1.2) would be added to investment, the rate of which would thereby increase from 20 to almost 23.5 percent: $[(20+4.8)/106] \times 100 = 23.5$. Such a policy could be continued year in, year out.

[21] See, for example, the novel by Vera Ketlinskaya, "Dni nashey zhizni" (The Days of Our Life), *Znamya*, no. 5 (1952), p. 82.

A simple arithmetic illustration does not purport to reproduce complex historical reality. Still, if one looks at Soviet economic history since the initiation of the five-year plans until, say, the middle of the fifties, it would be difficult to deny that an increase in the *rate* of investment and a corresponding decrease in the *rate* of consumption constituted perhaps the most significant feature of the period under review. This meant, however, that a good many relative disabilities of the Soviet economy, such as were described earlier, could be compensated for by the increased availabilities of capital, large portions of which, despite the increase in military expenditures, were devoted to productive investment. This policy provides perhaps the most important explanation for the Soviet success in keeping the rate of industrial growth after the war at a level altogether comparable to that of the thirties.

IV

But what about the immediate past and what about the future? As has been shown here, the record of former predictions is not particularly encouraging. Still, remembering Cournot's observation that the function of prediction is not to foretell the future, but rather to cast a sharper light upon the present,[22] a few general remarks may be ventured.

It would seem to follow from the discussion in the preceding pages that the continuous increase in the rate of investment is of crucial importance in maintaining a high rate of industrial growth. It should be clear that within the Soviet institutional framework there is no *economic* reason why the policy of a rising rate of investment could not be pursued ad infinitum, despite the phantasmagoric results such a policy would produce in the end. The Soviet economy could go on turning out steel in order to produce machinery with which to produce more steel in order to produce still more machinery; the economic reality offers, of course, a large variety of possible circuits. It should be remembered that by the early fifties industrial output in Russia may have increased sixfold since 1928, while wages still lagged miserably behind the level of 1928. That was the very essence of Stalin's policy of industrialization. It is noteworthy that Soviet leaders still proclaim, and Soviet economists still write books to assert,

[22] A. Cournot, *Souvenirs, 1760–1860* (Paris, 1913), p. 251.

the existence of a "law of economic development" according to which economic growth is said to be impossible unless output of producers' goods grows faster than output of consumers' goods.[23]

Taken as analytical propositions, assertions of this sort are of course nonsensical. Because of technological progress that can be introduced into the processes of replacement of worn-out machinery, a zero rate, or even a negative rate, of net investment can be perfectly compatible with economic growth, quite apart from the fact that positive growth rates are also a function of increased labor skills and of other factors which have little to do with the supply of investment goods.

Yet analytical absurdities can make very good political sense. For there is an intimate connection between the totalitarian dictatorship in Russia and an economic policy of investment for the sake of investment. It is a truism that a policy of high and rising investment rates could not be pursued in Russia unless by a ruthless and all-powerful dictatorship. But the obverse may also be true: such a policy provides a dictatorial government with a social function and a justification for its existence. It satisfies well its specific needs for dynamism. At the same time, a policy of rapid increases in the levels of consumption may, in the short run, bridge the political difficulties, but in the long run it is likely to create troublesome problems. Plentiful supplies of consumers' goods produce a climate of relaxation among the populace which is not congenial to dictatorships. Once the stress and strain have been reduced, the problem of political liberty is almost bound to arise.

Russia has traveled a good deal since the year of Stalin's death. Caught in the throes of a prolonged succession crisis, the government accorded not inconsiderable increases in the supplies of consumers' goods. The rates of growth of industrial producers' and consumers' goods do not appear any longer to be separated by a very wide margin. And yet the average rate of industrial growth which Khrushchev has envisaged for the decade of the sixties is — at 10.2 percent per year — only negligibly below the 1955–1960 rate of 10.5 percent.[24] It

[23] A. I. Pashkov, *Ekonomicheskii zakon preimushchestvennogo rosta proizvodstva sredstv proizvodstva* (The Economic Law Concerning the Faster Growth of Output of Producers' Goods) (Moscow, 1958).

[24] See *Pravda*, October 19, 1961, p. 3.

is true that for the decade of the seventies a lower average rate of 9.2 percent per year is projected, which may mean that the Soviet government is not unaware of the existence of the retarding factors. But the decade of the seventies is still too far off and no one will believe in the precision of a twenty-year projection. As far as the foreseeable future goes, the Soviet government is not prepared to acquiesce in any real retardation of the country's industrial growth. It is, therefore, not surprising that Khrushchev, in his speech to the Twenty-second Congress, declared that heavy industry would retain its leading position in the country's economic development.[25] The rate of growth of producer-goods output continues to exceed that of consumer-goods output. True, the differential between the two rates has become small, but, as has been mentioned before, it is a moot question to what extent the index for consumers' goods and the rate of growth it implies can be accepted at face value. It is, in fact, possible to surmise that the high projected rate of growth for total industrial output may not be attained unless the rate of growth of producer-goods output will be increased at the expense of the rate of growth of consumers' goods.

The Twenty-second Congress held in October 1961 devoted much of its time to the demoting and demonumenting of Stalin and some of his associates. One cannot help feeling, however, that behind the screen of the so-called de-Stalinization vigorous attempts were made in several important directions to return to the "normalcy" of the past. Whether one looks at the reversal of the decentralization movement in industrial organization; or at the attitudes displayed at the congress toward the "advent of communism"; or at the attacks launched against some timid libertarian tendencies in Soviet literature, one invariably gets the strong impression of forces at work struggling hard to restore the stability conditions of dictatorial power exercise. Those forces may be thwarted in the end. But if they are not, still another stability condition is likely to be successfully re-established. Then the plans for the output of consumers' goods will again remain systematically underfulfilled, as they were in the days of Stalin, while the aggregate rate of Soviet industrial growth may continue undiminished for a long time to come.

[25] *Ibid.*

I I

Industrial Enterprise in Soviet Russia

SOVIET Russia describes itself as a socialist country and its economy as a socialist economy. Those claims are seldom disputed. And yet, on reflection, they may well appear less valid than is generally assumed. In casting doubt upon them, our purpose is not merely to accuse the Russians of conceptual perversion and to defend some "correct" concept of socialism against Soviet encroachments. There may be indeed much need for, and justification of, tidier semantics; but what primarily matters within the present context is to elucidate some aspects of industrial enterprise and industrial management in Soviet Russia, and one way to approach the problems involved is to look briefly for the ideological antecedents of policies in the course of which the industrial organization in Soviet Russia has been shaped and reshaped.

To do this, let us have recourse to an expository device the attractiveness of which is attested by long centuries of use and abuse. Imagine an average Russian intellectual in the very early years of this century, preferably a university student, who, like a famous fictional figure of another age and continent, most likely would have "an insuperable aversion to all kinds of profitable labor." On the other hand, he would be passionately interested in politics and political debates and speculations and would consider himself an implacable enemy of the Russian autocracy. Imagine further that, like the princess in the Grimms' fairy tale, or like St. Vladimir's knight in the Russian ballad, or like the hero in Edward Bellamy's novel, he was put to sleep, say in 1902, and slept several decades in pleasant isolation from highly unpleasant world history, dreaming happily the dream of a future Russia, free from the stupors of starvation, drunkenness, and illiteracy. True to our patterns, let him awaken as the Kremlin chimes strike the first hours of the century's second half. Let us agree that time had stood still with him and that, unlike the Catskill villager who had taken such a deep draught out of the mysterious flagon, he found his youthful vigor undiminished. We can therefore at once dispatch him upon an extensive journey through the highways and byways of the Soviet industrial landscape. Finally, let us posit — making the most fantastic assumption of them all — that he is allowed to give free vent to his observations, comparisons, and reactions.

Our traveler's first impressions are general but very exciting. He quickly discovers that private property in capital goods has been abolished. He feels that this is indeed a negative but very convincing proof that the previous "system of capitalism" has been replaced by the "system of socialism." In forming this view he feels corroborated by what he remembers from his perusal not only of socialist books and pamphlets but also from very scholarly and quite nonsocialistic treatises of the subject.[1] They all regarded the question of ownership over the means of production as the separating line between the two economic systems, the great watershed clearly and firmly drawn on the maps of social geology. Our explorer not only fails to be shocked by the change but tends to welcome it. His previous political views are not ascertainable in great detail. It is clear, however, that despite his dreams he was not connected with any of the then existing socialist groups; a fact which tends to set him somewhat apart, since in those days the average Russian intellectual liked to view the world through socialist spectacles with a better than fifty-fifty chance that the precise hue of his glasses had a Marxian rather than an agrarian or populist tinge. Yet, although not a socialist, he tended to contemplate socialism in its different connotations with a good deal of sympathy. In this, no doubt, he was very Russian and very un-American. He never felt the average American's aversion to the term which Bellamy once expressed so well and so forcefully, inviting the inevitable *a minori ad maius* inference.[2]

---

[1] V. Pareto, *Les Systèmes socialistes* (Paris, 1902), I, 107; Karl Diehl, *Über Sozialismus, Kommunismus und Anarchismus*, 2nd ed. (Jena, 1911), p. 7.

[2] "The word socialist is one I never could well stomach. In the first place, it is

On the contrary, for our man socialism always has been a perfectly respectable and much respected term. He never doubted that socialist ideas contained considerable ethical values. He felt that the socialist movement tried to satisfy age-old yearnings for justice and goodness. He had heard others use and was himself not past using the sacral phrase: "In a sense, of course, we are all socialists." At the same time, perhaps paradoxically and inconsistently, he was also attracted by the anethical tenets of Marxism which stressed the inevitable rise of Russian society from the barbarous depths of a primitive agrarian economy to the heights of a civilized industrial community. It was pleasant to have the certainty of economic progress assured by what he, along with many members of the intelligentsia, was glad to regard as the "last word of modern science." [3] But neither respect for socialist values nor the thesis that Russia "was bound to pass through the stage of capitalism," to use the parlance of the time, had led him to a complete espousal of the socialist cause. What kept him from joining one of the many clandestine socialist groups, his strong individualism aside, were grave doubts as to the practicability and feasibility of the socialist system, particularly with regard to its ability to discipline and to organize.

Let us inject here that our man's surprise in seeing a socialist system established and working in his country is not paralleled by similar astonishment at the extent of industrialization which had taken place in the interval. He remembers well Count Witte's policy of rapid industrialization in the 1890s and his own conviction derived both from Witte's exploits and Marxian expositions that by mid-century Russia would become an industrialized country. When it is

---

a foreign word in itself and equally foreign in all its suggestions. It smells to the average American of petroleum, suggests the red flag, with all manner of sexual novelties, and an abusive tone about God and religion." Joseph Schiffman, "Mutual Indebtedness: Unpublished Letters of Edward Bellamy to William Dean Howells," *Harvard Library Bulletin*, XII (Autumn 1958), 370.

[3] "Later on, as a university professor, I had frequent opportunity in my seminars to argue against the theories of Karl Marx who at that time was the students' highest authority. Time and again, a freshman would tell me with a condescending smile: 'But, professor, Marx is the last word of science'; to which I usually replied: 'How do you know it to be the ultimate and not the penultimate word of science?' " Prince Evgeni Nikolayevich Trubetskoy, *Vospominaniya* (Memoirs) (n.p., n.d.), pp. 46–47. The period referred to is the turn of the century.

explained to him that the process of industrial growth had been interrupted by great wars, both foreign and civil, which left cruel destruction in their wake and presented vast and difficult problems for reconstruction, our traveler manages to requite this intelligence with a critique of a Russian statesmanship that did not know how to stay out of two world wars. Faithful to traditions of his youth, he is always willing to criticize the government. Yet his interests lie in a different direction. It is not the magnitude of the industrialization effort, which he persists in taking for granted, but the specific organization of Soviet industry that arouses his curiosity. Here he quickly discovers much reason for surprise.

As a young man, he used to read in many a treatise on political economy an expression of doubt that a socialist society would be able to increase or even to maintain its capital stock. Such a society, it was argued persuasively, would not be able to control its desires and would tend to squander its resources in excesses of consumption: "Men first feel necessity, then look for utility, next attend to comfort, still later amuse themselves with pleasure, thence grow dissolute in luxury, and finally, go mad and waste their substance." [4] This side circuit of Vico's *corsi e ricorsi* was felt to foretell the nature, and to spell the doom, of a socialist society. Indeed, the socialist literature had seemed to place all weight of emphasis on redistribution of wealth and greater equality of income. Its interest in growth of production seemed quite overshadowed by its interest in distribution. But the Soviet society seems never to have been in danger of overconsumption. The traveler learns with amazement that, over the period of almost a quarter of a century, industrial output increased about six times, whereas the real wages of industrial workers actually declined absolutely, even though statistics for the magnitude of the decline would vary depending on the system of valuations used in making the comparison. Some preliminary conclusions begin to form themselves, though vaguely, in the traveler's mind. He begins to think that possibly his concept of socialism requires some readjustment if it is to be made to fit Soviet reality.

As he wanders from factory to factory and gathers his impressions

[4] G. Vico, *The New Science*, tr. T. G. Bergin and M. H. Fisch (Ithaca, 1948), p. 70.

of the way in which the Soviet industrial enterprises are organized and managed, this need for conceptual reassessment becomes stronger and stronger. He finds out that the enterprises are managed by individuals called "directors," as they had been in presocialist times. He sees those directors arrive at the factories in large chauffeured automobiles. He hears them in their conversations with their subordinates employ the old feudal *ty* (thou) while they are being addressed with the respectful *vy* (you). His confusion grows as he hears them speak of "profits," a category he had thought quite alien to socialist economy and for a long time a central target for socialistic attacks upon capitalism. He is astonished to hear occasional references to "trusts," an organizational form which he was wont to associate with monopolistic exploitation of both workers and consumers by an aggressive capitalist enterprise.

He discovers that the director wields what in theory at least appears an undivided power within the plant. In explaining the director's position to him people use the term *yedinonachaliye,* and our explorer cannot help reflecting that, while the Russian language has a different word reserved for a rendition of the Greek word "autocracy" (that is, *samoderzhaviye*), the Greek version of the term actually employed to characterize the director's status would be *mono*cracy and, whatever the difference is between *auto*cracy and *mono*cracy, both seem sufficiently removed from *demo*cracy. Yet before he has absorbed the idea of a director of a socialist enterprise who acts so fully the part of master in his own house, our traveler is again jolted by hearing that the power of the director essentially consists in acting under orders and that his main function lies in being responsible for the exact execution of those orders. That, he is told, is the essence of socialist planning and the natural opposite of capitalist chaos. After having watched directors of huge enterprises upbraid their subordinates in a thunderous bass and immediately thereafter conduct a telephone conversation with their superiors in a softly ingratiating tenor, the tourist is ready to accept the fact of a duality in the director's social role. But while he marvels at the flexibility of human nature and the range potentiality of a man's voice, he finds it more and more difficult to bring his impressions into harmony with his admittedly preconceived ideas about the nature of the socialist system. In fact, he finds he has reached a point at which he must try to reread what the socialist literature had to say of the problems of management and entrepreneurship and to see how it may have influenced the creation of the enterprise system in Soviet Russia. Accordingly, he interrupts his industrial tour and betakes himself to a library, anxious to spend some time buried in volumes of ancient and not-so-ancient lore.

Unfortunately, the very next day as he tries to order Oskar Lange's brilliant pamphlet *On the Economic Theory of Socialism* he finds himself questioned about his interest in counterrevolutionary literature in general and bourgeois theories of socialism in particular. The interrogation is stern and menacing, and at its close the disenchanted explorer quickly resumes his enchanted sleep, expecting to reawaken in more civil and less bewildering times.

Even so, he has been able to arrive at some helpful though negative conclusions. It appears that the great figures of socialist literature had paid very little attention to the problems of enterprise and its management. To the extent that they did, the chief purpose was to separate "administrative wages" from "entrepreneurial profit" (that is, *Verwaltungslohn* from *Unternehmergewinn*).[5] The latter was seen as flowing from ownership over capital; the former included both managerial and entrepreneurial rewards and did not seem to constitute much of a problem. Marx may have praised in passing the "shrewd expert eye" of the capitalist selecting and combining the factors of production.[6] But the emergence of both the workers' producer cooperative and the joint-stock company made it perfectly clear to him that the exercise of the managerial guidance (*Oberleitung*) by the capitalist had become superfluous.[7]

Karl Hilferding, writing a generation after Marx's death, naturally had a great deal more to say on the joint-stock companies. He stressed their powerful role in the process of concentration of capital. They created, he said, a financial basis which was much broader than that usually available to unincorporated enterprise. He

[5] Karl Marx, *Das Kapital*, Volksausgabe, III (Moscow-Leningrad, 1933), part 1, 425.

[6] Marx, *Das Kapital*, Volksausgabe, I (Moscow-Leningrad, 1932), 193.

[7] Marx, *Das Kapital*, Volksausgabe, III, part 1, 422–423.

did not confine himself to stressing the "superfluity" of the capitalist within the joint-stock company, but went on to suggest that the corporate form opened far more fertile fields to entrepreneurial and managerial activity, permitting a greater degree of rationality, a faster discarding of obsolescent equipment, and a much more aggressive policy in widening the firm's market areas. According to Hilferding, a man who administered an enterprise that was not his could be presumed to act more vigorously, more boldly, and more rationally than an individual owner-entrepreneur, whom Hilferding believed to be restrained by anxieties and personal considerations of all kinds.[8]

The political implication of this appraisal for the future socialist economy was fairly clear. If the joint-stock enterprise had facilitated so much of the task of entrepreneurship and management, the socialist economy could have been expected to simplify it further. Despite all the differences in fundamentals and approach, Hilferding's conclusion came close to Schumpeter's view of the process. Schumpeter believed that the entrepreneurial function was losing its importance because generations of innovating entrepreneurs had firmly embedded the desirability of innovations within the social value system. As innovations became routine, special personal qualities and special efforts were no longer needed to overcome the resistances to change.[9] Unlike Schumpeter, the socialist writers did not treat entrepreneurs and innovations as independent variables in the process of economic growth. For them the process did not have to "become depersonalized and automatized";[10] it always had been viewed in those terms. But the final conclusion was the same: entrepreneurship and management could be taken for granted. As in so many other areas the problems of socialist management were assumed to be presolved in the course of the capitalist development. The Marxian literature was reluctant to indulge in detailed descriptions of the socialist system, but the general contours of the picture emerged with sufficient clarity: socialism meant organization of production not indeed by the state, which was to "wither away," but by the free collectives of "associated

[8] Karl Hilferding, *Das Finanzkapital* (Vienna, 1910), pp. 137ff.
[9] Joseph A. Schumpeter, *Capitalism, Socialism, and Democracy* (New York and London, 1942), pp. 132–133.
[10] *Ibid.*

producers," the tasks of management being discharged by salaried specialists. It was this image of the economy which inspired Lenin in 1917 as he stood at the threshold of power.[11]

These basic attitudes would well serve as an ideological introduction to the views expressed by Oskar Lange in his celebrated piece.[12] The tenor of the former is in perfect harmony with the spirit of the latter. Also for Lange the managerial problem was simple indeed. The Central Planning Board is to tell the managers to minimize average cost and to produce as much of each commodity as will equalize the price of product and its marginal cost. The managers are to bid for labor in the market; similarly, consumers' preferences are to determine prices of consumers' goods, while all other prices and the rate of interest is set by the Planning Board, as far as possible so as to equalize demand and supply of producers' goods and of loanable funds. Finally, the Planning Board determines arbitrarily the rate of net investment from planning period to planning period.[13]

This scheme for the organization of the socialist economy has one guiding principle and one basic aim: "to satisfy consumers' preferences in the best way possible." [14] There is every implication that, in determining "arbitrarily" the rate of net investment, the Planning Board is expected to be guided primarily by the welfare of the consumers and to operate with reasonable time-horizons.

It is, of course, not clear at all in the Lange scheme how it is assured that the manager will in fact observe the two fundamental rules with regard to methods of production and the composition of output. Neither a system of supervision of managerial activity nor a system of possible incentives to induce the managers to comply with the rules is included in the scheme. This omission, however regrettable, is perhaps not altogether incomprehensible. The point is not only that the market in consumers' goods, together with the emergence of surpluses and deficits in producers' goods and loanable funds, is thought to provide objective checks for the correct function-

[11] V. I. Lenin, *Gosudarstvo i revolutsiya* (State and Revolution), *Sochineniya* (Works), 4th ed. (Moscow, 1949), p. 398.
[12] Oskar Lange and Fred M. Taylor, *On the Economic Theory of Socialism* (Minneapolis, 1938).
[13] *Ibid.*, pp. 77–85.
[14] *Ibid.*, p. 75.

ing of the system; no less important is the implied supposition that in a system based on consumers' preferences the consumers should find ways and means to control the activities of the managers and to enforce compliance with the rules; similarly, there is the further supposition that consumers will know how to force the Planning Board not to substitute its own preferences for those of the consumers. And above it all hovers the feeling that an economy of this type would generate a social environment within which compliance with rules that are socially so desirable will be forthcoming readily and spontaneously. *Le socialisme c'est la bonté et la justice*, says one of Anatole France's heroes. It should not be difficult for such a society to find "just" and "good" managers to administer its economic enterprises. This has been the traditional view of socialism by socialists. And even Lenin, who envisaged the managers as standing under "control of the armed proletariat," considered such control quite a transitory measure. Lange's system *is* a socialist system in terms of the ideological history of the socialist movement and must be read and appraised in the context of that history. Compared with the basic stress on popular welfare, the question of collective versus individual ownership of means of production would seem altogether ancillary.

But if the Lange system of socialist economy can claim to be considered the consummate model of socialism, by the same token it impedes rather than furthers our comprehension of the Soviet system to view it as a socialist system. It is a general hazard of social science that the objects of our study time and again tend to confuse the scholarly observer by making statements about themselves. When those statements are supported by monopolistic dominance over communication media on the part of a powerful dictatorial government, their persuasive power is further enhanced. Nevertheless, however often Soviet Russia may introduce itself to the world as a socialist country, the fact remains that the social scientist may find it much more illuminating to consider Soviet Russia not as a socialist economy but as an economy which by the will of a ruthless totalitarian government has been kept in the process of a very rapid industrialization. "Accumulate, accumulate! This is Moses and the Prophets!" [15] Those are the words in which Karl Marx tried to describe the quintessence of

[15] Marx, *Das Kapital*, Volksausgabe, I, 624.

capitalism. There is every reason to doubt that there has been any economy on modern historical record to which these words would apply with greater justification than to the economy of the Union of the so-called *Socialist* Soviet Republics.

Predictions are precarious. Still, so firmly has the Soviet political system been wedded to the policy of a high *and growing* rate of investment that at least this observer of its evolution has felt tempted to conclude that no other economic policy would be easily compatible with the maintenance of the Soviet dictatorship; in other words, that a policy of rapid increases of consumers' welfare either would remain unacceptable to the dictators or, if accepted, would in all likelihood lead to the disintegration of the dictatorship. It matters little in this connection whether future history will verify or falsify this hypothesis. It is referred to here in order to throw into relief the antagonistic nature of an allegedly classless economy in which the investment interest of the government has been continually opposed by the consumption interest of the population.

To return to the problem of management and enterprise: the socialist literature could afford to pay scant attention to the problem of management because it operated with the vision — or illusion — of a harmonious society unrent by any serious cleavage of interest. The antagonistic Soviet society was forced to pursue a different policy. Far from being able to ignore or to take lightly the problem of management, the leaders of the Soviet government came to regard the search for the appropriate degree of managerial dependence as focal to their economic policy. The position of the manager proved to be the all-important nucleus of the broader problem of the appropriate degree of centralization within the Soviet economy. So far, the very nature of that economy has precluded a clear and lasting solution to either problem. Thence came the uneasy compromise between the preached principle and the tolerated practice; thence came also the continual wavering to and fro in organizational structure, in the course of which the lines of command were alternatively lengthened and shortened, loosened and tightened. Quite recently, the Soviet government has embarked upon a far-reaching scheme of organizational reform, thus making dramatically apparent the inherent instability of the previously existing arrangements. The remainder of this essay will be devoted to a sketch of those arrangements and an appraisal of the probable motivations and effects of the recent reforms.

The attempt is constantly made in Soviet writings to view the evolution of management and enterprise *over the whole Soviet period* as determined by one unvarying and unerring purpose. Such claims do not stand up under investigation. After the October Revolution, the institution of workers' control over economic enterprises was established by a rather perplexed and bewildered government. Even today the workers' control of those days (1918–1919) is still praised in Soviet literature as an important step on the road of Soviet managerial progress.[16] In reality workers' control very quickly led to the diffusion of syndicalist tendencies; it served to hasten the disintegration of the country's economy and, probably even more than the simultaneous resistance of factory owners, forced the government, then in the throes of the civil war, to proceed with an otherwise unintended nationalization of industrial enterprises.

On the other hand, during the New Economic Policy of the twenties, the centralized grip on industry was considerably relaxed, even though large-scale industry remained in the hands of the state. "Trusts" which combined a number of connected industrial enterprises assumed some managerial decisions, while at the level of individual enterprises managerial activity was largely exercised by the so-called triangle or trio (*troyka*), consisting of the director of the enterprise, the local party cell, and the local trade-union group. This tripartite organization of factory management no doubt reflected some general socialist ideas concerning democratization of management. In the West, such ideas were mildly articulated in the socialization debates after World War I and affected various legislative acts.[17] They continued to play a considerable part in the literature of the interwar period, in which "extension of democracy into the economic sphere"

[16] See, for example, *Ekonomika sotsialisticheskikh promyshlennykh predpriyatii* (Economics of Socialist Enterprises in Industry) (Moscow, 1956), p. 25.

[17] In Austria and in Germany, for instance, such ideas became reflected in the institution of work councils or shop stewards — see, for Austria, "Gesetz betreffend die Errichtung von Betriebsräten," May 15, 1919, *Staatsgesetzblatt*, no. 283, article 11, and, for Germany, the law of February 4, 1920 (Betriebsrätegesetz), and of February 5, 1921 (Bilanzgesetz). A. Shuchman, *Codetermination, Labor's Middle Way in Germany* (Washington, D.C., 1957), pp. 79–81.

was advocated.[18] After the last war, those modest beginnings were further amplified in the various codetermination or cooperation schemes which were designed to give the workers some sense of participation in the conduct of the enterprise.[19]

In Soviet Russia, this legacy of socialistic ideas did not survive the end of the NEP. It was clearly at variance with the policy of superindustrialization. "The year of the great change" was Stalin's apt description of the year 1929. It was in 1929 that the thorough purge of the Central Trade Union Council took place. The emasculation of the unions as a representation of labor's interests was the result. Thereafter, Soviet industrial labor appeared reduced to the passive role of a "factor of production" and the unions were transformed into an arm of management, designed — to use Marxian terms — to extract from labor the greatest possible amount of surplus value. The readjustment of the unions was swift and far-reaching, and neglect of the interests of labor quite unhesitating. It was left to Stalin a few years later to follow his usual practice and to shift the blame onto subordinate shoulders by stressing the forgotten connection between incentives and output. It was only then that the unions began to proclaim some concern for the workers' living needs, although dealing with them "chiefly if not exclusively in terms of production needs." [20]

It was the same year, 1929, in which the "triangle" was loudly denounced and the aforementioned principle of director's monocracy proclaimed. Henceforth neither the trade union nor the party cell was to interfere with the decisions of the manager. This "strengthening" of *local* authority naturally was not an act of decentralization but, on the contrary, an important precondition for a greatly enhanced centralization in the management of Soviet industry. Within the triangle the responsibility had been divided and was hence diffuse and elusive. Management was to become a stable, more easily supervised, and more readily apprehended recipient and executor of the orders

[18] Cf. Fritz Naphtali, ed., *Wirtschaftsdemokratie, Ihr Wesen, Weg und Ziel* (Berlin, 1929).

[19] Shuchman, chaps. 9, 10.

[20] J. V. Stalin, Speech, June 23, 1931, in *Sochineniya* (Works) (Moscow, 1951), XIII, 55–60. G. Bienstock, S. M. Schwarz, and A. Yugow, *Management in Russian Industry and Agriculture* (London, New York, Toronto, 1944), p. 37.

that came from the center. The intention no doubt was a fully centralized organization in which the factory manager was no more than a transmission belt in the formidable industrialization machine whose prime movers and control levers were concentrated in Moscow. It was in this spirit therefore that, in 1929, the individual enterprise was both solemnly pronounced an "independent productive and commercial unit," and made fully dependent upon the decisions in the administrative center. At the same time, the "center" was appropriately reorganized so as to establish the closest possible connection with the individual enterprises. As a part of this process, the Supreme Economic Council was split into three People's Commissariats (much later, in 1946, renamed Ministries) with a rapid proliferation in the following years of special commissariats for every important branch of Soviet industry. In 1934, the previously existing intervening links were abolished and, at least in the rapidly growing heavy industry, the enterprise became directly subordinate to the respective commissariats in Moscow, thus consummating the centralization of the industrial structure.[21]

The formidable effort at centralization is a historical fact. Nor is there any doubt that a complete subjugation of the manager of the individual enterprise was the aim. And yet, even for an omnipotent and ruthless dictatorship, the coefficient of "will enforcement" rarely equals unity. What is so striking about the outcome of this process is that dictatorial order and resistance inherent in men and things combined to produce an organizational structure whose lines possessed neither the charming simplicity of Oskar Lange's pair of rules nor the uncharming straightforwardness of an absolute "I order, you obey" economy. To understand the position of the manager as it was pressed into shape in Stalin's organizational rolling mill, it is advisable to present first an image of Soviet industrial management as seen through the wishful spectacles of the official theory of that

[21] It is not necessary for the purposes of this presentation to go into detailed description of the administrative structure and to dwell on the different types of People's Commissariats beyond saying that for the bulk of the heavy industry the commissariats were of the "all-union" type which allowed of no intermediary organs in the constituent republics of the USSR. Light industries were controlled by the so-called Union Republican Commissariats, for which, at least in theory, the relations with the enterprises were channeled through People's Commissariats in the individual republics.

period. One may proceed then to compare the image with a more concrete presentation of Soviet reality.

In the official view, the manager's activity in his enterprise was regulated by a linguistic monstrosity known as the annual *Tekhprom-finplan,* which was a complex of targets for the prospective plan period, comprising quantities and values of output, utilization of workers of different categories, use of different types of raw materials and fuels, magnitudes of gross and net investment, data on cost, prices and profits, and finally a description of technological and organizational innovations. That plan, prepared within the enterprise upon central directives and then approved by the central authority, was regarded as an integral part of the annual over-all plan for the development of the Soviet economy. For the manager it possessed the force of law.

An appropriate avenue leading to an understanding of the plan and the manager's official position within its framework may be found in the concept of profits, an obvious curiosity within an allegedly socialistic system, which caused so much surprise to the errant intellectual who haunted the introductory pages of this essay. Originally introduced for reasons of imitative respectability as a symbol of American businesslike matter-of-factness (*delovitost'*), the category of profits has become a carrying pillar of the system of economic accounting (*khozraschet*), which in turn is identified with the aforementioned "independence" of the enterprise. Having been supplied from the state budget with fixed capital, receiving a modicum of working capital from the state budget, and covering the balance of its needs in working capital through credits from the state bank, the manager of the Soviet enterprise as a rule is expected to husband his resources in such a way as to produce the planned quantity of output without exceeding the prescribed planned cost of that output; since, again as a rule, unit prices exceed unit cost and sales are assured, the enterprise is expected to achieve a certain planned profit. If, in addition, the enterprise should succeed in achieving some "unplanned" profit, so much the better and this achievement is appropriately rewarded. In this way, even though every industrial enterprise in Soviet Russia is owned by the state, its accounts are kept discrete from the state budget; the revenues and the expenditures of the firm do not enter the budget, except for the investment funds (and subsidies) received from and for taxes (on turnover and profits) paid into the government treasury.

What, then, is the function of profits within this system? A simple answer distilled from the official writings may be formulated as follows. Just as the main function of prices for producers' goods in the Soviet economy — prices for consumers' goods are a different matter — is said to lie in their role in planning output and in supervising the degree to which plans have been fulfilled, so the role of profits — as distinguished from taxes on turnover — lies in their serving as an index of the degree to which resources have been used in accordance with the plan. Needless to add, the indicator is a very crude one. Very different combinations of the individual cost factors are, of course, compatible with a given level of profits, and the planners' point of view of the desirability of the individual combination might differ very widely. Yet, such as it is, the category of planned profits has provided the central authorities with a simple global check on the use of resources by the individual enterprises.

To gauge an industrial manager's freedom of decision, it is useful to turn for a moment from planned profits to unplanned profits. Obviously in order to overfulfill the plan — be it in the quantity of output or in the sum of profits — the manager must be able to display freedom of initiative outside the area circumscribed by the prescriptions of the plan. But how can the manager increase profits beyond the level provided for? Theoretically, numbers of workers, wage rates, cost of available raw materials, selling prices, funds available for technological improvement — all those are circumscribed by the plan and must be regarded as "givens." The manager cannot vary any of those magnitudes as might his counterpart — the Western manager operating within a freer competitive structure. As long as total output is held constant, the only way open to a Soviet manager who wishes to achieve unplanned profits is through introduction of innovations which reduce cost while costing nothing. A more rational arrangement of men and machinery within a plant, less wasteful handling of materials and machines, insistence on greater diligence on the part of the workers — those are the primary methods of increasing unplanned profits at the disposal of a Soviet industrial manager, as pictured by official writings. It is difficult to avoid the conclusion that his range of freedom is severely limited.

It is true, of course, that output need not be considered constant. No Soviet manager in his right senses will contemplate an increase of profits by reduction of output below the planned level. On the other hand, overfulfillment of the plan is not only permissible; it is enthusiastically encouraged by multifarious rewards. An increase in output may increase or decrease profits, but it is fair to say that in all probability a Soviet manager will be willing to swap some decrease in profits for some increase in output; if an increase in output would bring the enterprise across the magic line that separates underfulfillment from overfulfillment, the probability becomes a certainty. Yet what has been said of higher-than-planned profits largely holds also of higher-than-planned output. How can a Soviet manager, officially described as narrowly circumvallated by the plan, find the labor, raw materials, semifabricates, and possibly also some investment goods that are needed in order to increase output? Would not overfulfillment of the output plan in one area of necessity lead in this fully employed system to underfulfillment of the plan in other areas? And if the plan provides, as is claimed, for balanced growth of the economy as a whole, would not such lopsided sallies beyond the plan targets disrupt the functioning of the economic system, leading to useless surpluses in some spots and badly missed deficits in others? Is it not correct to infer that in an economy in which individual enterprises are allowed to indulge in such disruptive activities, the position of those enterprises and particularly that of the leaders of those enterprises must be a good deal less restricted than might appear from our official image of the Soviet economy?

It is half a century since a brilliant German sociologist put on paper what certainly has proved to be a profound insight: "The elimination of any spontaneity in a subordinate position is in reality much rarer than one might assume from popular speech which uses very freely such terms and phrases as 'compulsion,' 'no other choice,' 'absolute necessity,' and so on. Even in the most cruel and oppressive states of subordination, there usually exists a considerable measure of personal freedom." [22] Modern studies on Soviet industrial man-

[22] Georg Simmel, *Soziologie* (Leipzig, 1908), p. 135.

agement by Western economists have well borne out the truth of Simmel's generalization.[23]

The conclusion is inescapable that the official theory is a poor guide in assessing the true role of Soviet industrial managers. Far from being bound, trunk and limbs, by the plan, the manager enjoys a large sphere of independent activity. On the one hand, he is able to influence the targets of the plan. In so doing he tries to maneuver in such a way as to achieve two disparate ends: to establish for himself a reputation of a bold administrator insisting on high rates of growth and at the same time to keep the planned rates of growth well within the capabilities of the enterprise so that they can be attained with a good deal of certainty and without undue stress and strain. In Soviet conditions where interindustry supplies have remained the weakest point of the whole economic system,[24] and where, on the other hand the policy of high rates of growth keeps the enterprises at a very low level of inventory, the managers are almost forced to hold hidden reserves. To carry on such a policy it is necessary first to convince the central authorities that the input-output coefficients are higher than they actually are; it is necessary, second, to engage in various strictly illegal dealings, in the course of which materials and goods produced are bartered away to neighboring factories in an attempt to provide substitutes for the shortcomings of the central system of allocations. To be able to do this effectively, the manager must also deceive the central authorities as to the actual level of his plant's output. Only in this way can he accumulate a stock of finished goods of which he can dispose through other than the planned channels.

Those who are interested in the details of these evasive arrange-

[23] See particularly, David Granick, *Management of the Industrial Firm in the USSR* (New York, 1954), and Joseph S. Berliner, *Factory and Manager in the USSR* (Cambridge, Mass., 1957).

[24] A Soviet journalist, Boris Polevoy — well but not always pleasantly known — a few years ago crossed the United States from coast to coast without apparently finding anything to excite his admiration. But in Los Angeles he was shown through a Chevrolet assembly plant and was told that the plant received its materials from twelve thousand different factories, some of them many hundreds of miles away from Los Angeles; still the assembly line moved on without interruption. This was so downright un-Soviet that Polevoy could no longer suppress a burst of enthusiasm. See *Amerikanskiye dnevniki* (American Diaries) (Moscow, 1956), p. 214.

ments may refer to the two excellent works by Berliner and Granick mentioned earlier. What matters here is only to throw light on a fundamental peculiarity of the Soviet industrial system — that is, the well-built-in discrepancy between plan and reality. In the light of this discrepancy it is easy to see that the manager as a rule has many ways of achieving unplanned profits, or of increasing output above the plan figures, or of deciding between the one and the other course of action. Thus the actual situation no doubt is a great deal more complex than it appears to be on the basis of the official descriptions of Soviet planned economy. It is safe to conclude that the Soviet government's power over the economy is somewhat less complete than Soviet literature would make us believe.

The reason for this bashfully concealed but nonetheless very real limitation on the power of a ruthless dictatorial government is not far to seek. The official view of the Soviet economy is premised upon the assumption of unrestricted knowledge and foreknowledge on the part of the central planners. Needless to say, this assumption is far from realistic. The stream of paper reports that flows from the plants to the central authorities may belittle the majesty of the Volga River, but it provides no assurance of real insight into the conditions within the individual plant. The fundamental ignorance of the central authorities restricts their ability to enforce their will. Obversely, it is the knowledge of the manager that assures for him his area of freedom. Once the assumption of complete knowledge is dropped, it becomes immediately clear why the Soviet planners in the past had frequent recourse to the price system of producers' goods, not just in order to check and supervise but also to change the allocation of scarce resources. Increases in prices of commodities such as oil or copper were cases in point. The purpose was to induce the managers of industrial enterprises to economize on those commodities in favor of the more plentiful substitutes. And the reason why the device of a price increase, so much less direct and so much less transparent in its effects than a change in quantitative allocations as among firms, was chosen must be sought precisely in the ignorance of the authorities, who were in the dark as to what allocation claims of what plants to accept or reject. Presumably, once the prices were changed and the managers adjusted their decisions accordingly, the plan targets for the utilization of the relevant materials were also appropriately adjusted. But the process reveals both the importance of the area of free managerial decisions and the *mirabilia* of such decisions' determining the plan, rather than vice versa — surely a rather perverse sequence from the point of view of the official theory.

The Soviet government is not known for its tolerance. Nor does it readily brook disobedience to its orders. If it has been asquiescing in a widely diffused system of plan evasion, the reason is that — aware of the extent of its ignorance — it has recognized that a measure of managerial freedom from the plan was a prerequisite to the fulfillment of the plan. The price it pays is not simply in terms of abdication in favor of abstract managerial independence. Up to a point, evasions of the plan are indeed designed to fulfill it. But some of the evasions are dictated by very different motives, including the managers' personal enrichment, something that is not easily compatible with the Soviet ethos of absolute devotion to the state.

Thus the Soviet system of industrial management defies an easy circumscription of its contours. For it has no fixed contours at all. The zone of managerial freedom is largely *extra legem*. Hence its boundary is in perpetual motion, being continually adjusted and readjusted. At the level of each individual enterprise, a managerial sally into greater independence is followed by a retreat toward greater obedience. Shifting the managers from factory to factory, maintaining a well-developed system of informers, increasing control over the "monocrat" by the local party organs — those are some of the devices by which the central authorities have often attempted to shorten a manager's tether or at least to control its length. Yet as managerial disobedience is eliminated, so is his free initiative. And since the latter soon proves indispensable for the successful operation of the enterprise, the rope must be played out again, starting a new cycle, the regularity of which would have surprised and delighted Polybius or Vico.

But is the Soviet government really doomed to keep this zigzag course, which no doubt is wasteful of time and effort? Must it continue living in fear of managerial autonomy? Cannot it rather face up to its necessity and mete out to managers an openly recognized generous measure of freedom? There is little doubt that tendencies in this direction have been present within the Russian economy long before Stalin quit the stage. This should not be surprising. Apart from the reasons just mentioned, the existence of a twilight zone of tolerated illegality agrees ill with the nature of Soviet dictatorship. And yet it is the mechanics of power exercise by the self-same dictatorship that make it so difficult to take the step from grudging acquiescence to open recognition.

It is very often not recognized that dictatorial power requires incessant exercise. It is maintained and asserted by ruling and regulating. A decrease in regimentation therefore tends to be tantamount to a decline in power. Even more important, however, is the previously mentioned connection between the dictatorship and the high rate of growth. If it is true that the Soviet dictatorship not only makes rapid industrialization possible but continually derives from it new strength and new vindication, then it is also true that the high rate of investment and, obversely, the low rate of consumption must remain characteristic of the Soviet economy. Yet, because of the relative neglect of consumption, the path of an industrial manager is strewn with manifold temptations. Wherever technically possible, there is a strong urge to deflect resources into consumption and away from investment. A recognized and firmly established sphere of managerial autonomy is therefore very likely to produce results that would be most undesirable from the point of view of the basic interests of Soviet dictatorship. To give an example: in 1934, the Soviets decided to grant increased freedom of action to so-called local industry, producing for the local market with the help of local fuels and local raw materials. Stalin spoke of the need to "liberate its initiative." Appropriate resolutions were adopted.[25] And yet after a short period the policy was abandoned, because even in the limited sphere of "local industry" freedom from regulation soon clashed with the basic principles of Soviet policy.

There were other similar oscillations. But what has been taking place in the Soviet Union during the past few years is an effort at organizational reform without precedent and parallel in the history of the country since the inception of central planning. It seems to introduce far-reaching changes in the distribution of economic author-

[25] Stalin, Report to the Seventeenth Congress, *Sochineniya*, XIII, 315–317.

ity and, possibly, to affect the position of industrial managers as it developed under Stalin and has been described in the preceding pages. The reform originated as an attack upon the central organs of economic administration which began within less than a year after Stalin's death and proceeded rapidly to gather momentum.[26]

About a year later (August 9, 1955), the scope of managerial rights was expressly expanded through a resolution of the Council of Ministers.[27] In this way, some of the activities previously proscribed, though tacitly tolerated, were solemnly legalized. Among these activities were unplanned purchases and sales of materials, equipment, and finished goods to other enterprises, as long as they remained on a small scale. Furthermore, the managers became entitled to more flexibility in adjusting wage rates and wage payments, and they also received the right to shift outlays from one category to another and from one period to another. All this was to be done within certain narrow limits. It is quite doubtful, therefore, that the resolution brought any substantive change into the management of the Soviet enterprise, even though it may have had the effect of providing to managerial consciences some relief from the burdens of evasions and collusions.

Finally, in May 1957, the Supreme Soviet of the USSR passed an act under the terms of which most of the central economic ministries were abolished.[28] The area of the USSR was divided into more than one hundred administrative regions, and in every region a National Economy Council (*Sovnarkhoz*) was entrusted with the local administration of industrial enterprises. The Sovnarkhoz reports to the Council of Ministers of the individual republic, which in turn is subordinated to the Council of Ministers of the USSR.[29]

[26] The first resolution in the matter was adopted by the Central Committee of the Communist Party on January 25, 1954. It was followed by the joint resolution on October 14, 1954, of the Central Committee and the Council of Ministers, which used little restraint in criticizing the bureaucratic confusion, inefficiency, and incompetence of the economic ministries and suggested and demanded various improvements without yet proposing any fundamental organizational changes. See *Direktivy KPSS i sovetskogo pravitel'stva po khozyaystvennym voprosam, 1917–1957 gody* (Directives of the Communist Party of the Soviet Union on Economic Matters) IV (Moscow, 1958), 155–156, 311–317.

[27] *Direktivy*, IV, 451–457.

[28] "Zakon o dal'neyshem sovershenstvovanii organizatsii upravleniya promyshlennost'yu i stroitel'stvom" (Act Concerning Further Organizational Improvement in the Administration of Industry and Construction), *Direktivy*, IV, 732–738.

[29] See A. N. Yefimov, *Perestroyka upravleniya promyshlennost'yu i stroitel'stvom*

The sphere of competence of the Sovnarkhozes as defined in a special charter is vast indeed.[30] Particularly striking is the right bestowed upon them to change both output and investment targets, apparently not merely by shifts as among enterprises of the same industrial branch but also by shifts as among industrial branches. At the same time, a considerable increase in "local industry" is envisaged, which is to be supervised by local rather than regional organs.

The central guidance of Soviet industry henceforth is to reside in the Council of Ministers and to proceed on the basis of a unified plan prepared by the State Planning Commission (*Gosplan*). The latter institution is called upon to watch over the "rational location of industry," to assure a unified policy in developing the leading branches of Soviet industry, to supervise the rate of economic progress, and so forth.[31] It is intended that the most crucial economic decisions for the economy as a whole should continue to be made in Moscow. In particular, the basic determination of the rate of investment and the rate of consumption remains reserved to the central organs. Similarly, the central quantitative allocation of scarce materials (which used to be called "funded commodities") is to continue, possibly even on a somewhat expanded scale. Khrushchev solemnly announced that the organizational reform would not weaken the central guidance of the Soviet economy.[32]

It cannot be the purpose of this essay to go into details in describing the organizational transformation that is being carried out. It is more important at this point to form some idea with regard to the possible motivations of the reform. In this connection it might be possible to appraise both the correctness of Khrushchev's prediction and the probable durability of the change.

In reviewing the possible aims of the reform, what comes to mind first is its potential military aspect: to split the Soviet economy into a large number of more or less watertight compartments may enhance its power of resistance in case of war. If this is true, the reform may be somewhat comparable in character, though not in

v SSSR (Reorganization of Administration of Industry and Construction in the USSR) (Moscow, 1957), *passim*.

[30] Resolution of the Council of Ministers of the USSR (September 26, 1957), *Direktivy*, IV, 784–805.

[31] Yefimov, p. 44.

[32] *Pravda*, March 3, 1957.

dimension, to the change in attitude adumbrated in the Third Five Year Plan with regard to scale of enterprise and location of industries. This explanation, however, is at variance with the reasonable hypothesis that the Russians indeed desire a continuation of the cold war, with its periodic recrudescence of tensions which are so congenial to dictatorial rule; but that at the same time they do not want "hot war" and feel safe in the knowledge that an attack upon them by the West is very improbable. This does not mean that the mechanics of dictatorial power might not at some juncture lead Russia into the impasse of an open military conflict, but it is unlikely that the Soviets should be willing to pay a heavy price in terms of economic cost for what must seem to them a remote contingency.

It is therefore more plausible to assume that the reform is a recurrence of the cyclical swing away from central control, except that the previous rate of Soviet economic growth as well as the great disturbances of the succession crisis served to magnify the cyclical swing out of all historical proportion. On the one hand, there was the feeling that the growing size of the Soviet industrial establishment rendered continuation of its direction from a single center more and more difficult. On the other hand, Khrushchev may have had very excellent reasons to rid himself of the ministerial bureaucrats, most of whom had been bred in loyalty to Khrushchev's competitors in the struggle for personal power. Nevertheless, if the aggregate weight of these considerations was sufficient to cause the change, it may not suffice to perpetuate it. For the centripetal forces, which for the moment seem subdued, almost inevitably will reappear and are likely to reassert themselves.

At the time of this writing (1959), the reform still receives high praise in Russia; it is even said to have accelerated the rate of industrial growth.[33] The satisfaction of having eliminated ministerial inefficiency dominates the picture. However, the new brooms of the Sovnarkhoz will also very soon be covered with bureaucratic cobwebs. Then the risks of decentralization, including the great difficulty of reconciling the vast decision-making power of the Sovnarkhoz with consistency in central planning, will become increasingly conspicuous. Hardly a few months passed before the Soviet press and literature

[33] *Sovetskaya Rossiya*, November 14, 1958.

became full of warnings against the dangers of "localism" (*mestnichestvo*). The intensified intraregional division of labor is likely to proceed at the expense of specialization on a national scale and to lead to a malallocation of resources. It was a peculiarity of the industrial managers' illicit activities that they were displayed within a narrow area bounded by personal connections and acquaintances. One consequence of the reform is to enhance further this quaint element of medieval narrowness within an economy whose "modernity" is so incessantly glorified.

And what about the position of the manager within the new organizational framework? Obviously, the Sovnarkhoz will be closer to the individual enterprise than were the abolished ministries in Moscow. But it is not obvious at all that it will be close enough to give the regional authorities a real insight into the inner workings of the enterprise. Some of the regions represent formidable industrial complexes.

Moreover, the reform began in an atmosphere in which increase rather than decrease in managerial freedom seemed to be the aim.[34] There is, for instance, no question that the managers were accorded more flexibility in their relations with the labor force. This is bound to intensify the inflationary pressures within the economy. It will be recalled that the wartime legislation which had tied the worker to the factory for long years after the war finally melted away in the years of the Soviet thaw. As a result, the managers are able to bid for labor, with the inevitable effect upon wage rates. It would seem that the greater flexibility inherent in decentralization will make it more difficult for the authorities to resist the enterprises' demands for additional funds. Even during its periods of strictly centralized administration, the Soviet authorities found the inflationary cost and price changes of the thirties a very real obstacle to their attempts to check on whether or not resources had been used in accordance with

[34] On the close relation between decentralization and increase in managerial freedom, see the novel, *The Brothers Yershov*, by V. Kochetov, for some time a Soviet bestseller, directed against so-called revisionist tendencies. There the point is emphatically made that merely increasing the number of economic ministries would have led indeed to a "more flexible and less cumbersome" organization; but "an unnatural centralization would remain and the managers' hands and feet would remain swaddled." V. Kochetov, "Brat'ya Yershovy," *Neva*, no. 7 (1958).

the plan. In conditions of decentralization, the inflationary change in yardsticks by which performances are measured must reduce the central authorities to a state of groping helplessness.

More fundamental, however, than the problem of inflation is that of a high rate of investment. In the past, it was the iron grip of central authorities that forced upon the economy the low rate of output of consumers' goods. It would seem that any step along the road of decentralization is likely to relax the grip and to jeopardize adherence to the traditional policy. The managers of industrial enterprises in all likelihood will be strongly tempted by the pent-up demands for consumers' goods, and it is not clear at all that the Sovnarkhoz will know how to resist that demand and will not become a sheltering wall between the central authority and the individual enterprise. If that should happen, however, central direction of the economy by means of the plan will become quite problematic and the urge to relieve the situation by an organizational reversal will be irresistible. Mergers of two or more Sovnarkhozes would appear the most natural first steps toward such a *restitutio in integrum*.

To be sure, it is at least imaginable that the Soviet government might decide upon a radical revision of its economic policy. A drastic increase in the rate of consumption would reduce the inflationary pressures *and* provide the preconditions for the successful perpetuation of a decentralized economy, subject to a limited but effective degree of planned control. A Soviet economy, so transformed, would be much more readily understood and appreciated by Western observers. It would prove much less confusing to our prerevolutionary intellectual, should he wish to return for a renewed inspection tour.

Yet the chances for such an evolution are slim indeed. In the West the transition from an industrialization economy to a consumption economy has been gradually achieved. *Sine littera* and with varying ingredients, the Western economies have come to combine liberal (in the original sense) and socialist elements — that is to say, the elements of the two humanitarian movements that dominated the nineteenth century. It is doubtful that a consumption economy can be established in Soviet Russia. A decentralized economic system geared to a steady rise in levels of consumption would leave the Soviet dictatorship without a social function, without a justification for its existence. It is much more likely that the dictatorship will continue the policy of willfully provoking one international crisis after the other and of maintaining a high rate of investment as the economic pendant to such a policy. Then a renewed curtailment of such managerial freedoms as have been granted since Stalin's death,[35] followed by a general reversal of the decentralization policy, should be only a matter of time, and enterprise and management in Russia should once more return to the normalcy of Soviet mercantilism, concealed beneath a generous veneer of socialist phraseology.

[35] It may be significant in this connection that the theses of Khrushchev's speech to the Twenty-first Congress (the Seven Year Plan) speak of increased local initiative on the part of labor and technical personnel but fail to mention the need for managerial initiative. Thus the process of curtailment already may have begun. *Sovetskaya Rossiya*, November 14, 1958. [In May 1961 the Soviet government embarked upon a further reform of industrial organization by establishing seventeen regional councils, designed to supervise and to coordinate the activities of the individual Sovnarkhozes. This does seem to be more than the first station on the road to renewed centralization of the Soviet industrial structure. See *Sovetskaya Belorussiya*, July 1, 1961, and *New York Times*, February 24, 1962. For Khrushchev's somewhat bashful reference to the new reform, see his speech to the Twenty-second Congress, *Pravda*, October 19, 1961, p. 3. A. G., 1962]

I 2

A Neglected Source of Economic Information
on Soviet Russia

CAN fiction be considered a serious source of information on *modern* economic history? In an article on English novels in the 1840s, William O. Aydelotte points out that such information in the works of the four most important social novelists of that decade (Dickens, Kingsley, Disraeli, and Mrs. Gaskell) "is highly suspect for the scholar's purpose" because "it is spotty, impressionistic, and inaccurate." [1] This is a harsh verdict. Yet, in a somewhat milder form, it may well prove generally valid. The truth probably is that the economic historian of modern times does not need the aid of contemporaneous novels or plays. The social historian may indeed be greatly interested in finding out why certain novels were written and why they were read. But this is a different matter.

No economic historian needs Balzac's *Le Curé de village* in order to understand the working of the Napoleonic laws concerning inheritance. Inquiry into financial developments under the Second Empire does not require perusal of Zola's *L'Argent* or *La Curée;* and a student of the "merchant-employer" system in Silesia may safely forego reading Gerhart Hauptmann's *Die Weber.* No additional contribution to the knowledge of peasant conditions in Russia was made either by Turgenev, or Grigorovich, or Tolstoy; and the effects of the dust bowl on the rural population of Oklahoma would not

---

[1] "The England of Marx and Mill as Reflected in Fiction," *Journal of Economic History*, Supplement VIII, 1948 (New York, 1949), 43.

have been less clear had Steinbeck's *Grapes of Wrath* remained unwritten. Each of these authors was indeed referred to time and again in professional studies of the respective subjects, but the purpose was one of communication with the reader, that is, to strike a familiar note in the reader's mind, rather than to supply additional evidence.

Nonetheless, a fairly strong case can be made for increased preoccupation with Soviet novels, short stories, and plays on the part of Western economists who work in the field of Soviet economy. Not that the material to be found in Soviet fiction is less "spotty, impressionistic, and inaccurate" than that of Dickens' and Kingsley's. In fact, the opposite may be true. But the situation is profoundly different in other respects. Information supplied by a novelist can be disdained only if the flow from other more important sources is plentiful. This, of course, is not the case with Soviet Russia.

It has become a common practice for students of the Soviet economy to preface their writings on the subject with some sort of apology. This is understandable. Anyone devoting time and thought to problems of Soviet economic development must be painfully aware both of the narrow limits to the scope of his own knowledge and of the distressing gaps in available information. This lack of knowledge stems essentially, although not exclusively, from the restrictive information policy of the Soviet government. Since the middle of the thirties the volume of data supplied has been steadily declining. During the war an almost complete blackout prevailed; and what has been published since its end is still very inadequate even in comparison with the low point of 1940.[2] It is not the quantitative information alone that has deteriorated. The general descriptive Soviet literature on economic subjects has also suffered a great deal. While the volume of such literature on various portions of the current five-year plan has been very considerable, its contents on the whole have been confined to a jejune repetition of official pronouncements. As a result, the innumerable books and pamphlets all seem alike. Walter Bagehot once said, "When you have seen one Fuegian, you have seen all

[2] The text, written in 1949, presents a fair picture of the situation in Russia well into the fifties. Since 1956, the amount of economic information has greatly increased, surpassing both in volume and (to a lesser extent) in quality what was available at the end of the 1930s. [A. G., 1962]

Fuegians — one Tasmanian, all Tasmanians." [3] The current economic literature in Soviet Russia is primitive indeed.

There is no point in exaggerating what doubtless is a very unsatisfactory situation. It is quite true that over the last decade or so a number of Western economists have impressively demonstrated that patience, imagination, and ingenuity can succeed in extracting valuable results even from such a scarce and resistant material as Soviet statistics. In order to achieve these results, the economists concerned had to pile assumption on assumption, to piece together small fragments of uncertain information into a perhaps still less certain whole, to extrapolate and interpolate, and to unfold long inferential chains from a casually given Soviet figure or statement. Even though very often these scholars must have felt like participants in the famous game of billiards from Gilbert and Sullivan's *Mikado,* which was being played

> On a cloth untrue
> with a twisted cue,
> and elliptical billiard balls,

there is no doubt that their labors have materially widened our knowledge and increased our understanding of Soviet Russia.

In many respects, however, it is precisely this increase in our grasp of the Soviet economic system that reveals and aggravates the

[3] Walter Bagehot, *Works,* IV (Hartford, 1891), 500. The Russians are not unaware of this degradation of their economic literature. K. V. Ostrovityanov, who was Varga's successor in the reformed Institute of Economics, said at a session of the Scientific Council of the Institute: "The fear of committing an error in posing and elaborating new problems causes economists to move away from analyses of contradictions arising in the process of development of socialist economy and reduces scholarly work to a mastication of existing resolutions, or to publication of propaganda articles and pamphlets, while serious scholarly investigation of the economic problems of socialism is avoided." He added that only a few of the recent dissertations for the degree of candidate and doctor of economics were published, because the authors did not relish having their theses printed (*Voprosy ekonomiki,* 1948, no. 8, p. 74). The probable effectiveness of the speaker's admonitions for a "bolder, bolshevist approach to economic research" must be judged in the light of the sweeping and severe decree concerning disclosure of state secrets (*Pravda,* June 10, 1947), and Ostrovityanov's immoderate strictures in the same speech of "errors" committed by a number of Soviet economists.

Since 1956, there have been some narrowly confined, but not unimportant, improvements in Soviet economic literature. [A. G., 1962]

economist's predicament. As a foundation is being laid for a scholarly study of Soviet economy with the help of tools of modern economic and statistical analysis, a growing number of new and exciting problems is brought within the purview of the economist. In the process, he becomes even more conscious of the inadequacy of his material and of a basic limitation which lies in the virtual impossibility of gaining understanding of economic processes in the Soviet Union from personal association with men who are actively engaged in these processes. The planner in the Gosplan, the banker in the Gosbank or in one of the special investment banks, the manager and the union representative of an industrial plant, the chairman of a collective farm — they all are, and, barring a radical change in Soviet policy, will remain, out of reach of the Western research worker.[4] A scholar studying the economy of the first socialist country has not only to forego the wealth of documents which the student of capitalism once found in the British Museum; it is also unthinkable for him to have a close friend who is in charge of an industrial enterprise in the Soviet Union and moves in the very hub of the industrial life of the country. In these circumstances, no source of information, however uncertain, can be lightly rejected, and the quest for such sources deserves serious attention.

Conversations with Soviet citizens who, after the end of the war, found themselves outside Russia and her zone of influence in Europe may indeed provide valuable information. In fact, it is highly regrettable that little has been done so far to collect and to analyze information from that source, and every attempt should be made to utilize it. The matter is urgent. Memories of individuals who have suffered great tribulations in the intervening years are likely to become blurred. As time passes, and the process of their adaptation to Western ways proceeds, they must tend to lose their original viewpoints and the value of their testimonies will diminish accordingly. Finally, the accessibility of the persons concerned is dwindling

[4] Changes have taken place in this respect as well. But neither the larger flow of economic information nor the opportunities for personal contacts nor the considerable change in various institutional arrangements has been such as to invalidate, or even to alter materially, the position taken in this essay on the significance of Soviet literature as a source of economic information. Still, the reader will want to keep in mind that the present essay was written thirteen years ago. [A. G., 1962]

through their emigration to South America, Australia, and other distant regions. At any rate, whatever information can be gleaned from this source does not transcend the years of the war. For the postwar period and for the future, one must have recourse to other sources.

The remainder of this essay is devoted to a brief discussion of the possibilities of obtaining useful information from Soviet novels and plays and to a few illustrations taken from such recent Soviet productions.

The first question to be raised is whether or not the subject matter of Soviet literary productions is such as to arouse the economist's interest in them. The answer must be in the affirmative. Since the days of Fedor Gladkov's *Cement,* a new type of industrial novel has developed in Soviet Russia and has been subsequently paralleled by the emergence of collective-farm novels. Very deliberately and no doubt under pressure by the government, literature has been increasingly placed in the service of the economic policies of the Soviet government. Love, friendship, the inner struggles of the individual have been pushed far into the background and sometimes eliminated altogether. Construction of factories, railroads, pipelines, and power stations; increases in mining and industrial output; application of improved methods of farming — these are the subjects to which Soviet novelists have primarily addressed themselves, if the very substantial recent crop of military novels may be disregarded. Soviet belles-lettres have been dedicated to economic problems to an extent altogether unprecedented in the history of world literature, with the possible exception of the hunting songs of primitive folklore. This is a development which an economist working in the Soviet field cannot ignore.

This shift in the sphere of interest of Soviet writers, undertaken as it was under extraneous pressure, doubtless proceeded at the expense of the artistic value of their works. A pattern of monotonous uniformity has developed. Voltaire, who accepted every literary genre except the boring one, would have refused to read the average Soviet novel or play, but this is of little concern to the economist who is in search of things less exciting and more tangible than artistic values. The real problem from his point of view is whether or not this literature has been so subordinated to the propaganda interests of the government as to become worthless as a reflection of Soviet economic reality. The present writer would like to answer the question in the spirit of restrained optimism.

That Soviet literature is not only subject to a preventive censorship, but also is positively controlled and guided by the government seems reasonably certain. Otherwise it would be difficult to explain the rapidity of literary responses to changes in the party line. A governmental action in the field of philosophy coupled with a campaign against Western influences immediately calls forth novels like Grigori Konovalov's *University* [5] with its brazen glorification of Russian philosophy in the face of the still valid dictum of Vladimir Solovev that "what is philosophical in Russian works on philosophy is not Russian, and what is Russian in these works has no relation to philosophy." [6] The line turns against the United States and almost instantly plays like Konstantin Simonov's *Russian Question* or Kozhevnikov and Prut's *The Fate of Reginald Davis* are turned out.[7] The "uprooted cosmopolitan" is put under fire, and without delay Simonov serves up another play, *The Foreign Shadow*,[8] where the dangers of international scientific cooperation are depicted in the darkest colors, the cosmopolitan is unmasked as a spy, and, in addition, the government's policy of secrecy is glorified.

The present writer has no knowledge as to the exact nature of the actual connection: does a governmental agency actually present individual writers with specific assignments or is reliance on servility of the writers, in conjunction with general exhortation, considered sufficient? But strong as the ascendancy of the government is, it can hardly be absolute: a certain margin of freedom must be allowed, as is shown by savage postpublication attacks in the press.[9] And this

[5] "Universitet," *Oktyabr'*, 1947, nos. 6, 7; subsequently published in book form.

[6] "Natsional'nyi vopros v Rossii" (The National Question in Russia), *Sobranie sochinenii* (Collected Works), V (St. Petersburg, n. d.), 88.

[7] K. Simonov, "The Russian Question," *Soviet Literature*, February 1947; V. Kozhevnikov and I. Prut, "Sud'ba Redzhinal'da Devisa," *Zvezda*, 1947, no. 4.

[8] K. Simonov, "Chuzhaya ten'," *Znamya*, 1949, no. 1.

[9] At times such attacks lead to discontinuation of the publication of a work of fiction which has been appearing serially; see, for instance, the case of Y. German's novel "Podpolkovnik meditsinskoy sluzhby" (Lt. Col. of Medical Service), *Zvezda*, 1949, no. 1.

stands to reason. Complete regimentation might easily result in such an additional decline in the value of Soviet literary output as would defeat the government's purposes altogether.

Soviet discussions of socialist realism versus socialist romanticism may be pertinent in this connection. Divested of a good deal of inane phraseology, the problem seems to be whether a Soviet writer should depict his heroes as they are or as they ought to be from the point of view of the official ideal. Presentation of society composed of Soviet *chevaliers sans peur ni reproche* should appeal to the instincts of the literary police. It may appeal to the self-preservation instincts of the authors. The result would be the "conflictless" novel as it is called in Soviet discussions of the subject.[10] This is romanticism with a vengeance: E. T. A. Hoffmann's *Die Elixire des Teufels* without the devil. But fortunately this ideal seems to be unattainable.

Soviet economy has been one of intensive internal conflicts. As long as the ratio between investment (including military expenditures) and consumption remains so heavily weighted in favor of the former, the day-to-day economic processes in Soviet Russia are characterized by a continuous struggle between the government and the population. There is nothing sensational about these struggles. Least of all are they political in nature. But nonetheless they are very real. The government must fight the worker who is unwilling to sustain the tempo of work in the face of inadequate increases in levels of consumption and who is trying to keep the production norms as low as possible; the government must fight the manager of industrial plants who is trying in a variety of ways to evade the plan and who, conscious of inflationary pressures in the economy, is trying to hoard raw materials so as to achieve unplanned profits and the bounties and promotions which follow in the wake of such achievements; the government, in fine, must fight the collective farms, which are unwilling to surrender to the government substantial portions of their produce at prices greatly below the kolkhoz market prices and which are employing every imaginable device to evade the obligation imposed on them.

It is not suggested that these struggles imperil the stability of the

---

[10] See, for instance, the article by N. Gribachev, "Za novyi pod'em sovetskoy poesii" (For a New Upsurge of Soviet Poetry), *Znamya*, 1949, no. 1, p. 171.

government. All that is suggested here is that a literature, which tries to present as "conflictless" an economy still subject to a high degree of stress and strain, must inevitably and very quickly transcend the limits of verisimilitude; and that thereby literary production becomes impossible. Not necessarily so, because a strike of authors should be the answer. As Chekhov once remarked, "If you beat a hare for a sufficiently long time it may learn how to use a photographic camera." It should not be too difficult to badger a Soviet writer into submission. But the unbridgeable gulf between the conflictless society in the novel and on the stage and the conflict-pregnant reality would destroy all the propaganda effect of literature. The Soviet discussions of romanticism and realism may perhaps be taken both as a mild form of rebellion against too great a regimentation of literature and as a sign that the regimentation is not absolute. To repeat: a certain margin of freedom must remain.

But is it possible for the non-Russian reader of Soviet works of literature to separate the wheat from the chaff, the reality from its distortion? And will the grains of truth be numerous enough to warrant the economist's search for them? A brief presentation of a number of illustrations from a few recent works of Soviet literature may be helpful in suggesting at least tentative answers to these questions.[11]

It may be advisable to mention first a rather singular case in which the validity of facts as supplied by the novelist was capable of being tested.

In 1948, the literary journal *Oktyabr'* published a novel on gold

[11] Most Soviet works of fiction are first published in one of the literary journals of which the following should be noted: *Novy Mir, Oktyabr', Znamya,* and *Zvezda.* The first three journals appear in Moscow and the last one in Leningrad. For years, Vera Aleksandrova has been publishing reviews in Russian on current Soviet fiction in various periodicals, most notably in the *Sotsialisticheskii vestnik,* the magazine of the Russian Social Democratic Party in exile, now appearing in New York. While Mrs. Aleksandrova's interests do not lie specifically in the economic field, in general she addresses herself to the social significance of Soviet belles-lettres, and economists interested in the problems raised in this essay will find her reviews a most excellent introduction to Soviet fiction. It is, incidentally, very regrettable that these reviews are inaccessible to those who have no reading knowledge of Russian. A translation into English of at least a selection of these reviews would be desirable indeed.

mining in Soviet Russia.[12] This novel was finished just before the outbreak of the war, after its author had spent seven years in Siberia as a party functionary in one of the mines. The novel describes the efforts made to increase the output of gold at a trans-Baikalian mine sometime during the thirties. The difficulties which confronted the administration of the mine and its workers are graphically presented: the inadequacy of food supplies to the miners who had been induced to move to the permafrost region by extravagant promises; the resulting low effort on the part of the workers; the hopeless primitiveness of the technological equipment; the aloofness of engineers who preferred to stay away from the mine; the deflection of sizable portions of output into illegal channels. All this is not new to the Western economist, but this is precisely why Ganibesov's novel is of interest for the purposes of this discussion. For the Russian author's description coincides strikingly with the story of gold mining in Russia as told by a perfectly trustworthy source: John J. Littlepage, the American engineer who had served for many years in a responsibile capacity in the Soviet gold mine administration.[13] There also exists a professional Soviet discussion of the subject,[14] and it is curious to see that in many respects Ganibesov's novel provides a much clearer and franker insight into the situation.

Ever since the beginning of the First Five Year Plan, the trend in the Soviet Union has been for increased power of managers of industrial plants. "Unity of control" (*yedinonachaliye*) implied vesting in the manager of the enterprise the responsibility for carrying out its plan, for all matters relating to output and to hiring and firing of workers and salaried employees of the plant. Neither the trade union through the factory committee nor the party cell were thenceforth supposed to interfere directly in the administration of industrial enterprises. This development has raised a number of interesting problems, and economists have every reason to search for evidence permitting them better to assess the present position of the manager within the framework of the Soviet economy. Soviet fiction does

[12] V. Ganibesov, "Starateli" (The Placer Miners), *Oktyabr'*, 1948, no. 3.

[13] John J. Littlepage, *In Search of Soviet Gold* (New York, 1938).

[14] A. P. Serebrovski, *Na zolotom fronte* (On the Gold Front) (Moscow-Leningrad, 1936).

shed some light on this question. A novel by Vera Panova, *Kruzhilikha* (the name of a plant), which was first published in 1947,[15] contains interesting material on various aspects of the question. A good deal of the novel is devoted to the relations between the manager and the chairman of the factory committee. The latter does not have much luck in his attempts to assert himself:

Usdechkin [chairman of the factory committee] . . . came to Listopad [manager] with a number of demands concerning working conditions in the factory.

"No, you stay out of these matters," said Listopad. "You leave all that to me."

"Sorry, comrade manager," said Usdechkin, "but don't you know that this is a direct function of the trade union?"

"No, I don't," said Listopad . . . "It's your business to know what your functions are" (p. 9).

The chairman of the factory committee shows some fighting spirit. He attacks the manager in the meetings of the city party committee. But the effect is nil. The manager is unassailable, and the reason is clearly shown in the novel: he has succeeded in regularly overfulfilling the production plan. The chairman of the factory committee may protest ever so loudly against the manager's transforming the "principle of unity of control" into the "principle of autocracy." The manager knows that, if the chairman should become too bothersome to him, he will not find it too difficult to get rid of this elected representative of the workers (p. 7). But would not the workers support their representative against the manager? Apparently not. And the reason is not necessarily the manager's proficiency in production. For Panova supplies an additional fact which also should be of interest to the economist. The manager had built up a secret organization of special agents who are distributed throughout the villages of the region. They watch closely the process of deliveries of agricultural products by collective farms to the governmental procurement agencies. As soon as the quota is fulfilled and a collective farm has received the right to sell its products on a free market, representatives of Kruzhilikha, who had been informed by their agents, appear on

[15] *Znamya*, 1947, nos. 11, 12. Subsequent page references are to the edition in book form (Moscow-Leningrad, 1948).

the scene, conclude the contracts, and cart away grain, potatoes, and vegetables for the factory ORS (division of workers' supplies). By the time the other factories were officially informed of completion of deliveries to the government, Listopad had bought up the available surpluses.

The action of the novel takes place in 1945; nevertheless, this practice sheds an interesting light on the operation of the "kolkhoz market" in conditions of scarcity. Such operations may have been preserved well beyond the abolition of rationing in 1947 to the extent that the latter did not necessarily mean immediate elimination of food scarcities.

It is not unlikely that the scarcities of the war period in general contributed to strengthening the position of the manager as against the workers, thus supplementing such increases in his power as resulted from the labor legislation which tied the worker to the factory and which is referred to in the novel as "wartime legislation," even though it is still on the statute book.[16] In Panova's novel, a youth working in the factory absents himself without permission for a week. The manager can surrender him to the court. In this particular case, he decides to place no strain on the quality of mercy, and this again seems to be illuminating: the manager's power to bind and to loose must have greatly contributed to equipping him with new paternalistic traits. It is therefore not surprising to find in *Kruzhilikha* and elsewhere in Soviet fiction that the manager, in addressing subordinates, uses the time-consecrated feudal *ty* (thou) while the subordinates use the respectful *vy* (you).

A manager who is overfulfilling production plans acquires an impregnable position because of the support of his economic ministry. But Panova's novel touches on an even more important problem: the basic strength of the manager in relation to the central authorities. It describes how difficult it was to dismiss Listopad's predecessor, although, according to the novel, he had proved unable to meet the wartime plans. The manager claimed that the plans exceeded the

---

[16] The legislation which made it a penal offense for a worker to quit his job was not abrogated until May 1956. See *Direktivy KPSS i sovetskogo pravitel'stva po khozyaystvennym voprosam* (The Directives of the Communist Party of the Soviet Union on Economic Matters) (Moscow, 1958), pp. 620–626. [A. G., 1962]

factory's capacity. And in this, Panova informs us, he found support even from some members of the local party committee who thought that "it would not be so bad if the plan were to be cut by about fifteen percent. Everything would become much easier; the factory would show better performance, and come into good standing with the narkomat [ministry]" (p. 115).

The local party functionary began a struggle against the manager, in which he was not countenanced by the city party committee. Its chairman felt that this was a delicate matter to be decided between the narkom and the manager. According to the novel, the local party man in the plant succeeded in enlisting the help of some engineers, foremen, and skilled workers and prepared a report for submission to a special commission sent to the plant by the ministry. His opinion prevailed, but the story carries strong implications that without this help from inside the factory the ministry would have acquiesced in the lowering of plan goals.

Similarly, in a play by A. Sofronov, *Beketov's Career*,[17] combines which have been produced by a large Soviet factory regularly break down in the fields. The ministry in charge of the factory sends down a representative who instantly dismisses the manager of the factory. But the ministry's action has been provoked by a series of anonymous letters written by the factory's chief engineer, who has been aspiring to the manager's position.

This is a point well worth dwelling upon. Very frequently, in professional presentations of the modus operandi of the Soviet economy, the impression is created of a completely centralized framework within which the manager of the individual enterprise receives binding orders by the central plan as to composition and size of the plant's inputs and outputs. This may tend to disguise important developments. Even the pioneering work by Bienstock, Schwarz, and Yugow,[18] in which a good deal of information on the sphere of autonomy of industrial plant managers has been analyzed, perhaps underestimates the actual scope of that autonomy. It would seem that, in appraising the way in which the Soviet economy works and

[17] "Kar'era Beketova," *Novy Mir*, 1949, no. 4.
[18] Gregory Bienstock, Solomon M. Schwarz, and Aaron Yugow, *Management in Russian Industry and Agriculture* (New York, 1944).

the degree of its centralization, it may be advisable to distinguish between the administrative surface and the economic core of the problem. There is no question that the Soviet administration of the economy by central planning covers overwhelmingly large parts of that economy. It is conceivable, however, that a good deal of what formally sails under the name of central planning is in fact based on decisions taken on the level of plant management.[19] It is conceivable that in reality there are considerable limitations on the knowledge and foreknowledge of central authorities as to the actual conditions and developments in the individual plants. An economist who has been wondering about relationships like those touched upon in note 19 may feel that the material contained in Panova's novel or in Sofronov's play does in some measure enhance the validity of the questions raised.

In this connection another play by Sofronov, which, like *Kruzhilikha*, was awarded a Stalin Prize, is also revealing.[20] The

[19] An example may serve to illustrate the point. Production and consumption of copper is centrally planned. Copper is included in what is called in Russia "material balances," that is, balance-sheet-like juxtapositions of output and consumption of individual commodities in terms of physical quantities. In Soviet literature very much emphasis is placed on this method of planning through material balances. It is said to assure absence of disproportionalities. Now, copper remained in short supply throughout most of the thirties. Domestic production grew at too slow a rate; imports remained substantial; and the Soviet government attempted for years to reduce the consumption of copper by introduction of substitutes in less essential lines of production. These attempts showed but a moderate degree of success, until, in 1937, the government decided to increase drastically the price of copper while keeping constant the planned cost of commodities in the production of which the metal was used. Apparently, the effect was all that could be desired. Copper was thenceforth confined to more essential uses, and substitutes began to be utilized on a significant scale. See G. Kozlov, *Khozyaystvennyi raschet v sotsialisticheskom obshchestve* (Economic Accounting in Socialist Society) (Ogiz, 1945), p. 65.

This obviously raises a question: why did not the central-planning authority simply change the pattern of copper consumption in its material balances? Why did the Soviet government have to have recourse to the indirect device of a price increase, which surely is more uncertain and less transparent in its effects? There is a strong presumption in favor of believing that the Soviet government could not use the more direct method because *it did not know* in what segments of the copper-using industry and to what extent the restrictions should and could be applied. In other words, the central authority accepted decisions of the managers of the individual plants. Presumably, *after* the rise in price, the pattern of copper consumption in the material balances was adapted to the new situation.

[20] "Moskovskii kharakter" (The Moscow Character), *Oktyabr'*, 1949, no. 1.

central figure of the play is again a successful industrial manager, Potapov. His plant, which specializes in machine-tool production for construction of agricultural machines, has been overfulfilling the plan. The play begins with Potapov's decision to fulfill the factory's current (Fourth) Five-Year Plan in three-and-a-half years. Immediately thereafter, however, he is presented with a request from the manager of a nearby textile plant. Potapov is asked to devote some of his capacity to the output of textile machinery for the neighboring enterprise. The whole plot of the play turns around the request. Potapov first refuses and it takes full four acts of suasion and persuasion, including a decision of the district party committee, to make him acquiesce in the wishes of the textile plant.

The details of the play need not occupy us, although some of them are illuminating (such as the attitude of humorous resignation which the average Russian displays toward government and party slogans). Nor is it necessary to concern ourselves with the moral of the play, the intended propaganda effect of which is clear: the Soviet government and the Communist Party are interested in production of investment goods not only for further investment but also for immediate use in consumption-goods industries; and the play contains sharp strictures on the feeling of superiority shown on the part of representatives of heavy industry toward those of light industry, a feeling presumably intensified during the war. But while all this is certainly significant, what is of interest here is that throughout the play an important decision with respect to the production program is assumed to lie within Potapov's discretion: "If you agree, the Ministry won't have any objections!" (p. 110). And, it is interesting to note, the resolution of the party committee does not urge the ministry to *instruct* Potapov to accept the order of the textile factory, but merely urges the ministry to *allow* him to do so.

This illustrates the supposition that large portions of industrial output may be in fact only very imperfectly controlled by the plan, if they are controlled at all; that the manager, and particularly the plan-overfulfilling manager, enjoys a considerable sphere within which he can make basic decisions with respect to both the type of goods to be produced and the mode of their disposal. The latter, incidentally, becomes to a large extent a matter of personal connections. As such it introduces an element of chance and narrowness into the allocation of resources as an alternative both to the comprehensive decision of the central planner and to the objective price mechanism of the market. Later we shall supply some additional illustrations for this role of personal connections in Soviet economy. Suffice it to say here that the problem is well worth further note. Could it be that the limitations on effective central planning in conjunction with absence of a free and broad market for industrial goods produce within the Soviet economy certain aspects of localism which were peculiar to the narrow economy of the medieval city?

Sofronov poses the managerial problem in Soviet Russia with a good deal of clarity, when he lets Potapov's wife tell him reproachfully: "Why do you say so often 'my factory,' 'I am the manager,' 'I am the *khozyain*' [owner, boss]? You are a *khozyaistvennik* [a responsible economic functionary], but the state, the people — that's the *khozyain*." [21] This indeed is the problem: the degree to which a *khozyaistvennik* tends to become a *khozyain*. Both Panova's novel and Sofronov's play provide interesting fragments of information on this problem.

The increase in the power of managers of Soviet industrial plants is sometimes regarded as an irresistible evolution, which will continue unabated in the years to come. Others may feel that such strengthening in the position of the manager as has taken place in the past has been a temporary phenomenon, occasioned primarily by the fact that development of institutional machinery designed to supervise the execution of the plan has lagged behind development of an apparatus for plan making. Naturally, fiction will provide no answer to such speculations. But the attention that at present is being devoted to the problem by Soviet fiction may be indicative of its importance and perhaps even adumbrate the approach of a period of critical decisions with regard to the relations between managers and central authorities. [22]

[21] For a very similar retort by which a manager of a railroad is reprimanded, see the play by A. Surov, "Zelenaya ulitsa" (The Green Street), *Oktyabr'*, 1949, no. 5, p. 118.

[22] As mentioned elsewhere in this volume (Chapter 11, note 33), the organizational reform in Soviet industry (1957) was duly reflected in Soviet novels. For additional treatment of the problems surrounding industrial management, see

Soviet postwar literature includes a considerable crop of collective-farm novels and plays. Many of them serve to illustrate the fact that the struggle of the peasants to evade the obligation to deliver grain to the procurement agencies has continued unabated. Both the play by Virta, *Our Daily Bread*, and the novel by Babayevski, *Knight of the Golden Star*,[23] refer to the collective-farm practice of hiding grain by adding it to the "seed fund" which in the case described by Virta came to exceed the plan threefold (p. 46). In Babayevski's novel the chairman of a collective farm becomes apprehensive of a possible inspection of the seed fund and distributes the surplus among the members of the kolkhoz. His purpose is to keep the grain for sale on the kolkhoz market until the spring when prices will be high. In addition, in Virta's play, a kolkhoz chairman hides the grain by letting it escape into the offals during threshing with the intention of recovering it later in the winter. Such episodes must be viewed in the light of the fact that grain deliveries from collective farms to the government are legally computed not on the basis of harvest, and not even on the basis of area sown (as was the custom until 1940), but on the basis of the aggregate arable land of the kolkhoz; computations in relation to area sown apparently either led to a diminution of the area under cultivation in relation to total arable land or at least prevented an increase in that ratio. In 1947, the system was rendered more flexible by varying the "delivery norms" in accordance with the existing relations between total arable land of the individual kolkhoz and the number of able-bodied workers available to it.[24] But the principle of government deliveries on the basis of the land available rather than on the basis of the harvest was fully maintained.

The question then arises as to the purpose pursued by kolkhozes in hiding their grain. It should be noted that the deliveries mentioned in the preceding paragraph constitute only a portion of the centralized deliveries to the government. A very substantial share of the aggre-

---

Alexander Gerschenkron, "The Changeability of a Dictatorship," in *World Politics*, July 1962. [A. G., 1962]

[23] Nikolai Virta, "Khleb nash nasushchny," *Zvezda*, 1947, no. 6; Semen Babayevski, "Kavaler zolotoy zvezdy," *Oktyabr'*, 1947, nos. 4, 5.

[24] *Pravda*, March 7, 1947.

gate [25] is delivered by the kolkhoz in the form of a payment in kind for work performed for it by the Machine Tractor Station (MTS). Such payments are computed on the basis of the harvest, but for the most part the computation is made on the basis of the biological (field) yield rather than on that of the actual (barn) yield. It is only the reaping and threshing operations for which the payment is calculated in accordance with quantities actually reaped or threshed. The aim of these arrangements obviously was to render purposeless the various devices by which the kolkhozes tried to evade their obligations. It is therefore useful to note the interest which Soviet fiction takes in those devices and to speculate as to how their continued use might be reconciled with a legal framework that *a priori* seemed to have rendered them inapplicable.

Possibly, the farm hiding grain avoids the pressure to deliver *additional* grain to the government under the so-called decentralized deliveries. More likely is the supposition that the rigid stipulations of the legislation are impossible of practical implementation and that in reality grain deliveries are determined by taking, in some manner, account of the actual production of grain. Still another possibility is that by concealment of grain the kolkhoz hopes to achieve a reduction of future obligations. Finally, there may be, of course, outright bribery of officials in charge of supervising the process of grain deliveries. In Virta's play, the maleficent chairman of the kolkhoz even goes so far as to bribe the director of the MTS station into issuing a falsified certificate concerning the quantity of grain threshed and the employee of the procurement agency into issuing a fictitious receipt for grain that never has been delivered.

In the postwar collective-farm fiction, the role of the hero is assigned to the homecoming veteran, who immediately upon his return acquires a dominant position in the collective farm or in the local soviet and with great energy leads the kolkhoz on the road of adjustment to peacetime conditions. Both in the novel and in the play, the respective heroes are able to uncover the malefactors and to reform the kolkhoz. Neither fiction nor any other source, naturally, can pro-

[25] For instance, 50 percent in 1937; see L. S. Galimon, *Dokhody mashino-traktornykh stantsii* (The Revenues of the Machine Tractor Stations) (Moscow, 1948), p. 8.

vide an answer to the question of the over-all quantitative significance of evasions of government regulations by the collective farms.

Of some interest is the efficient way in which Babayevski's Knight of the Golden Star, who has become chairman of the local soviet, dismisses the guilty administration of the kolkhoz. He makes up his mind as to who should succeed the old chairman and, at a late hour of night, convokes a meeting of kolkhoz membership and has the satisfaction of seeing that the person of his choice is spontaneously nominated by the assembly and instantly elected. This sidelight on the operation of kolkhoz elections is of some importance. So is the fact that at least one person in the novel protests against it and considers it a breach of the kolkhoz covenant.

In collective-farm fiction considerable attention is devoted to the problem of individual plots of land of the kolkhoz members and to the more intensive work devoted to these plots as compared with the work on kolkhoz fields. In Babayevski's novel an interesting theory is even developed by two kolkhoz chairmen independently of each other to the effect that greater sowing of cereals on individual plots would tend to spread the risk, so that a crop failure on kolkhoz fields would be compensated for by a good harvest on the individual plots. While the logical persuasiveness of this theory is probably not too great, the fact that it is being expounded provides some additional insight into the attitudes of collective farmers.

An interesting problem suggested by perusal of Soviet fiction refers to the existence of "leading" kolkhozes. A good deal of the novel by V. Ilenkov, *The High Way*, is devoted to this question.[26] The difference between the leading kolkhoz, which is managed by the father of the hero of the novel, and another one not far away is striking: "We distribute 12 kilograms of grain and in addition 4½ rubles per working day,[27] and there [in the poorer kolkhoz] it is years since they had enough bread to eat." [28]

The problem undoubtedly is a delicate one. The government naturally favors those kolkhozes showing an extraordinary perform-

---

[26] "Bol'shaya doroga," *Oktyabr'*, 1949, nos. 1, 2.

[27] "Working day" is a conventional measure of work performed by the members of the kolkhoz and is not identical with a calendar day.

[28] Ilenkov, p. 93.

ance. Within a certain margin, they serve as a model for the remainder of collective farms in the region or district. The record performance, as often as not, is the result of a deliberate governmental policy. The previously quoted play by Virta shows how the local soviet can affect the production results as among the individual kolkhozes by directing, in crucial moments, trucks and tractors to one kolkhoz in preference to others. Again, it may be noted parenthetically, the problem of personal connections comes in: in Ilenkov's novel one person expresses the opinion that unless at least the first secretary of the district party committee, who is the actual boss of the chairman of the regional soviet and, in fact, of the whole region, is invited to the planned bear-hunting expedition of the kolkhoz, it might be difficult to obtain gasoline for tractors during the summer.[29]

But the problem is a much broader one. The record performance of one kolkhoz may be achieved at the expense of losses by other kolkhozes which are greatly in excess of the increment in output realized through the record performance. During the last war the shipyards in California from time to time would produce a Liberty boat within twenty-four hours instead of the usual eighteen to twenty-one days. Impressive as such performances were, they were bought at the cost of delaying output for some fifteen boats in construction in the respective yard because all scarce equipment, such as cranes, was concentrated on the record boat. The great importance which is attributed to record performances in Soviet Russia doubtless constitutes a serious problem from the point of view of allocation of scarce resources, and one may be grateful to Soviet fiction for supplying some sidelights on the question. It may be rewarding to look for analogous literary illustrations in the field of industry and mining where the problem may well be much more acute.[30]

A similar difficulty appears, in a slightly different form, in Babayevski's novel. The hero proposes an electric-power station to be built by his village, which consists of three collective farms. In

[29] *Ibid.*, p. 59.

[30] The previously cited play by Surov, "The Green Street," pivots around a sharply criticized attempt on the part of a railroad administration to establish a record of performance merely for window-dressing purposes in lieu of sustained improvements in the speed of transportation and the volume of goods carried. See *Novy Mir*, 1949, no. 5.

the course of the execution of this proposal, he is promoted to chairmanship of the district soviet executive committee and immediately decides to increase the capacity of the power station so as to make it serve the whole district. This action dismays the neighbors in his own village, because they had gone to great trouble in floating lumber down the river to the village for the construction of the station, and they are willing to share neither the fruits of their labor nor the glory of being the first electrically lit village of the region. The curious thing, however, is that, when the hero is approached by a representative of a neighboring district who asks him to increase the capacity of the station further, so that it may serve more than one district, he refuses bluntly. None of the arguments on the virtues of cooperation and the dangers of selfishness with which he so eloquently allayed the misgivings of his neighbors seems to occur to him now. And the question is left uncertain except for a slight hint that the secretary of the district party committee may take up the matter. The desire to monopolize achievements in the Soviet economy is thus rather strikingly illustrated. The double aspect of monopolistic developments — which both promote and retard progress — may appeal to the dialectically trained minds of the Soviet leaders, but it also constitutes a grave problem calling for difficult practical decisions.

Perhaps it is permissible to return for a brief moment to the role of personal connections which was touched upon earlier. For Babayevski's novel provides some additional material on the subject. When the village needs lumber for the construction of the power station, the first (although ineffectual) attempt to obtain it leads the Knight of the Golden Star to undertake a journey to a personal friend of the manager of the district consumers' cooperative, who is said to be in a position to arrange dealings of this sort: "There is no point in going to regional administration. They can't do anything without Moscow's consent . . . You had better go to Pyatigorsk. I have a friend there . . . a wonderful fellow. I'll write to him, and he'll do everything." [31] When that manager is subsequently sent to Moscow to secure equipment for the station, he emphasizes in his report of the trip how helpful were the personal connections he had established, and he suggests to the Knight that "a certain volume of butter," if

[31] Babayevski, p. 5.

taken along, "would be extremely helpful in further attempts to purchase needed materials."

In a rather similar manner, it may be added, operates Grigori Kondrashev, an architect in Simonov's novel, *The Smoke of the Fatherland;* [32] an additional element in this case seems to be that Kondrashev, while using personal connections for the needs of his housing projects under construction, does not forget his own person and manages to derive personal benefits from his various transactions. Interestingly enough, Simonov volunteers the information that the period of postwar distortion was particularly propitious for men of Kondrashev's type, but that Kondrashev had operated in essentially the same way before the war.

In Ilenkov's novel, the chairman of the kolkhoz, while trying to obtain copper wire, proceeds by applying to the factory in which his brother works as a foreman. It is worth noting that the request is refused because in the past the chairman of the kolkhoz had refused to release to the factory in question twenty kolkhoz members. One is struck time and again by how much economic activity is carried out independently of the plan and of central supervision.

It has not been attempted in the preceding discussion to go into the novelist's or playwright's attitude to the occurrences he relates. This is a more difficult problem and perhaps a not too relevant one from the point of view of this essay. Naturally, Babayevski and Virta both disapprove of farmers' concealing grain from the government. The perpetrators are surrendered to what presumably will be swift and merciless justice. We are told in plain words that Sofronov's manager should have complied with the demand of the textile factory and produced for them the presses they need. But it would be much more difficult to state clearly whether, for instance, Panova's sympathies are with the manager of the plant or the pathetic representative of the union whom the former bullies and badgers to his heart's content. And still more difficult would it be to express such a judgment with regard to the little facts of everyday economic life as related in fiction. Revealing as they may be to the foreign observer, the Soviet writer often takes their existence for granted and therefore

[32] "Dym otechestva," *Novy Mir,* 1947, no. 1, esp. pp. 32–37.

does not feel under any compulsion to label them "good" or "bad."

If some positive conclusion may be drawn from the preceding discussion, it is that it does not seem too difficult to discern in Soviet fiction descriptions of facts and relations which appear both plausible and instructive. A good deal of material an economist may find in Soviet fiction he ought to be able to place within the framework of hypotheses and questions which he has formulated on the basis of professional studies of the Soviet economic scene. While his perusal of the works of fiction will not lead to any "proofs" of his hypotheses or unambiguous answers to his questions, the cumulative effect of recurring fragments of information, all pointing in the same direction, will tend to strengthen in some measure such tentative generalizations as he may have ventured upon. And contrariwise he may find Soviet fiction rather suggestive, and, very often, it may be from this side that the student of Russia's present economy may receive impulses and viewpoints which he may wish to apply in his study of the professional literature.

But the significance of Soviet fiction seems even to go beyond this. Fadeyev's *Young Guard* or Popov's *Steel and Slag* [33] may be but indifferent novels, but they still give a most vivid description of the period of evacuation in the Donbas before the wave of advancing Germans, and such a description provides an invaluable background against which the economist may place such quantitative data on evacuation of factories as are, for instance, contained in Voznesenski's book on the Soviet war economy. And, similarly, Pavlenko's *Happiness* allows at least a glimpse of the great migrations that must have taken place in Soviet Russia upon the conclusion of the war.[34] It is such Soviet fiction that opens to the economist the road to acquiring some sense of the everyday atmosphere of Soviet economic life and of its human fabric, without which any scholarly study must remain a lifeless shell.

[33] A. Fadeyev, *Molodaya gvardiya* (Moscow, 1947); V. Popov, "Stal' i shlak," *Znamya*, 1949, nos. 1, 2.

[34] P. Pavlenko, "Shchast'e," *Znamya*, 1947, no. 7.

I3

Reflections on Soviet Novels

THERE is every likelihood that future historians of the Russian novel will praise the Soviet period for the record number of volumes produced and blame it for an equally unprecedented decline in artistic standards. Yet one may hope that the twenty-first-century critic, in fairness to an unhappy past, will not overlook a redeeming feature of the Soviet novel: its considerable anthropological value. The present reflections about a few recent or fairly recent Soviet novels do not deal with their literary qualities. They are concerned exclusively with the light these novels cast upon various aspects of everyday life in Soviet Russia, including, it may be added, the life of the novel makers themselves.

I

Leonid Leonov's *Russian Forest*,[1] written between 1950 and 1953, provides perhaps more illumination and more food for thought than any other Soviet product in the field since the end of the last war. (Because of its public repudiation in Russia, if not for other reasons, Pasternak's *Doctor Zhivago* may be safely excluded from the list of *Soviet* novels.) *Russian Forest* has both an apparent and a real theme. Though the latter is much more important, the former is by no means without interest. In addition, there are a number of political judgments strewn over the pages of the novel, some of which are worth noting.

[1] *Russkii les*; the page references in the text are to *Sobraniye sochinenii* (Collected Works), VI (Moscow, 1956).

The theme apparent is writ large over the title page: it is the problem of Soviet forestry politics. The hero of the novel, a professor of forestry, loves the forest and wishes the forest-covered areas of the country to be maintained unreduced and unthinned. He would not only preserve the aggregate extent of the forest, but also freeze the existing geographic distribution of forest lands. In defending his position, the professor adds to the long list of Soviet claims to invention by asserting that the concept of "sustained yield" (the concept of a forest which is "normal" as to age structure and produces year in, year out, a harvest maximized in some rational fashion) was developed by Russian students of forestry (p. 318).

In temperament and Weltanschauung, our professor — his name is Virkhov — is a direct descendant of Doctor Astrov in Chekhov's *Uncle Vanya*, except that Chekhov's *médecin de campagne* expressed himself simply, using good Russian, while the Soviet professor prefers a dubious jargon. "The forest," he teaches and preaches, "is the sum of productive forces and not of production forces" (p. 251). This obscure formulation in pseudo-scientific style sounds very much like a quotation from the official Soviet textbook of economics. But the tenor of the professor's pronouncements does imply some criticism of Soviet policy. The official Soviet line consists, first, of accusing the prerevolutionary government of barbarous destruction of forests and, second, of demonstrating how after the revolution the traditional prerevolutionary principles of forest conservation prevented, for a number of years, full utilization of timber resources. This is not a very consistent position, but it is a fact that in 1929, when Soviet policies were radically revised, forest utilization was completely subordinated to the general policy of high-speed industrialization and the amount of lumber cut for domestic use and for export came greatly to exceed natural growth.[2]

Thus Professor Virkhov may be regarded as a critic of Soviet policy. To be sure, the criticism is very mild. First of all, except for charges of poor workmanship, it never is made quite explicit. Nor are the Soviets likely to be very sensitive to strictures in this area. Con-

---

[2] See, for example, V. A. Popov, *Lesnaya promyshlennost' SSSR* (The Forest Industry of the USSR), 1, *Lesoekspluatatsiya* (Forest Exploitation) (Goslesbumizdat, 1957), pp. 15, 33.

sidering the extent of their general trespasses upon sound principles of resource conservation, the predatory use of forests would seem the least grievous of Soviet sins. Some permanent reduction in extent or density of forests, of course, may well have been justifiable. The problems of rational forest utilization are in general much more complex, and the choices to be made involve many more factors than Leonov and his professor seem to grasp. Not that there is any evidence that the Soviet government was guided by an accurate calculus. On the contrary, some of the elements involved, such as a reasonable "forest percent" (an interest rate with the help of which the optimum rotation, or felling age, can be determined), were proscribed in Soviet Russia for ideological reasons. Soviet ideas of forest exploitation were gross and crude. Still, quite apart from permanent changes in rotation that can be quite sensible, temporary deviations from "normalcy" are a regular phenomenon in forestry policies and can be as rational as normalcy itself. At any rate, the losses suffered need not be irreparable. Some of them can be remedied by afforestation. A log is not like a chunk of iron ore. It can be replaced, even though at some cost. It is also quite possible, and in fact likely, that by the beginning of the 1950s, when Leonov wrote his novel, the Soviet government was getting ready for a change in its forestry policy and Leonov's novel was a welcome — if not a government-inspired — vindication of the new policy.

However this may be, the wish to protect the Russian forest is painted over in the novel with such a heavy coat of Soviet patriotism that the light touches of criticism tend to disappear beneath it. Some of Leonov's interpretations of recent events are gems of Soviet metaphysics and historical accuracy and should not be overlooked. We are treated, for instance, to an analysis of the feelings of the Soviet population in the summer of 1941 after Hitler's attack on Russia: "Behind regrets about construction work that had to remain unfinished, one could discern contempt for the enemy — for this immediate enemy and also *for the other — the main and hidden enemy who got scared of peaceful competition between the two systems*" (p. 105; italics added). Apparently the reference is to the mythical being known as "capitalism." Or is it to the United States? The ambiguity seems intentional and the purpose is to suggest, subtly and darkly, that the United States had stood behind Hitler's aggression and that, in doing so, it was moved by fears of Soviet achievements. In this connection, also, a perceptive view of American national character is helpful. In a conversation between Professor Virkhov and a friend who is an old Bolshevik and a model of a revolutionary hero, the latter describes some uncivilized acts which, he says, have been committed by the American army. The professor, duly horrified, asks the deeply probing question: "Who are they then? — soldiers or robbers?" and promptly receives an illuminating answer: "They are merchants. Soldier is the great title of a man who knows how to die for an idea . . . But name for me at least one idea which in the course of the last hundred years has emerged from the merchant class and was implemented in the name of life [*sic*] . . . Merchants, at the very best, grow to be pirates" (p. 680).

One must wonder whether Leonov himself realized that his perfect Communist repeated almost verbatim ideas from Werner Sombart's *Händler und Helden* (Merchants and Heroes), a book of "patriotic cogitations" written in Germany during World War I and directed against England (Munich, 1915). Even Leonov's style in those paragraphs with its nebulous haecceities sounds very much like a rendition into Russian of reactionary German writings.

In view of these deplorable characteristics, it is not surprising to learn how despicably the Americans acted during the war. Day in, day out, Professor Virkhov and his neighbors wonder where the second front will be opened; they continue to speculate for nine hundred days, until on the nine hundred and first, when the Germans attacked in the Ardennes, the Muscovites smilingly read the telegraphic prayers for help which come from their allies (p. 718). Thus the Anglo-American forces apparently managed to get to the Ardennes without ever opening a second front. The moronic effrontery of this presentation of the course of World War II in the West would be difficult to surpass. It is also hard to believe that the average Soviet reader is, or that Leonov believes him to be, so stupid, ignorant, and gullible as to accept Leonov's counterfeits for true coins. In general, it is probably more reasonable to assume that statements of this sort are to be taken within the context of Soviet mores as part of a ritual; as a somewhat pompous affirmation, that is, of loyalty to the regime.

But Leonov does seem to go further than is required by the Soviet code of proper behavior for a writer. In addition to mistreatments of the past his novel also contains some glimpses of future history. Varya, the ideal heroic figure of a young Soviet girl who loses her life fighting the Germans, places the last war in its proper historical perspective: "You see," she explains to her friend, the professor's daughter, "the fascists are just an episode in a great historical competition . . . Remember your history: if it took a full thirty years to settle the trifling dynastic conflicts between the Red and the White Roses, then it should not be surprising if it takes a century to decide the great argument between the Red and White halves of mankind. But you may assume that we have done the first twenty percent of the job" (p. 129).

This is very strong stuff indeed, and one can only conclude that the insurance premiums which Soviet writers must pay are high. Still, it seems advisable to be overinsured rather than underinsured. A writer who shows such fervent loyalty *in magnis* surely must be permitted a fleeting moment of eccentric independence of judgment *in parvis silvanis*. Leonov is widely regarded as one of the foremost Soviet novelists. It is almost frightening to see a man who aspires to the reputation of a great Russian writer cast aside all pretenses at historical veracity, and common sense, and common decency. The Soviet novel does reveal the predicament of the Soviet writer and, through him, that of the Soviet system.

All this is by no means devoid of interest. There is more to Leonov's novel, however, than cheap sentimentality in the style of Otto Ludwig's *Erbförster*, or semiliterate ideas about rational calculus of forest utilization, or shameless distortions of historical truth. It is only in a very superficial sense that Leonov's novel deals with the vicissitudes of the Russian forest. Its actual subject is the vicissitudes of Soviet man. For it is a novel about the *Lebenslauf*, the span of life, the human biography in Soviet Russia. This is the real theme of the novel and a much more rewarding one.

Professor Virkhov's forestry theories may be flat, but his view of human biography probes deeply into the very core of the Soviet social system. Progress, our professor believes, consists in an increase of moral duties which must proceed *pari passu* with an increase in the volume of material goods; only the perfect man can achieve perfect happiness. "Hence everybody must make it his business to have a perfect biography" (p. 59). This is indeed a sentence full of significance. Unfortunately, its translation in English does not do justice to the Russian style, which uses a phrase taken from the archaic language of the tsarist ukazy. In fact, for a moment the reader hesitates, not knowing whether Leonov and his hero really mean what they say. The concept of perfect biography and the way in which it is expressed are irresistibly reminiscent of Shchedrin's celebrated satirical sallies against Imperial Russia in which he glorified *yedinomysliye*, perfect conformity in thinking, as the great ideal of the rulers of Russia. But the reader's doubts are out of place, for Leonov is very much in earnest. The problem of perfect biography is indeed a crucial problem of Soviet society. Not that it originated in Soviet Russia; but it is there that it acquired an extent and a significance which it had never possessed before. It would seem useful, therefore, to clarify the concept, before examining its application in Leonov's novel.

There are many possible criteria for classifying societies and civilizations. But the prevailing attitude toward a man's biography is far from the least important among those criteria. For it is related to another and perhaps more widely noted distinction, that between settled and migratory or immigration societies. The settled society, as the term is understood here, is one in which the whole life of an individual as a rule is passed within one fairly narrow social circle. In such societies there is no caesura in a man's ideal biography. His biography is perfect in the very specific sense in which a settled society values such perfection: it achieves a unity of life. According to a Russian proverb, no word can be thrown out of a song. No part, however small, can or need be thrown out of a man's biography in a settled society.

The values of a migratory society are radically different. This is a society in which the process of the stranger's losing his alien quality is perennially undone or renewed by the influx of new strangers. The migratory society may coincide with one growing industrial city; it may comprise a region like the valley of the Ruhr or a huge country like the United States. A society can be more or less "migratory" depending *inter alia* on its geographic extent or its rate of growth or on the distance separating it from the areas whence the migrants come and the degree of irreversibility inherent in the act of migration. But the likelihood is that the attitude to a man's life of such a society will tend to differ greatly from that of a settled society. Naturally, such an attitude does not emerge instantaneously. In a sense, the puritanism of New England in several of its aspects was an attempt to negate the basic experience of migration. To become fully migratory, the American society had to shed much of puritan provincialism. Just because the ideas of the "old country" travel with the migrants and are brought in as specific "brain-case" imports, establishment of a migratory society is a long process even in a young country such as the United States. Once such a society has been established, however, and a new ideology peculiar to it has developed, the migratory society acquires easily discernible traits. In such a society a unity of life, a perfect biography, cannot be regarded as the ideal. The very fact of the migration, the very transformation of a peasant into a city dweller, of a European into an American, create a hiatus in biography. They tear it asunder and force the man to begin a new life. It is not an accident that it was an American philosopher who emphasized the moral characteristics of the twice-born.[3] In a sense, emigration is death. The emigrant, as the Parisian argot has it, *ravale son bulletin de naissance*; the naturalization certificate attests the second birth.

The newcomer to a migratory society may have very weighty reasons to forget his past. By suppressing the memory thereof he liberates himself from a record of failure or crime or humiliation. He may want to dismiss his past simply because the burden of nostalgic sentiments is too heavy to carry; or because he feels that the memories lame his energies and thwart his will in an environment that invites action and places high value upon the will to act. In such circumstances, the scriptural injunction against looking backward is filled with new significance. Goethe's urgent advice, "Stirb und werde!" should be written over the gates of immigration societies. The immigrant must obey it or pay the penalty of becoming, again in Goethe's words, "ein trueber Gast auf der dunklen Erde."

The specific "migratory" attitude toward unity of life affects

[3] William James, *The Varieties of Religious Experience* (New York, 1903), esp. pp. 166f.

many areas of behavior and endeavor. Examples are not far to seek. The manners of an immigration society do not favor inquiries into a man's past. One of the causes for the temporary success of Senator McCarthy must have lain in the pleasure of overstepping in public an ancient taboo, a well-established rule of private life. Business life provides many an instance of differences between settled and migratory societies. In the former, bankruptcy is likely to end a businessman's career. Even a protested bill of exchange is extremely hard to live down. In an immigration milieu, failure does not block the road to subsequent success and, in fact, success, once achieved, either obliterates the memory of the failure or even tinges it with glory. In a settled society, the jack of all trades is presumed — has been presumed since the days of the Homeric or pseudo-Homeric *Margites* — to be a tyro in all and is looked upon with disdain. The man who keeps changing from one trade to another is expected to fail; indeed, given the prevailing attitude, he is most likely to fail. In a migratory society, the virtues of specialization tend to remain unrecognized and unrewarded. The feeling of being up to any task, of being "a man and not a mollusc," is the specific attribute of a man in such a society, as was discovered by the French worker whose report about his downright un-French experience in California was quoted by Marx.[4] It is another matter that the organization of modern factories often requires the worker to perform a single recurring operation. Such operations are quickly learned and, in a growing and mobile society, they are as quickly abandoned and forgotten.

In an immigration society, a second marriage is much more likely to repair a previous marital failure. At any rate, the milieu does not diminish the second marriage's chance of success by refusing to accept it. (It may be easily ascertained by appropriate comparisons that specific religious injunctions are quite insufficient to explain the difference in attitudes.) An even clearer case is provided by marriages of widowed persons. They are frowned upon and viewed as attestations of disloyalty in a settled society and greeted with gladness in a migratory society. To be sure, differences in family structure, the resulting differences in the position of aged people, fear of loneliness in one case and social approval of solitude in the other — all these

[4] *Das Kapital*, Volksausgabe, I (Moscow, 1932), 513.

affect the social judgment of remarriage. Still, it is the willingness to forget — the refusal to place a high value upon unity of life — that makes possible the position assumed in immigration societies. It is not surprising, therefore, that the propensity to write memoirs is so much more widespread in a settled society than in a migratory society. At the same time, such memoirs as do get written in an immigration society are much less in the nature of autobiographies in the proper sense of the word. They tend to deal with events, not with the span of a unique life. Maeterlinck once said that it is memory that presupposes and constitutes the unity of life. In the settled society it is the memoirs that as a rule are concerned with revealing a man's life as a straight line placed within limits that are both narrow and predetermined by the fixed coordinates of birth, family, social set or class, and professional endeavor.

These are significant differences which penetrate deeply into man's customs and feelings. They are the threads from which the fabric of everyday life is woven. They stem from the nature of the society in which they exist and they themselves exert a powerful influence upon the mobility and fluidity of social bodies. There is little doubt that they have direct bearing upon much of modern economic history. An immigration society and an industrial society are not coterminous. Obviously, there were immigration societies that had nothing to do with modern industry. On the other hand, a developed industrial society may have shed most of the qualities of an immigration society. Certain elements of such a shedding process have been clearly perceptible in the United States over the last quarter of a century or so. This is particularly true with regard to some of the aspects mentioned above. And yet one way of looking at the industrial evolution of the eighteenth and nineteenth centuries is to regard it as a change from a settled society to an immigration society. Every industrialization which was more than a mere development of manorial handicraft or a growth of cottage industry almost naturally tended to partake of the elements of an immigration society. Industrialization was destructive of provincialism. It metropolized the society. It broke the unity of man's life and, by so doing, tended to reduce the value attached to it.

It is true, of course, that within the old established political entities the transformation was slower and often less complete. To some extent, preindustrial values have been adjusted to new conditions rather than abandoned altogether. Still, no one can compare the habits of the population, say, in the teeming cities of the Ruhr Valley with those of the little towns in Mecklenburg or in any two similarly comparable areas in France, Italy, or any other European country without registering a profound difference in attitude toward a man's life. What is so peculiar about the Soviet type of industrialization is that it represents an attempt to build up an industrial society while preserving the basic features of a settled society. Revolutions, civil strife, and foreign wars have convulsed the land. The countryside has disgorged millions and millions of muzhiks into industrial employment. Large cities have been built in places where not even a tiny hamlet had anticipated the urban future. Tremendous migrations over the face of the enormous country have taken place. And still throughout this period of unprecedented change the government which has been responsible for most of the change has refused, as it were, to recognize its impact upon the course of individual lives. To repeat, this refusal is the real theme of Leonov's novel, to which we may now return.

In accordance with the established custom in Soviet novels, the "positive" hero, Professor Virkhov, has an antagonist, Professor Gratsianski. This bearer of a family name which was chosen to indicate descent from the Russian clergy bitterly attacks Virkhov's views on forestry policies. Unlike Virkhov, who is a conservationist, his opponent is in favor of placing the forest at the service of industrialization. This is reasonably straightforward. The substantive arguments used are much less so. Some of them are mere abuse and inconsistent abuse at that. While Virkhov accuses the bourgeoisie of destroying the Russian forest, Gratsianski refuses to be "scared" by the conservative rules of forest utilization invented by the bourgeoisie for its own purposes (p. 421). But there is no need to seek for clarity; arguments do not matter in reality. It is not by puncturing the opponent's logic or erudition that an argument can be won, but by puncturing his biography. Gratsianski derives most of the support for his point of view from the fact that Professor Virkhov as a boy had received a present of twenty-five rubles (about $12.50 in old gold dollars) from a wealthy businessman (p. 143). Furthermore, while he was a student, several payments of twenty-five rubles were made to him from a source that remained unknown. Gratsianski explains that it would be unrealistic to believe in pure philanthropic motivations on the part of the mysterious donor; it is much more natural to assume that he had some long-term designs and hoped to be recompensed at the cost of national properties at some remote future time when the former student would be holding a responsible position in forest administration. Furthermore, Virkhov had married a girl who had been raised on a gentry estate, and this circumstance, too, is used to refute Virkhov's ideas on what to do with the forests. Finally, there is an even more potent, seemingly incontrovertible argument which Gratsianski is holding in reserve as a secret weapon for the moment of the real showdown: this is his knowledge of the fact that Virkhov had adopted and raised the child of a "dekulakized" peasant.

This array of far-fetched nonsensicalities may be quite irrelevant to the point at issue. Yet they are taken seriously. Professor Virkhov's young and virtuous daughter, when informed of her father's dubious past, and particularly of the unexplained twenty-five rubles, is plunged into black despair. She tries to change the pronunciation of her name by shifting the accent to the first syllable so as to dissociate herself from her father; and she wonders whether acquaintance with the daughter of a tainted man will not be detrimental to her friend Varya. The technical expression used throughout the novel for damaging a person's reputation by associating with him or her is "to cast a shadow upon somebody."

It would be pleasant, and in fact almost liberating, if one could regard all this as a satire directed against the Soviet attitudes to biography. But unfortunately this is not possible. First of all, Leonov's "positive" character himself is the inventor of the concept of perfect biography. Second, the plot of the novel, divested of the incidentals of partisan fighting and air raids on Moscow, consists of nothing but the gradual unmasking of Gratsianski. His theories of forestry are confounded by showing that in his student days he had seduced and then heartlessly abandoned a girl and her child that was also his. And the *coup de grâce* falls when, through a series of contrived coincidences, it transpires that Gratsianski, again in his student days, stood up an audience of workers to whom he was supposed to deliver a lecture and, in addition, betrayed to the police (somewhat unwittingly, it appears) a mutual friend of his and Virkhov's, the great revolutionary, who, as we have seen, later on was to become a student of Sombart's theories. Once these events of some thirty years ago have been revealed or are close to being revealed, Gratsianski is finished. A richly deserved punishment is in store for him, while Virkhov is rewarded by a medal and in addition recovers the wife who had left him many years earlier. (The separation, incidentally, had seemed final; still, mindful of the unity of their respective biographies, neither the professor nor his spouse entered into any new relationships.) But a man with Gratsianski's biography does not even know how to wait patiently for just retribution from society, as represented by the appropriate organs of the Soviet government. He remains an obdurate individualist and, after having composed a monograph on suicide, he himself chooses this "most despicable way of deserting from life" (p. 673). Thus virtue has triumphed and the battle of biographies has been satisfactorily decided by the victory of the less imperfect life story.

To summarize: this is an unattractive book. It contains unlearned disquisitions on forestry, brazen distortions of historical truth in supine obedience to the wishes of the dictators, a preposterous search for closets filled with skeletons, and characters drawn with the tritest means. And all this is presented in a pretentious, perfectly unnatural style and is spread thinly over nearly eight hundred pages of dense print — with frank disregard of all counsels of artistic economy. And yet it is an important book which makes a real contribution to our understanding of Soviet society. In dealing with the curiosities of imperfect biographies, it actually reveals the imperfections of Soviet industrialization.

It is not the first time in Russian history that economic development designed to close the gap between Russia and the West has westernized Russia in some respects while keeping it oriental or even "orientalizing" it in others. The reforms of Peter the Great were a great step toward westernization. But the simultaneous curtailing of the liberty of all classes of the population was a step away from the West. The unevenness of Soviet progress is its most outstanding trait.

Soviet industrialization conducted under the auspices of a ruthless dictatorship has not received its economic consummation: the Soviet government cannot afford to let its population enjoy the fruits of industrialization in the form of a rapid increase in the levels of consumption. But just as consumption is kept close to preindustrialization levels — thus, in effect, ignoring the changes that have taken place in the size of capital stocks, in the knowledge of technological processes, and in the skill of the workers — so the evaluation of human beings is still kept at a level consonant with small and stable preindustrial settlements rather than with the large and rapidly growing industrial centers. These provincial attitudes have been perpetuated with a vengeance. Just as serfdom in Russia was conjoined with a modern police state and hence approached outright slavery to a degree unknown in the West, the ubiquitousness of the Soviet dictatorship has raised provincialism to the level of a national dogma and, in so doing, has made it more destructive of individual freedom and happiness than genuine provincialism ever was.

It is the essence of preindustrial societies to stand upon traditionalism, to live in the past and according to the past and to value it highly. It is the essence of industrial, or at least industrializing, societies to let bygones be bygones, to live in the present and to think of the future. It is paradoxical indeed that the Soviet society, which is so strongly bent upon change, has shown such a high rate of economic growth, and claims to live for the future, should unceasingly probe into the past of its individual members; it is strange that a system which has discovered for itself that only falsifying the past yields perfect history should persist in clamoring for perfect biography. If the Soviet writers were allowed to notice these inconsistencies and to discuss them publicly, they might well be tempted to speak of "dialectics" and "historical contradictions." As it is, they prefer to think in absolutes. The government establishes a categorical distinction between good and evil in a man's past and makes it operational through the instrument of the questionnaire — the Soviet substitute for, and improvement upon, memoir writing. Perfect memory is enforced by law. The *Ivany Nepomnyashchiye*, the nonremembering Ivans, who used to roam over the Russian plain and were the bane of the tsarist police, are still not allowed to plead poor memory. They have been taught to read and write. Accordingly, they must read the questions and write the answers, weaving the flimsy web of a flawless life story.

One does not need Leonov's book in order to know that the life of the average Russian citizen is dominated and kept in perennial jeopardy by the questionnaire — this embodiment of and the perennial menace to perfect biography. But Leonov's novel does show how the institution of the ubiquitous questionnaire translates itself into men's thinking about men, how it becomes an institutionalized and internalized piece of social ideology and, as such, an instrument of domination. It is perhaps not pretty to see a writer of reputation extol and glorify the tools of police oppression. But whatever our judgment of Leonid Leonov, his book has both clarified and enriched our judgment of the social system that exists in Soviet Russia.

II

Relations between the sexes present an obvious field for exercises in perfect biography. Marital fidelity is of course well suited to epitomize the unity of life and to stress the stability of a provincial society. Accordingly, Soviet literature as a rule has shown no interest in matrimonial deviations and sexual irregularities. For a long time the novelists went on mass-producing cheap figurines of Baucis and Philemon, dressed up in Soviet style, and sometimes even had recourse to the Soviet Olympus for appropriate substitutions for the roles of Zeus and Hermes in the Greek story. It is one thing, however, to track down and to expose the possessor of an impure biography. It is another thing blandly to deny his existence. By depicting Soviet citizens, male and female, either as fierce virgins or monogamous maniacs, Soviet novels inevitably came into conflict with reality, which, in these particular areas, was neither fierce nor maniacal.

Fortunately, there are limits to this decline of Russian literature to the level of penny — or kopek — novelettes. Presumably, the tradition of the Russian novel — which means its competition with the Soviet novel for the interest of the modern reader — is a strong force in keeping the Soviet novel within the bounds of verisimilitude. As a result, there have been two or three ethnographically more valuable treatments of marriage in Soviet Russia. First, the novel *Ivan Ivanovich* by Antonina Koptyayeva (Moscow, 1949) produced surprise among Soviet readers by demonstrating the incredible fact that a marriage of two perfectly decent people can fall apart; and that even an energetic intervention on the part of the local party boss (first secretary of the Raykom) may fail to put it together again. Koptyayeva then wrote a second novel, *Druzhba* (Friendship; Moscow, 1956), in which the tradition of the happy ending — even more deeply rooted in the Soviet novel than in the Hollywood movie — emerged triumphant. In the inferno of besieged Stalingrad, the hero, Ivan Ivanovich, a surgeon by trade and an abandoned husband by misfortune, manages to form a new attachment after having saved the life of his former wife through a skillful operation and having wavered for some time among several attractive candidates. These novels, too, contain some expressions of opinion on international politics and the course of world history. Such cogitations fully deserve to be placed beside those of Leonov which have been quoted earlier. The two books provide some sidelights on the grasping arrogance of the local party boss, who even tries to prescribe the types of operations which a surgeon may or may not perform in the local hospital; the way in which these ambitions are curbed by a successful appeal to higher party authorities is no less instructive than the threat of criminal prosecution to which a wrong diagnosis seems to expose the physician. But the novels' main interest stems from their having blazed the trail for a fuller and freer treatment of Soviet marriage.[5]

Such a presentation is contained in Galina Nikolayeva's *Bitva v puti* (Battle on the Road), a novel which appeared seriatim in 1957 in the journal *Oktyabr'*.[6] This no doubt is one of the most revealing products of recent Soviet belles-lettres. It is not simply a novel about the risks of Soviet matrimony. Like most Soviet novels, *Battle on the Road* provides valuable insights into aspects of Soviet life which, although unflattering, are so common within the system that they are

[5] In what appears to be her latest novel, *Derzaniye* (Daring; Moscow, 1959), Koptyayeva proceeds to wreck the second marriage of the surgeon, who leaves his wife in order to correct an error of choice made in Stalingrad a decade earlier. Fortunately for the abandoned wife, she too is put on the road to an alternative happiness.

[6] Nos. 3–7; in subsequent references, only the issue and page numbers will be cited.

considered perfectly natural, and their inclusion in a work of fiction is simply a sort of *Kleinmalerei*. For the same reason, they escape the blades of the censor's scissors. But Nikolayeva's novel offers a good deal more than a collection of *obiter pincta*. It bears the clear stamp of having been written after the Twentieth Party Congress, at the apogee of the rebound from the restraints of the Stalinist era. Both in being deliberately critical and in disregarding taboos, this novel is quite unusual and probably much more significant than Dudintsev's *Not by Bread Alone*, which happened to catch the eye of the reading public within and without Soviet Russia.

The novel supplies a broad canvas of Soviet life. In many respects, it confirms impressions previously gained of the way Soviet factories and collective farms operate. We have heard before about the problem of managerial honesty. Still it is interesting to note that the successful factory manager, in reporting the percentage of flawed goods in total output, deducts the permissible amounts, thus producing a more favorable picture by false means (no. 7, p. 120). A chairman of a kolkhoz caught in various prevarications insists that it is his honesty that makes him lie: "Honesty requires me to manage the *kolkhoz* in such a way as to yield profit to the State and to the *Kolkhozniks*. But planning sometimes is plainly directed against profit." And the writer dots the "i"s by adding that "the errors of planning and the trammels upon initiative" make it necessary for alert and dedicated men "to lie and to act deviously" (no. 5, p. 43). This is not in any sense novel information. We have known for a long time that illicit activities of the managers are designed both to evade the plan and to make its operation possible. But it is perhaps the first time that a Soviet writer has stated the complexity of the situation so sharply and so frankly.

The factory manager has an "exchange fund," that is to say, concealed stacks of goods which he can offer to the railroads as a consideration for extra-quick service; alternatively, he lets his factory shops perform special and quite unscheduled repair work for the railroads (no. 5, pp. 26, 27, 92). This again is a well-known phenomenon — a part of the Soviet concept of *blat* or *blatmeysterstvo*, terms which originally referred to the underworld and underworld operations but which in Soviet Russia have come to connote illicit economic operations.[7] But the description of these conditions is given a very modern, post-Stalin twist in the novel. The director of the factory, which manufactures tractors, returns from Moscow to announce that the factory will henceforth contribute its share to the output of consumers' goods by establishing workshops producing beds, frying pans, stove parts, and similar commodities. The decision reflects the promises to improve the levels of consumption made first by Malenkov and then by Khrushchev. But the reason for the director's readiness to add output of pots and pans to that of tractors should be noted: to have consumers' goods at his disposal will greatly increase his bargaining position in various *blat* operations. And equally enlightening is the fact that the director's opponent in the factory, the chief engineer — the "positive" hero of the novel — combats inclusion of consumers' goods in the production program because what Soviet factories need is efficient specialization in a few well-defined operations rather than dissipation of energies in attempts to produce a wide variety of articles. According to the chief engineer, it is bad enough that the factory must continue to produce the smallest and simplest parts that go into a tractor engine instead of receiving them from the outside (no. 5, p. 67). The difficulties in organizing efficient interfactory cooperation have long been a very sore point in Soviet industrialization. It is quite instructive to see how the half-sincere attempts to satisfy consumers by makeshift arrangements, while avoiding the requisite structural changes, are received within Soviet factories.

Nikolayeva's critique does not confine itself to the relative safety of local conditions in the factory. The target has been widened to include the powerful first secretary of the Obkom, the virtual boss of a huge region and of the ministry to which the tractor factory reports and which is accused of having lost its grasp of the enormously expanded productive machinery. In the end, the struggle within the factory is satisfactorily resolved. Both the director of the factory and the first secretary of the regional party committee are exposed and demoted. The secretary, who is described as having worshipped the infallible, mysterious, incomprehensible power of one man, the chosen

---

[7] Etymologically, the term *blat* comes from the German *Platte* — gang (of criminals or rowdies). It probably fits well into the Russian language because of the subconscious association with the Church-Slavonic *blato*, swamp or filth.

vessel of wisdom (no. 6, p. 44), tries to speak of the "magnificent construction of our era" which make it inevitable for the Ivan Ivano-vich Ivanovs to restrict themselves and even to make some sacrifices (no. 7, p. 115). But the chairman of the Central Committee meeting which sets everything right cuts the secretary short: "But some people regard those sacrifices as a grave and temporary necessity which must be terminated as quickly as possible; others regard them as a natural law which it does not pay to think about and which it is harmful to talk about" (p. 115). The practical effect of the two positions may be identical. But this remark spells the doom of the secretary and the director. The chief engineer becomes the director of the factory, eager to remedy past errors and omissions and in particular to do something about the main evil of Soviet factories and collective farms: "the mechanization without organization" (no. 4, p. 73; no. 5, p. 113; no. 7, p. 129), which certainly is an aphoristically felicitous way — thrice repeated — of pointing to a crucial problem of Soviet economic de-velopment, a disability to which much attention is likely to be devoted in the next few years.

To appreciate the full breadth of Nikolayeva's criticism, add to the foregoing, first, the fact that the husband of the heroine, a devoted party member, is arrested and executed as an "enemy of the people"; then the description of the general atmosphere of shivering cowardice, including the suggestion that members of the secret police are not above taking advantage of the wives of arrested men; and, finally, the expulsion of the heroine, even prior to her husband's execution, from the Communist youth organization on charges of being over-dressed at a meeting and of having failed to greet her fellow members properly (no. 4, pp. 28–33).

Some of Nikolayeva's strictures simply justify certain reforms of the Khrushchev era. The attacks upon economic ministries which adumbrate Khrushchev's decentralization are of this kind. But, on the whole, her criticism has been bold, comprehensive, and far-reaching. To be sure, she has remained true to the Soviet tradition and has served up a happy ending in which rewards and retributions are distributed to each according to his deserts. The reader is left with the strong suggestion that the change for the better within the tractor factory is bound to be duplicated over the whole range of the Soviet economy. The fateful knocks on the door in the dead of night belong to the past. The Soviet citizen can sleep quietly, and the future seems bright.

And yet the peculiarity of Nikolayeva's novel is that her happy ending is confined to the public sphere, as it were. At the level of private relations and in terms of individual happiness, the novel ends in gloom and despair.[8] It is at this level that Nikolayeva's novel represents a real innovation in Soviet literature, being the first whose central theme is adultery. The subject is introduced and treated with circumspection. "Socialist people are not made for adultery," says the hero (no. 7, p. 93). There is no description of the pleasures of the flesh. But there is human truth in the irresistibility of the attraction which the hero — the chief engineer — and the heroine — an engineer in the same factory — feel for each other. An oft-told story is related with simplicity and dignity, and the long years of spinsterly modesty enforced upon literature by a government that trod under foot all laws of decency elevate the appearance of this story to the rank of a political sensation.

Its primary significance, however, does not lie in providing a high point on the gauge by which fluctuations in post-Stalinist liberalism can be measured. Much more important is the unusual glance into the more permanent and more stable structure of the Soviet value system which Nikolayeva's story affords. The happiness of the lovers finds a sudden termination in the fashion standardized by the second-rate French novel of the nineteenth century. By accident, the deceived wife surprises the sinful pair in the *pied-à-terre* which they have rented on the periphery of the town. By the next morning the story is the talk of the town. The party cannot remain indifferent, and the new first secretary of the Obkom hastens to the factory to comfort the new director, who bravely exhibits the "face of a fighter." And the woman? Alas, no one comforts her. She cannot return to the factory and must leave town, which she promptly does, after having confessed her sin

[8] In this respect, the present novel is very different from Nikolayeva's earlier novel, *Zhatva* (Harvest), for which, in 1950, she received a Stalin Prize. The high award was richly deserved. For in that fully standardized and altogether uncritical presentation of life on a postwar collective farm, public and private happy endings were indeed one and indivisible.

to her husband and having received from her lover three hundred rubles for travel expenses.

Once more the provincialism of the Soviet value system has been exposed. A settled society has little respect for privacy. Neither the town nor the factory nor the party boss is willing to regard the episode as the private affair of those immediately concerned. But what is even more striking is that in this case Soviet provincialism has not only the same form but also the same substance as the time-honored provincialism of the so-called bourgeois societies. It is the woman whose biography has received the indelible stain. The man can escape unscathed, the beauty blemish hardly affecting the perfection of his biography. His marital life will go on as before and the unity of his life will remain unbroken. Again, one can only marvel at the paradoxical complexity of Soviet society. It has allowed women to become engineers in steel mills and to perform physical jobs which in less socialistic countries are entrusted to men, and preferably to machines. But right and wrong in sexual relations are still distributed in patterns that were formed in the days when the village blacksmith was the main exponent of industrialization. Thus, when the provincial quest for perfect biography is somewhat relaxed, the underlying provincialism of the value system becomes even more apparent and even more surprising.

III

Thanks to Nikolayeva's critical attitude, the curtain has been lifted to allow at least a glance at some hitherto concealed sides of Soviet life. It would be quite erroneous, however, to assume that novels lacking in critical spirit are necessarily uninformative and unilluminating. Vsevolod Kochetov's novels are a case in point. Here is a writer raised and steeped in the atmosphere of Soviet conformity. Through his novels, beginning with *Pod nebom rodiny* (Under the Sky of the Fatherland; Leningrad, 1955), which was written between 1947 and 1950, usually passes a member of the secret police who is a truly fine chap, possessed of all kinds of virtues. Even in a discussion between two agronomists on the structure of relative prices in the United States and Soviet Russia — the price ratio of cars and horses in the two countries is at issue — the hero quickly confounds his adversary by a thinly veiled threat of denunciation to the GPU (*Pod nebom rodiny*, p. 124). It is natural for Kochetov to deprecate increases in the standard of living of the Soviet population: what matters, he says, is increase in the productivity of labor (p. 259).

In prerevolutionary Russia there was a type of writer generally characterized as belonging to the school of *Chego izvolite?* — "What can I do for you, sir?" Kochetov's servility has been remarkable even under Soviet conditions. In his second novel, *Zhurbiny* (The Zhurbins; Leningrad, 1953), published in the last year of Stalin's life, the novelist was quick to notice the rising tide of Soviet anti-Semitism, and he obliged by assigning to a Jew the role of the only unreformed scoundrel in the book. Some scholars have preferred to withdraw from the pressures of life in Soviet Russia into pure theory. Again, Kochetov's watchful eye is upon them — and in his third novel, *Molodost' s nami* (Youth Is with Us; Moscow, 1957), this contemptible behavior is appropriately castigated (p. 93). In the fourth novel, *Brat'ya Yershovy* (The Yershov Brothers), which is said to have sold several hundred thousand copies, Kochetov rushed to the defense of the dictatorship against the critics of the post-Stalin era.[9]

In a sense, the book is a deliberate retort — novel for novel — to Dudintsev. If the latter tried to show how factory management, government bureaucracy, academic experts, and even judicial organs conspired in order to suppress an invention and punish the inventor, Kochetov puts the conspiratorial shoe on the other foot and serves up a fraudulent inventor who is engaged in criminal intrigues directed against the factory director and the party bosses. In addition, he also manages to insert into his novel (no. 6, p. 97) some brief mockery of Ehrenburg's *The Thaw*, which was one of the first, if not the first, literary expressions of dissatisfaction with Stalin's era. He is anxious to issue warnings against the tendency to accept with open arms the returnees from jails and forced-labor camps: "One must distinguish between those who suffered innocently and those who were released out of generosity . . . The Soviet government has a generous soul . . . It is generous because it is strong . . ." (p. 20). In short, Kochetov is a faithful servant of the regime, its willing mouthpiece. And still his novels contain much more than just a few grains of useful infor-

[9] *Brat'ya Yershovy* appeared in 1958 in *Neva*, nos. 6–7; in subsequent references only the issue and page numbers will be cited.

mation, the value of which is all the greater since one must assume that it has been imparted quite unwittingly. A few examples may be in order here.

It is *Brat'ya Yershovy* that most impressively and quite effortlessly gives the reader some feeling of the extent of informing and denouncing which thicken the air in Soviet Russia. The city boss, the first secretary of the Gorkom, Gorbachev, is presented as a person of excellent standing and impeccable reputation. But the enemy is on the march. The wily and false inventor composes a denunciatory epistle in which Gorbachev is accused of having used city snow plows in order to clear the street in front of his daughter's house on the day of her wedding. The denunciation goes to the next higher party authority, the first secretary of the Obkom. The latter knows that the maligned person has a weak heart; there is no doubt about the trifling character of the complaint. But the Soviet code of action prescribes paying full attention to every accusation. Gorbachev is shown the letter, suffers a heart attack, and dies (no. 7, pp. 119 f). It is truly impressive to observe Kochetov's uncharming naïveté which makes him believe and make believe in his turn that it is the anti-Soviet inventor who has killed Gorbachev rather than the defenselessness of the dictatorial police state against informers.

That informing is a problem not even Kochetov can pretend to ignore. Another member of Kochetov's collection of ideal GPU men suddenly breaks out in a long tirade against the "slanderers, careerists, . . . whose denunciations clog the machinery of the party, of the soviets, and of the judiciary." He adds, "I am afraid of them" (*Molodost' s nami*, p. 433). The colonel's further suggestion that "there should be a law against informing" may be a helpful one, provided that the law also institutes a different attitude to human biography.

It is in the same novel that incidentally, by way of explaining the weakness of a character, Kochetov refers to an earlier episode in his life. The character, a professor, in filling out a questionnaire, had represented himself as the son of an artisan when in reality he was the son of a miller. An amateur hunter for inconsistencies in questionnaires discovered and denounced the falsification. A long investigation followed in which an unbelievable number of various governmental agencies and party authorities participated. It was the professor's wife whose boundless energy and perseverance beat off the attack, but not before she had gone to the Central Committee. Her husband was saved, but he never recovered from the experience (pp. 218–19).

Nor is it merely the state and the party that are on the lookout for biographical chinks. The private citizen is well trained to do his own private investigating, as it were, in a supplementary fashion. One of the brothers of the Yershov family was a prisoner of war of the Germans. After his return to Russia he spent years in a forced-labor camp. When, finally, he is allowed to return to his home town, his own brothers subject him to a grueling, humiliating, and pointless crossexamination (no. 6, p. 80). These are indeed useful illustrations of Leonid Leonov's ideal of a perfect biography and of what it means when the concept is shifted from abstract theory to everyday life. Soviet novels explain both Soviet life and Soviet novels. With the help of Kochetov's novels one can place Leonov's ideal of a perfect biography in a perfect society in its proper perspective and learn to distinguish more clearly between the mechanics of power exercised within a dictatorial system and the trappings of an outworn ideology.

There is much said in *Brat'ya Yershovy* about art and literature. One gets some idea as to how far-reaching has been the dissatisfaction with the official art and official literature, and how important was the wave of fresh air that came rushing in from Poland and Hungary. "They say in Poland that socialist realism is good for nothing but plywood constructions," says one of the heroes in Kochetov's novel (no. 7, p. 84), possibly one of those who, again according to Kochetov, kept their mouths shut for decades and now after Stalin's dethronement have been emboldened to raise their voices in criticism (p. 94). Will this movement of long-suppressed protest bear some permanent fruit? Or will the Kochetovs and those behind them — and above them — continue to keep Russian literature within the pinfold of socialist realism under the watchful eye of dictatorial censorship? The prospect may be as cheerless as the retrospect. There is no doubt that the Soviet government can effectively preclude the revival of the Russian novel. But it is quite unlikely that it can fully succeed in obstructing the Soviet novel's revelatory function. This is the conclusion that emerges *a minori ad maius* from Vsevolod Kochetov's literary exercises.

14

Notes on Doctor Zhivago

Сквозь прошлого перипетии
И годы войн и нищеты,
Я молча узнавал России
Неповторимые черты.
            Борис Пастернак
            ("На ранних поездах")[1]

Россия, страна моя . . .
Облеченная солнцем жена . . .
            Андрей Белый
            ("Христос Воскрес")[2]

О Русь моя! Жена моя!
            Александр Блок
            ("На поле Куликовом")[3]

AT TIMES, nothing fails like success, and art appreciation by ballot is often precarious. The vote of the Swedish Academy was swiftly followed by the landslide vote in the marketplace. As a result, the novel *Doctor Zhivago*, the strangest stranger among bestsellers,

[1] There are two alternative translations of these four lines from Boris Pasternak's poem "On Early Trains":

Through all the trials of the past,	But brooding over past reverses
The years of war and hardship,	And years of penury and war,
I silently identified	In silence I discern my people's
Russia's inimitable features.	Incomparable traits once more.
(Translated by George Reavey)	(Translated by Eugene M. Kayden)

Neither rendition brings out clearly Pasternak's personification of Russia.

[2] "Russia, my country . . .
    The woman clad in sun rays . . ."
                Andrey Bely, "Christ Has Arisen"

[3] "Oh my Russia! My wife!"
        Alexander Blok, "On the Kulikovo Battlefield"

came into countless hands that never should have touched it and was presented to minds that were totally unprepared for its meaning and significance. The unreasoned success was bound to end in an unreasonable failure. As the din of the bazaar, produced by political journalism and inane sensationalism, is dying down, one can at length hear the multilingual chorus of literary criticism. It is saddening, but not surprising, to find that the voices of the detractors ring out so much more clearly and firmly than those of the admirers; and that they seem to be listened to approvingly by many a disappointed reader. Unfortunately, the strictures are as obtuse as has been the praise.

I hear it said over and over again that *Doctor Zhivago* is not "a great novel" and that *War and Peace* is incomparably "greater." I am not certain that Ibsen or Chekhov may no longer be regarded as great playwrights, once their inferiority to Shakespeare has been demonstrated. Moreover, the only safe test, the acid test of a book's greatness, is its inclusion, a century after publication, in a Harvard course on great novels. Let us be patient, therefore. For my part, I am content to leave the decision to posterity in the hope, of course, that the twenty-first century will not turn out to be even more barbarous than its miserable predecessor.

Hence I do not propose to waste my time on a discussion of the obvious, but not very interesting, shortcomings of the novel. It would have been more pleasant if Dr. Zhivago's and his partners' conversational style were not so hopelessly stilted. It would have looked better if the large chunks of which the novel consists were not nailed together in such a crude and haphazard way, leaving the large clefts in motivations and events either uncalked or filled by hastily contrived coincidences. Over the last generation or so, the technique of writing novels has been enormously improved and employed to great advantage by writers who had little or nothing to say. Accordingly, the modern reader has been raised to believe that the "structure of the novel" is everything and to forget that fine carpentry may betray the hand of a skilled artisan but not the touch of a great artist. Pasternak is not a Tolstoy, nor is he a Shakespeare; but a good deal of this type of faultfinding recalls Tolstoy's preposterously persuasive attempt to show the complete absence of "naturalness," "logic," and "common sense" in *King Lear*. As Shakespeare survived Tolstoy's contumely, Pasternak in all likelihood will survive the strictures of our less illustrious contemporaries.

Nor do I wish to participate in micrological expeditions through Pasternak's pages in search for real or imaginary allusions. Again, I realize that modern poets have conditioned this weak and suggestible generation to confuse appreciation of art with a merry egg hunt. The maker of verse or stories — a parental figure — hides a number of eggs, very small in size and of varying degrees of freshness, and lets them be joyously discovered by the readers, who get thoroughly rejuvenated in the process. To refer to a thought expressed in a recent seminar discussion,[4] Pasternak's Lara may, through negligent pressing, let her whole wardrobe go up in holy smoke, and still the proposition may be false that the farther a critic has to go to fetch a tortured egg the better it will taste. *Laissons ces enfantillages!*

For the purpose of these remarks, *Doctor Zhivago,* then, is neither a bluebook to be graded nor a collection of puzzles over which to exercise our ingenuity and to exhibit our erudition. If any eggs are to be found in the following, their size will be extra-large. Most of what I have to say is related to my belief that in several important respects the novel is a return to the Russian literary tradition that only a short time ago seemed to be dead and buried and forgotten, at least by the members of the Union of Soviet Writers. It is easy, if one so desires, to regard *Doctor Zhivago* as an anti-Soviet novel. The letter of rejection which the former editorial board of *Novy Mir* claims to have addressed to Pasternak may be genuine or a latter-day falsification, wholly or in part. Still, unless the thaw of those days was to be followed by a real spring (which, of course, it never was), there was every political reason not to publish the novel in Soviet Russia. The editorial board's instinct for self-preservation was blissfully undeceived about that. And yet much more important than the *anti*-Soviet character of *Doctor Zhivago* is its *pre*-Soviet

---

[4] The suggestion is that Lara's name alludes to St. Larisa, who was tortured and burned at the stake and that this is indicated in the novel by smoke or the smell of smoke around Lara.

character; or, to put it somewhat differently, what is so anti-Soviet about the novel is its being so clearly pre-Soviet. Its language, its central figure, and its main theme all belong to a main strain of Russian literature of the nineteenth century.

The language above all! The translation by Max Hayward and Manya Harari is excellent indeed. Edmund Wilson may have scored a dozen times in pointing out omissions, weaknesses, and errors. What are they compared with thousands — literally thousands — of cases in which most difficult problems of rendition have been solved successfully and often brilliantly? The English translation of *Doctor Zhivago* supplies one of the strongest pieces of corroborative evidence for the "translatability thesis" which Georges Mounin has expounded with such zeal (and strangely un-French pedantry) in *Les belles infidèles* (Paris, 1955). Nonetheless, as one listens to criticism of the novel by those who have read it in English, one almost wonders whether it might not have been the better part of wisdom to leave the novel untranslated — into English or any other language. Such thoughts must be suppressed as soon as they are uttered, but the point remains that certain things about the novel that seem to bear crucially upon its meaning and message are lost beyond retrieve in translation. The novel must be read in Russian, and both the knowledge of contemporary literary Russian style and the remembrance of Pasternak's more remote antecedents must be strong upon the reader. Only then can he perceive and appreciate the miracle of Pasternak's language.

After a generation of Russian writers have debased themselves and their craft in writing Russian with a Georgian accent; after every unhackneyed word or unusual phrase, artistic image, or anything that surpassed the literary ability — or debility — of the dictator has come to be regarded as prima-facie evidence of counterrevolutionary conspiracy, one finds in Pasternak's novel the old Russian language in all its pristine glory, emerging unreduced and unweakened from the long years of its bewitched sleep. How can any translator hope to render the wonders of this reawakening?

In George M. Trevelyan's *History of England* (Book I, chap. 8), there is an inspired passage on the vicissitudes of the English language. For three centuries after the Conquest it had been trodden under foot as the villainous jargon of an illiterate peasantry, only to return transfigured, with added grace and suppleness and force, in Chaucer's *Tales* and Wycliffe's *Bible*. All analogies limp. One generation is not ten, and Pasternak's language may be an echo of the past rather than the reveille of the new day. Still, the reappearance of the despised "jargon" of the Russian intelligentsia after several decades and after millions of pages of the dreariest prose in the history of world literature bears witness to the immortality of the spirit:

> Nicht alle sind tot, die begraben sind;
> Denn sie töten den Geist nicht, ihr Brüder!

In Pasternak's work, literary Russia (like England in Taine's phrase[5]) has recovered her voice. The translation can reveal Dr. Yuri Zhivago as the central figure. It cannot reveal the fact that the "Word," the language of the novel, is its hero in a sense that is antecedent and basic to Zhivago's role. For this story of a Russian intellectual, that is to say, the story of the Russian intelligentsia, is conveyed through a medium which was created by generations of Russian intellectuals to be continually recreated and remolded.

Even so, the theme of the novel and its philosophical problem, though perhaps not the solution offered, are recreations of Russian literary tradition. In particular, Pasternak must remain unintelligible without Blok. Pasternak has called *Doctor Zhivago* a "novel in prose." [6] But the allusion, properly understood, should be to Alexander Blok rather than to Alexander Pushkin. The novel should be seen as a "poem in prose," a retelling, that is, of a poem by Blok.[7]

---

[5] H. Taine, *Histoire de la littérature anglaise*, I (Paris, 1866), 162.
[6] *An Essay in Autobiography* (London, 1959), p. 119.
[7] I have not seen an English translation of this poem. The following French translation (by Serge Karsky) may serve as an ersatz:

> Russie, miséreuse Russie. . . .
>
> Je ne sais pas te plaindre
> Et porte ma croix précieusement . . .
> A l'enchanteur que tu voudras
> Fais don de ta beauté sauvage!

Россия, нищая Россия . . .
Тебя жалеть я не умею,
И крест свой бережно несу . . .
Какому хочешь чародею
Отдай разбойную красу!
Пускай заманит и обманет—
Не пропадешь, не сгинешь ты,
И лишь разлука затуманит
Твои прекрасные черты . . .

Is this not Dr. Zhivago talking to Lara and saying things he never was made to say so clearly in the novel? Was not Lara tempted and carried away by the two sorcerers, Komarovski and Antipov-Strel'nikov? Komarovski's features were etched in steel by the very course of Russia's social and economic history: selfish and possessive, pleasure-loving and cruel, he is responsible for the death of Zhivago's father and for Lara's debasement; yet, intelligent and efficient, though neither farsighted nor wise, he appears as a savior in the hour of danger, offering travel on comfortable trains to a life of material contentment at the expense of brutally erased memories and frustrated yearnings. Not evil enough and not great enough to be "ein Teil von jener Kraft, die stets das Böse will und *stets* das Gute schafft," he does not shrink from sinning frequently and grievously, while his atonements are rare and ambiguous. Twice he tried to hold Lara and failed.

By contrast, Antipov's charms — his *chary* — are not of this world. He is the incarnation of purity and goodness. The filth of his lowly origins left no spot on his white garments. Nor was his rise from abject poverty marred by greed for money or power. Learning is the way of the righteous. It liberated and elevated Antipov and made him worthy to be chosen by Lara. But without creative power, knowledge — in two disciplines — is barren, and the desperate resort to heroism and self-sacrifice in war and civil war only shows the futility of destroying *because* one cannot create.

Qu'il te séduise et qu'il te trompe
Tu ne sombreras pas dans le néant,
Seul le souci déposera un voile
Sur les traits si beaux. . . .

From Nina Berberova, *Alexandre Blok et son temps* (Paris, 1947), pp. 232–33.

Thus the two *charodei* with whom Lara was united in marriage have no power over her. The charms are soon broken. A *razboynaya krasa* — a lawless beauty — is not made for matrimony blessed by church or state. Neither the vigor of capitalism nor the dreamlike image of proletarian virtue has lasting attraction. What does last is the free bond with Dr. Zhivago, the bond between real Russia and the intelligentsia. For Lara *is* real Russia. She is not westernized Russia as is Tonia, the wedded wife, who is so properly shunted away to France where she belongs. "I was born to make life simple and to look for sensible solutions; she to make life more complicated and create confusion," writes Tonia in her farewell letter to Zhivago. But her complaints are futile, and Western rationalism has no chance. Its recipes are wholesome but inapplicable. For the torture of crucifixion is not sensible, and the miracle of resurrection is not simple. Hence the future, the resurrection, and the life in Russia belong to the child of Zhivago's creative spirit and Lara's passive beauty.

General Evgraf Zhivago, the *good* go-getter and trouble-shooter (as distinguished from Komarovski, whose efficiency was not accompanied by high ethical standards) will serve as the guardian angel of the new generation — an arrangement which makes very good sense. Since capitalism proved less than perfectly satisfactory and socialism so altogether unsatisfactory, it would seem quite natural to entrust the young (or rejuvenated) woman to the cares of the army.

Thus the main theme of *Doctor Zhivago* goes back to Blok and beyond Blok to the great Russians of the past century. In one form or another, Russia's historical road and the intelligentsia's task always were the dominating problem. Pasternak's novel is an addition to a long series of *geschichtsphilosophische Betrachtungen* in the guise of novels. It came after a long hiatus. The hiatus itself was filled to the brim with world history. One must not be surprised, therefore, that while *Doctor Zhivago* raises the traditional questions, the answers it gives are somewhat different from those to which the generations of the nineteenth century had listened so eagerly.

In a sense, Dr. Zhivago (the man, not the novel) is still another picture in the crowded gallery of *lishniye lyudi* — "the superfluous people" of Russian literature. Onegin and Pechorin, Beltov and Oblomov, Rudin and Nezhdanov — these are some of Zhivago's

347

literary predecessors. All of them were failures as men of practical action, unable to help Russia and the Russian people. Zhivago was "superfluous" in the revolution and civil war of which he was a casual observer. It is not for nothing that Tonia charged him with "complete absence of will." If he had not died in 1929, he would have been as superfluous in the task of Soviet superindustrialization as was his creator. But at this point the continuity breaks or, at least, seems to break. A hundred years ago Russian novelists considered the superfluousness of a Russian intellectual a burden and a curse. Useful life was life dedicated to the collective, to the people. For Pasternak, this type of redundancy has deep and positive meaning. An *Umwertung der Werte* has occurred.[8] For the Russian radicals of the 1860s a pair of good boots was a far more useful commodity than the Venus de Milo. For Pasternak and his alter ego, one poem may be more important than all the problems of economic progress. To write poetry and, perhaps, to cure men — did not Christ speak in parables and heal the lame and the blind? — this is the true meaning of life, and what may seem superfluous to the collectively organized world may be a deeply felt necessity to the individual.

In a deeper sense, however, the continuity is still unbroken. However strong the intelligentsia's commitment to the weal of the people and to an ideal society, its Weltanschauung was always conceived as free decisions of free men and as such reflected the intelligentsia's fundamental individualism. It is not paradoxical to suggest that, precisely because its thinking was so often warped by a "false ambition of consistency" and thereby driven into many a dogmatic

---

[8] Perhaps nothing epitomizes the change more succinctly than a comparison of Turgenev's and Pasternak's views on Hamlet. For Turgenev, Hamlet was a superfluous intellectual, a selfish skeptic, eternally and uselessly preoccupied with himself (I. S. Turgenev, "Gamlet i Don-Kikhot," *Sobraniye sochinenii* [Hamlet and Don Quixote, Collected Works], XI [Moscow, 1949], 8, 13). But for Pasternak, *Hamlet* is a drama of "duty and self-denial" and Hamlet himself "a judge of his time" and "a servant of the future" (Boris Pasternak, "Translating Shakespeare," *I Remember* [New York, 1959], pp. 130–31). In the very first of Dr. Zhivago's poems, the figure of Hamlet the son merges with that of the Son of Man. For a perceptive interpretation of this deep and difficult poem in which also Hamlet as dramatis persona and the actor who plays the part tend to become one, as do Pasternak and his hero, see Nils Åke Nilsson, "Life as Ecstasy and Sacrifice: Two Poems by Boris Pasternak," *Scando-Slavica*, V (Copenhagen, 1959), 191–98.

impasse, the intelligentsia could not exist except in an atmosphere of free creative activity. When that freedom vanished, decay, disintegration, and, finally, death became inevitable. It is therefore not an accident that Zhivago's last years resemble the *Lebensabend* of the most superfluous of all the "superfluous" characters produced by Russian literature, that is, that of Goncharov's Oblomov. Nor is it surprising that Zhivago dies in 1929, the year so well described by Stalin as *god velikogo pereloma* — the year of the Great Break. In the world in which Stalin, the very negation of freedom and individual dignity, emerged victorious, there was no room for the intelligentsia. Its heart broke when its creative powers were destroyed.

Zhivago's death, however, is not a mere dissolution and disappearance. Nor is it just the predetermined effect of blindly working forces; it is not simply the angina pectoris within him and the anguish of life in Stalin's Russia around him that kills Pasternak's hero. His death is also an act of will, although a sacrifice rather than a suicide. This I take to be the meaning of the last poem appended to the novel, "The Garden of Gethsemane." [9]

> Но книга жизни подошла к странице,
> Которая дороже всех святынь.
> Сейчас должно написанное сбыться
> Пускай же сбудется оно, аминь.
>
> Ты видишь, ход веков подобен притче
> И может загореться на ходу.
> Во имя страшного ее величья
> Я в добровольных муках в гроб сойду.
>
> Я в гроб сойду и в третий день восстану.

[9] The American edition of *Doctor Zhivago* (Pantheon, 1958) contains the following informative translation of these lines by Bernard G. Guerney:

> But now the book of life has reached a page
> Which is more precious than all holies.
> That which was written now must be fulfilled.
> Fulfillèd be it then. Amen.
>
> Seest thou, the passing of the ages is like a parable
> And in its passing it may burst to flame.
> In the name then of its awesome majesty
> I shall, in voluntary torments, descend into my grave.
> I shall descend into my grave. And on the third day rise again.

When the hour on the Mount of Olives had drawn to its close; when all the doubts have been resolved, the fears suppressed, and the last hopes extinguished; when what has been written is about to be fulfilled, it is still "in voluntary pain" to glorify "the terrible majesty" of what has been preordained as the "march of centuries" that Jesus is ready for his cross.[10] And this is the last word and the

[10] Here again, Alexander Blok's poem has been the guiding beacon:

Когда в листве сырой и ржавой
Рябины заалеет гроздь,—
Когда палач рукой костлявой
Вобьет в ладонь последний гвоздь,—

Когда над рябью рек свинцовой,
В сырой и серой высоте,
Пред ликом родины суровой
Я закачаюсь на кресте,—

Тогда—просторно и далеко
Смотрю сквозь кровь предсмертных слез,
И вижу по реке широкой
Ко мне плывет в челне Христос,

В глазах такие же надежды,
И то же рубище на нем.
И жалко смотрит из одежды
Рука пробитая гвоздем,

Христос! родной простор печален!
Изнемогаю на кресте!
И челн твой—будет ли причален
К моей распятой высоте?

The following translation is by Babette Deutsch (*A Treasury of Russian Verse*, ed. A. Yarmolinski [New York, 1949], pp. 150–51):

When mountain ash in clusters reddens,
Its leafage wet and stained with rust,
When through my palm the nail that deadens
My bony hands is shrewdly thrust,

When o'er the rippling, leaden river,
Nailed to the cross, in agony,
Upon the wet gray height I quiver,
While, stern, my country watches me,

Then far and wide in anguish staring
My eyes, grown stiff with tears, will see
Down the road river slowly faring,
Christ in a skiff approaching me.

summary of the parable which is this novel. As Renato Poggioli has so rightly pointed out (in his essay in *Partisan Review*), the philosophy of *Doctor Zhivago* is very different from that of *War and Peace*. The short spring term which Pasternak had spent in Marburg at the feet of Hermann Cohen was never forgotten. Cohen taught him well "was der Alte meinte" [11] in propounding the Third Antinomy in the *Critique of Pure Reason*. The causal determination of the phenomena and the normative freedom of the noumena receive their active resolution in the methodological dichotomy of *Sein und Sollen*.[12] Man is a norm-making creature. He may know a great deal about the causal world; he may be deeply impressed with the grandeur of the creation and with what he believes to be the world's predetermined course, and he may mold his norms accordingly. Yet the attempt to obliterate the duality of causality and imputation by substantive *Gleichschaltung* must fail. Norm-making in its deepest essence is and remains a free activity. Whatever the strength of the causal world and its power over the individual, it cannot destroy the normative world of individual freedom. Also, *amor fati* is a revocable act of choice. At times, the Russian intelligentsia may have masochistically abused its freedom in this respect — in addition to overestimating its own ability to scrutinize the paths of destiny; but its history, taken for all in all, bears eloquent witness for its aversion from tyranny in all forms. Thus, Osip Mandelstam, whose life thread

---

> And in his eyes the same hopes biding,
> And the same rags from Him will trail,
> His garment piteously hiding
> The palm pierced by the final nail.
>
> Christ! saddened are the native reaches.
> The cross tugs at my failing might,
> Thy skiff — will it achieve these beaches,
> And land here at my cruciate height?

Note the manifold significance of *ryabina* — the rowan tree or mountain ash — in *Doctor Zhivago*, and see in this connection the penetrating remarks by Renato Poggioli in "Boris Pasternak," *Partisan Review*, XXV, no. 4 (1958), 551.

[11] Boris Pasternak, *Safe Conduct* (New York, 1958), p. 75.

[12] I. Kant, *Kritik der reinen Vernunft, Werke in sechs Bänden* (6 vols.; Leipzig, Insel Verlag, n.d.), II, 498. The concept of the noumenon may be "problematic," "marginal," and only "negative," but the specific reality of the *Reich des Sollens* is neither problematic nor merely negative. Hermann Cohen, *Kants Begründung der Ethik* (Berlin, 1877), pp. 31, 115.

is said, for one fateful moment, to have become intertwined with Pasternak's, may have (in 1918) "glorified the intolerable oppression of the regime":

Прославим власти сумрачное бремя,
Ее невыносимый гнет!

But it was his epigrams against the dictator that brought prison, banishment, and death upon that lover of Ovid.

It is, then, in "voluntary acceptance" of its fate that the Russian intelligentsia descended into the grave, secure in the knowledge of resurrection: the kingdom of human freedom will come. This, I think, is Pasternak's message. Its fate is uncertain. Imbedded in the context of the novel, it may pass unnoticed; torn out of it, it will hardly convince the skeptic. A message that appeals to faith can be confounded by doubt. Army generals are not necessarily the most trustworthy guardians of intellectual liberty. Yuri Zhivago is dead, and the hour of resurrection may never strike. Yet the novel called *Doctor Zhivago*, I believe, will not betray its name [13] and will live on as a monument to an art that, turning its back upon "les muses d'État," [14] refused to be "made tongue-tied by authority" and fearlessly proclaimed the eternal truth that creative genius and freedom are as inseparable as human life and human breath.

[13] The Church-Slavonic name "Zhivago" relates to "life" and "living."
[14] Victor de Laprade, *Poèmes civiques* (Paris, 1873), pp. 107–109.

The Approach to European Industrialization:
A Postscript

The gradual evolution of this writer's views on the industrial history of Europe has been presented in the first eight chapters of this volume. The purpose of the following pages is to offer a brief summary of those views; to point out certain inconsistencies, difficult to avoid in research processes which extend over a number of years and whose results are published seriatim; and most importantly, to say something about the crucial problem of the limitations to which the approach is subject and about the type of research that can profitably lead beyond those limitations.

The origin of this approach lies in two basic observations that can be formulated as follows. The map of Europe in the nineteenth century showed a motley picture of countries varying with regard to the degree of their economic backwardness. At the same time, processes of rapid industrialization started in several of those countries from very different levels of economic backwardness. Those differences in points — or planes — of departure, were of crucial significance for the nature of the subsequent development. Depending on a given country's degree of economic backwardness on the eve of its industrialization, the course and character of the latter tended to vary in a number of important respects. Those variations can be readily compressed into the shorthand of six propositions.

1. The more backward a country's economy, the more likely was its industrialization to start discontinuously as a sudden great spurt proceeding at a relatively high rate of growth of manufacturing output.[1]

[1] The "great spurt" is closely related to W. W. Rostow's "take-off" (*The Stages*

353

2. The more backward a country's economy, the more pronounced was the stress in its industrialization on bigness of both plant and enterprise.

3. The more backward a country's economy, the greater was the stress upon producers' goods as against consumers' goods.

4. The more backward a country's economy, the heavier was the pressure upon the levels of consumption of the population.

5. The more backward a country's economy, the greater was the part played by special institutional factors designed to increase supply of capital to the nascent industries and, in addition, to provide them with less decentralized and better informed entrepreneurial guidance; the more backward the country, the more pronounced was the coerciveness and comprehensiveness of those factors.

6. The more backward a country, the less likely was its agriculture to play any active role by offering to the growing industries the advantages of an expanding industrial market based in turn on the rising productivity of agricultural labor.

As stated in Chapter 2, the differences in the levels of economic advance among the individual European countries or groups of countries in the last century were sufficiently large to make it possible to array those countries, or groups of countries, along a scale of increasing degrees of backwardness and thus to render the latter an operationally usable concept. Cutting two notches into that scale yields three groups of countries which may be roughly described as advanced, moderately backward, and very backward. To the extent that certain of the variations in our six propositions can also be conceived as discrete rather than continuous, the pattern assumes the form of a series of stage constructs. Understandably enough, this result obtains most naturally with regard to factors referred to in proposition 5, where quantitative differences are associated with qualitative, that is, institutional, variations. Then, for instance, the

---

of *Economic Growth*, Cambridge, Mass., 1960, chap. 4). Both concepts stress the element of specific discontinuity in economic development; great spurts, however, are confined to the area of manufacturing and mining, whereas take-offs refer to national output. Unfortunately, in the present state of our statistical information on long-term growth of national income (see Appendix III to this volume), there is hardly any way of establishing, let alone testing, the take-off hypotheses.

relationships existing with regard to sources of capital supply, as sketched in Chapter 1, can be expressed as follows:

Stages	Advanced area	Area of moderate backwardness	Area of extreme backwardness
I	Factory	Banks	State
II		Factory	Banks
III			Factory

Such an attempt to view the course of industrialization as a schematic stagelike process differs essentially from the various efforts in "stage making," the common feature of which was the assumption that all economies were supposed regularly to pass through the same individual stages as they moved along the road of economic progress. The regularity may have been frankly presented as an inescapable "law" of economic development.[2] Alternatively, the element of necessity may have been somewhat disguised by well-meant, even though fairly meaningless, remarks about the choices that were open to society.[3] But all those schemes were dominated by the idea of uniformity. Thus, Rostow was at pains to assert that the process of industrialization repeated itself from country to country lumbering through his pentametric rhythm. Accordingly, Soviet Russia was like everybody else and rather confidently expected in the end to be propelled by the "Buddenbrooks dynamics" into the fifth stage of "high mass consumption."[4] Leaving erroneous literary allusions aside, there is, within a fairly wide margin, nothing wrong in principle with an approach which concentrates upon the interspatial similarities in industrial development. The existence of such similarities is very real.[5] Their study yields attractive simplicities, but it does so at the price of dismissing some refractory facts which a historian will ignore at his own peril. Those who see the essence of industri-

---

[2] See, for example, Bruno Hildebrand, *Die Nationalökonomie der Gegenwart und Zukunft und andere gesammelte Schriften*, I (Jena, 1922), 357.

[3] See Rostow, *The Stages of Economic Growth*, pp. 118f.

[4] Rostow, chap. 7 and p. 162. In kindness to the memory of Thomas Mann, it should be mentioned that *Buddenbrooks* is a novel dealing with the biological decay of a family whose vitality declines from generation to generation.

[5] See the discussion of this point in Chapter 1.

alization in the establishment of a strong and independent manufacturing enterprise need only to look diagonally across the previous tabulation in order to find such an enterprise in existence everywhere — in advanced England as well as in lagging Germany or in very backward Russia. Seen *in latum et in longum* — which are the easy dimensions — Russia is like Germany and Germany is like England. But to say this is to debar oneself from looking into the *depth* of history, that is to say, from perceiving the industrialization in the making. What is the story of Central European industrializations without the role of the banks in the process? What is the Russian industrialization of the 1890s without the Ministry of Finance?

The point, however, is not simply that these were important occurrences which have just claims on the historian's attention. What matters in the present connection is that observing the individual methods of financing industrial growth helps us to understand the crucial problem of prerequisites for industrial development.

The common opinion on the subject has been well stated by Rostow. There is said to be a number of certain general preconditions or prerequisites for industrial growth, without which it could not begin.[6] Abolition of an archaic framework in agricultural organization or an increase in the productivity of agriculture; creation of an influential modern elite which is materially or ideally interested in economic change; provision of what is called social-overhead capital in physical form — all these are viewed as "necessary preconditions," except that some reference to the multifarious forms in which the prerequisites are fulfilled in the individual areas are designed to take care of the "unique" factors in development.[7] Similarly, the existence of a value system favoring economic progress and the availability of effective entrepreneurial groups basking in the sun of social approval have been regarded as essential preconditions of industrial growth.[8]

These positions are part and parcel of an undifferentiated ap-

[6] Rostow, chap. 3. The author expressly excludes from his generalizations the United States and some British Dominions, but this is of no interest in the present context which is confined to the industrial history of Europe.

[7] *Ibid.*

[8] It is in this sense that the discussion of entrepreneurship in economic development in Chapter 3 of this volume may be regarded as a contribution to the problem of prerequisites of industrial growth.

proach to industrial history. But their conceptual and empirical deficiencies are very considerable, even though it is by no means easy to bid farewell to this highly simplified way of viewing the processes of industrialization. It took the present writer several years before he succeeded in reformulating the concept of prerequisites so that it could be fit into the general approach premised upon the notion of relative backwardness. This, it is feared, is the area within the present volume that is most open to the charge of inconsistency. To give an example, several times the statement is made (as in Chapters 1, 6, and 7) that abolition of serfdom in Russia was a necessary or even an absolute prerequisite for industrialization.[9] What was meant was that the emancipation of the peasants in Russia of the 1860s very materially aided the subsequent process of industrialization. This is by no means wrong, but it should have been possible to express that thought without mobilizing high-sounding but meaningless terms. There should be a fine on the use of words such as "necessary" or "necessity" in historical writings. As one takes a closer look at the concept of necessity as it is appended to prerequisites of industrial development, it becomes clear that, whenever the concept is not entirely destitute of meaning, it is likely to be purely definitional: industrialization is defined in terms of certain conditions which then, by an imperceptible shift of the writer's wrist, are metamorphosed into historical preconditions.[10]

The recourse to tautologies and dexterous manipulations has been produced by, or at any rate served to disguise, very real empirical difficulties. After having satisfied oneself that in England certain factors could be reasonably regarded as having preconditioned the industrialization of the country, the tendency was, and still is, to elevate them to the rank of ubiquitous prerequisites of all European industrializations. Unfortunately, the attempt was inconsistent with two empirical observations: (1) some of the factors that had served as prerequisites in England either were not present in less advanced countries or at best were present to a very small extent; (2) the big

---

[9] These chapters were written before Chapter 2, in which the concept of prerequisites has been discussed in a more orderly fashion.

[10] It is not surprising, therefore, to see Rostow at one point (p. 49) mix conditions and preconditions of industrial development very freely.

spurt of industrial development occurred in those countries despite the lack of such prerequisites.

If these observations are not ignored or shrugged away, as is usually done, they quite naturally direct research toward a new question: in what way and through the use of what devices did backward countries *substitute* for the missing prerequisites? This crucial question, on which Chapter 2 of this volume is based, has yielded significant answers. It appears, on the one hand, that some of the alleged prerequisites were not needed in industrializations proceeding under different conditions. On the other hand, once the question has been asked, whole series of various substitutions become visible which could be readily organized in a meaningful pattern according to the degree of economic backwardness. To revert once more to the illustration shown in the previous tabulation, it is easy to conceive of the capital supplied to the early factories in an advanced country as stemming from previously accumulated wealth or from gradually plowed-back profits; at the same time, actions by banks and governments in less advanced countries are regarded as successful attempts to create *in the course* of industrialization conditions which had not been created in the "preindustrial" periods precisely because of the economic backwardness of the areas concerned.

It was shown in Chapter 2 that the area of capital supply is only one instance of substitutions for missing prerequisites. As one looks at the various patterns of substitution in the individual countries, taking proper account of the effects of gradually diminishing backwardness, one is tempted to formulate still another general proposition. The more backward was a country on the eve of its great spurt of industrial development, the more likely were the processes of its industrialization to present a rich and complex picture — thus providing a curious contrast with its own preindustrial history that most often was found to have been relatively barren. In an advanced country, on the other hand, the very richness of its economic history in the preindustrial periods rendered possible a relatively simple and straightforward course in its modern industrial history.

Thus, the concept of prerequisites must be regarded as an integral part of this writer's general approach to the industrial history of Europe. At the same time, it is important to keep in mind the heuristic nature of the concept. There is no intention to suggest that backward countries necessarily engaged in deliberate acts of "substitution" for something that had been in evidence in more advanced countries. Men in a less developed country may have simply groped for and found solutions that were consonant with the existing conditions of backwardness. In fact, one could conceivably start the study of European industrializations in the east rather than in the west of the Continent and view some elements in English industrial history as substitutions for the German or the Russian way of doing things. This would not be a very good way to proceed. It would make mockery of chronology and would be glaringly artificial. True, some artificiality also inheres in the opposite approach. It is arbitrary to select England as the seat of prerequisites. Yet this is the arbitrariness of the process of cognition and should be judged by its fruits.

The main advantage of viewing European history as patterns of substitutions governed by the prevailing — and changing — degree of backwardness lies, perhaps paradoxically, in its offering a set of predictabilities while at the same time placing limitations upon our ability to predict. To predict is not to prophesy. Prediction in historical research means addressing intelligent, that is, sufficiently specific, questions as new materials are approached.

When this writer embarked upon a study of Italian industrial development, his research was magistrally directed by the expectation of finding investment banks playing a central role in the process. This substitution pattern could be "predicted" on the basis of earlier studies of industrial growth in other countries in Central Europe, primarily in Germany. As is shown in Chapter 4, this particular prediction was well borne out by the study of the available archival materials. It might be noted that neither the contemporaneous nor the later-day literature on Italian industrial growth before World War I had contained adequate appreciation of the contribution which the banks had made to industrialization.

As the Italian case shows, substitution patterns of this kind can spread from country to country through deliberate importation. Yet it is equally true that the very concept of substitution is premised upon creative innovating activity, that is to say, upon something that is inherently unpredictable with the help of our normal apparatus of

359

research. This alone should raise the important problem of the limits to which the present approach is subject. But there are other reasons as well.

Historical hypotheses are not general or universal propositions. They cannot be falsified by a single exception. Testing them largely means trying to discover the boundaries of the area within which they seem reasonably valid. When research pushes against such boundaries and the deviations from expectations become significant, there are normally two ways of meeting the situation: either the hypothesis may be discarded — not necessarily as being "wrong" but as having exhausted its explanatory value; or the deviations found can be systematized and incorporated in the hypothesis, thus enriching it and providing stimulus for further research. In this way, the developed hypothesis may come to be far removed from its origins. In a sense, the general approach as presented here can be considered as an attempt to systematize the deviations from the English paradigm by relying on the degree of backwardness as the organizing concept. But this approach, too, can and should be pushed to the limits of its applicability.

As has been intimated before, a historical approach usually has competitors for the treatment of a given set of data. Within the scope of the essays in the present volume, the individual elements of the great industrial spurt in Russia of the 1890s have been viewed as essentially determined by the backwardness of the Russian economy. It has been argued, for instance, that the Russians favored producers' goods as against consumers' goods because of the importance of technological borrowings to a very backward country in conjunction with the accidental circumstance that technological progress in the immediately preceding period had been more vehement in the production of capital goods.[11] This lopsidedness in the industrial structure, natural in conditions of backwardness, is said then to have been merely *accentuated* by the policies of the Russian government.

It is quite possible, however, to attempt a primarily political

[11] See Chapters 1 and 6. Today, having been influenced by Albert Hirschman's studies, I should add that producers' goods possessing elaborate "forward linkages" are of particular importance in a very backward country where the internal market is narrow and where the existence of active "investment for investment's sake" circuits can be of major importance in sustaining the great spurt. Albert O. Hirschman, *The Strategy of Economic Development* (New Haven, 1958), chap. 6.

approach to the industrial history of the period and to see the stress on producers' goods as essentially determined by the immediate military needs of the government. As shown before, such an approach has long historical antecedents and certainly would be capable of considerable elaboration. It so happens, however, that, after having considered the industrial evolution in Russia not only in the 1890s but also in the years preceding the outbreak of World War I, the case for considering Russia as an integral part of an all-European pattern of industrial development has seemed very strong, and this writer at least has felt that his general approach as presented here offers a fuller and more plausible explanation of the total development. And still the fact remains that certain aspects of that development, such as some phases of railroad construction, or certain techniques of fiscal administration, or governmental decisions with regard to the field commune, would be much more naturally explicable in terms of a set of political rather than economic hypotheses.[12] This, no doubt, must be considered as a limitation upon the main explanatory scheme.

Some other limitations have been mentioned in the individual essays. The present approach deals with the industrial development of Europe. Yet there are geographic limitations within Europe. Throughout, the individual country has been used as a unit of observation. This does not mean, however, that industrial development in any backward European area representing an organized statehood can be expected to conform to the expectations set forth in the preceding pages. The economy of a small sovereign country may be so much enmeshed in the economy of another, more advanced, country as to be virtually an integral part of the latter area. Its economic evolution may therefore proceed without any serious discontinuities, the gradualness of its industrial growth simply mirroring the course of events in the larger country. With the lack of anything resembling a big spurt, the other specific elements of industrializations in conditions of backwardness are also likely to be absent. This appears to be the case of Denmark as referred to in Chapter 1.

On the other hand, the case of the Bulgarian industrialization

---

[12] Curiously enough, in such an explanation much weight would have to be given to a usually neglected factor: the relations between the Ministry of Finance and the Ministry of Interior.

dealt with in Chapter 8 deserves to be mentioned in this connection. For it illustrates well the fact that the present approach is not at all designed to predict that a great spurt of industrialization will occur. Such predicting — in the technical sense of the term — as is possible must remain conditional. If Bulgaria had gone through a spurt of industrial development, it would have been natural to look for certain paraphernalia thereof, including some patterns of substitution. Since the great spurt failed to materialize, all our approach can do is to attribute that failure to the inability or unwillingness of the government to discover and apply the appropriate pattern of substitution. It is plausible indeed that in the case of Bulgaria that pattern may well have consisted of a concentrated simultaneous effort by both banks and government. It is useful to be guided into these problems and to formulate some of those suppositions. Yet the main value of the Bulgarian experience lies in the fact that it strongly suggests the notion of *missed opportunity*. This would seem to be the most important aspect of the problem of limitations.

In Chapter 1 of this volume, the period in a backward country preceding the great spurt has been described as one of mounting tension between the prevailing economic conditions and the promise offered by rapid industrial developments. This accumulation of potential energies [13] was not seen as a merely gradual process. Significant political events, such as national unification or thoroughgoing judicial or administrative reforms, could indeed lead to relatively sudden multiplication of the existing opportunities [14] and might at times trigger the great spurt. At the same time, however, the flow of technological progress in more advanced countries kept enriching the fund upon which the backward country could draw for its technical equipment and know-how. In its technological borrowings the back-

[13] The present writer was pleased recently to come across a passage in a forgotten pamphlet by the great German sociologist, Georg Simmel (*Der Krieg und die geistigen Entscheidungen*, Munich-Leipzig, 1917, pp. 22–23), containing a very similar conception of German industrial development. Simmel speaks explicitly of the immense accumulation of *wirtschaftliche Spannkräfte*, which for a long time could not be discharged.

[14] Dealing with the optimistic forward-looking world of the nineteenth century, one was on the whole less ready to consider the contingency of *decreases* of tension consequent upon destructive wars or anti-industrial legislation.

ward country was to utilize decades or even centuries of progress most of which had proceeded *occulto aevo* — in the quiet lapse of time. In the light of this process, the tension preceding the great spurt appeared ever-increasing and the backward country was seen as steadily accumulating the advantages of backwardness.

This view of the development would seem in need of some reconsideration in the light of the Bulgarian and Italian studies; the latter is particularly relevant here. In Chapter 4, some attention has been devoted to the question of why the rate of industrial growth in Italy during 1896–1908 did not climb to still higher levels, which might have been reasonably expected in view of the degree of Italy's economic backwardness at that time. In discussing the problem, some weight had to be attributed to the ill-advised economic policies of the Italian government which persisted in favoring less promising branches of industrial endeavor at the expense of those in which the country's comparative advantage was greatest. But there were also other factors. In particular, it was suggested that the virtual completion of railroad construction prior to the initiation of the great spurt in the mid-nineties exercised a damping effect upon the subsequent rate of growth. The intensification of labor conflicts worked in the same direction. In this view, Italy's industrial development had its great chance in the 1880s; but the upswing of those years remained abortive, mainly, it is believed, because the modern investment bank had not yet been established in Italy.

If this conception is at all correct, it would mean that accumulation of "advantages of backwardness" can, at least at times, be paralleled by an accumulation of disadvantages of backwardness. If the latter proceeds at uneven rates, then certain historical moments in a country's development should be considered as particularly propitious for industrialization, as its *Sternstunden*. To change — and to lower — the metaphor, the bus that is supposed to take a country across its great spurt of industrialization sometimes comes at odd hours and can be missed. And the next bus may not be as large or as convenient or as fast as its predecessor. At any rate, the wait for it can be fairly long. In other words, both the timing of a country's great spurt and its character can be affected.

There is little doubt that "missed opportunities" can constitute real limitations upon this general approach to the industrial development of Europe. Some of those opportunities vanish in a way that is erratic and unpredictable, at least from an economist's point of view. The manifold structural difficulties and disabilities of the interwar period in a country like Bulgaria are a case in point. They were essentially political in nature or the consequence of political events. There are, however, other situations and other factors which are likely to lend themselves better to organized study and be more amenable to generalized conclusions.

Shifting attention to the study of the difficulties and obstacles that accumulate with the increase in the degree of economic backwardness may well lead to the formation of a more general concept of "nodal points" at which the advantages of backwardness reach optimal levels and beyond which lies at least a limited period of declining promise and growing disability. Such a study would involve *inter alia* a much closer scrutiny of the relations that exist between the pace of technological progress and the dominant innovations, on the one hand, and their impact upon the industrializing economies of backward countries, on the other. The present research plans of this writer do indeed point in this direction.

It is possible that, as a result of such additional explorations, the deviations from the norm once more would be brought into a system and our approach to the industrial history of Europe rendered more complex but also more illuminating. Yet, as has been said before, the nature of the deviations may be such as to require and perhaps suggest an organizing principle very different from the variations in the degree of backwardness. This would mean the end of an approach. But farewell to it would be said in a grateful mood. For what more can be expected of any historical hypothesis than to have stimulated research to the point of becoming the stepping stone to a new hypothesis and to new research?

APPENDIX I

Description of an Index of Italian Industrial Development, 1881-1913

TWO PREVIOUS ATTEMPTS

As far as this writer has been able to ascertain, there have been two previous attempts to construct an index of Italian industrial output for a period extending back into the nineteenth century: one by Jean Dessirier and the other by Guglielmo Tagliacarne.[1] Dessirier's index appears in his study, "Indices comparés de la production industrielle et de la production agricole en divers pays de 1870 à 1928."[2] The description given by Dessirier is sketchy. The index is said to include the following entries: (1) mining (lignite, iron ore, zinc ore, sulphur); (2) metalmaking (cast iron and steel); (3) engineering (calculated on the basis of steel consumption); (4) textiles (cotton and wool consumption and production of silk); and (5) chemicals (sulphuric acid, superphosphates, calcium carbide). The author is even less specific with regard to the question of the weights employed. He says: "The index of [Italian] industrial output has been

[1] Upon the completion of the work which is described here, still another and very interesting attempt has come to this writer's attention: the index computation by Silvio Golzio, published in his book *Sulla misura delle variazioni del reddito nazionale italiano* (Turin, n.d., probably 1951 or 1952). This computation, which in many ways is far superior to its two predecessors and in part employs the same devices as are used in the present index, shows a degree of coverage which is considerably higher than that of the present index. Nevertheless, it is less suitable for the purpose of studying Italian industrial development prior to the outbreak of the First World War because weights pertaining to a much later period (1938) are used and because the data are presented in terms of five-year averages, which tends to blur the exact delimitations of the individual subperiods of development and accordingly makes it difficult to ascertain the rates of growth from period to period. Since Golzio's index had not become available to this writer until the present descriptions had been written, some footnote references to it have been inserted throughout, and a more detailed presentation of his methods and results has been included in a final section.

[2] *Bulletin de la Statistique Générale de la France*, XVIII, no. 1 (October–December 1928), 65–110.

calculated by combining the individual series approximately in proportion to the numbers of workers employed in each industry in 1913."

It remains unexplained how the author proceeded in aggregating his subseries within the five industries included. Neither those subseries nor the numerical weights appear in the study. Nor does it contain any quantitative information on the coverage of the index. That the year 1913 rather than the census year 1911 has been chosen as the base-weighting year is somewhat surprising. Finally, it is not clear at all whether Dessirier carried out any adjustment of weights to take into account at least the considerable divergences between employment and mechanical power that existed among the industries concerned. Since there is no way of retracing the author's computations, the index must be regarded as a "take-it-or-leave-it" proposition. Still, until after the last war this was the only index of Italian production available, and so it is not surprising that the League of Nations staff in preparing its study, *Industrialization and Foreign Trade* (1945), decided to "take" it. Dessirier's year-by-year series begins in 1898 (the year, incidentally, when chemical-industry output was for the first time included in his index); for the period prior to 1898, only three numbers are given: for the years 1870, 1880, and 1890. In the League of Nations study the annual series on Italian industrial output begins in 1880, and the numbers for the years 1881–97 have been interpolated on the basis of Italian coal consumption (p. 176). It is not mentioned whether an attempt has been made to deduct from total consumption of coal the amounts used for nonindustrial purposes and particularly those for railroad locomotives and bunker coal. It may be noted, for example, that in 1889 industrial coal consumption in Italy amounted to only about 26 percent of total coal consumption.[3] The movement of the latter is therefore hardly apt to measure the rate of industrial change. So much for the Dessirier index. We shall return later to the rates of growth implied therein.

Tagliacarne's index was prepared for inclusion in a government document that was submitted to the Italian Constituent Assembly; it is contained in the section of that document entitled "Lo sviluppo dell'industria italiana ed il commercio estero." [4] Tagliacarne's index has the great advantage of being accompanied by a much more explicit statement concerning the method of its construction. Its main features are as follows.

The index includes the following series and subseries:

[3] L. Bodio, *Di alcuni indici misuratori del movimento economico in Italia* (Rome, 1891), p. 42. Incidentally, the League of Nations figure contains a typographical error: the number for 1899 should be 60 rather than 66; furthermore, the numbers for 1899 and 1898 are Dessirier's original figures and are not results of interpolations, as is erroneously indicated in the study (p. 132).

[4] Ministero per la Costituente, *Rapporto della Commissione Economica presentato all'Assemblea Costituente: II. Industria, I. Relazione, II* (Rome, 1947), 80.

Series	Subseries
(1) Raw silk	—
(2) Raw cotton imports	—
(3) Beer and sugar	Beer and sugar
(4) Metalmaking and mineral processing	Pig iron, iron and steel, lead and mercury
(5) Mining	Iron ore, lead ore, zinc ore, mineral fuel, iron pyrites, sulphur
(6) Shipbuilding	—
(7) Sulphuric acid	—

The series (3), (4), and (5) contain subgroups which in all cases have been combined by a simple, that is, unweighted, addition of tonnage data in which the original data were expressed. Accordingly, beer and sugar have been added ton per ton, as have been iron ore and raw sulphur or lead, pig iron, and iron and steel. This, of course, is a rather crude procedure which, along with some other disabilities of the index, must be explained in terms of great pressures for the speedy completion of an *ad hoc* assignment.

Tagliacarne does not provide an exact derivation of the weights by dint of which he combined his seven series into an index of aggregate industrial output. He says that in some cases payroll data and in others the amount of horsepowers installed have been used for the purpose; these data, he adds (p. 48), were obtained from the 1938 census. But he does supply a full tabulation of the weights used (pp. 48, 80–81):

Series	Weights	Weights in percent
Silk	1	4.8
Cotton	2	9.5
Foodstuffs	4	19.0
Metalmaking and mineral processing	5	23.9
Mining	3	14.3
Shipbuilding	4	19.0
Chemical products	2	9.5
	21	100.0

With the help of these weights, the individual series have been combined through weighted geometric averages. Something more will be said later about Tagliacarne's results and the rates of growth implied in his series.

The index shows a number of prima-facie shortcomings. The main questionable points are these:

(1) The previously mentioned unweighted aggregation of subseries.

(2) The attempt to measure the rate of progress in the engineering industry by the rate of change in a single branch of that industry — ship-

building. Since the group contained a fair number of new and rapidly developing industries, the use of a series pertaining to an older industry as a gauge for the change of the group as a whole seemed patently inadequate.

(3) The representation of the foodstuffs industry by only two series: beer and sugar. Since beer output was very small, the course of the series was determined by the sugar industry alone which, from the turn of the century on, grew at a most rapid pace.

(4) The use of a single series (sulphuric acid) to picture the rate of change in the whole group of the chemical industry.

(5) The use of a set of weights pertaining to the extreme end (1938) of an index period extending over more than half a century (1881–1937).

(6) Existence of some computational errors in the preparation of the index.

The decision to construct the present index was essentially determined by the desire to eliminate at least some of the deficiencies just mentioned. Nevertheless, it must be noted that some of those deficiencies appear as such only from the writer's specific interest in Italian industrial development before the outbreak of World War I. Moreover, while most of the series were obtained directly from the original sources, some portions of Tagliacarne's work have been taken over bodily into the present index. In general, the existence of that index provided a most valuable guide in the construction of the present one, which in many respects should be considered a mere modification and revision of its predecessor. This is true even though the results of the two computations differ substantially.

The Present Index: General Characteristics

The main features of the present index may be summarized as follows:

(1) The number of the main industrial groups is the same as in Tagliacarne's index.

(2) The combination of the subgroups was as a rule carried out by the use of the 1898 average unit value of output of the commodities concerned.

(3) Wherever possible, an attempt was made to eliminate double counting (thus, the pig-iron series was excluded from the index of metal-making and, in addition, gross values of output of some products were diminished by the values of at least some of the raw materials consumed in the process of production).

(4) The series of the foodstuffs industry has been "stabilized" by the introduction of a subseries reflecting changes in the output of flour mills, the latter being a dominant component of the industry, particularly with regard to its share in horsepowers used.

(5) The engineering industry has been represented by an index of

Italian steel consumption reduced by the amounts of steel consumed in the Italian production of rails and related materials.

(6) The sets of weights used in combining the six main series pertain to the years 1902–03, the basic data having been gleaned from the Italian industrial survey of those years. This survey, to which reference is made below, was not a real census of Italian industrial output, the first such census being taken in 1911. The survey is based on a series of monographic investigations of Italian industry which began in 1885 and were subsequently brought up to date so as to focus on the years 1902–03. The main set of weights used represents value-added estimates, prepared on the basis of the survey. In addition, two more indices have been computed by using 1902–03 data on employment and horsepower, respectively.

The other changes made in comparison with Tagliacarne's index, such as the inclusion of some additional subseries and the exclusion of others, are of lesser importance. They are reported fully in the following section.

The Present Index: Subseries

Mining

The mining industry is represented by seven subgroups: (1) iron ore, (2) zinc ore, (3) lead ore, (4) copper ore, (5) solid mineral fuel, (6) sulphur, and (7) pyrites.

(1) *Iron-ore output.* The basic output data in tons were obtained from *Annuario Statistico Italiano,* abbreviated in the following as *Annuario.* The references are as follows: for 1881–98, *Annuario* 1900, p. 477; 1899–1905, *Annuario* 1905–07, p. 434; 1906–09, *Annuario* 1911, p. 125; 1910–13, *Annuario* 1915, p. 148. The value of product in 1898 was 2,746,239 lire (*Annuario* 1900, p. 477), yielding an average unit value of 14.5 lire per ton; this price was applied to the series in tons for 1881–1913, as shown in the following table.

IRON-ORE OUTPUT

Year	1,000 tons	Value (1,000 lire)	Year	1,000 tons	Value (1,000 lire)
1881	421	6,104.5	1892	214	3,103.0
1882	242	3,509.0	1893	191	2,769.5
1883	204	2,958.0	1894	188	2,726.0
1884	225	3,262.5	1895	183	2,653.5
1885	201	2,914.5	1896	204	2,958.0
1886	209	3,030.5	1897	201	2,914.5
1887	231	3,349.5	1898	190	2,746.0
1888	177	2,566.5	1899	237	3,436.5
1889	173	2,508.5	1900	247	3,581.5
1890	221	3,204.5	1901	232	3,364.0
1891	216	3,132.0	1902	241	3,494.5

IRON-ORE OUTPUT (*cont.*)

Year	1,000 tons	Value (1,000 lire)	Year	1,000 tons	Value (1,000 lire)
1903	375	5,437.5	1909	505	7,322.5
1904	409	5,930.5	1910	551	7,989.5
1905	367	5,321.5	1911	374	5,423.0
1906	384	5,568.0	1912	582	8,439.0
1907	518	7,511.0	1913	603	8,743.5
1908	539	7,815.5			

(2) *Zinc-ore output.* The source references for the physical quantities of output and for the unit value in 1898 are the same as specified above for iron-ore output, except that the page reference for 1881–1913 is p. 479. The value of product in 1898 was 12,062,000 lire, yielding an average unit value of 91.3 lire per ton; this price was applied to the series in tons for 1881–1913, as shown in the following table.

ZINC-ORE OUTPUT

Year	1,000 tons	Value (1,000 lire)	Year	1,000 tons	Value (1,000 lire)
1881	72	6,573.6	1898	132	12,062.0
1882	91	8,308.3	1899	151	13,786.3
1883	100	9,130.0	1900	140	12,782.0
1884	105	9,586.5	1901	136	12,416.8
1885	107	9,769.1	1902	132	12,051.6
1886	108	9,860.4	1903	158	14,425.4
1887	93	8,490.9	1904	148	13,512.4
1888	87	7,943.1	1905	148	13,512.4
1889	97	8,856.1	1906	156	14,242.8
1890	111	10,134.3	1907	161	14,699.3
1891	121	11,047.3	1908	152	13,877.6
1892	130	11,869.0	1909	130	11,869.0
1893	133	12,142.9	1910	146	13,329.8
1894	132	12,051.6	1911	140	12,782.0
1895	122	11,138.6	1912	150	13,695.0
1896	118	10,773.4	1913	158	14,425.4
1897	122	11,138.6			

(3) *Lead-ore output.* The source references for the physical quantities of output and for the unit value in 1898 are the same as specified above for iron-ore output, except that the page reference for 1881–98 is p. 479. The value of product in 1898 was 5,221,240 lire, yielding an average unit value of 153.57 lire per ton; this price was applied to the series in tons for 1881–1913, as shown in the following table.

LEAD-ORE OUTPUT

Year	1,000 tons	Value (1,000 lire)	Year	1,000 tons	Value (1,000 lire)
1881	40	6,142.8	1898	34	5,221.2
1882	46	7,064.2	1899	31	4,760.7
1883	46	7,064.2	1900	35	5,374.9
1884	46	7,064.2	1901	43	6,603.5
1885	40	6,142.8	1902	42	6,449.9
1886	40	6,142.8	1903	42	6,449.9
1887	38	5,835.6	1904	43	6,603.5
1888	35	5,374.9	1905	39	5,989.2
1889	37	5,682.0	1906	41	6,296.3
1890	32	4,914.2	1907	43	6,603.5
1891	30	4,607.1	1908	47	7,217.7
1892	33	5,067.8	1909	38	5,835.7
1893	29	4,453.5	1910	37	5,682.0
1894	30	4,607.1	1911	38	5,832.7
1895	31	4,760.7	1912	42	6,449.9
1896	34	5,221.3	1913	45	6,910.6
1897	36	5,528.5			

(4) *Copper-ore output*. The source references for the physical quantities of output and for the unit value in 1898 are the same as specified above for iron-ore output, except that the page reference for 1881–1913 is p. 478. The value of product in 1898 was 2,131,497 lire, yielding an average unit value of 22.43 lire per ton; this price was applied to the series in tons for 1881–1913, as shown in the following table.

COPPER-ORE OUTPUT

Year	1,000 tons	Value (1,000 lire)	Year	tons 1,000	Value (1,000 lire)
1881	26	583.2	1895	84	1,884.1
1882	24	538.3	1896	90	2,018.7
1883	24	538.3	1897	93	2,086.0
1884	27	605.6	1898	95	2,131.0
1885	27	605.6	1899	95	2,131.0
1886	25	560.8	1900	96	2,153.3
1887	44	986.9	1901	108	2,422.4
1888	47	1,054.2	1902	101	2,265.4
1889	48	1,076.6	1903	115	2,579.4
1890	50	1,121.5	1904	158	3,543.9
1891	53	1,188.9	1905	149	3,342.1
1892	102	2,287.9	1906	147	3,297.2
1893	96	2,153.2	1907	168	3,768.2
1894	93	2,086.0	1908	107	2,400.0

COPPER-ORE OUTPUT (*cont.*)

Year	1,000 tons	Value (1,000 lire)	Year	1,000 tons	Value (1,000 lire)
1909	90	2,018.7	1912	86	1,928.9
1910	68	1,525.2	1913	89	1,996.3
1911	68	1,525.2			

(5) *Output of solid mineral fuel.* The data refer to output of anthracite, lignite, bituminous schist, and fossil timber. The source references for the physical quantities of output and for the unit value in 1898 are the same as specified above for iron-ore output, except that the page reference for 1881–1913 is p. 482. The value of product in 1898 was 2,429,825 lire, yielding an average unit value of 7.13 lire per ton; this price was applied to the series in tons for 1881–1913, as shown in the following table.

SOLID MINERAL FUEL

Year	1,000 tons	Value (1,000 lire)	Year	1,000 tons	Value (1,000 lire)
1881	135	962.5	1898	341	2,429.0
1882	165	1,176.4	1899	389	2,773.5
1883	214	1,525.8	1900	479	3,415.2
1884	223	1,590.0	1901	426	3,037.4
1885	190	1,354.7	1902	414	2,951.8
1886	243	1,732.6	1903	345	2,459.9
1887	327	2,331.5	1904	362	2,581.1
1888	366	2,609.5	1905	412	2,937.5
1889	390	2,780.7	1906	473	3,372.5
1890	376	2,680.8	1907	453	3,229.9
1891	289	2,060.6	1908	480	3,422.4
1892	295	2,103.4	1909	555	3,957.2
1893	317	2,260.2	1910	562	4,007.0
1894	271	1,932.2	1911	557	3,971.4
1895	305	2,174.6	1912	664	4,734.3
1896	276	1,967.8	1913	701	4,998.1
1897	314	2,238.8			

(6) *Sulphur* (*minerali di zolfo*). The source references for the physical quantities of output and for the unit value of output in 1898 are the same as specified above for iron-ore output, except that no data for the commodity were available prior to 1895 and that the page reference for 1895–98 is p. 483. Since it was found that data on output of raw sulphur for the years 1895–1913 corresponded closely to that of minerali di zolfo over the same period, it was assumed that the same correspondence obtained in the years 1881–94. Accordingly, the tonnage data for these years were

obtained by applying to the 1895 output of the latter commodity the percentage changes in the output of raw sulphur for the years 1881-94 (for data on output of raw sulphur, see *Annuario* 1900, p. 489). The value of product in 1898 was 40,375,152 lire, yielding an average unit value of 12 lire per ton; this price was applied to the series in tons for 1881–1913, as shown in the following table.

SULPHUR OUTPUT

Year	1,000 tons	Value (1,000 lire)	Year	1,000 tons	Value (1,000 lire)
1881	2,522	30,264	1898	3,363	40,356
1882	2,993	35,916	1899	3,763	45,156
1883	3,027	36,324	1900	3,628	43,536
1884	2,758	33,096	1901	3,727	44,724
1885	2,859	34,308	1902	3,582	42,984
1886	2,522	30,264	1903	3,690	44,280
1887	2,287	27,444	1904	3,539	42,468
1888	2,522	30,264	1905	3,761	45.132
1880	2,487	29,844	1906	3,274	39,288
1890	2,455	29,460	1907	2,788	33,456
1891	2,657	31,884	1908	2,848	34,176
1892	2,825	33,990	1909	2,827	33,924
1893	2,791	33,492	1910	2,815	33,780
1894	2,724	32,688	1911	2,683	32,196
1895	2,381	28,572	1912	2,504	30,048
1896	2,737	32,844	1913	2,452	29,424
1897	3,314	39,768			

(7) *Pyrites*. The source reference for the physical quantities of output for 1881–98 and for the unit value of output in 1898 is *Annuario* 1900, p. 482; for 1899–1906, *Annuario* 1905–07, p. 435. The references for the remaining years are as specified above for iron ore output. The value of product in 1898 was 828,051 lire, yielding an average unit value of 12.36 lire; this price was applied to the series in tons for 1881–1913, as shown in the following table.

PYRITES

Year	1,000 tons	Value (1,000 lire)	Year	1,000 tons	Value (1,000 lire)
1881	6	74	1886	17	210
1882	7	86	1887	18	222
1883	7	86	1888	15	185
1884	8	98	1889	17	210
1885	11	135	1890	15	185

PYRITES (*cont.*)

Year	1,000 tons	Value (1,000 lire)	Year	1,000 tons	Value (1,000 lire)
1891	20	247	1903	101	1,248
1892	28	346	1904	112	1,384
1893	29	358	1905	118	1,458
1894	23	284	1906	122	1,507
1895	39	482	1907	127	1,570
1896	46	569	1908	132	1,632
1897	58	716	1909	132	1,632
1898	67	828	1910	166	2,052
1899	77	952	1911	165	2,039
1900	72	890	1912	278	3,436
1901	89	1,100	1913	317	3,918
1902	93	1,149			

Summation of the seven subseries yielded the following aggregate series for mining, at constant prices of the year 1898.

Year	Millions of lire (at 1898 prices)	Present index (1900 = 100)	Year	Millions of lire (at 1898 prices)	Present index (1900 = 100)
1881	50.7	71	1898	65.8	92
1882	56.6	79	1899	63.0	88
1883	57.6	80	1900	71.7	100
1884	55.3	77	1901	73.7	103
1885	55.2	77	1902	71.3	100
1886	51.8	72	1903	76.9	107
1887	48.7	68	1904	76.0	106
1888	50.0	70	1905	77.7	108
1889	51.0	71	1906	73.6	103
1890	51.7	72	1907	70.8	99
1891	54.2	76	1908	70.5	98
1892	58.7	82	1909	66.6	93
1893	57.6	80	1910	68.4	95
1894	56.4	79	1911	63.8	89
1895	51.7	72	1912	68.7	96
1896	56.4	79	1913	70.4	98
1897	64.4	90			

It will be noted that the present index contains the same subseries as Tagliacarne's, except that a series for copper-ore output has been added here. As will be shown later, the behavior of the two indices differs very considerably.

Metalmaking (including oil refining).

This industry is represented by three subgroups: (1) iron and steel, (2) copper, and (3) lead. A fourth group on output of refined petroleum products — difficult to house elsewhere — has been added.

(1) *Output of iron and steel.* The source references for the physical quantities of iron output are as follows: for the years 1881–98, *Annuario* 1900, p. 487; 1899–1906, *Annuario* 1905–07, p. 440; 1907–09, *Annuario* 1911, p. 127; and 1910–13, *Annuario* 1915, p. 151. The data from 1902 on do not include output of small furnaces. Accordingly, the figures for 1902–13 have been increased by 10 percent, in order to render them roughly comparable with those of the preceding years. The value of product in 1898 was 40,865,825 lire yielding an average unit value per ton of 243.97 lire; this price was applied to the series in tons for 1881–1913, as shown in the following table.

IRON OUTPUT

Year	1,000 tons	Value (1,000 lire)	Year	1,000 tons	Value (1,000 lire)
1881	95	23,177	1898	167	40,866
1882	91	22,201	1899	198	48,306
1883	125	30,496	1900	191	46,598
1884	120	29,276	1901	181	44,159
1885	141	34,400	1902	181	44,159
1886	162	39,523	1903	195	47,574
1887	173	42,207	1904	199	48,550
1888	177	43,183	1905	226	55,137
1889	182	44,403	1906	260	63,432
1890	176	42,939	1907	273	66,604
1891	153	37,327	1908	333	81,242
1892	124	30,252	1909	309	75,387
1893	138	33,668	1910	342	83,438
1894	142	34,644	1911	333	81,242
1895	164	40,011	1912	197	48,062
1896	140	34,156	1913	157	38,032
1897	150	36,595			

The source references for the physical quantities of steel output are the same as those for iron output. The value of output in 1898 was 27,085,481 lire, yielding a price per ton of 309.66 lire; this price was applied to the series in tons for 1881–1913, as shown in the following table.

STEEL OUTPUT

Year	1,000 tons	Value (1,000 lire)	Year	1,000 tons	Value (1,000 lire)
1881	3.6	1,115	1883	3.0	929
1882	3.4	1,053	1884	4.6	1,424

STEEL OUTPUT (*cont.*)

Year	1,000 tons	Value (1,000 lire)	Year	1,000 tons	Value (1,000 lire)
1885	6.4	1,982	1900	115.9	35,889
1886	23.7	7,339	1901	123.3	38,181
1887	73.0	22,605	1902	108.9	33,722
1888	118.0	36,540	1903	154.1	47,719
1889	158.0	48,926	1904	177.1	54,841
1890	108.0	33,444	1905	244.8	75,804
1891	76.0	23,534	1906	333.0	103,117
1892	57.0	17,650	1907	347.0	107,452
1893	71.0	21,986	1908	438.0	135,631
1894	55.0	17,031	1909	609.0	188,582
1895	50.3	15,576	1910	671.0	207,781
1896	65.9	20,406	1911	698.0	216,142
1897	63.9	19,787	1912	802.0	248,347
1898	87.5	27,085	1913	846.0	261,972
1899	108.5	33,598			

The output figures for iron and steel (in 1898 lire) in the two preceding tables were then reduced by the values of imported pig iron, imported scrap, and pig iron produced, so as to exclude at least some double counting and to take account of such changes in technical coefficients as may have taken place over the period under review. Data on import quantities have been obtained from *Movimento Commerciale* for the respective years and valued at 1898 unit values. Unfortunately, it proved impossible to ascertain, and similarly to deduct, the quantities of coal consumed by the iron and steel industry. An attempt to compute these quantities indirectly on the basis of some information concerning the average coal:iron and coal:steel production coefficients had to be abandoned because of the many uncertainties involved.

The calculations made are based on the assumption that the deducted portions of value of raw materials bear roughly the same ratios to value added as those that remained undeducted.

PRODUCTION OF PIG IRON

Year	1,000 tons	Value (1,000 lire)	Year	1,000 tons	Value (1,000 lire)
1880	17.3	1,813	1886	12.3	1,289
1881	27.8	2,913	1887	12.3	1,289
1882	24.8	2,599	1888	12.5	1,310
1883	24.3	2,547	1889	13.5	1,415
1884	18.4	1,928	1890	14.3	1,499
1885	16.0	1,677	1891	11.9	1,247

PRODUCTION OF PIG IRON (*cont.*)

Year	1,000 tons	Value (1,000 lire)	Year	1,000 tons	Value (1,000 lire)
1892	12.7	1,330	1904	89.3	9,359
1893	8.0	838	1905	143.1	14,997
1894	10.3	1,079	1906	135.3	14,179
1895	9.2	964	1907	112.2	11,758
1896	7.0	734	1908	112.9	11,832
1897	8.4	880	1909	207.8	21,771
1898	12.4	1,300	1910	353.2	37,015
1899	19.2	2,012	1911	302.9	31,744
1900	24.0	2,515	1912	380.0	39,824
1901	15.8	1,656	1913	427.0	44,750
1902	30.6	3,207	1914	385.3	40,379
1903	75.3	7,891			

IMPORTS OF PIG IRON

Year	1,000 tons	Value (1,000 lire)	Year	1,000 tons	Value (1,000 lire)
1880	29	2,467	1898	169	14,377
1881	46	3,913	1899	192	16,333
1882	40	3,403	1900	161	13,696
1883	74	6,295	1901	160	13,611
1884	68	5,785	1902	155	13,186
1885	55	4,679	1903	127	10,804
1886	81	6,891	1904	150	12,761
1887	231	19,651	1905	136	11,570
1888	90	7,656	1906	170	14,462
1889	169	14,377	1907	231	19,651
1890	130	11,059	1808	254	21,608
1891	109	9,273	1909	248	21,097
1892	101	8,592	1910	205	17,439
1893	114	9,698	1911	235	19,991
1894	119	10,123	1912	267	22,714
1895	132	11,230	1913	222	18,886
1896	119	10,123	1914	220	18,715
1897	156	13,271			

IMPORTS OF SCRAP

Year	1,000 tons	Value (1,000 lire)	Year	1,000 tons	Value (1,000 lire)
1880	54	4,333	1884	82	6,580
1881	52	4,173	1885	78	6,259
1882	70	5,617	1886	116	9,309
1883	81	6,500	1887	174	13,963

IMPORTS OF SCRAP (*cont.*)

Year	1,000 tons	Value (1,000 lire)	Year	1,000 tons	Value (1,000 lire)
1888	165	13,241	1902	199	15,969
1889	157	12,599	1903	206	16,531
1890	168	13,482	1904	246	19,741
1891	137	10,994	1905	276	22,149
1892	146	11,716	1906	345	27,686
1893	177	14,204	1907	363	29,130
1894	157	12,599	1908	326	26,161
1895	180	14,445	1909	416	33,384
1896	162	13,000	1910	387	31,057
1897	131	10,513	1911	393	31,538
1898	138	11,074	1912	344	27,606
1899	245	19,661	1913	326	26,161
1900	197	15,809	1914	255	20,463
1901	148	11,877			

The value series in the three preceding tables have been added, shifted forward six months (by adding one half of the figure for the preceding year to one half of the figure for the following year) to take account of lags, and then deducted from the aggregate gross values of iron and steel output, as shown in the following table (in thousands of lire).

Year	Total iron and steel output	Imports of pig iron plus imports of scrap plus production of pig iron (moved 6 months forward)	"Net" output of iron and steel
1881	24,292	9,806	14,493
1882	23,254	11,309	11,945
1883	31,425	13,480	17,945
1884	30,700	14,817	15,883
1885	36,382	13,454	22,928
1886	46,862	15,052	31,810
1887	64,812	26,196	38,616
1888	79,723	28,555	51,168
1889	93,329	25,299	68,030
1890	76,383	27,215	49,168
1891	60,861	23,777	37,084
1892	47,902	21,576	26,326
1893	55,654	23,189	32,465
1894	51,675	24,270	27,405
1895	55,587	25,220	30,367
1896	54,562	25,248	29,314
1897	56,382	24,260	32,122

Year	Total iron and steel output	Imports of pig iron plus imports of scrap plus production of pig iron (moved 6 months forward)	"Net" output of iron and steel
1898	67,951	25,607	42,344
1899	81,904	32,278	49,626
1900	82,487	35,013	47,474
1901	82,340	29,582	52,758
1902	77,881	29,753	48,128
1903	95,293	33,794	61,499
1904	103,391	38,543	64,848
1905	130,941	45,288	85,653
1906	166,549	52,521	114,028
1907	174,056	58,433	115,623
1908	216,873	60,070	156,803
1909	263,969	67,926	196,043
1910	291,219	80,881	210,338
1911	297,384	84,392	212,992
1912	296,409	86,708	209,701
1913	300,004	89,970	210,004

(2) *Output of copper and copper alloys.* The values of copper output at 1898 prices have been computed as follows. The average unit value of 1898 was applied to the series in tons for the years 1884–1913 (no copper output registered prior to 1884). Thereupon the resulting values were diminished by the value of copper-ore output plus net imports and minus net exports of copper ore (all at 1898 prices). The source references are as follows. Copper output in tons: for the years 1884–97, *Annuario* 1900, p. 488; 1898–1906, *Annuario* 1905–07, p. 440; 1906–10, *Annuario* 1911, p. 127; 1911–13, *Annuario* 1915, p. 151. The value of product in 1898 was 20,108,258 lire, yielding an average unit value per ton of 1,719 lire. For data on copper-ore output, see above. The (relatively small) values of copper-ore imports and exports were obtained from *Movimento Commerciale* for the pertinent years. The foreign-trade data were valued at 1898 prices and moved forward six months to take account of lags. The following table presents the results of these computations.

COPPER AND COPPER ALLOYS

Year	1,000 tons	Gross value (1,000 lire)	Value of copper-ore output plus or minus net imports or net exports of ore (1,000 lire)	"Net" value of copper output (1,000 lire)
1881	—	—	334.23	—
1882	—	—	322.97	—
1883	—	—	338.67	—

381

COPPER AND COPPER ALLOYS (*cont.*)

Year	1,000 tons	Gross value (1,000 lire)	Value of copper-ore output plus or minus net imports or net exports of ore (1,000 lire)	"Net" value of copper output (1,000 lire)
1884	0.4	687	354.38	332.62
1885	1.6	2,750	338.68	2,411.32
1886	2.2	3,781	334.26	3,446.74
1887	3.1	5,378	750.26	4,627.74
1888	5.3	9,110	837.75	8,272.25
1889	6.9	11,861	891.55	10,969.45
1890	6.4	11,001	909.54	10,091.46
1891	5.9	10,142	964.60	9,177.40
1892	6.0	10,314	2,060.24	8,253.76
1893	6.9	11,861	1,932.26	9,928.74
1894	9.7	16,674	1,902.07	14,771.93
1895	8.5	14,611	1,758.49	12,852.51
1896	10.3	17,705	1,935.71	15,769.29
1897	11.5	19,768	2,042.26	17,725.74
1898	11.7	20,108	2,156.79	17,951.21
1899	10.2	17,533	2,184.83	15,348.17
1900	10.4	17,878	2,218.35	15,659.65
1901	9.6	16,502	2,591.75	13,910.25
1902	10.2	17,533	2,494.19	15,038.81
1903	11.2	19,253	2,790.24	16,462.76
1904	11.8	20,284	3,740.16	16,543.84
1905	16.1	27,676	3,496.87	24,179.13
1906	15.5	26,645	3,464.30	23,180.70
1907	17.5	30,083	4,073.25	26,009.75
1908	18.3	31,458	2,767.85	28,690.15
1909	20.0	34,380	2,310.29	32,069.71
1910	22.5	38,677	1,723.71	36,953.29
1911	21.3	36,615	1,674.36	34,940.64
1912	28.7	49,335	2,074.70	47,260.30
1913	26.2	45,037	2,077.05	42,959.95

(3) *Lead output.* The process of computing "net" lead output strictly paralleled that of computing "net" copper output as described in the foregoing. The source references for the physical quantities of output are as follows: for 1881–98, *Annuario* 1900, p. 489; for the subsequent years, the references are the same as those for copper output. The value of product in 1898 was 8,234,323 lire, yielding an average unit value of 336.09 per ton. For data on lead-ore output, see above. The net import and net export values for lead ore were obtained from *Movimento Commerciale* for the pertinent years, expressed at 1898 prices, and moved forward six months. The following table presents the results of these computations.

LEAD

Year	1,000 tons	Gross value (1,000 lire)	Value of lead-ore output plus or minus net imports or net exports of ore (1,000 lire)	"Net" value of lead output (1,000 lire)
1881	11.7	3,932	3,447.65	484.35
1882	13.2	4,436	4,292.26	143.74
1883	13.5	4,537	4,008.16	528.84
1884	15.0	5,041	4,238.51	802.49
1885	16.5	5,545	3,647.29	1,897.71
1886	19.5	6,553	4,691.56	1,861.44
1887	17.8	5,982	5,021.68	960.32
1888	17.5	5,881	4,230.80	1,650.20
1889	18.1	6,083	4,791.29	1,291.71
1890	17.8	5,982	4,084.92	1,897.08
1891	18.5	6,217	3,954.43	2,262.57
1892	22.0	7,393	5,182.98	2,210.02
1893	19.9	6,688	5,113.85	1,574.15
1894	19.6	6,587	5,482.45	1,104.55
1895	20.3	6,823	5,474.80	1,348.20
1896	20.8	6,990	5,781.83	1,208.17
1897	22.4	7,528	6,695.63	832.37
1898	24.5	8,234	6,465.12	1,768.88
1899	20.5	6,889	5,550.26	1,338.74
1900	23.8	7,999	6,127.39	1,871.61
1901	25.8	8,671	7,409.74	1,261.26
1902	26.5	8,906	6,695.61	2,210.39
1903	22.1	7,427	5,989.19	1,437.81
1904	23.5	7,898	6,019.93	1,878.07
1905	19.1	6,419	5,405.63	1,013.37
1906	21.3	7,159	5,666.66	1,492.34
1907	23.0	7,730	6,388.51	1,341.49
1908	26.0	8,738	7,578.59	1,159.41
1909	22.1	7,427	6,265.69	1,161.31
1910	14.5	4,873	5,628.25	—
1911	16.7	5,612	4,872.89	739.11
1912	21.5	7,225	5,336.52	1,888.48
1913	20.5	6,889	5,981.50	907.50

(4) *Petroleum products.* The series on petroleum products, the output of which was relatively small during the period under review, was left unadjusted for imports of crude oil which are not sufficiently specified in the Italian trade statistics of the period. Output in the decade of the eighties was negligible. Source references for the physical quantities of output are as follows: for the years 1890–98, *Annuario* 1900, p. 490; 1899–1906, *Annuario* 1905–07, p. 440; 1907–10, *Annuario* 1911, p. 127; 1911–13,

Annuario 1915, p. 151. The value of products in 1898 was 1,979,105 lire (*Annuario* 1900, p. 490), yielding an average value per ton of 392.68 lire; this price was applied to the series in tons for the years 1890–1913, as shown in the following table.

PETROLEUM PRODUCTS

Year	1,000 tons	Value (1,000 lire)	Year	1,000 tons	Value (1,000 lire)
1881	—	—	1898	5.0	1,979
1882	—	—	1899	5.3	2,081
1883	—	—	1900	6.1	2,395
1884	—	—	1901	4.2	1,649
1885	—	—	1902	4.4	1,727
1886	—	—	1903	4.6	1,806
1887	—	—	1904	6.6	2,591
1888	—	—	1905	9.9	3,887
1889	—	—	1906	10.9	4,280
1890	0.3	118	1907	10.5	4,123
1891	0.8	314	1908	10.9	4,280
1892	1.6	628	1909	11.0	4,319
1893	2.6	1,021	1910	12.3	4,830
1894	1.6	628	1911	15.5	6,087
1895	4.2	1,649	1912	13.8	5,418
1896	2.7	1,060	1913	7.5	2,945
1897	3.4	1,335			

Summation of the four series yielded the following aggregate series for metalmaking (including oil products) at constant prices of the year 1898.

METALMAKING

Year	Value (1,000 lire)	Present index (1900 = 100)
1881	14,977	22
1882	12,089	18
1883	18,474	27
1884	17,018	25
1885	27,237	40
1886	37,118	55
1887	44,204	66
1888	61,090	91
1889	80,291	119
1890	61,275	91
1891	48,838	72
1892	37,418	56

METALMAKING (*cont.*)

Year	Value (*1,000 lire*)	Present index (*1900 = 100*)
1893	44,989	67
1894	43,909	65
1895	46,217	68
1896	47,351	70
1897	52,015	77
1898	64,043	95
1899	68,394	101
1900	67,400	100
1901	69,579	103
1902	67,104	99
1903	81,206	120
1904	85,831	127
1905	114,733	170
1906	142,981	212
1907	147,097	218
1908	190,933	283
1909	233,593	346
1910	252,221	374
1911	254,759	377
1912	264,268	392
1913	256,846	381

It will be noted that the present index of metalmaking differs in its composition from Tagliacarne's index. The present index contains no series for pig iron and mercury. On the other hand, it contains the copper (and oil) series which is not included in Tagliacarne's index. A comparison between the two indices is given further below.

Textiles

As in Tagliacarne's index, the rate of change in the textile industry is represented by two series: (1) output in physical quantities of raw silk, and (2) net imports in physical quantities of raw cotton. For quantitative data on silk output, see Tagliacarne, p. 82. Data on net imports of cotton have been taken from *Movimento Commerciale*. The two series have been combined into a single index in the following fashion.

According to the report for the 1902–03 survey, the gross value of raw silk produced in 1899–1904 amounted on an average to 284 million lire (Direzione Generale della Statistica, Statistica Industriale, *Riassunto delle notizie sulle condizioni industriali del Regno*, Rome, 1906, part 1, p. 153; in the following cited as *Survey*). In 1903–04, the production of cocoons amounted to 50.4 million kilograms (p. 152). Adding to this the share of imported cocoons in total output (about 17.9 percent of domestic production on an average in 1899–1904), a total quantity of cocoons of 59.4 million kilograms is obtained. (p. 157) The price of cocoons in 1903 was 391.50 lire per quintal (see Ernesto Cianci, *Dinamica dei prezzi delle merci in Italia dal 1870 al 1929*, Annuali di Statistica, Serie VI: XX, 1923, 270), yielding a total value for cocoons of 232.6 million lire, which leaves an amount of "net" value in raw silk production of approximately 50 million lire. Gross value of silk fabrics produced was estimated at 100 million lire (*Survey*, p. 156). Applying to that figure the U.S. 1899 ratio of 42 percent of value added to value of product in silk fabrics, the value added by manufacturing silk fabrics in Italy in 1903–04 has been estimated at 42 million lire. There remains the item of silk waste, the price of which on the basis of U.S. statistics of the period was about 20 percent of that of raw silk, which on the basis of previously given data yields an amount of about 10 lire per kilogram. (See also, Ratan C. Rawley, *Economics of the Silk Industry, A Study in Industrial Organization*, London, 1919, p. 153.) Applying this price to the output of 8 million kilograms, an amount of 80 million lire results, which should contain about 16–17 million lire of value added. To sum up: the Italian silk output presents itself as follows.

	Million lire
Raw silk	50
Fabrics	42
Waste	17
Total value added	109

The gross value of cotton fabrics produced in 1900 is given at 301.6 million lire (*Survey*, p. 171). To this may be added the small value of exported cotton yarn amounting annually to about 2.2 million lire, yielding a total of 303.8 million lire. Applying to this figure the U.S. 1899 ratio of value added to value of product in the production of cotton goods at 47.9 percent gives a figure of 145.5 million lire for value added in cotton. Accordingly, the relative cotton:silk weights are 1.33:1 (145.5:109). Tagliacarne combined the cotton and silk series in the proportion of 2:1; this would seem to give too low a weight to silk in terms of the situation existing at the turn of the century. Such a proportion would result if one were to correct the American silk:cotton ratios for the differences in horsepower equipment as between the two industries in Italy. But in view of the very low number of horsepowers per Italian silk worker (0.6), this would almost imply that further reduction of this scarce horsepower would tend to reduce output to zero, which would be altogether unrealistic for the conditions of the period. On the other hand, it is quite reasonable that the ratios accepted for the present index imply a cotton:silk ratio of value added *per worker* in Italy of 2.1:1,

$$\frac{145.5}{138.88} \cdot \frac{109.0}{191.6},$$

as against a U.S. 1899 ratio of only 1.28:1. This seems true in view of the fact that the American silk industry of the time was much more advanced in relation to the American cotton industry than was the Italian silk industry in relation to the Italian cotton industry.

The next table presents the two original series for cotton and silk and the combined index resulting from imparting to cotton and silk the weights of 1.33 and 1, respectively, and computing the arithmetic average of the two. It may be noted that the use of a weighted geometric average does not result in any significant differences.

It will be noted that no attempt has been made to adjust the cotton-import series for the movement of stocks within the country. Such information is available for some portions of the period,[5] and one receives the

Year	Raw silk (index 1900 = 100; weight = 1)	Raw-cotton imports (net) (index 1900 = 100; weight = 1.33)	Aggregate silk-cotton (index 1900 = 100)
1881	90	27	54
1882	69	41	53
1883	94	38	62
1884	84	39	58
1885	74	51	61
1886	94	43	65
1887	98	54	73
1888	99	53	73
1889	81	63	71
1890	92	71	80
1891	85	63	73
1892	79	67	72
1893	106	69	85
1894	99	89	93
1895	99	88	93
1896	97	92	94
1897	86	99	93
1898	92	109	101
1899	99	107	104
1900	100	100	100
1901	98	110	105
1902	106	120	114
1903	90	126	111
1904	110	126	119
1905	108	135	124

[5] See, for example, Carlo di Nola "La crisi cotoniera e l'industria del cotone in Italia," *Giornale degli Economisti*, June 1912, p. 528.

Year	Raw silk (index 1900 = 100; weight = 1)	Raw-cotton imports (net) (index 1900 = 100; weight = 1.33)	Aggregate silk-cotton (index 1900 = 100)
1906	118	149	136
1907	120	177	153
1908	107	168	142
1909	110	156	136
1910	95	142	122
1911	92	155	128
1912	101	174	142
1913	92	165	134

impression that stocks on the whole were rather small in relation to output and that consideration of them, except in certain individual years, would not have affected the index significantly. At any rate, it has proved impossible to obtain a consistent stocks series for the period as a whole. On the other hand, it was felt that in this case the use of some smoothing-out device might have blurred not insignificant variations in output.

Engineering

In default of pertinent detailed information, it has been decided to use the changes in Italian iron and steel consumption in 1881–1913 as representing an index of machinery output in the country. The method is open to many strictures, but an immediate and obvious difficulty stems from the fact that a certain proportion of iron and steel produced and imported was consumed by the nonindustrial segments of the economy, such as railroad construction and maintenance. It was necessary, therefore, to obtain information on Italian production of rails and related materials during the index period. These data have been obtained from three sources: for the years 1886–94: L. Bodio, *Di alcuni indici misuratori del movimento economico in Italia* (Rome, 1896), p. 67; for the years 1895–99, the data were supplied by courtesy of the Studies Department of ILVA-Genoa; the data for the years 1900–13 were taken from ILVA, *Alti forni e acciaierie in Italia, 1897–1947* (Bergamo, 1948), p. 356. Accordingly, the output of rails and related materials (*rotaie e armamento*) was deducted from the quantities of steel produced in Italy in each of the years of the period.

No data on output for rails and related materials were available prior to 1886, the year when production of such materials was begun at Terni. But output during 1881–85 must have been quite negligible and so was, for that matter, the total output of steel. Accordingly, a very crude simplifying assumption was made with regard to that period, as can be seen from the following tables. After having obtained the "net" figures for steel output and valuing them at 309.66 lire per ton (see above, under

"NET" OUTPUT OF STEEL

Year	Steel output (1,000 tons)	Output of rails and related materials (1,000 tons)	"Net" output of steel (1,000 tons)	Value of "net" output of steel (1,000 lire)
1881	3.6	—	—	1,100
1882	3.4	—	—	1,100
1883	3.0	—	—	1,100
1884	4.6	—	—	1,100
1885	6.4	—	—	1,100
1886	23.7	20	3.7	1,146
1887	73.0	30	43.0	13,315
1888	118.0	67	51.0	15,792
1889	158.0	105	53.0	16,412
1890	108.0	70	38.0	11,767
1891	76.0	47	29.0	8,980
1892	57.0	31	26.0	8,051
1893	71.0	39	32.0	9,909
1894	55.0	25	30.0	9,290
1895	50.3	26	24.3	7,525
1896	65.9	22	42.9	13,594
1897	63.9	23	40.9	12,665
1898	87.5	30	57.5	17,805
1899	108.5	21	87.5	27,095
1900	115.9	8	107.9	33,412
1901	123.3	25	98.3	30,440
1902	108.9	19	89.9	27,838
1903	154.1	46	108.1	33,474
1904	177.1	23	154.1	47,718
1905	244.8	23	221.8	68,682
1906	330.0	65	265.0	82,060
1907	347.0	90	257.0	79,583
1908	438.0	84	354.0	109,620
1909	609.0	141	468.0	144,921
1910	671.0	147	524.0	162,261
1911	698.0	123	575.0	178,055
1912	802.0	147	655.0	202,827
1913	846.0	174	672.0	208,091

"INDUSTRIAL" IRON AND STEEL CONSUMPTION (ENGINEERING)

Year	Value of "net" steel output (1,000 lire)	Value of iron output (1,000 lire)	Value of steel and iron imports (1,000 lire)	"Industrial" iron and steel consumption (1,000 lire)	Index
1881	1,100	23,177	49,545	73,822	62
1882	1,100	22,201	66,886	90,187	76
1883	1,100	30,496	78,034	109,630	92

"INDUSTRIAL" IRON AND STEEL CONSUMPTION (ENGINEERING) (*cont.*)

Year	Value of "net" steel output (*1,000 lire*)	Value of iron output (*1,000 lire*)	Value of steel and iron imports (*1,000 lire*)	"Industrial" iron and steel consumption (*1,000 lire*)	Index
1884	1,100	29,276	76,486	106,862	90
1885	1,100	34,400	76,486	111,986	94
1886	1,146	39,523	76,641	117,310	98
1887	13,315	42,207	85,157	140,679	118
1888	15,792	43,183	78,189	137,164	115
1889	16,412	44,403	54,191	115,006	96
1890	11,767	42,939	39,482	94,188	79
1891	8,980	37,327	28,024	74,331	62
1892	8,051	30,252	24,773	63,076	53
1893	9,909	33,668	25,547	69,124	58
1894	9,290	34,644	26,631	70,565	59
1895	7,525	40,011	26,166	73,702	62
1896	13,594	34,156	26,476	74,226	62
1897	12,665	36,595	28,489	77,749	65
1898	17,805	40,866	26,918	85,589	72
1899	27,095	48,306	30,324	105,725	89
1900	33,412	45,598	40,256	119,266	100
1901	30,440	44,159	44,126	118,725	100
1902	27,838	44,159	45,055	117,052	98
1903	33,474	47,574	47,223	128,271	108
1904	47,718	48,550	47,688	143,956	121
1905	68,682	55,137	48,462	172,281	144
1906	82,060	63,432	58,371	203,863	171
1907	79,583	66,604	87,789	233,976	196
1908	109,620	81,242	103,890	294,752	247
1909	144,921	75,387	91,350	311,658	261
1910	162,261	83,438	83,142	328,841	276
1911	178,055	81,242	82,524	341,821	287
1912	202,827	48,062	83,453	334,342	280
1913	208,091	38,032	78,808	324,931	272

steel), these figures were added (1) to the value of iron produced between 1881 and 1913 and (2) to the value of iron and steel imports. The latter were obtained as follows: for the years 1880–98, *Annuario* 1900, p. 616; 1899–1905, *Annuario* 1905–07, p. 551; 1906–13, *Movimento Commerciale*, annual reports. The import figures were uniformly valued with the average Italian steel price for 1898 (309.66 lire per ton), and the series was moved forward six months to take account of import-output lags (it should be noted that these imports of iron and steel did not, of course, include imports of rails, which constituted a special item in Italian statistics of foreign commerce). The foregoing adjustments and their results are shown in the preceding two tables, together with an index for adjusted iron and steel consumption.

It will be noted that the foregoing adjustment is rather crude. No attempt has been made to diminish the iron and steel consumption further by deducting quantities of ferrous metals consumed in housing construction. While the quantities involved were minor prior to 1914, they seem to have been increasing fairly rapidly in the last years of the index period. It would have been desirable to deduct from iron and steel consumptions the indigenous production of other materials (wire, and such) which are consumed primarily outside the engineering industry. But the available data did not warrant such a computation, except perhaps for the very last years of the index period. In addition, there still may have been some small amount of iron rails produced for use on secondary tracks. Deficiencies of this kind must be kept in mind in appraising the validity of the method followed here for developing a gauge of machine-building output during 1881–1913.

It may be of interest to compare the adjusted iron and steel consumption series as given in the preceding with the unadjusted series of iron and steel consumption. This is done in the following table.

IRON AND STEEL CONSUMPTION

1900 = 100

Year	Adjusted	Unadjusted
1881	62	60
1882	76	73
1883	92	89
1884	90	87
1885	94	92
1886	98	101
1887	118	122
1888	115	129
1889	96	120
1890	79	94
1891	62	72
1892	53	59
1893	58	66
1894	59	64
1895	62	67
1896	62	66
1897	65	69
1898	72	77
1899	89	91
1900	100	100
1901	100	103
1902	98	100
1903	108	116

391

IRON AND STEEL CONSUMPTION (*cont.*)

Year	Adjusted	Unadjusted
1904	121	123
1905	144	146
1906	171	183
1907	196	213
1908	247	261
1909	261	289
1910	276	305
1911	287	310
1912	280	309
1913	272	309

Something more will be said later on the rates of change implied in the two indices.

Foodstuffs industry

The output of the foodstuffs industry has been represented by the subgroup outputs: beer industry, sugar industry, and flour mills. On the first two, data on output are available for the whole period under review. The source references are as follows. Beer: 1881–98, *Annuario* 1900, p. 556; 1899–1906, *Annuario* 1905–07, p. 504; 1907–10, *Annuario* 1911, p. 145; 1910–13, *Annuario* 1915, p. 172. Sugar: 1881–1906, *Annuario* 1905–07, p. 505; 1907–10, *Annuario* 1911, p. 131; 1911–13, *Annuario* 1915, p. 155.

The beer price for 1898 of 10 lire per hectoliter was obtained as the unit value of beer imports increased by the tariff and some allowance for cost of distribution. The sugar price of 142.17 lire per quintal was obtained from E. Cianci, *Dinamica dei prezzi delle merci in Italia dal 1870 al 1929* (Rome, 1933), p. 490. The data on tonnage and value for the two commodities are shown in the following table.

BEER AND SUGAR OUTPUT

Year	Beer output (1,000 hl.)	Sugar output (1,000 q.)	Beer output (1,000 lire)	Sugar output (1,000 lire)	Beer and sugar output (1,000 lire)	Index (1900 = 100)
1881	127	0.6	1,270	85	1,355	1.7
1882	131	1.9	1,310	270	1,580	2.0
1883	122	3.3	1,220	469	1,689	2.2
1884	130	6.5	1,300	924	2,224	2.8
1885	163	1.1	1,630	156	1,786	2.3
1886	164	1.5	1,640	213	1,853	2.4

BEER AND SUGAR OUTPUT (*cont.*)

Year	Beer output (*1,000 hl.*)	Sugar output (*1,000 q.*)	Beer output (*1,000 lire*)	Sugar output (*1,000 lire*)	Beer and sugar output (*1,000 lire*)	Index (*1900 = 100*)
1887	148	1.6	1,480	227	1,707	2.2
1888	162	4.0	1,620	568	2,188	2.7
1889	145	5.7	1,450	810	2,260	2.8
1890	161	7.1	1,610	1,001	2,711	3.4
1891	158	13.1	1,580	1,862	3,442	3.8
1892	106	10.6	1,060	1,507	2,567	3.3
1893	109	10.3	1,090	1,464	2,554	3.2
1894	90	18.8	900	2,672	3,572	4.5
1895	107	23.8	1,070	3,384	4,454	5.6
1896	103	20.7	1,030	2,943	3,973	5.1
1897	112	30.0	1,120	4,265	5,385	6.8
1898	123	58.6	1,230	8,331	9,561	12.1
1899	134	207.5	1,340	29,500	30,840	39.0
1900	154	541.7	1,540	77,013	78,553	100.0
1901	159	664.2	1,590	94,429	96,019	122.0
1902	168	856.5	1,680	123,048	124,728	159.0
1903	185	1,151.2	1,850	163,666	165,516	211.0
1904	230	712.3	2,300	101,267	103,567	132.0
1905	238	855.6	2,380	121,640	124,020	158.0
1906	315	954.0	3,150	135,630	138,780	177.0
1907	401	1,212.0	4,010	172,310	176,320	225.0
1908	423	1,506.0	4,230	214,108	218,338	278.0
1909	566	1,380.0	5,660	196,195	201,855	257.0
1910	554	1,420.0	5,540	201,881	207,421	264.0
1911	695	1,659.0	6,950	235,860	242,810	309.0
1912	646	1,784.0	6,460	253,631	260,091	331.0
1913	679	2,519.0	6,790	358,126	364,916	465.0

Since direct data on flour-mill output are not available, it was decided to represent the movement of output of flour mills by a series of wheat consumption in the country. Such a series is given for the years 1884–1905 in *Annuario* 1905–07, p. 499; 1906–10, *Annuario* 1911, p. 144; 1910–13, *Annuario* 1915, p. 171. The series is based on domestic production minus seeds plus net imports. It was further reduced by using data on wheat utilization in Italy for feed as contained in *Wheat Studies* (Food Research Institute), XI, no. 7 (March 1935), 302. The data for the years 1881–83 were estimated. The resulting series was smoothed by using four-year moving averages. Information on changes in carryover was not obtainable. These computations and the index series are shown in the following table.

FLOUR-MILL OUTPUT (WHEAT CONSUMPTION FOR FOOD)

Year	Production minus seeds plus net imports (Millions of quintals)	Feed (Millions of quintals)	Available for food consumption (Millions of quintals)	Index 1900 = 100 (Smoothed by four-year moving averages)
1881	32.6	1.0	31.6	71
1882	33.6	1.1	32.5	73
1883	34.6	1.1	33.5	76
1884	35.6	1.1	34.5	78
1885	36.2	1.2	35.0	77
1886	38.5	1.2	37.3	76
1887	40.0	1.3	38.7	75
1888	32.9	1.1	31.8	75
1889	34.6	1.1	33.5	77
1890	37.1	1.3	35.8	79
1891	39.0	1.3	37.7	78
1892	37.8	1.3	36.5	76
1893	38.6	1.3	37.3	77
1894	34.6	1.2	32.4	72
1895	36.8	1.3	35.5	74
1896	39.5	1.3	38.2	75
1897	29.1	1.0	28.1	77
1898	37.5	1.3	36.2	88
1899	39.3	1.3	38.0	92
1900	42.5	1.4	41.1	100
1901	50.0	1.6	48.4	104
1902	45.9	1.5	44.4	105
1903	53.7	1.7	52.0	111
1904	50.0	1.6	48.4	110
1905	51.4	1.6	49.8	110
1906	57.6	1.8	55.8	112
1907	51.4	1.6	49.8	109
1908	50.9	1.6	49.3	109
1909	55.8	1.8	54.0	112
1910	51.0	1.5	49.5	113
1911	51.0	1.5	49.5	121
1912	58.1	1.7	56.4	123
1913	57.6	1.7	55.9	129

The beer and sugar index and the flour-mill index were combined by attributing a weight of .109 to the former and a weight of .891 to the latter. These weights were estimated on the assumption that the value-added-per-worker ratios between the cotton industry, on the one hand, and the sugar and the flour-mill industry, on the other, were similar to those which prevailed between these industries in the United States in 1899 (see above). Naturally, this procedure involves no assumption with regard to absolute productivity levels in the United States and in Italy. For the value added per worker in the Italian cotton industry, see the section on textiles. The computed data on value added per worker were then multiplied by the respective labor-force figures and the ratios of the products (total value added) used as weights in combining the two indices. The final index is as follows.

FOODSTUFFS INDUSTRY

Year	Index (1900 = 100)
1881	63
1882	65
1883	68
1884	70
1885	69
1886	68
1887	67
1888	67
1889	69
1890	71
1891	70
1892	68
1893	69
1894	65
1895	66
1896	67
1897	69
1898	80
1899	86
1900	100
1901	106
1902	111
1903	120
1904	112
1905	115
1906	119
1907	122
1908	127
1909	128
1910	130
1911	141
1912	146
1913	166

Chemical industry

Tagliacarne used a single series — output of sulphuric acid — to represent the output of the chemical industry. Patently inadequate as this procedure is, it was accepted in the present index. The tonnage series, taken over from Tagliacarne, p. 83, and the index series with the base year changed to 1900 are as follows.

CHEMICAL INDUSTRY (SULPHURIC ACID)

Year	Output (*1,000 tons*)	Index (*1900 = 100*)
1881	20	8.7
1882	25	10.9
1883	30	13.1
1884	35	15.2
1885	40	17.4
1886	45	19.6
1887	50	21.8
1888	55	24.0
1889	60	26.1
1890	65	28.3
1891	64	27.9
1892	62	27.0
1893	59	25.9
1994	71	31.1
1895	96	41.7
1896	111	48.5
1897	129	56.1
1898	139	60.7
1899	165	72.1
1900	230	100.0
1901	235	102.4
1902	252	109.8
1903	263	114.6
1904	278	121.0
1905	302	131.6
1906	365	158.9
1907	425	185.2
1908	524	228.4
1909	590	256.9
1910	645	280.8
1911	596	259.7
1912	634	276.4
1913	645	280.9

THE PRESENT INDEX: WEIGHTS

The six index series described in the preceding section were combined to an aggregate index of Italian industrial output by the alternative use of three sets of weights pertaining to the census year 1903.

Employment

The relevant data were obtained from the survey (*Riassunto delle notizie sulle condizioni industriali del Regno*, Rome, 1906, part 1, table 4, pp. 12f). They are reproduced in the following table.

WORKERS IN SELECTED ITALIAN INDUSTRIES
(PRESENT-INDEX INDUSTRIES) IN 1903

Branch	Numbers	Weight
Mining and mineral processing	71,633	7.79
Metalmaking	34,580	3.75
Engineering	101,684	11.05
Textiles	452,969	49.24
Foodstuffs	223,980	24.34
Chemicals	34,994	3.83
	919,840	100.00

Horsepowers

The relevant data were obtained from the *Survey*. They are reproduced in the following table.

HORSEPOWERS INSTALLED IN SELECTED INDUSTRIES
(PRESENT-INDEX INDUSTRIES) IN 1903

Branch	Number	Weight
Mining and mineral processing	14,657	2.90
Metalmaking	48,075	9.44
Engineering	47,680	9.39
Textiles	137,803	27.08
Foodstuffs	214,187	42.09
Chemicals	46,498	9.10
	508,900	100.00

Value-added estimates, 1903–04

The third set of weights was obtained through a series of value-added estimates.

Mining and mineral processing. It was assumed on the basis of comparable information from other European countries that the ratio of value added to value of product was 70 percent. According to the *Survey* (p. 28), the value of product in 1903 amounted to 85,204,934 lire, and the value added was estimated at 60 million lire. While this results in a fairly high amount of value added per worker (1,000 lire), it was not considered implausible in view of the large share of sulphur in the total and the monopolistically high price which at that time attached to the mineral. On the other hand, the value added in the small group of mineral processing, of which processing of sulphur was again the largest part, was assumed to produce a much lower value added per worker, estimated in the aggregate at 5.7 million lire.

Metalmaking. The two main groups of the industry were iron and steel and copper, the former dominating the field. The value of product in iron and steel amounted in 1903 to about 80 million lire. Applying to this figure the 1899 U.S. ratio of value added to value of product in the iron and steel industry of a little less than 30 percent, the amount of 23.5 million lire was obtained. The value of product in the Italian copper industry in 1903 amounted to 22,043,000 lire. Applying to this sum the 1899 ratio of value added to value of product in the United States of 25.5 percent, an amount of 5.64 million was obtained. The value added in iron and steel plus copper, amounting to 29.14 million lire in 1903 (23.50 + 5.64), when divided by the number of workers in the two industries, yields a value added per worker of 1,356 lire. It was assumed that the remaining number of about 13,000 workers, mostly employed in small shops, contributed a value added of 500 lire per worker, giving a total for metalmaking outside iron and steel and copper of 6.5 million. Adding up the three subgroups results in a value-added sum of 35.64 million lire for the series of metalmaking.

Textiles. In the previous section some value-added estimates were used in order to combine the silk and cotton indices. The value added in the Italian wool industry can be similarly estimated. Value of product in the wool industry amounted in 1903 to 110 million lire (*Survey*, p. 163). Applying to this figure the 1899 U.S. ratio of value added to value of product in the American wool industry of 39 percent, a value added by Italian wool manufacturing of 42.9 million lire is obtained. The average value added per worker in the silk, cotton, and wool industries can be accordingly computed as follows.

Branch	Number of workers	Estimated value added (million lire)	Value added per worker (lire)
Silk	191,651	109.0	568.74
Cotton	138,880	145.5	1,048.0
Wool	37,744	42.9	1,136.6
	367,275	297.4	809.74

Total workers in textile industry	452,969
Total workers in silk, cotton, and wool industries	367,275
Balance	85,634

Applying to the remaining branches of the textile industry the average per worker value added by manufacturing in the three main subgroups yields an amount of value added of 69.4 million lire. Adding this sum to the amounts previously computed gives a total value added in the textile industry of 366.8 million lire.

Engineering. The number of workers occupied in the Italian machinery industry can be broken down as follows:

Big machinery factories	38,104
Shipbuilding	25,936
Various machinery	19,560
Small specialized shops	18,357
	101,957

Since no data on Italian value of produce in engineering were available, the following method of estimation was applied. The 1899 U.S. value added by manufacture per worker was computed for individual branches of the American machinery industry. Thereafter, the ratio of the results to value added per worker in the American cotton industry was obtained. Finally, these ratios were applied to the lire amount of value added by manufacture in the Italian cotton industry.

For the first group, the ratio of value added per worker in the American metalworking machinery output ($868) was used. This amount exceeded the corresponding magnitude in the American cotton industry ($537.04) by a coefficient of 1.53. Applying this coefficient to the value added per worker in the Italian cotton industry (1,048.3 lire) yields an amount of 1,603 lire per worker.

The corresponding 1899 American ratio for the shipbuilding industry was 1.45 ($781:$537.04), which yields a value-added estimate for Italy of 1,520 lire (1.45 times 1,048.3 lire).

For the group of various machinery in Italy in which bicycle production was a strong component, the data on U.S. bicycle output in 1899 were used and similarly related to the value added per worker in the American cotton industry, yielding a coefficient of 1.37 ($734:$537.04). Applying this coefficient to the value added per worker in the Italian cotton industry yields an amount of 1,436 lire (1.37 times 1,048.3 lire).

It was assumed that the balance of the engineering industry in Italy, in which small but highly specialized shops prevailed, showed a similarly high value added per worker, which was estimated at 1,500 lire.

Accordingly, total value added for the Italian machinery industry was estimated as follows.

VALUE ADDED IN ENGINEERING, 1903

Branch	Workers	Value added per worker (lire)	Total value added (million lire)
Big machinery factories	38,104	1,603	61.08
Shipbuilding	25,936	1,520	39.42
Various machinery	19,560	1,436	28.09
Small specialized shops	18,357	1,500	25.54
			156.13

Foodstuffs industry. The method of estimating the amounts of value added was analogous to that used for the same purpose with regard to the engineering industry. The value added per worker in the Italian sugar industry was estimated to bear the same value-added-per-worker relation to the Italian cotton industry as in the United States ($1,050:$537.04 times 1,048.3) thus equaling 2,044 lire, which resulted in a total for value added produced of 25.5 million lire. As to the most important single component — flour mills — it seemed excessive to accept the full American mill:cotton ratio of about 4 to 1; in view of the less modern character of Italian flour mills in relation to Italian cotton manufacturing, the ratio was reduced to 3:1, yielding a value added of 208.1 million (3,144 lire times 66,191 workers).

It was assumed that the rest of the industry, occupying 145,320 workers but a very small proportion of the industry's horsepower, produced a value added of 500 lire per worker, yielding a total of 72.65 million. Summing up the three groups (208.1+25.5+72.65) gives a total value added for the foodstuffs industry of 306.25 million lire.

Chemical industry. The 1899 U.S. ratio of value added per worker in phosphate production to value added per worker in cotton-goods output ($1,355:$537.04) of about 2.5 was applied to the value added per worker in the Italian cotton manufacturing, yielding the amount of value added of 2,620 lire per worker and 89.1 million lire for the whole industry (2,620 times 34,994).

The weights for the six industries which were obtained in the described fashion are summarized in the following table.

VALUE-ADDED ESTIMATES FOR SELECTED INDUSTRIES
(PRESENT-INDEX INDUSTRIES) IN 1903

Branch	Amount (million lire)	Weight
Mining and mineral processing	65.70	6.43
Metalmaking	35.64	3.49

VALUE-ADDED ESTIMATES FOR SELECTED INDUSTRIES
(PRESENT-INDEX INDUSTRIES) IN 1903 (*cont.*)

Branch	Amount (*million lire*)	Weight
Engineering	156.13	15.27
Textiles	366.80	35.86
Foodstuffs	306.25	29.99
Chemicals	91.68	8.96
	1,022.20	100.00

THE RESULTS

The six index series of Italian industrial output have been combined into an aggregate index through arithmetic averages as applied to the three sets of weights that have been discussed in the foregoing pages. The results are as follows.

AN INDEX OF ITALIAN INDUSTRIAL OUTPUT, 1881–1913

Year	Value-added weights	Employment weights	Horsepower weights
1881	53.86	55.46	51.91
1882	56.81	57.56	53.83
1883	63.91	64.99	60.09
1884	62.68	62.66	59.57
1885	64.78	64.96	61.92
1886	67.00	67.82	64.51
1887	72.92	73.92	69.23
1888	73.66	74.75	71.54
1889	71.85	73.35	72.91
1890	72.34	75.49	72.16
1891	66.55	69.53	66.58
1892	63.94	67.38	63.21
1893	69.83	74.79	68.50
1894	71.98	77.91	69.31
1895	73.37	78.47	71.09
1896	75.18	80.11	72.82
1897	77.83	81.80	75.28
1898	85.91	90.23	89.94
1899	92.30	95.38	91.32
1900	100.00	100.00	100.00
1901	104.06	100.00	100.00
1902	108.82	109.61	108.99
1903	113.65	113.04	115.57
1904	116.83	116.88	116.76
1905	125.65	124.81	126.64
1906	138.84	136.89	140.39
1907	151.95	149.67	151.40

AN INDEX OF ITALIAN INDUSTRIAL OUTPUT, 1881–1913 *(cont.)*

Year	Value-added weights	Employment weights	Horsepower weights
1908	163.34	155.09	165.31
1909	168.10	157.02	173.87
1910	169.23	154.40	177.19
1911	174.18	160.09	182.68
1912	182.03	169.15	190.98
1913	184.14	169.12	195.96

It is possible now to show the rates of growth implied in our index series for the index period as a whole and for portions of that period. That raises the problem of the choice of appropriate subperiods into which the total index period should be divided.

It is not easy to select appropriate subperiods, at least for some stretches of the index period. Tagliacarne used the following division: 1881–91, 1891–96, 1896–1913. In order to make the rates of the present index comparable with Tagliacarne's results, figures for the same subperiods have been computed. But this division has certain shortcomings. The period 1881–91 throws together the years of the upswing to 1887 or 1888 and the years of stagnation and decline thereafter. On the other hand, the period 1896–1913 again combines the period of rapid growth to 1908 with a period of slower advance thereafter. Accordingly, rates have been also computed for the periods 1881–88, 1888–96, 1896–1908, 1908–1913, and finally also for the whole period 1881–1913.

As to the method of rate of growth computations, it has been decided to use a "two-point" rate which links the first and the last year of the given period by the compound-interest formula. A rather extensive experimentation with the alternative method of fitting a straight line to the logarithms of the index data and using the slope of the line as the average rate of growth for the given period did not result in sufficiently large discrepancies between the two rates.

The annual average rates of growth which are implied in the three indices presented in the last table are as follows.

ANNUAL AVERAGE RATES OF GROWTH OF ITALIAN INDUSTRIAL OUTPUT, 1881–1913 AND SUBPERIODS

Period	Value-added estimates	Employment	Horsepower
1881–1888	4.6	4.4	4.7
1888–1896	0.3	0.9	0.3
1881–1896	2.2	2.5	2.3
1881–1891	2.1	2.3	2.5

ANNUAL AVERAGE RATES OF GROWTH OF ITALIAN INDUSTRIAL OUTPUT,
1881–1913 AND SUBPERIODS (*cont.*)

Period	Value-added estimates	Employment	Horsepower
1891–1896	2.5	3.9	1.8
1896–1908	6.7	5.7	7.1
1908–1913	2.4	1.7	1.1
1896–1913	5.4	4.5	6.0
1881–1913	3.8	3.5	4.3

Computed on the assumption of a geometric rate of growth between the first and the last years of the specified periods.

The comparison of the three indices shows two obvious features. (1) The index based on value-added weights in almost all cases comes to lie between the indices based on horsepower and employment, respectively. It thus constitutes a compromise between the latter two which does not seem unreasonable in terms of the underlying economic relations. (2) The index based on horsepowers shows, in comparison with the index based on employment, a faster rise during the good periods and a slower rise during stagnation periods, thus suggesting that industries with more capital equipment are more sensitive to cyclical variations, which again is something that one would expect.

The rates shown in the preceding table should be viewed against the rates of increase (or decrease) in the individual component series of the present index. These rates are shown in the following table.

ANNUAL AVERAGE RATES OF GROWTH IN THE SIX INDEX INDUSTRIES

Branch	1881–1888	1888–1896	1881–1891	1891–1896	1896–1908	1908–1913	1881–1913
Mining	0.0	1.30	0.7	0.8	1.8	0.0	1.0
Metalmaking	22.50	−3.24	12.6	−0.5	12.4	6.1	9.3
Textiles	4.40	3.20	3.1	5.2	3.5	−1.2	2.5
Engineering	9.20	−7.40	0.0	0.0	12.2	2.0	4.7
Foodstuffs	0.9	0.0	1.1	0.9	5.5	5.5	3.1
Chemicals	15.1	9.4	12.0	11.8	13.7	1.8	11.3

Computed on a compound basis using the first and the last years of the specified periods.

The following facts may be gleaned from the preceding table.

(1) The rate of growth in mining was steady but very low throughout the whole period under review.

(2) Metalmaking showed an extremely high rate in the eighties and a very high rate in the period 1896–1908. It was severely affected during the early nineties, showing a decline of output between 1888 and 1896. A reduced but still very respectable rate of increase continued after 1908.

(3) The older textile industry had a steadying and stabilizing effect on the rate of industrial growth by developing at a medium speed. The depression of the nineties failed to affect it seriously, the revival coming as early as 1893. But the decline in output between 1908 and 1913 did reflect a serious crisis in the cotton industry and a rather precarious situation in the silk industry.

(4) Engineering output showed a very rapid increase in the eighties, but was immediately and profoundly affected by the depression. It will be noted how Tagliacarne's choice of periods disguises both the rise and the fall in output. After 1896, the industry shows a very high rate until 1908, but it proves quite sensitive to the following recession while retaining a positive rate of growth. As far as the period 1896–1908 is concerned, it is engineering and metalmaking that are mainly, if not solely, responsible for the big industrial movement of those years.

It is useful at this point to compare the rates of growth implied in the engineering index (iron and steel consumption minus production of rails and related materials) with the rates of growth of the unadjusted iron and steel consumption in the country.

AVERAGE ANNUAL RATES OF GROWTH OF
IRON AND STEEL CONSUMPTION

Period	Adjusted	Unadjusted
1881–1888	9.20	8.04
1888–1896	−7.40	−8.00
1881–1891	0.00	1.85
1891–1896	0.00	−1.17
1896–1908	12.20	12.20
1908–1913	2.00	3.4

This comparison reveals that in the depression of the nineties railroad building and maintenance not only failed to exert a steadying effect on the economy but even accentuated the downward trend. This is true whether the depression period is represented by the years 1888–96 or, as Tagliacarne does, by the years 1891–96. This throws interesting light on the general policies pursued during the period. By contrast, the period of slower development, 1908–13, is characterized by a faster growth of iron and steel consumption, including railroad-building materials. In 1905, the major Italian railroads were taken over by the government and considerable modernization programs were begun a few years later.

(5) The foodstuffs industry fared poorly in the eighties and even showed declines in the nineties. The explanation lies in the composition of the series. The Italian sugar industry had not yet begun its rapid development and flour-mill output, being represented by wheat alone rather than

by wheat and corn, appears less depression-resistant than it probably was in reality. From 1896 on, the food industry shows a fairly high rate of increase, its output continuing to grow after 1908 at the same rate — essentially because of the increasing weight of sugar output.

(6) The chemical industry mirrors the rapid rise of sulphuric-acid production. Throughout the eighties it developed at a very high speed and continued almost unabated through the depression of the nineties into the following period. It was, however, particularly affected by the recession after 1908, its rate having been reduced to a fraction of its former level.

AN APPRAISAL OF THE INDEX

The foregoing detailed description of the way in which the present index has been constructed makes it unnecessary to present more than a brief discussion of its weaknesses.

The following tabulation shows the coverage of the index made under the — somewhat spurious — assumption that the indirect measures used for the engineering and cotton series yield a complete coverage.

COVERAGE OF THE INDEX

Branch	Number of workers (1903)		Percent of industry included to imputed	Horsepowers (1903)		Percent of industry included to imputed
	Included	Imputed	imputed	Included	Imputed	imputed
Mining and mineral processing	60,147*	71,633	84*	9,800*	14,657	67*
Metalmaking	34,580*	34,580	100*	48,075*	48,075	100*
Engineering	101,684*	101,684	100*	47,680*	47,680	100*
Textiles						
Silk 191,651						
Cotton 138,880	330,531	452,969	73	98,929	137,803	72
Foodstuffs						
Mills 66,191						
Sugar and beer 12,469	78,660	223,980	35	178,311	214,187	83
Chemicals	8,000*	34,994	23*	35,000*	46,498	75*
	613,602	919,840	67	417,795	508,900	82
Outside the index		488,301			268,927	
		1,408,141			777,827	
Percent of included to total			44			54
Percent of imputed to total			65			65

* Approximately

Despite the generous assumptions, the picture is far from comforting. No less than 35 percent of Italian industry has remained outside the scope of the index. The excluded segments comprise many "diverse" industries from hat making to output of musical instruments. They comprise the paper industry with its 28,000 horsepowers installed and the straw-working industry employing almost 125,000 workers (all figures refer to 1903–04). The output of the paper industry amounted to about 1 million quintals at the end of the nineteenth century; it was close to 3 million quintals before the outbreak of World War I.[6] A great deal of modernization of the industry occurred at that time. If the industry had been included in the present index, the latter's rate of growth probably would have increased somewhat during the period 1896–1913. That period, however, is marked by the first stage of rapid development of electric-power production. The first large power-producing plants were built in the last years of the century. Consumption of electric power in Italy rose from 60 million kwh. in 1891 to 160 million kwh. in 1896; by 1908 a level of consumption of 1,009 million kwh. was reached, and this amount was further doubled in the remaining years until 1913 (2,312 million kwh.); the weight to be attributed to the industry before the First World War was probably not excessively large. (In 1938, after an unprecedented further upswing, the total value added produced by the industry was still below that of the chemical industry, which developed very fast but less impetuously than did power production.) Still, there is no doubt that inclusion of electric-power output would have raised the rate of growth in the period 1896–1913 in a perceptible manner. On the other hand, many an excluded industry probably showed a rather low rate of change.[7]

As for the industries included in the present index, it may be said that mining and metalmaking are fairly well covered as far as the important branches of the two industries are concerned. The percentages of included branches to imputed branches are high for mining, both for labor and for horsepower. What has remained outside is essentially the processing of minerals. The metalmaking index must be considered as almost complete. It must be remembered that aluminum output, which is not included, was first recorded in 1907 and remained very small until the 1920s.

The main problem with regard to engineering lay in the aptitude of a steel-consumption index to reflect correctly the changes in value of output in that industry. Since the process of industrialization presumably consists in growing amounts of value added per weight unit of steel consumed, the engineering series probably tends to understate the industry's rate of growth.

[6] See *Industria Italiana alla meta del secolo XIX*, Confederazione Italiana dell' Industria Italiana (n.p., n.d.), p. 8.

[7] It is, however, comforting to see that the larger coverage of the Golzio index does not show strong differences in the rates of growth between the present-index industries and the rest of industrial output. See the final section on the Golzio index.

The same should apply, though less strongly, to the cotton industry, which is represented by imports of raw cotton. Production of raw silk is, of course, a poor measure of progress achieved in silk weaving, which was slow to develop in Italy. In addition, it must be noted that the raw-silk-output series itself does not include treatment of imported raw silk for further processing that is still confined within the raw-silk stage of production.[8] This consideration apart, the fact that the silk and cotton industries have both been represented gives a high ratio of included to imputed coverage for the textile industry as a whole, 72–73 percent, for both labor and horsepower.

The foodstuffs industry with its three series for sugar, beer, and flour mills is much less well represented. The coverage with regard to labor is only 35 percent, though, thanks to the flour-mill industry, it is 83 percent with regard to horsepower.

It would have been desirable to have the flour-mill industry represented by a combined wheat-corn input series rather than by wheat alone. (It is true that, in addition to wheat and corn, Italian mills also ground some oats and rye, though not barley, but the quantities involved were very small.) It was somewhat difficult, however, to obtain the requisite data. Though the published sources contain the amounts used for seeds, they do not record quantities of corn used for poultry feed and alcohol production, and such data would be indispensable for computing corn-milling availabilities as a residuum. By the time a series on corn-milling availabilities was made available to this writer by the much-appreciated courtesy of Professor Benedetto Barberi (director general of Istituto Centrale di Statistica, Rome), it was too late for inclusion of these data into the body of the present computations. Still, it was possible to compute the index of the foodstuffs industry including both wheat- and corn-milling availabilities and also to see whether such an inclusion affects the annual average rates of growth of the aggregate index as presented in the preceding section. This is done in the following computations.

CORN-MILLING AVAILABILITIES (IN MILLIONS OF QUINTALS)

1881	13.4	1889	11.1
1882	10.1	1890	12.0
1883	12.3	1891	10.5
1884	13.1	1892	10.1
1885	14.7	1893	10.3
1886	11.8	1894	10.7
1887	12.1	1895	9.0
1888	11.6	1896	10.9

[8] See "L'Industria dell seta in Italia," *Statistica Industriale, Annali di Statistica*, Serie IV (Rome, 1891), p. 21.

CORN-MILLING AVAILABILITIES (IN MILLIONS OF QUINTALS) (*cont.*)

1897	11.5	1906	11.3
1898	11.1	1907	10.5
1899	12.7	1908	10.2
1900	12.3	1909	11.4
1901	10.8	1910	12.8
1902	11.3	1911	13.3
1903	9.5	1912	12.1
1904	10.8	1913	12.0
1905	10.8		

These data have been combined with the (comparable) wheat series by using as weights the average wheat-corn price ratio for the years 1896–1904 (24.5:15.5). The price data have been obtained from Cianci, *Dinamica dei prezzi delle merci in Italia dal 1870 al 1929*, pp. 357–8, 363–4.

The combined data were smoothed by using four-year moving averages, and thereupon they were combined with the series of beer and sugar output as described earlier above. The result was a new index of foodstuffs industry. In the following tabulation this index is compared with the index as included in the present index.

FOODSTUFFS INDUSTRY INDEX OF OUTPUT, 1881–1913 (1900 = 100)

Year	Including corn available for milling	Excluding corn available for milling
1881	64.7	63
1882	66.0	65
1883	72.6	68
1884	74.6	70
1885	72.9	69
1886	71.4	68
1887	70.3	67
1888	70.0	67
1889	71.4	69
1890	73.0	71
1891	71.2	70
1892	70.0	68
1893	70.8	69
1894	67.4	65
1895	69.2	66
1896	71.3	67
1897	72.9	69
1898	81.8	80
1899	88.3	86
1900	100.0	100

408

FOODSTUFFS INDUSTRY INDEX OF OUTPUT, 1881–1913 (1900 = 100) (*cont.*)

Year	Including corn available for milling	Excluding corn available for milling
1901	104.8	106
1902	109.6	111
1903	120.0	120
1904	110.7	112
1905	113.8	115
1906	118.8	119
1907	120.9	122
1908	127.2	127
1909	128.5	128
1910	130.0	130
1911	136.3	141
1912	139.9	146
1913	155.6	166

Similarly, it is possible to compare the annual average rates of growth which are implied in the aggregate index of Italian industrial output *including* corn availabilities with the aggregate index as given above (which does not include such availabilities). This is done in the following table.

ANNUAL AVERAGE RATES OF GROWTH OF
ITALIAN INDUSTRIAL OUTPUT

Period	Including corn-milling availabilities	Excluding corn-milling availabilities
1881–1888	4.6	4.6
1888–1896	0.3	0.3
1881–1896	2.2	2.3
1881–1891	2.1	2.1
1891–1896	2.5	2.7
1896–1908	6.7	6.5
1908–1913	2.4	2.1
1896–1913	5.4	5.2
1881–1913	3.8	3.9

We may conclude, therefore, that inclusion of corn-milling availabilities does not affect the index of the foodstuffs industry significantly, except during the last three years of the index period 1881–1913. Naturally, the rates of growth of the aggregate index are affected even less.

The series of the chemical industry probably is the least reliable of the six. It is represented by a single product (sulphuric acid), and it requires a good deal of stretching even to arrive at the ratio of 23 percent for included-to-imputed output with regard to horsepower. On the whole, it must be assumed that the series of the chemical industry overstates the rate of growth of the industry. This must be true of the period 1881–96. But the degree of overstatement may not be unduly large for the years after 1896. The production of fertilizers in general (for which sulphuric acid is an important material) grew at an almost similar pace. In addition, with the beginning of the century a number of new products was taken up by the industry (caustic soda and others) which showed very high rates of increase. On the other hand, the rate of increase plummeted to a low level after 1908. To sum up, at least for the later portions of the index period (after 1896), the use of sulphuric acid to represent the industry as a whole may be somewhat less hazardous than appears at first glance.

Still, when everything is said and done, the final conclusion of the table, according to which 67 percent of the labor force in the six index industries and 82 percent of their horsepowers have been included directly or indirectly in the index, must be taken with a grain of salt. And even this figure implies that less than 50 percent of the aggregate industrial labor force has been included in the present index.

That the mode of combining both the subgroups and the six main series is open to question should be obvious. The use of prices (unit values) rather than value added per unit for aggregating the subgroups in mining and metalmaking and the beer and sugar subgroup is approximate indeed, even though in principle it is much preferable to Tagliacarne's ton-per-ton summation. Furthermore, for reasons of consistency, prices (unit values) pertaining to the year 1898 had to be used, while the weights combining the main series pertained to the survey years 1902–03. The latter, however, may be regarded more in the nature of a beauty blemish inasmuch as a check on those 1903 prices (unit values) that were obtainable failed to produce any significant changes in price structure.

The value-added weights used for the main aggregation are of course uncertain. Time and again recourse had to be had to the data of the American census of 1899 and to the assumption that the ratios of value added per worker in the individual industries were roughly the same in the two countries. This artificial assumption is sweeping in the extreme. True, nothing is assumed about the absolute levels of productivity as between the two countries. But, as a rule, no attempt has been made to adjust for the differences in the comparison of the labor force by sex and age in the two countries, for the length of the working day, or for the differences in the composition of output. Moreover, where a variety of nonhomogeneous goods is produced, as in the engineering or chemical industry, it was necessary to select as basis of comparison some subgroup or subgroups of products and to assume that the computed value-added ratios applied to the larger segments of the industry as well.

The weights computed on the basis of employment and horsepower might be expected to be more reliable than the computed value-added weights, and in a sense they probably are. But even here it should be noted that the Italian survey of 1902–03 was far from being as complete as the later censuses. Actually, the first real industrial census in Italy was not taken until 1911. It is significant that an attempt to compute, with the help of the present index, changes in labor productivity between 1902–03 and 1911 had to be abandoned precisely because the 1911 census "discovered" a large number of workers in small enterprises, particularly in metalmaking and engineering. As a result, the number of workers per shop was greatly reduced which led, in metalmaking, to quite implausible *declines* in productivity of labor over the period concerned. There is no assurance, of course, that the inadequacy of ascertaining the labor force and horsepowers installed in the 1902–03 survey was necessarily the same in all the industries considered.

As said before, the six series were combined through the use of arithmetic rather than geometric averages. This need not be considered a disadvantage, even though Tagliacarne makes strong assertions to the contrary (p. 53). An attempt to compute geometric averages of index numbers for the beginning and ending years of the period 1881–1913 and for subperiods thereof has not yielded significantly different results. The following table compares the rates of growth computed on the basis of two sets of index numbers, those averaged arithmetically and those averaged geometrically.

PRESENT INDEX: THE RATES OF GROWTH IN ITALIAN INDUSTRY, 1881–1913
(VALUE-ADDED WEIGHTS)

Period	Weighted arithmetic average	Weighted geometric average
1881–1891	2.1	2.4
1891–1896	2.5	2.7
1896–1908	6.7	6.9
1908–1913	2.4	2.3
1881–1913	3.8	3.7

Computed on a compound basis using the first and the last years of the specified periods.

It is easily seen that, with one exception (1908–13), the differences are fairly minor. It is, of course, natural for rates resulting from geometric averages of index numbers *below* the base year to be *higher* than rates resulting from arithmetic averages. Since both series show 100 in the base year (1900) and since each single geometric average is lower than its arithmetic counterpart, the former must rise faster than the latter in order to reach equality in the base year. For the years subsequent to the base year the position is reversed.

While the use of weighted arithmetic averages need not be regarded as a deficiency of the present index, the shortcomings listed before are, no doubt, very real ones. And it must also be considered that the listing does not include a discussion of the reliability of the underlying basic data in terms of physical quantities. The standards of statistical accuracy improved rather slowly in the course of the index period, and it should be clear that no absolute faith can be placed in the series concerned.

All these deficiencies must be fully recognized. They are no doubt very serious and, with regard to the rate of growth, the present writer finds it difficult to state whether on balance the present index tends to understate or overstate the aggregate rate of growth. The probable understatements in cotton manufacturing and engineering must be set against some probable overstatement in the chemical industry throughout the index period and in the foodstuff industry during its second half. Nor is it clear to the writer that the present index is sufficiently refined to react in a very significant manner to a change in weights so that use of weights pertaining to an earlier (or later) period would relevantly raise (or lower) the rate of growth. To achieve that result a much more detailed index of engineering weighted by values added per unit, or at least prices, would probably be necessary. (But compare the discussion of the Golzio index in the final section.)

The present index is probably capable of being improved by further study. But such improvements would be spotty. Possibly one or two additional subgroups could be added to the chemical industry; introduction of a series on wool output would make the index of the textile industry more complete. The data on steel consumption might be further refined. Above all, a series for electric-power production might be introduced, although the problem of finding an appropriate weight for it would be fairly difficult. Finally, one might experiment with the use of 1911 weights and perhaps even with 1876 weights, although the survey of that year is even much less comparable to that of 1902–03 than is the 1911 census. But despite all these amplifications and emendations, the main features of the present index would remain unchanged and so would its shortcomings.

However, nothing can be gained by exaggerating those shortcomings. Whatever their extent, the resulting indices reveal a pattern that is altogether meaningful in terms of our qualitative knowledge of Italian industrial development. It is, furthermore, of considerable importance that the use of three alternative sets of weights yields results which, by and large, are quite similar to each other. In particular, they lead to the view that the golden age of Italian industrialization prior to 1914, such as it was, falls into the long period 1896–1908; thereafter some decline in the rate of growth took place throughout the remaining years until 1913. In this the present index agrees both with the results of Tagliacarne and with those of Dessirier, despite significant discrepancies between these two indices and the present index with regard to the absolute level of rates and particularly with respect to the very different picture the three indices present for the period 1891–96.

The three variants of the present index and the two previous indices, expressed by the rates of growth implied in them, are compared in the following table.

ANNUAL AVERAGE RATES OF GROWTH, 1881–1913 AND SUBPERIODS

	Present index				
Period	Value-added weights	Employment weights	Horse-power weights	Tagliacarne* index	Dessirier index
1881–1891	2.10	2.30	2.50	5.10	4.70
1891–1896	2.50	3.90	1.80	−4.00	4.90
1896–1908	6.70	5.70	7.10	11.40	5.80
1908–1913	2.40	1.70	1.10	6.30	1.25
1881–1913	3.80	3.50	4.30	6.10	4.60

All rates computed on a compound basis using the first and the last years of the specified periods.

* Tagliacarne also supplied the results of his computations of the rates of growth on the basis of an arithmetically weighted average. They are as follows: 1881–91, 6.5; 1891–96, −3.6; 1896–1913, 22.8. This rate of growth for the period 1896–1913 contrasts with Tagliacarne's rate for the same period computed on the basis of weighted geometric averages of 9.80. The 1896–1913 rate of growth implied in the present index is 6.7, 5.7, and 7.1 for the three sets of weights. The difference is striking. Unfortunately, it cannot be put down to the vagaries of the weighted arithmetic average. The present writer recalculated the rate of growth on the basis of Tagliacarne's indices, applying a weighted arithmetic average, and found the resulting rate to be more than 50 percent below the rate computed by Tagliacarne, 22.8 percent, which is quite reasonable in relation to his geometric rate. It is clear that pressures causing haste in preparation must have been responsible for this error.

TAGLIACARNE'S INDEX AND THE PRESENT INDEX: COMPARISON OF THE COMPONENT SERIES

A comparison of the rates of growth in the index constructed by Tagliacarne with its modification in the present index may serve to underscore some important features of the latter and to provide some additional explanation for the behavior of the aggregated series in the present index. The rates of growth implied in the seven groups of Tagliacarne's index are as follows.

COMPONENT SERIES

Industry	1881– 1888	1888– 1896	1881– 1891	1891– 1896	1896– 1908	1908– 1913	1881– 1913
Silk	1.1	−0.1	−0.7	2.5	0.5	−1.1	0.0
Cotton	6.4	5.2	6.7	4.0	5.2	−0.5	4.6
Beer and sugar	1.6	−1.2	1.5	−2.7	26.6	11.0	11.1
Metals and minerals	12.9	−4.0	6.5	−2.1	11.7	10.4	7.6
Mining	0.0	−0.5	0.2	0.6	4.2	4.3	2.4
Shipbuilding	−3.8	−2.0	2.4	−14.0	7.0	4.0	1.8
Sulphuric acid	15.1	9.4	12.0	11.8	13.7	1.8	11.3

Computed on a compound basis using the first and the last years of the specified periods.

The first thing to be noted is that the chemical industry shows exactly the same rates of growth in the two indices, being represented in both by the same single series of sulphuric acid (see the tabulation on p. 403 for this and other rates). Nor is the impact of the series upon the aggregate index different in the two cases. Tagliacarne assigned to the chemical industry a weight of 9.5 percent, while in the present index a weight of 8.96 percent (value-added weights) is attached to it.

In the field of mining the differences are more important, though not before 1896. In the preceding periods both indices tend to record a close-to-zero rate of change in the industry, although the present index rises better than 1 percent a year between 1888 and 1896. Thereafter, however, Tagliacarne's index shows a high participation of mining in the upswing 1896–1908 and lets the industry's growth continue unreduced until 1913 with the annual rates of growth of 4.2 and 4.3 percent, respectively. The present index indeed shows an improvement in 1896–1908, but no change at all between 1908 and 1913. The explanation probably lies partly in the very crude weights in which the subseries for the industry were combined in Tagliacarne's index, giving much too low a weight to the extraction of zinc ore and much too high a weight to iron ore and sulphur; partly in the exclusion of copper-ore mining from Tagliacarne's series.

The series of the metalmaking industry shows discrepancies more in the level of rates than in their variation from period to period. These discrepancies, too, are to some extent explicable in terms of the difference between unweighted and weighted methods of combining the subseries. In addition, they must be also attributed to the fact that Tagliacarne's index contains output of pig iron, which has been deliberately excluded from the present index. To some extent, the very high rate of growth which Tagliacarne's index reveals between 1896 and 1908 is the result of an exaggerated drop which his series shows between 1891 and 1896.

The series of the engineering industry (Tagliacarne's shipbuilding) shows very far-reaching discrepancies. First of all, there is the deep plunge of the nineties, with an annual rate of *decrease* of 14 percent between 1891 and 1896. (The difference between the rates for 1881–88 and 1888–96, on the one hand, and 1881–91 and 1891–96, on the other, is due to the sudden brief rise which the shipbuilding index takes around 1891.) All the more surprising is the failure of the series to show a comparable rate of increase during the following period 1896–1908. The rate of 7.0 percent per year is high but much below the rate shown by the present index, and it also lies far below the rate shown by Tagliacarne's series for metalmaking (11.7 percent). The reason is fairly obvious: shipbuilding is hardly apt to picture correctly the behavior of output of the many new machinery industries which showed a strong upward drift after 1896. By contrast, the adjusted steel-consumption series in the present index assigns a strong role to engineering throughout 1896–1908 (12.2 percent per year). These differences appear to be quite important for the interpretation of the signal features of the period 1896–1908.

The textile industry in the present index is a combination of Tagliacarne's series on raw-silk output and raw-cotton imports. What is different is the impact of the two series upon the aggregate index, because Tagliacarne's weights assign less importance to silk than is done in the present index. Tagliacarne's weight attribution, pertaining as it does to a much later period, does not seem to do justice to the relative conditions prevailing around the turn of the century.

Finally, there are the truly enormous differences in the foodstuffs industry. Tagliacarne's index shows in 1896–1908 quite a fantastic annual rate of 26.6 percent for that industry. This is the result of letting the industry be represented by sugar output (to which the small tonnage of beer output was added). This series fairly dominates Tagliacarne's index, even though the weight attached to it is relatively low in terms of the situation around 1900. It is interesting to note that Tagliacarne's aggregate rate of growth for the period 1896–1908 of 11.4 percent per year would be reduced to 9.2 percent if his series of the foodstuffs industry were to be excluded.

To sum up: the effects of the depression of the early nineties appear to be exaggerated in Tagliacarne's index. This is particularly true of engineering and, to a much smaller degree, of the metalmaking and foodstuffs industries. The subsequent upswing is essentially dominated by the foodstuffs industry, while the much more basic development in engineering appears to be unduly understated.

THE INDEX OF SILVIO GOLZIO

The distinguishing feature of the Golzio index is its wide coverage. In addition to the series included in the present index, it contains the following series: (1) cement and lime, (2) wood, (3) paper, (4) tanneries, (5) clothing, (6) printing, and (7) rubber. Moreover, some of those series which are contained in both Golzio's index and the present index comprise a larger number of subseries. Thus, the foodstuffs industry includes, in addition to beer, sugar, and the flour-mill industries (the latter represented, as in the present index, by a wheat series), indirect representations of the wine and olive-oil and fruit-and-vegetable canning industries. (The introduction, from 1911 on, of a meat and milk series is of less importance for a pre-1914 index.) The textile industry, in addition to silk output and cotton imports, also takes (as did Dessirier's index) the imports of wool into account.

The subseries in the textile industry and in the foodstuffs industry have been combined by using constant prices. Unfortunately, Golzio does not reveal the year to which these prices pertain, which makes it impossible to gauge their appropriateness for the periods preceding 1914. Developing a comparable set of prices must have raised some interesting problems. Futhermore, nothing at all is said on the mode of combining the subseries in mining, metalmaking, and cement and lime. It is possible, therefore, that these series have been combined in the same fashion as was done by Tagliacarne, that is to say, by an unweighted addition of tonnage data.[9] This would be unfortunate in a study which does not have Tagliacarne's excuse of considerable time pressures. Some of the indirect measurements used by Golzio are very ingenious. Thus, his series for the clothing and shoe industries is represented by a combination (through geometric averages) of the textile-industry series, a series on imports of wool and a series on availabilities of hides and skins.

The engineering industry is represented by the production plus net imports of iron and steel. This corresponds to what was done in the present index, except that no attempt was made to eliminate from the series the consumption of iron and steel for railroad construction and maintenance. Furthermore, *along* with the series on engineering, Golzio presents a series on shipbuilding and it is not at all clear how the two series were merged in the final computation of a total index. The use of an independent series for shipbuilding would have made it all the more important to carry through adjustments in the iron and steel series.

Ingenious as are Golzio's attempts to mirror output through indirect series, he seems at times to go much too far. Thus, his fruit-and-vegetable canning series is based (if his laconic statement on p. 53 means what it says) on a series of fresh fruit and vegetable output, which is obviously a very inadequate measure of the process of growth in the canning industry.

[9] In fact, this is more than a mere possibility. Upon adding up the figures on output of mines for the individual products for several five-year periods as given in *Annuario* 1949–50, one finds a very close correspondence between the ratios of the resulting sums and Golzio's index for mining.

In addition, it is not clear what constant price of what commodity could have been applied to combine this series with the other subseries in the foodstuffs industry. The computation of changes of output in the leather industry on the basis of availabilities of hides seems quite justified in itself, but these availabilities had to be estimated and Golzio does not reveal the bases of his estimates (p. 53).

Finally, it might be mentioned that it is not clear whether or not Golzio used *net* cotton imports for his cotton-industry series. Since he speaks of imports *tout court,* the presumption cannot be rejected that, like Tagliacarne, he used gross imports, which, if true, would tend to falsify the picture for the earlier years very considerably.

After having obtained his subseries, Golzio applied to them the respective 1938 lire amounts of net product (as obtained from the 1937–39 census). These amounts are as follows.

Industry	Billions of lire	Percentage
Mining	.79	2.29
Foodstuffs	7.50	21.80
Hides and leather	.42	1.20
Textiles	5.36	15.54
Clothing, etc.	1.42	4.12
Wood	1.12	3.25
Paper	.67	1.94
Printing	.75	2.18
Metalmaking	2.29	6.64
Engineering	8.83	25.62
Nonmetallic minerals	1.03	2.99
Chemicals	3.29	9.54
Rubber	.52	1.50
Others	.48	1.39
	34.47	100.00

Within the confines of industries included in the present index Golzio's set of weights is as follows.

WEIGHTS IN GOLZIO'S INDEX
(PRESENT-INDEX INDUSTRIES)

Branch	Present index (1903)	Golzio index (1938)
Mining and mineral processing	6.43	6.25
Metalmaking	3.49	7.86
Engineering	15.27	30.35

Branch	Present index (1903)	Golzio index (1938)
Textiles	35.86	18.40
Foodstuffs	29.99	25.82
Chemicals	8.96	11.32
	100.00	100.00

Changes of this nature would seem to be a natural result of the industrialization over a period of three and half decades. It is, of course, to be expected that the weight of engineering should increase, while the weight of textiles and foodstuffs in total industrial output should decline. Still, one cannot help wondering why the weight of textiles should decline so much more than the weight of foodstuffs, while the weight of chemicals should increase so little. It is true that the value-added estimates for 1902–03 are approximations and as such much less reliable than the value-added (or net-product) amounts obtained by the 1937–39 census. But it does not seem that the explanation lies necessarily with the 1903 estimates.

Since Golzio very conveniently computed output of individual industries in terms of 1938 lire (from lustrum to lustrum of his index period), it is interesting to observe the composition around 1903 according to his data. Since he presents his data in five-year averages, one is forced to take the period 1901–05 as comparable with 1903. For that period he shows the following distribution of output.

Branch	Golzio value of net output (million 1938 lire)	Per-centage	Present-index weights
Mining and mineral processing	506	4.36	6.43
Metalmaking	303	2.62	3.49
Engineering	1,661	14.30	15.27
Textiles	3,175	27.34	35.86
Foodstuffs	5,463	47.04	29.99
Chemicals	505	4.34	8.96
	11,613	100.00	100.00

This comparison is instructive. The weights of the Golzio index do not seem appropriate to the years around the turn of the century. To impute to the foodstuffs industry a weight of 47 percent for 1903 does not seem reasonable in the light of the available data on both labor and horsepower, particularly if it is considered that the value added per horsepower must be a good deal lower in the foodstuffs industry than in the other industries of the present index. On the other hand, the weight for engineering for 1903 as implied in the Golzio index would seem to be very close to that of the present index. Finally, the weight of the chemical industry is a good deal below that of the present index. One is tempted to say that this is a natural result of applying "postindustrialization" weights or, at any rate, applying weights pertaining to a later stage of industrialization to an earlier period thereof. The effect of industrialization is to make the products of traditional industries dearer in terms of those of more modern industries. In fact, one would have expected the weight of engineering in the Golzio index to lie a good deal below that of the present index.

But what is not at all clear and appears rather unexpected is that the textile industry should show a lower rather than a higher weight in the Golzio index as compared with the present index. A possible explanation is that in Italian conditions, with the upsurge of artificial fibers in the 1920s, the textile industry remained a "new" industry and behaved accordingly with respect to both output and prices. On the other hand, the failure of engineering — a typically new industry in this sense — to show a much lower Golzio weight in 1903 may be the result of the monopolistic price structure of the industry. However that may be, we might perhaps conclude on the strength of the great weight differential in the foodstuffs industry that the Golzio index should reveal a lower rate of growth for the prewar period as compared with the present index, although this index-number effect might appear mitigated by the "unorthodox" behavior of the weight ratios in engineering and, particularly, in textiles.

It is obvious, however, that the weights can tell only a part of the story. In addition, there is the problem of coverage. The industries which are excluded from the present index may have grown at a lower rate than the industries which remained excluded from the present index but which are included in Golzio's computations. And, finally, there is the question of the correspondence between the actual series in the two indices. Thus, though *a priori* one should expect the Golzio index to yield a lower rate of growth, this cannot be taken as a foregone conclusion. A comparison of the two indices may follow first (1881 = 100).

Period	Present index	Golzio index
1881–1885	112	117.1
1886–1890	135	138.5
1891–1895	129	135.8
1896–1900	160	150.0
1901–1905	211	184.4
1906–1910	294	250.3

Golzio's index and the present index show roughly parallel developments until 1896–1900. Prior to that, the present index proves to be a little bit more sensitive to the depression of the early nineties. The great difference, however, begins after 1900. In 1906–10, the present index is almost 50 points above the Golzio index. This can be attributed to two factors: (1) the drag of the more slowly developing indices which are included in the Golzio index; (2) the effect of Golzio's using a "post-industrialization" weight system. To separate the two factors, a tabulation of the Golzio figures is presented which is confined to industries contained in the present index. The result is as follows (1881 = 100).

Period	Present index	Golzio index (Present-index industries)	Golzio total index
1881–1885	112	122	117.1
1886–1890	135	145	138.5
1891–1895	129	139	135.8
1896–1900	160	153	150.0
1901–1905	211	191	184.4
1906–1910	294	256	250.3

This is an interesting result. Excluding the "other industries" from Golzio's index makes surprisingly little difference. The "other industries" retarded a little the growth of the eighties. They, being more stable, made Golzio's total index somewhat less sensitive to the depression of the early nineties. But, apart from those minor variations, the important conclusion is that they did not appreciably change the character of the upswing years after 1900 as pictured in Golzio's index. In 1906–10, Golzio's index, liberated from the presumable downward pull of "other industries," rises only 6 points above his total index.

This is a rather comforting result from the point of view of the present index. The latter's more restricted coverage may be a smaller deficiency than is likely to appear at first sight. On the other hand, a comparison of the component series in Golzio's index and the present index shows not unimportant, and to some extent surprising, discrepancies. The data for both indices are given in the following table (P = present index; G = Golzio index).

COMPARISON OF COMPONENT SERIES

Period	Mining		Metal-making		Textiles		Engineering		Foodstuffs		Chemicals	
	P	G	P	G	P	G	P	G	P	G	P	G
1881–1885	108	97	120	112	107	111	134	113	107	133	144	150
1886–1890	100	104	382	218	134	147	163	151	108	142	247	317
1891–1893	109	103	297	171	154	159	95	96	107	143	342	353
1896–1900	127	126	401	213	182	182	146	115	128	146	551	774
1901–1905	147	149	561	316	223	219	184	161	179	175	1289	1330
1906–1910	135	170	1299	696	255	275	371	350	199	182	2467	2550

The discrepancy is most surprising in the case of the chemical industry, since both index series are based on the single sulphuric-acid series of output. Unless Golzio used a series of output not accessible to the present writer, the discrepancy is likely to be the result of errors in computation. Golzio's series outruns that of the present index until 1896–1900, whereupon its growth is much slower than that of the present index. Taking 1896–1900 as equal to 100, the Golzio index reaches 330 in 1906–10, whereas the present index almost hits the 450 mark. The foodstuffs series does not show similar discrepancies, except in the earlier periods. But its growth, too, is slower between 1896–1900 and 1906–10 (128 as against 155). The engineering series in the two indices run fairly parallel, but here the Golzio series shows a much faster rise during the later periods, which probably is the result of the Golzio series not being liberated from the weight of steel consumption by railroads. Such consumption naturally is extraneous to what the series purports to measure.

The textile series develops, on the whole, *pari passu* in the two indices, although the Golzio series shows a jump ahead in the last five-year period. The same is true of his mining series. By contrast, the series on metal-making shows a very great lag in the first portions of the index period. In the second half of that period, the two indices move at almost exactly the same pace. The earlier discrepancy may find its explanation in the use of unweighted aggregation of the component subseries.

The final conclusion may, therefore, be stated as follows: (1) The differences in coverage do not seem to cause discrepancies betwen the two indices. (2) The Golzio index receives some legitimate downward bias as a result of using weights pertaining to a very late date. (3) It would seem that the lags which Golzio's index shows in the later subperiods in the chemical industry and in the foodstuffs industry are likely to have further accentuated the downward bias inherent in his index.

APPENDIX II

Industrialization in Bulgaria:
Basic Data and Calculations

NET OUTPUT OF STATE-ENCOURAGED INDUSTRY,
DATA AND CALCULATIONS (TABLES 1–9)

Table 1. Number of enterprises

Industry	1909	1929	1937
Textiles	61	198	197
Flour mills	62	313	157
Other foodstuffs	38	155	118
Metals	16	136	103
Leather	22	54	46
Chemicals	25	104	96
Woodworking	18	48	46
Pottery	10	101	87
Paper	3	4	4
Energy	2	45	48
Total	257	1,158	902
Total without energy	255	1,113	854

Source: Glavna Direktsiya na Statistikata, *Statisticheski Godishnik na Búlgarskoto Tsarstvo*, 1910 (Sofia, 1911), p. 253; 1931 (Sofia, 1931), pp. 230–237; 1939 (Sofia, 1939), pp. 384–389. Hereafter cited *Godishnik*, with references to year and page.

Table 2. Number of workers employed

Industry	1909	1929	1937
Textiles	4,064	16,368	24,313
Flour mills	660	2,747	1,442
Other foodstuffs	907	4,369	3,671
Metals	892	5,469	4,603
Leather	398	1,029	864
Chemicals	432	1,767	2,618
Woodworking	1,130	1,165	1,144

Table 2. Number of workers employed (cont.)

Industry	1909	1929	1937
Pottery	1,158	3,834	3,772
Paper	152	338	972
Energy	18	908	699
Total	9,973	37,994	44,098
Total without energy	9,955	37,086	43,399

Source: see Table 1.

Table 3. Number of horsepowers used

Industry	1909	1929	1937
Textiles	3,722	17,884	31,186
Flour mills	3,721	22,827	17,794
Other foodstuffs	2,101	23,674	26,717
Metals	379	7,543	9,399
Leather	506	3,056	3,537
Chemicals	454	3,719	6,591
Woodworking	689	1,853	3,296
Pottery	661	13,259	14,718
Paper	233	1,512	8,932
Energy	4,734	56,538	114,292
Total	17,200	151,865	236,462
Total without energy	12,466	95,327	122,170

Source: see Table 1.

Table 4. Number of workers per enterprise

Industry	1909	1929	1937
Textiles	66.6	82.7	123.4
Flour mills	10.6	8.8	9.2
Other foodstuffs	23.9	28.2	31.1
Metals	55.7	40.2	47.7
Leather	18.1	19.1	18.8
Chemicals	17.3	17.0	27.3
Woodworking	62.8	24.3	24.9
Pottery	115.8	38.0	43.4
Paper	50.7	84.5	243.0
Energy	9.0	20.2	14.5
Total	38.8	32.7	48.9
Total without energy	39.0	33.2	50.8

Source: Tables 1 and 2 of this appendix.

Table 5. Number of horsepowers per worker

Industry	1909	1929	1937
Textiles	.92	1.1	1.3
Flour mills	5.64	8.3	12.3
Other foodstuffs	2.32	5.4	7.3
Metals	.42	1.4	2.0
Leather	1.27	3.0	1.3
Chemicals	1.05	2.1	2.5
Woodworking	.61	1.6	2.9
Pottery	.57	3.5	3.9
Paper	1.53	4.5	9.2
Energy	263.00	62.3	164.2
Total	1.72	4.0	5.3
Total without energy	1.25	2.6	2.8

Source: Tables 2 and 3 of this appendix.

Table 6. Value of net output in 1909
(in thousands of current leva)

Industry	Value of product	Cost of raw materials	Cost of fuel	Net output
Textiles	17,445	11,687	576	5,182
Flour mills	32,598	27,448	416	4,734
Other foodstuffs	7,883	3,249	702	3,932
Metals	2,147	833	85	1,229
Leather	4,539	3,361	64	1,114
Chemicals	2,463	1,574	45	844
Woodworking	2,699	1,585	25	1,089
Pottery	1,792	219	265	1,308
Paper	461	178	57	225
Energy	928	6	71	851
Total	73,134	50,320	2,306	20,508
Total without energy	72,206	50,314	2,235	19,657

Source: *Godishnik,* 1910: data on output, p. 277; data on raw materials, p. 276; data on fuel, p. 275.

Table 7. Value of net output in 1929
(in millions of current leva)

Industry	Value of product	Cost of raw materials	Cost of fuel	Cost of power	Net output
Textiles	2,340	1,604	44	10	682
Flour mills	1,788	1,671	30	5	82
Other foodstuffs	1,432	760	54	4	614
Metals	601	322	15	4	260
Leather	408	331	5	2	70
Chemicals	575	359	12	3	201
Woodworking	137	87	.5	.2	49
Pottery	419	46	72	33	268
Paper	53	18	3	2	30
Energy	198	3	18	—	177
Total	7,951	5,201	254	63	2,433
Total without energy	7,753	5,198	236	63	2,256

Source: *Godishnik*, 1931, pp. 230–237.

Table 8. Value of net output in 1937
(in millions of current leva)

Industry	Value of product	Cost of raw materials	Cost of fuel	Cost of power	Net output
Textiles	2,634	1,692	45	44	853
Flour mills	1,077	900	18	11	148
Other foodstuffs	1,057	733	35	8	281
Metals	539	299	15	11	214
Leather	311	230	3	3	75
Chemicals	533	311	9	8	205
Woodworking	110	78	1	1	30
Pottery	365	44	37	31	253
Paper	194	104	6	6	78
Energy	337	76	48	—	213
Total	7,157	4,467	217	123	2,350
Total without energy	6,820	4,391	169	123	2,137

Source: *Godishnik*, 1939, pp. 384–389.

Table 9. Ratio of net output to value of product in state-encouraged industry
(in percent at current prices)

Industry	1909	1929	1937
Textiles	29.70	29.15	32.35
Flour mills	14.52	4.59	13.84
Other foodstuffs	49.86	42.87	26.48
Metals	57.20	43.12	39.56
Leather	24.54	17.04	23.95
Chemicals	34.27	34.90	38.34
Woodworking	40.33	36.00	27.37
Pottery	73.01	64.12	69.37
Paper	49.15	55.57	40.14
Energy	91.77	89.00	84.64
Total	31.19	30.65	34.28
Total without energy	30.11	29.17	31.81

CALCULATION OF NET OUTPUT OF STATE-ENCOURAGED INDUSTRY AT CONSTANT PRICES, VOLUME OF OUTPUT, AND RATES OF GROWTH (TABLES 10–17)

Table 10. Price index numbers of selected commodities, 1929
(base period 1908–1912 = 1)

Commodity	Index number
Beer	36.95
Flour	38.97
Raw hides	30.00
Men's clothing	36.68
Clothing materials	45.47
Underwear	30.84
Coal	26.84
Construction timber (boards)	35.39

Source: All the following references are from *Godishnik*, 1931: For beer, p. 335. Flour, p. 334. Raw hides, no figure available for 1929; the index for 1928 stood at 31.40 (p. 334); since the price for livestock (oxen) in 1929 was about 3 percent below the preceding year, the index number for raw hides was reduced from 31.40 to 30.00. Men's clothing, clothing materials, and underwear price indices as given in official statistics are based on August 1915; the 1929 index numbers were 26.20, 32.48, and 22.03, respectively (p. 339); they were reduced here to 1908–1912 by the use of the general price-level index: 1908–12 = 1; 1915 = 1.4; accordingly, the index numbers in the tables are the result of multiplication of the three numbers as given in this note by 1.4. Coal, p. 335. Construction timber, p. 335; the index number of 32.96 given in *Godishnik* refers to 1928; it was changed to 1929 by the ratio of the general price index for 1929:1928 (p. 335) — accordingly, (35.49/33.05) × 32.96 = 35.39.

Table 11. Price indices of selected commodities, 1937
(base year 1929 = 100)

Commodity	Index number
Sugar	85.70
Flour	45.71
Raw hides	71.74
Pig iron	122.00
Wool yarn	65.17
Cotton yarn	69.00
Caustic soda	90.38
Window glass	55.80
Construction timber	85.95
Coal	85.87
Paper	105.70

Source: All the index numbers in Table 11 have been computed from data given in *Godishnik*, 1939, pp. 554 and 555.

The data from Tables 10 and 11 were used to represent the price changes in the respective industrial branches. The allocation of the individual commodity prices to branches of industry was as follows:

Industry	Period 1908/12–1929	Period 1929–1937
Textiles	Unweighted average of men's clothing, clothing materials, and underwear	Unweighted average of wool yarn and cotton yarn
Flour mills	Flour	Flour
Other foodstuffs	Beer	Sugar
Metals	General price index	Pig iron
Leather	Raw hides	Raw hides
Chemicals	General price index	Caustic soda
Woodworking	Construction timber	Construction timber
Pottery	General price index	Window glass
Paper	General price index	Paper
Energy	Coal	Coal

The indices for the two periods were spliced in 1929. The consolidated result is shown in Table 12.

Table 12. Price indices for branches of state-encouraged industries

Industry	1908–1912	1929	1937
Textiles	1	38.26	25.67
Flour mills	1	38.97	17.81
Other foodstuffs	1	36.95	31.66
Metals	1	35.49	43.30
Leather	1	30.00	21.52
Chemicals	1	35.49	32.08
Woodworking	1	35.40	30.42
Pottery	1	35.49	19.80
Paper	1	35.49	37.51
Energy	1	26.84	23.04

Since Bulgarian price statistics were presented in terms of 1908–1912 prices, and prices for the sole year 1909 were not available, it has been assumed that the prices of 1908–1912 are representative of those of 1909. Inspection of few scattered price data for 1909 seemed to justify the assumption fairly well. The following Table 13 contains the results of deflating the net-output data from Tables 6, 7, and 8 by price index numbers as given in Table 12, using the weights of the year "1909."

Table 13. Net output of state-encouraged industry at "1909" prices

Industry	1909		1929		1937	
	1,000 leva	Percent	1,000 leva	Percent	1,000 leva	Percent
Textiles	5,183	25.27	17,834	25.97	33,201	35.20
Flour mills	4,734	23.08	2,110	3.07	8,371	8.87
Other foodstuffs	3,931	19.16	16,610	24.19	8,839	9.38
Metals	1,229	5.99	7,300	10.63	4,922	5.22
Leather	1,114	5.43	2,317	3.37	3,460	3.66
Chemicals	844	4.12	5,655	8.23	6,366	6.75
Woodworking	1,089	5.31	1,398	2.04	992	1.05
Pottery	1,308	6.38	7,574	11.03	12,794	13.56
Paper	227	1.10	829	1.22	2,071	2.20
Energy	852	4.15	7,041	10.25	13,310	14.11
Total	20,511	100.00	68,668	100.00	94,327	100.00

Deflation of net-output data in Tables 6, 7, and 8 by price index numbers as given in Table 12, using the weights of the year 1929, yields the following result (Table 14).

Table 14. Net output of state-encouraged industry at 1929 prices

Industry	1909		1929		1937	
	1,000 leva	Percent	1,000 leva	Percent	1,000 leva	Percent
Textiles	198,297	26.46	682,328	28.07	1,270,559	38.24
Flour mills	184,478	24.62	82,168	3.38	326,150	9.81
Other foodstuffs	145,237	19.38	613,743	25.24	326,550	9.83
Metals	43,614	5.82	259,092	10.65	174,679	5.25
Leather	33,410	4.46	69,505	2.86	103,803	3.12
Chemicals	29,963	4.00	200,688	8.25	225,950	6.80
Woodworking	38,525	5.14	49,473	2.03	35,115	1.06
Pottery	46,436	6.20	268,813	11.06	454,062	13.66
Paper	8,040	1.08	29,435	1.22	73,499	2.22
Energy	21,286	2.84	175,948	7.24	332,632	10.01
Total	749,286	100.00	2,431,193	100.00	3,322,999	100.00

Deflation of net-output data in Tables 6, 7, and 8 by price index numbers, as given in Table 12 and using the weights of the year 1937, yields the following result (Table 15).

Table 15. Net output of state-encouraged industry at 1937 prices

Industry	1909		1929		1937	
	1,000 leva	Percent	1,000 leva	Percent	1,000 leva	Percent
Textiles	133,044	25.01	577,056	27.98	852,291	35.22
Flour mills	84,310	15.85	37,559	1.82	149,083	6.16
Other foodstuffs	124,444	23.40	525,978	25.50	279,853	11.56
Metals	53,212	10.00	316,093	15.32	213,108	8.81
Leather	23,966	4.51	49,863	2.42	74,468	3.08
Chemicals	27,084	5.09	181,382	8.79	204,214	8.44
Woodworking	33,115	6.23	42,522	2.06	30,185	1.25
Pottery	25,907	4.87	149,971	7.27	253,321	10.47
Paper	8,498	1.60	31,112	1.52	77,688	3.21
Energy	18,279	3.44	151,087	7.32	285,631	11.80
Total	531,859	100.00	2,062,623	100.00	2,419,842	100.00

In the following Table 16, the data presented in Table 13 have been converted to indices at prices of "1909."

Table 16. Indices of net output of state-encouraged industry at "1909" prices

Industry	1909	1929	1937
Textiles	100	344	641
Flour mills	100	45	177
Other foodstuffs	100	423	225
Metals	100	594	401
Leather	100	208	311
Chemicals	100	670	754
Woodworking	100	128	91
Pottery	100	579	978
Paper	100	366	914
Energy	100	827	1,563
Total	100	335	460

The average annual rates of growth of industrial output as implied in the data in Table 16 have been computed on a compound basis, using the initial and terminal years of the respective periods. In alternative computations, the Balkan wars and World War I have been taken into account by an arbitrary reduction of the respective periods by four years. The results are shown in the following Table 17.

Table 17. Average annual percentage rates of growth of net output
of state-encouraged industry
(based on "1909" prices)

Industry	1909–1929 (20 years)	1909–1929 (16 years)	1929–1937 (8 years)	1909–1937 (28 years)	1909–1937 (24 years)
Textiles	6.38	8.03	8.08	6.86	8.05
Flour mills	−3.85	−5.00	18.80	2.05	2.40
Other foodstuffs	7.47	9.42	−9.65	2.94	3.44
Metals	9.32	11.78	−3.61	5.08	5.95
Leather	3.70	4.68	5.15	4.13	4.84
Chemicals	9.98	12.62	1.50	7.48	8.78
Woodworking	1.26	1.58	−4.19	−.33	−.40
Pottery	9.18	11.60	6.77	8.48	9.97
Paper	6.70	8.45	12.12	8.22	9.66
Energy	11.14	14.11	7.97	10.22	12.03
Total	6.23	7.85	4.05	5.60	6.56

L. Berov's computation of investment in fixed industrial capital yielded the following series at constant prices of 1939.

Table 18. Gross investment in fixed capital in Bulgarian industry, at 1939 prices

Year	1,000 leva	Year	1,000 leva
1880	5,584	1910	277,552
1881	7,190	1911	229,397
1882	4,927	1912	295,038
1883	2,689	1913	342,595
1884	5,589	1914	236,733
1880–84	25,979	1910–14	1,381,315
1885	23,373	1915	8,719
1886	15,462	1916	11,695
1887	40,915	1917	34,357
1888	36,375	1918	30,541
1889	51,645	1919	6,346
1885–89	167,770	1915–19	91,658
1890	93,896	1920	42,581
1891	49,764	1921	120,653
1892	60,493	1922	132,652
1893	62,518	1923	214,708
1894	126,782	1924	296,905
1890–94	393,453	1920–24	807,499
1895	88,120	1925	394,170
1896	56,109	1926	400,269
1897	111,691	1927	427,710
1898	82,986	1928	559,963
1899	23,470	1929	691,631
1895–99	360,376	1925–29	2,473,743
1900	35,802	1930	451,818
1901	52,751	1931	470,433
1902	76,577	1932	488,711
1903	78,711	1933	393,179
1904	97,836	1934	274,360
1900–04	341,677	1930–34	2,078,501
1905	108,153		
1906	142,431		
1907	198,541	1935	462,756
1908	214,023	1936	634,738
1909	286,376	1937	1,434,936
1905–09	949,524	1935–37	2,532,430

Source: "Kúm vúprosa za tempovete na kapitalisticheskata industrializatsiya na Búl-gariya" (On the Question of the Rates of Capitalist Industrialization in Bulgaria), Bulgarska Akademiya na Naukite, *Isvestiya na Ikonomicheskiya Institut*, VIII, nos. 3–4 (Sofia), 158–161.

The fixed-capital stock in Bulgarian industry (at 1939 prices) was computed from the data in Table 18 on the basis of the following assumptions: (1) that the value of capital stock in industry in 1879 was negligible (hence equal to zero); (2) that the capital invested depreciated discontinuously at the rate of 25 percent at the end of every quinquennium. The calculation based on these assumptions is shown in Table 19.

Table 19. Capital-stock computations
(in 1,000 leva at 1939 prices)

(1) Quinquennium	(2) Gross investment	(3) Depreciation multiplier	(4) Capital stock (2) times (3)
		1880–1909	
1880–84	25,979	$.75^5$	6,164
1885–89	167,770	$.75^4$	53,082
1890–94	393,453	$.75^3$	221,318
1895–99	360,376	$.75^2$	202,711
1900–04	341,677	$.75$	256,258
1905–09	949,524	—	949,524
	Capital stock at the end of 1909:		1,689,057
		1909–1937	
–1909	1,689,057	$.75^6$	300,616
1910–14	1,381,315	$.75^5$	277,929
1915–19	91,658	$.75^4$	29,002
1920–24	807,499	$.75^3$	340,664
1925–29	2,473,743	$.75^2$	1,391,480
1930–34	2,078,501	$.75$	1,558,757
1935–37	2,532,430	—	2,532,430
	Capital stock at the end of 1937:		6,430,088

The data on capital stock, as computed in Table 19, refer to the whole complex of Bulgarian industry rather than to the state-encouraged sector alone. They must be related, therefore, to comparably comprehensive data on labor and output. Such data are available for 1937: The labor force amounted to 90,621 workers (*Godishnik*, 1939, p. 391). Value of product amounted to 10,956,472,000 leva. The sum total of the value of raw materials, fuel, and power used amounted to 7,080,407,000 leva. This left a balance of net output of 3,876,065,000 leva (*ibid.*, pp. 392–393).

Comparable data are not available for 1909. It has been assumed, therefore, that the ratio of output and labor in "total industry" to output and labor in state-encouraged industry was the same in 1909 as in 1937 (all value figures at 1937 prices). Accordingly: Net output of "all industry" in 1909 equals output of "all industry" in 1937 times output of state-encouraged industry in 1909, divided by output of state-encouraged industry in 1937, or:

$$\frac{3,876,065,000 \times 531,859,000}{2,419,842} = 851,923,000 \text{ leva}$$

(for net output of state-encouraged industry in 1909 and 1937, see Table 15 of this appendix).

Similarly, the labor force in "all industry" in 1909 equals the labor force in "all industry" in 1937 times the labor force in state-encouraged industry in 1909, divided by the labor force in state-encouraged industry in 1937, or:

$$\frac{90,621 \times 9,973}{44,098} = 20,494 \text{ persons.}$$

Neglecting the small inconsistency between capital-stock data, which are expressed in terms of 1939 prices, and net-output data, which are expressed in terms of 1937 prices, the double set of three basic data may be summarized in Table 20.

Table 20. *Labor force, fixed capital stock, and net output in all industry in 1909 and 1937*

Data	1909	1937
Labor force	20,494	90,621
Capital stock (1,000 leva)	1,689,057	6,430,088
Net output	851,923	3,876,065

These data are then inserted into a production function of the Cobb-Douglas type: $O = F \times L^k \times C^{1-k}$, where:

$O =$ industrial output,
$F =$ productivity factor,
$L =$ labor force (number of workers employed),
$C =$ capital stock,
$k =$ labor's share in industrial output (assuming it is rewarded at its marginal productivity).

Since data on k are not available, the following four alternatives are presented:

(1) $k = .75$
(2) $k = .65$
(3) $k = .50$
(4) $k = .25$

Solving for F — the productivity factor — in each of the four cases yields the following result:

433

(1) $k = .75$, hence: $F = \dfrac{O}{L^{.75} \times C^{.25}}$.

$$F_{1937} = \frac{3,876,065,000}{90,621^{.75} \times 6,430,088,000^{.25}} = 2,621.$$

$$F_{1909} = \frac{851,923,000}{20,494^{.75} \times 1,689,057.000^{.25}} = 2,454.$$

$$\frac{F_{1937}}{F_{1909}} = \frac{2,621}{2,454} = 1.0685.$$

(2) $k = .65$, hence: $F = \dfrac{O}{L^{.65} \times C^{.35}}$.

$$F_{1937} = \frac{851,923,000}{90,621^{.65} \times 6,430,088,000^{.35}} = 858.$$

$$F_{1909} = \frac{851,923,000}{20,494^{.65} \times 1,689,057^{.35}} = 791.$$

$$\frac{F_{1937}}{F_{1909}} = \frac{858}{791} = 1.0847.$$

(3) $k = .50$, hence: $F = \dfrac{O}{L^{.50} \times C^{.50}}$.

$$F_{1937} = \frac{3,876,065,000}{90,621^{.50} \times 6,430,088,000^{.50}} = 160.6.$$

$$F_{1909} = \frac{851,923,000}{20,494^{.50} \times 1,689,057^{.35}} = 144.8.$$

$$\frac{F_{1937}}{F_{1909}} = \frac{160.6}{144.8} = 1.1090.$$

(4) $k = .25$, hence: $F = \dfrac{O}{L^{.25} \times C^{.75}}$.

$$F_{1937} = \frac{3,876,065,000}{90,621^{.25} \times 6,430,088,000^{.75}} = 9.84.$$

$$F_{1909} = \frac{851,923,000}{20,494^{.25} \times 1,689,057^{.75}} = 8.55.$$

$$\frac{F_{1937}}{F_{1909}} = \frac{9.84}{8.55} = 1.1512.$$

Using the results just obtained, the average annual rate of change in the productivity factor for the period 1909–1937 (28 years) may be computed as follows:

$$(1) \quad \frac{\log 1.0685}{28} = 100.24.$$

$$(2) \quad \frac{\log 1.0847}{28} = 100.29.$$

$$(3) \quad \frac{\log 1.1090}{28} = 100.37.$$

$$(4) \quad \frac{\log 1.1512}{28} = 100.50.$$

APPENDIX III

Problems in Measuring Long-Term Growth in Income and Wealth

"Acceptable long-term records of national income and wealth and of their customarily distinguished components constitute indispensable minimum information in the study of economic growth." Few would take exception to this statement by Simon Kuznets in his introduction to the present volume, and this reviewer agrees emphatically.[1] Without knowledge of basic aggregates, economic history at best would remain confined to easy but unsubstantiated generalizations. Most likely, it would relapse into legal and political history, into essays in biography, and into sociological schematism and sociological impressionism. In short, economic history would contain everything but one thing — economics. It is another matter that, once the pertinent *economic* questions have been posed and the requisite empirical information has been assembled and placed within economically significant frameworks, interpretation of the findings inevitably would call for recourse to various noneconomic factors and accordingly to disciplines other than economics. What is at stake, of course, is not professional provincialism but methodological clarity with regard to the specific subject matter of economic history.

For the most part, the volume under review purports to summarize the state of our knowledge of long-term trends of national output and wealth with regard to four major and two smaller countries: the United Kingdom, France, Germany, Japan, Denmark, and Hungary. Some of the essays, however, embody a good deal of original work on the part of the authors. The character and the quality of the individual contributions are not uniform. Nor is the availability and reliability of the basic data. It is partly for this reason that the high initial expectations with which one begins the perusal of the volume are soon tempered by disappointments. No doubt much remains to be done before the results can be used conveniently and confidently for the purposes of historical interpretation within the

---

[1] This appendix was a review of *Income and Wealth*, V, Simon Kuznets, ed. (International Association for Research and Wealth, 1955). It appeared in the December 1957 issue of the *Journal of the American Statistical Association*.

individual countries; the road to meaningful comparisons among them would seem even much longer.

The first paper, by James B. Jefferys and Dorothy Walters ("National Income and Expenditure of the United Kingdom, 1870–1952"), is modestly presented by the authors as a review of progress made. It is more than that, since the process of fitting together and reconciling the various existing estimates involved much additional and original work.

From a statistical point of view, this paper is the most mature of the six contributions. Both the income side and the expenditure side of social accounts are presented. The discrepancies between them are frankly and carefully discussed, and the reader can form an opinion of his own with regard to the reliability of the estimates. It is gratifying to see that after 1890 the disparity between the two series is reduced to quite tolerable proportions. The last section of the paper contains a brief but not inadequate discussion of the methods used in constructing the component series. The weakest point of the calculations seems to lie in the conversion of estimates at current prices into constant prices of 1912–13. Apparently, no attempt has been made to use different deflators for different types of consumers' goods. Nothing is said about the weights employed in the construction of the various price indices which the authors had to link in order to obtain consecutive price series for the whole period. Accordingly, it is not clear at all what weights actually underlie the income series allegedly expressed at prices of 1912–13. To obtain an index of physical volume at constant prices of one period, the deflator for each year's current values, properly speaking, should be a price index based on weights pertaining to that year. In other words, a consistent base-year volume index requires given-year price indices as deflators. In what sense "output values at constant prices of one year" as presented here can be regarded as actually aggregated on the basis of the price structure of that year is anybody's guess. The comparability among the individual subperiods as well as the rate of growth for the period as a whole remains problematic under these circumstances, for the data for the individual years must be subject to a *varying degree* of distortion. The authors might well have included an investigation of the distortions inherent in the series in their list of various "gaps" to be filled by further study. They are careful to point out that their series is not adequate for the purposes of short-term analysis. But as long as we have no idea as to the direction and probable extent of those distortions, the degree of retardation or acceleration over longer periods is also quite elusive. This is a serious limitation on any historical interpretation of the results, although it must be admitted that the deflating techniques used in this paper are greatly superior to those used in some other contributions to this volume.

On the other hand, it is to be welcomed that the authors have presented their data at current prices for each year of the period under

437

review and have made it possible for the interested reader to compute the national income at constant prices in the same fashion. The mechanical presentation, by calendar decades or quinquennia, be they overlapping or not, is hardly adequate for many problems raised in historical analysis — in particular, for the all-important problem of relation between structural spurts of growth and the intervening cyclical fluctuations. Nor is there much doubt that such an analysis would call for much more detailed breakdowns of growth by production sectors than the ones used in this paper to obtain the aggregate income figures.

From any historical point of view, one must also join the authors in the regret that their series begins at such a late point in the nineteenth century. This is particularly so if one recalls the lower reliability of the data for the seventies and the eighties and the interruptions of continuity by the two great wars. Still, this point must not be overemphasized. There are reasonable limits to ingratitude, and this reviewer should not like to cross them.

François Perroux, the author of the paper on French economic growth ("Prise de vues sur la croissance de l'économie française, 1780–1950"), shows much less interest in the description of statistical techniques and much more concern with broader historical problems. In particular, his distinction between "active" and "passive" components of national income in the process of its growth is very helpful in providing direction and orientation for quantitative research. In Perroux's words, it is "reasoned history" that must inhale meaning into statistical analysis. That in reality there is, and must be, a steady interaction, and that questions addressed to the facts are just as important as questions raised by the facts, is another matter. Unfortunately, the author's dictum has a special meaning because it is designed to convey his distrust of the quantitative data which he makes available: if the latter are at variance with what we should expect from general historical knowledge, they should be rejected.

The reader is unable to pass judgment on this attitude, for the author does not allow him any glimpses into the statistical kitchen in which the estimates have been brewed, beyond giving references to some previous studies. We are not even told just what concept of national income is embodied in the series presented, except that the data have been based on production statistics. The only statistical point on which the author is explicit is his criticism of the methods used to deflate current values to constant price magnitudes. After what has been said before, one can only agree that the job of conversion, should its results make sense, must be regarded as a much more arduous one than is usually assumed. While Perroux does not advert to the basic weighting problem mentioned above, in a special section of his paper he vents bitter contempt on the impropriety of deflating heterogeneously composed values by some specific price index and is eager to show how the use of unsuitable deflators at times results in curious and unwarranted irregularities in the deflated series which reflect nothing but some spasmodic movements in the deflator chosen.

It is very useful to have all this said, since it should draw much needed attention to the problem and reduce the willingness to engage lightheartedly in mechanical deflations. But Perroux draws a practical consequence. He abandons all pretense at obtaining comparable values at constant prices and decides to take changes in values at current prices as representing changes in physical volume of output. He supports and justifies this procedure by the fact that the period between the reign of Napoleon I and the First World War was free from major monetary disturbances and, accordingly, current values are at least as good as deflated values for that period. It might be noted that Walther Hoffmann arrived at a similar conclusion in his study of British industrial output. The trouble, however, is that to reach such a conclusion reliably, one would have to have correct deflators; in their absence the actual relation between value and volume is quite uncertain. Thus, the rates of growth as given by Perroux must be taken with extreme caution. The margin between maximum and minimum rates of growth shown by Perroux is fairly narrow, and it is quite conjectural just how much importance can be attributed to comparisons among them.

The rhythm of long-term development, as it emerges from the data, is certainly not inconsistent with opinions generally held on the course of French economic history in the nineteenth century. But as long as quantitative research must be tested by vague and impressionistic ideas rather than the other way round, the progress achieved cannot be regarded as impressive.

Perhaps nothing reveals Perroux's skepticism so clearly as his discussion of whether or not French society was economically progressive in the course of the last century and a half. He answers the question in the negative. A progressive economy is one in which "technological inventions are translated into economic innovations with a minimum of delay and a minimum of social cost" involving use of all the human and material resources considered as an entity (p. 72). This, he says, was not the case in France. One must wonder about the relevance of such considerations in a paper of this sort. It is not clear at all that they are presented to explain why the rate of growth was not higher than it actually was, and the value of concepts not adapted to the nature of the material presented is dubious. According to the data given, French national output increased more than fourfold between 1825 and 1909, which surely is a considerable rate of progress for a "nonprogressive" economy. It would seem that in a quantitative study, progressiveness — or the lack of it — must, at least in the first instance, be conceived in quantitative terms and that qualitative concepts should be brought in to explain the results rather than to negate them.

If this is *not* done, it must be taken to mean that quantitative research is not yet able to produce trustworthy results.

The paper on Germany by Paul Jostock ("The Long-Term Growth of National Income in Germany") is much less reticent concerning the nature of the estimates presented. The text contains some discussion of the methods used and more is said in a special appendix. The picture is approximately as follows. For the period before World War I detailed computations of national income exist for one year only, 1913. In addition, there are official extrapolations for the years 1891–1913 on the basis of income-tax returns for Prussia and Saxony only. For 1860–1890 the author prepared an estimate of his own for five years (1860, 1870, 1877, 1883, and 1890) and interpolated values for the intervening years. The "benchmark" years' income was variously estimated. For instance, the value of net industrial output was calculated as follows: a previously available index of *gross* value of industrial output at current prices (which, incidentally, was derived by the multiplication of an index of physical output by an index of wholesale prices) was multiplied by a (previously available) figure of net industrial output in 1913. The implicit assumption as to the constancy of the gross-net ratios over fifty-three years may not be so very implausible since the data are at current prices and the higher degree of fabrication is likely to have been offset by the relative decrease in prices of value-added components. The uncertainty, however, about the mutual appropriateness of weights in the two underlying series may be much more serious.

The computations for national income produced by agriculture are even cruder. As to the remaining sectors of the economy, their contribution for 1890 was estimated roughly as a residual by first extrapolating roughly the official rough estimate for total national income for 1891 back to 1890. For earlier years, "the necessary estimates had to be roughly approximated" by relying "on knowledge of general developments" (p. 120). It must be noted that what was being estimated in this fashion was said to amount to no less than 50 percent of national income in 1890.

The data for 1925–1941 are no doubt much more reliable and, in fact, the best of the whole series. Much less so are those relating to the years after the last war which have been computed by applying production indices to the 1936 census. All current values from 1913 onward have been deflated to constant values by dint of a single cost-of-living index. The data for the years before 1913 were deflated by a single wholesale-price index. The result is said to be a physical-output series at 1928 prices. After what has been said about the problem of weight correspondence between the divisor index and the resulting quotient index and bearing in mind Perroux's strictures, it should be fairly clear that the homogeneity of the physical-volume series is a highly doubtful one, to say the least. It should not be forgotten that all these problems precede, as it were, the real index-number problem. It is only after the correct weights have been obtained and output values have been consistently expressed in terms of a given period that one can begin to wonder what would happen to the index and the rates of growth implied in it, and to the component series, if another more remote or more proximate period were chosen for the purposes of weighting.

After having presented his data, the author goes into an exploration of a number of interesting and relevant problems. He discusses the meaning of the index in terms of various structural changes in the economy, such as the shifts away from household production, changes in age distribution of the population, expansion of "unproductive" activities, role of military expenditures, and territorial changes. He also tries to adjust his series by taking into account price-level differentials existing among localities of various size. The adjustment, however, is quite mechanical, and the author is well aware of its limitations. To assume constant price differentials among towns of different size over a period of some eighty years is really quite hazardous. Moreover, since the expenditure side of national income is as yet unexplored and the division between consumption and investment unknown, the adjusted data refer to per-capita national income rather than to per-capita consumers' expenditures. In addition, the paper includes an attempt to estimate the value of increased leisure; it investigates the change in income per capita of gainfully engaged population; it provides information on the changing ratio of industrial and agricultural output; and, at least for the post-1913 period, it has something to say on the changes in distribution of income.

All these problems, largely posed or inspired by Simon Kuznets' work, are of course most worthwhile. Yet one cannot shed the feeling that the time for discussing them has not arrived. When one considers that the only really consecutive historical period for which long-term change is meaningful is that from 1860 to 1913; when one recalls the nature of the estimates for that period and the degree of their reliability and deflates thereby the elaborations made and the conclusions reached, the resulting real income in terms of safe historical knowledge cannot be very large.

The paper on Denmark by Kjeld Bjorke ("The National Product of Denmark, 1870–1952") provides complete year-by-year estimates of national income from 1870 to 1952. These estimates are divided, on the one hand, into agriculture and "other industries" and, on the other, into consumption and gross investment. The latter, which does not include working capital, has been estimated separately for building, construction, machinery and equipment, and transportation. Consumption appears to be computed by adding the net surplus in the balance of payments to the gross-investment figure and then deducting the resulting sum, representing "gross saving," from the independently made estimates of total national income. The latter have been derived from income-tax returns adjusted for tax-exempted incomes for the years 1870–1920 and from production statistics for 1921–1952. It is only from 1930 on that an official series began to be computed. There is little opportunity for the reader to gauge the reliability of the methods used. What is made clear, however, is that the physical-output series, that is, national output in terms of 1929 prices, cannot be really regarded as such, except with strong reservations. The data for 1914 to 1928 have been converted into 1929 values by means of a cost-of-living index, except that for the years 1914–1921 an average of a cost-of-living index and a wholesale-price index was used. No attempt has been made to deflate separately for agriculture and "other industries." For 1929–1952, the existing official series at 1935 prices was reduced to 1929 prices by a cost-of-living index. Again, the problem of weighting is shrouded in silence. But the most remarkable part of the procedure is the deflation of the pre-1914 figures. The 1913 data were converted to 1929 prices via the cost-of-living index. Thereupon, the series at current prices for the years 1870–1913 was adjusted by the ratio of the 1913:1929 price relatives. In other words, the data for 1870 to 1913, while adjusted by that ratio, still reflect all the price fluctuations experienced during those forty-three years!

The paper on Hungary by Alexander Eckstein ("National Income and Capital Formation in Hungary, 1900–1950") is by far the most detailed piece in the volume. It is very explicit and careful in the discussion of the concepts employed, and there is no attempt to pass over lightly the techniques employed and the procedures followed. This is the only paper in the volume in which the conversion into constant prices is discussed more freely. While the actual conversion in itself may not be very superior, credit must be given for the attempt to use different deflators for different components of national income, both for the post-World War I period and for connecting the prewar data to the 1938–39 price base. But the deflation of the 1900–1914 figures is fairly dismal. An unweighted price index, based in part on price quotations from other parts of the Hapsburg Monarchy, is used for the purpose.

In general, this is probably the most original of the six contributions. The study of Hungarian national income over a long period presents particular difficulties because of the drastic territorial retrenchment after 1918 and the profound organizational change in the economy and in the prevailing official views regarding coverage of national income after the last war. Though previous studies have been used as far as possible, a great many adjustments and improvements have been introduced by the author. The most independent part of the study refers to capital formation for the years 1924/25–1949. Starting from an existing monograph for the years 1937–40, the author constructed estimates of capital formation for the remaining interwar years and for the first postwar years. As was to be expected, the worth of individual estimates is subject to variation. The important capital formation in industry, for instance, is based on much less than perfectly convincing methods and there is at least a hint of a possible double counting. Nevertheless, the criteria and the methods developed in the study will certainly be basic to all further progress in this area. An additional advantage lies in the author's willingness to engage in some historical interpretation both with regard to the rate of growth by sectors and to the investment trends. Like Perroux, the author stresses the role of the "active" or "motive" components of national income. He may be mistaken in his belief that the early stress on iron and steel as well as machinery output was peculiar to Hungary alone among the European industrializations, but the attempt to see changes in national income within a broader historical framework is certainly most helpful. All in all, the volume would have gained greatly if some of the authors of the other papers had set for themselves equally high standards of critical analysis and kindliness to the reader.

The last paper, by Yuzo Yamada ("Notes on Income Growth and the Rate of Savings in Japan"), is a brief report on the discrepancies which at present exist among a number of different estimates, including those by the author. These discrepancies are large indeed for the decades of the nineteenth century and the first years of the present century. Nevertheless, the author presents some provisional conclusions, mainly in correction of Colin Clark's estimates which are said to be excessive with regard to the average rate of growth and especially with regard to the rate of savings. Since Japanese economists are eagerly engaged in attempts at reconciling the discrepancies and in improving the nature of the estimates, the present contribution must be considered even more provisional than the other papers in the volume.

It has seemed necessary to dwell at some length on the individual contributions to this volume. The subject matter of these essays is of fundamental importance and the suggestive power of a printed figure is great. It cannot, therefore, be stressed too emphatically that for the most part the long-term rates of growth are much too uncertain to allow of any reliable intertemporal and, least of all, interspatial comparisons. A great deal of work remains to be done and, in particular, the problems of conversion of value to volume must be explored much more painstakingly before the results can be used in any responsible fashion. What this reviewer has found discouraging about the present essays is not so much the present low level of reliability of the deflating procedures as the absence of a clear conception of the problems involved and of any insistence upon the need for constructive solutions. To turn away in disgust, as does Perroux, is perhaps an understandable but not too helpful an attitude. One must consider that price and cost-of-living indices so far have been constructed by scholars and institutions interested mainly in changes in prices and cost of living for their own sake. Those engaged in investigating long-term trends in national income and its components cannot hope to arrive at satisfactory results unless they embark upon construction of price indices especially designed to serve the needs of their work. Naturally, it will be very helpful to develop a number of specific deflators for as many subgroups as possible. Since in practice each subgroup will still contain very many commodities with very different rates of change of output and price, the need for correct conversion of each subgroup by the given year's deflators will still remain. Moreover, in many cases one will have to continue operating with just one or two comprehensive price indices. In either situation it may be impossible to construct as many price indices as there are years in a long time series. But there is every probability that by constructing price indices for a considerable number of short subperiods, each of them weighted by magnitudes pertaining to a year within each subperiod, we should come reasonably close to a consistent volume index. It would seem that research on long-term-income estimates has reached a stage where this task should receive the highest priority. This at least is the conclusion which emerges rather forcefully from the present volume. It is only when the job has been done and meaningful "physical output" series have been obtained that one will be able to proceed to an investigation of the alternative vantage points in viewing long-term change. The better understanding of the index-number problem will not eliminate the arbitrariness of our approaches, but it will make it possible to gauge its extent and reveal the historical significance of the weighting choices which are made.

All this of course must not diminish our gratitude to the editor and the contributors. There is no intention to deny the importance of the findings summarized here or to overlook the labor invested and the ingenuity displayed. The volume shows with much clarity where we stand now. The very weakness of some of the results can be relied upon to instigate further elaborations and improvements. Our ability to use past experience for the comprehension and solution of present problems largely depends upon the success of this enterprise.

Index

Prepared by Margarita Willfort